SALT

The Essential Mineral
& Its Medicinal Benefits

SALT

The Essential Mineral
& Its Medicinal Benefits

Margaret Briggs

Abbeydale Press

ISBN 978-1-86147-232-8

1 3 5 7 9 10 8 6 4 2

Published by Abbeydale Press
an imprint of Bookmart Ltd
Registered number 2372865
Trading as Bookmart Ltd
Blaby Road, Wigston, Leicester
LE18 4SE, England

Produced for Bookmart Limited
Illustrations by Tegan Sharrard
Cover design by Omnipress Ltd

Printed in Dubai

ABOUT THE AUTHOR

Margaret Briggs was a teacher for 30 years, working in Kent,
Germany, North Yorkshire and Sussex.

Since leaving teaching she has had more time for gardening and
cooking and has embarked on a second career as a freelance
writer, researcher and editor, alongside her writer husband, Lol.
Six years ago the couple bought a dilapidated house in south-
west France. The house is now restored and Margaret and Lol
divide their time between Sussex and the Gironde, with two
contrasting gardens to develop.

Margaret has written four other books in this series, *Vinegar —
1001 Practical Uses, Gardening Hints and Tips, Porridge — Oats
and their Many Uses* and *Honey — and its Many Health Benefits.*

CONTENTS

Introduction   7

What is salt?   9

Salt throughout history   25

The industrial uses of salt   51

Salt: kill or cure?   73

Salt in customs, religions and rituals   91

Cooking with salt   107

Hints and tips   141

Fascinating facts   151

Introduction

For many people salt is just a white granular substance you sprinkle from a salt cellar onto your chips. Using salt to season food is a habit that many adults acquired as children, from parents. We just use it because it is there. How many people have you seen reach for the salt, even before tasting the food placed in front of them? It seems to me an assumption that the food won't be tasty unless smothered in sodium chloride. What about other flavours that are completely covered by the salt?

Salt is a commodity that we cannot do without. Every species of living creature needs the sodium in salt, but through changes during evolution, social groupings and civilisation we now consume far more than we need. In fact, too much salt can cause as much or more harm than too little. I can't recall hearing of many people in my experience suffering salt deficiency, whereas I know plenty with high blood pressure.

The salt on the table is just the tip of the iceberg. It is everywhere in our daily lives.

Its industrial uses are phenomenal. In fact, only a small percentage of the salt produced in the world is used for food preservation or seasoning. It may yet contribute in some way to renewable energy sources.

Historically, salt has been the cause of wars, uprisings and revolutions. It has been taxed all over the world, used as money and has been a powerful force in the economic rise and fall of civilisations. Religions, ceremonies and rituals rely on salt. You can't really ignore it.

This book explores many themes in a light-hearted fashion. While we can learn from history and we can take advice from scientists, now is, perhaps, the time to listen to advice and evidence from the medical world and not take their words with a pinch of salt!

What is Salt?

The term salt also specifically refers to sodium chloride, or common table salt, which is a crystalline compound. It has widespread uses as a food preservative and for seasoning. It is formed by the action of sodium on dry hydrogen gas and chlorine, which causes sodium chloride crystals to form. The chemical name for sodium chloride is NaCl. The 'Cl' part is easy to understand, but it doesn't really help explain why sodium is called Natron, so we'll go back a bit in terms of chemical understanding and historical evidence, to explain a little about sodium and natron; knowing a little about the properties of sodium helped me to understand why sodium chloride is such an important substance, and why, like so many other trails in this series on basic substances and their many benefits, we have a lot to thank the Ancient Egyptians for.

SODIUM

Sodium exists as more than a trace element in the stars and the sun and is the sixth most abundant element on the earth's crust, making up an estimated 2.8%. Sodium, along with potassium, is classed as a soft metal but is not found naturally as a metal. It is found in a wide distribution as compounds with other substances, the most familiar being sodium chloride or table salt. Other salts of sodium are found in many rocks and in nearly all soil types. These include halides, silicates, carbonates, sulphates and nitrates. Sodium occurs throughout the rocky crust of the earth as feldspar, a silicate of sodium, and in various other rocks. Like potassium, sodium is a soft metal with a silvery white lustre. It tarnishes in the air and is one of the most reactive of metals.

Early civilisations knew about the benefits of sodium, although as potassium compounds were very similar in appearance, they thought they were the same substance. Records exist of saltpetre from potassium being used to make glazes for pots in Mesopotamia 17 centuries BC and the Egyptians used sodium carbonate 16 centuries BC for making glass. They also used natron for embalming and preserving.

The ancient Egyptians appreciated beauty so much they protected and preserved it even after death by mummification with natron, a white crystalline mixture of sodium bicarbonate, sodium carbonate, sodium chloride and sodium sulphate. It was mined from dry lake beds and from the banks of the River Nile. The area of Wadi-el-Natrun lies 23 metres (25 yards) below sea level and gets its name from the natron. Known to be mildly antiseptic as well as a good exfoliant and drying substance, it was, all in all, a perfect base for adding oils and fragrances used to preserve the dead. The fragrances exemplified spirituality and beauty and served to cover up the foul odours of decaying flesh, which conjured up or summoned particular deities. So you not only had to look good but also smell divine, even in the intense heat of Egypt, without refrigeration or air conditioning!

Sodium chemicals today are used widely in synthetic chemistry as drying agents and reducing agents. Sodium has also been used in the manufacture of photoelectric cells. Its high heat capacity and conductivity make it useful as a heat transfer medium. It is lighter than water and can be cut with a knife at room temperature. It reacts with water to give hydrogen and sodium hydroxide, so it is an extremely active chemical which easily unites with oxygen. The metal is, therefore, usually kept immersed in an inert liquid for safety. It is used in some nuclear reactors and sodium lights give that characteristic yellow illumination to many of our roads and towns. This works by gaseous sodium glowing in a tube which has voltage passed through it.

PROPERTIES OF SODIUM CHLORIDE

Sodium chloride forms symmetrical crystals. A salt in chemical terminology is produced by the reaction of an acid with a base. A salt is a positive ion of a base and the negative ion of an acid, producing a neutral product. The larger chloride ions form a cube arrangement while the gaps are filled with smaller sodium ions. Each ion is therefore surrounded by six ions of the other type.

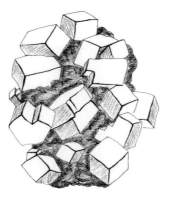

The same structure is found in many other minerals. The crystals are said to be isometric, meaning that they have three axes of symmetry, all equal in length and lying at 90 degrees from each other. The colour of the salt is dependent on its purity, but it is normally colourless to white. It may also be light blue, dark blue, yellow, orange, green, grey and pink. The colour is determined by bacterial debris trapped inside the lake or water source which evaporated. These coloured crystals are highly sought after by rock collectors.

THE SOLUTION
Salt's affinity for water means that it can be easily dissolved in a solution, as any upper Key Stage 2 Primary pupils will tell you. Evaporation of water content will return the salt to its previous solid condition. At 20°C (68°F) 100 grams (4 fluid ounces) of water will dissolve 36 g of salt. The higher the temperature of the water, the greater the amount of salt that will be dissolved.

SPECIFIC GRAVITY
The specific gravity of salt is 2.165, which means that salt is 2.165 times heavier than water at 0°C, 32°F.

MOHS SCALE OF HARDNESS
The Mohs scale of mineral hardness characterises the scratch resistance of various minerals through the ability of a harder material to scratch a softer one. It was created in 1812 by the German mineralogust Friedrich Mohs and is based on ten minerals that are readily available:

Talc is 1, gypsum is 2, calcite has a hardness of 3 and diamond, the hardest mineral, 10. Halite has a hardness of 2.5, meaning that you can scratch it with a fingernail but not with a bronze coin.

MELTING POINT
Salt will melt at 427°C (800°F) and vaporise beyond this temperature. I haven't, obviously, put this to the test, being mainly concerned with Primary Science, but it might be of interest further up the scale of scientific enquiry!

BOILING POINT
Boiling point is 1,413°C. Again, I take this on trust, having neither the means, nor the inclination, to put it to the test.

ELECTROLYSIS OF SALT
Under an electrical current, molten salt decomposes to form metallic sodium and chlorine. When salts dissolve in water they are called electrolytes.

Salt is hygroscopic, which means that it will absorb water from damp atmospheres, above 75% relative humidity. Below this, it will dry out.

SOURCES OF SODIUM CHLORIDE
There are three ways of extracting salt for processing:

- Rock salt, called halite
- Evaporated sea salt
- Natural brines

ROCK SALT

Halite, the mineral form of sodium chloride, occurs in rocks, commonly mudstones, but is present in a range of rocks from different geological eras, as masses and beds. The deposits are the residue of evaporated seas, lakes and salt flats. A bed of rock salt lying near the surface can be excavated like any other mineral. Some of the beds can be 350 metres (383 yards) thick and lie under wide areas of landscape. High quality deposits need only to be ground and sieved for processing. Deposits with impurities may be melted and leached with dilute hydrochloric acid.

The salt is then washed, first with brine and then with fresh water, dried and ground to give crystals of the desired size. Deeper deposits can be extracted by pumping water down under pressure to dissolve the salt deposits before the brine is collected and treated.

Thirty per cent of the salt produced in the UK is from rock salt, produced mainly for de-icing roads. The rest is produced from brine, mostly by the chemical industries as a raw material. Some is evaporated to produce white salt. Britain has huge reserves of salt, mainly located in England, with some in Northern Ireland. Some of the largest halite deposits in Europe are to be found in the UK, Germany, France, Poland, Hungary, Romania and Austria. Other huge deposits are found in the USA and Canada, particularly the Appalachians, under New York, Ontario, the Michigan basin, Utah, Ohio, Kansas, New Mexico and Nova Scotia. Pakistan, Iran, Russia and China also have important salt deposits. Another important halite deposit is to be found in salt domes.

SALT DOMES

Salt domes are formed when beds of rock containing quantities of evaporate minerals, such as halite, gypsum and anhydrite, are squeezed up through other rocks above. They intrude or push up vertically through the overlying, sedimentary rocks, creating pip-like masses of salt, or diapirs, because they are more buoyant, low density rock types. As they push up, they pierce the rocks above and create anticlines or upward folds in the surface of the earth. The mushroom-shaped domes produced make traps for hydrocarbons, such as natural gas, oil and coal. Salt domes are found along the coasts of Texas and Louisiana in the USA, Germany, Spain, the Netherlands, Romania and Iran. Naturally, the presence of a salt dome can arouse interest from oil and petroleum companies.

SALT GLACIERS

If these rising salt domes or diapirs breach the surface of the earth they can produce salt glaciers, as are found in the Zagros Mountains of Iran. The salt may be mixed with clay and will move more during the winter months when there is more moisture around, than in the summer. Movement of salt will mean that the flow spreads in tongue-like masses downward by gravity into the surrounding area for many kilometres, just like real glaciers.

SALT PANS

Salt pans are desert features, usually appearing as a shiny white expanse of flat land covered in salt and other minerals which have accumulated over thousands of years. They signify where there was once water which, unable to drain away, was evaporated faster than any precipitation could collect. The crust of salt may cover a muddy trap underneath, so should be treated with care. They have provided ideal conditions for aircraft runways and various land speed attempts, as at the Bonneville Rock Desert in Nevada. Another site in Nevada hosts an annual arts festival called the Burning Man Festival. The largest salt pans in the world is Salar de Uyuni, near Potosi in Bolivia. It covers 10,582 square kilometres (4,085 square miles) and is 25 times bigger than the Nevada flats.

Salt pans are found next to large areas of water, such as coasts, lake shores or river deltas. They flood during storms and mixtures of minerals result. The deposits can appear zoned, like rings around a dirty bath. Sulphates and carbonates collect around the edges, with sodium chloride in the centre. Playa (Spanish for beach) or dry lakebeds are the remains of the shore of a dried-up endorheic lake. An endorheic lake is a closed basin, where there is no water flowing in or out on the surface as rivers or underground through rocks. This means that the only water added to the lake is from rain or other precipitation. The Dead Sea is an example of such a lake. They can be found all over the world but are mostly associated with deserts. The Black Sea was one such lake until the Mediterranean Sea broke through the land separating the two. Such basins often have extensive salt pans although some are seasonal. Human activity in areas that were previously too dry for habitation means that many such lakes have been made smaller because of the building of dams. This may lead to higher salinity, concentrations of pollutants and disruption to ecosystems.

EVAPORATED SEA SALT

Sodium chloride is the chief chemical compound responsible for the saltiness of the sea. Four litres (1 gallon) of seawater contains between 1% and 5% solids, and sodium chloride is the most abundant of the salts in solution: over three-quarters of the solids are sodium chloride. Some seas are saltier than others. The polar seas have less salt content, whereas the Mediterranean and Red Seas, which are more enclosed, have much higher concentrations than open seas and oceans.

Specialised sea salts are produced in France, Ireland, Colombia, Sicily and the USA. These have different mineral contents and give a different flavour from table salt, which is pure sodium chloride. They are used in the cosmetics industry as well as in 'gourmet' cooking, although the actual salt content varies little from table salt.

Mineral	Average % of solids in sea water
Sodium chloride	77
Magnesium chloride	10
Magnesium sulphate	5
Calcium sulphate	3
Potassium chloride	3
Magnesium bromide	Trace
Calcium carbonate	Trace

NATURAL BRINES

Naturally occurring deposits of salt water are called brines and vast areas are found in the Dead Sea as well as parts of the USA (Death Valley), India, Australia and parts of Africa.

The Dead Sea covers an area of 1,049 square kilometres (405 square miles). It is fairly free from sulphates and has a high percentage of potassium (38% of solids), magnesium (53% of solids) and bromine. Less than 8% is sodium chloride. Weather conditions and temperatures mean that solar evaporation is possible for eight months of the year to process potassium and bromine as well as sodium chloride.

The brine from Kharaghoda in India is like sea water, but much more concentrated. In fact the brine is nearly saturated, meaning that the water has dissolved as much salt as possible. British brines contain chlorides of barium and strontium, not usually found in brines. These were found at great depths during test drilling for petroleum. Similar brines have been discovered in deep wells in locations in the USA.

EXTRACTION OF SODIUM CHLORIDE AND THE MANUFACTURE OF SALT

At one time nearly all the salt used commercially was produced from the evaporation of sea water. Today 10% of the world's salt requirements is produced by solar evaporation. It is the least complicated of mineral industries, needing only a source of salt water or rock salt and sunlight to evaporate the water content. Commercial production of salt comes from rock salt, sea water and natural brines. Artificial brines are created by pumping water into underground salt beds and a considerable amount of commercial salt is derived from this method.

SOLAR EVAPORATION

Solar evaporation is the oldest method of producing salt, having been used for thousands of years and probably originating along the shores of the Mediterranean and Red Seas. Its use is only practical in warmer climates where the evaporation rate exceeds the amount of rainfall by about 75 centimetres (30 inches). This is called a negative evaporation rate. Basically the brine is allowed to evaporate to a specific gravity of about 1.21. This means that the brine is 1.2 times as dense as water. Impurities can be removed during this stage. The brine is then fed into three or four pans or shallow ponds for evaporation by the sun to start crystallisation and where the concentration of salt gradually increases. In the final pan the specific gravity rises to 1.25 or 1.26. The salt crystals are washed with saturated brine and then fresh water. The principle is the same, whether in the USA, West Indies, India or Africa. The salt, called bitterns, can then be used to make potash, bromine, magnesium chloride and magnesium sulphate (Epsom salts). The equipment might be more upmarket, but the method is the same. In the Dead Sea area, dye is added to the water to allow more heat to be absorbed. Solar evaporation can take from one to five years to produce salt.

The solar evaporation ponds in San Francisco Bay produce

about 700,000 tons per year. Commercial production began in 1854, although Native Americans had collected salt long before then. The brine is only 2.5% sodium chloride compared with 3.5% in sea water. Evaporation continues through a series of ponds until the brine is saturated and it is then fed into the crystalliser. The salt crystals collect in the bottom of the bed. The remaining dark red liquid brine, packed with magnesium and other minerals, is drained off to leave pure sodium chloride in a layer about 10 to 20 centimetres (5 to 8 inches) thick. Huge machines like snowploughs scrape the salt up for processing. Salt harvesting in this way is seasonal, usually lasting from September until December, with a 24-hour operation in place to harvest before bad weather sets in.

This same cycle operates in the Camargue region in the south of France. The huge delta where the River Rhone meets the Mediterranean Sea is made up of inland salt lakes and marshes. Sea salt is the most important harvest of the region. Salt forms as the huge brine pans evaporate over the summer months and result in enormous mounds of salt crystals up to 8 metres (26 feet) high, called camelles. During the summer up to 15,000 tons per day may be produced, when these salt plains look like a desert. Such salt marshes provide wonderful sites for wildlife, wildfowl and plant species adapted to salt water.

In the UK a very small amount of sea salt is produced by evaporation of sea water at Maldon in Essex.

METHODS USING OTHER FORMS OF HEAT

In areas where the salt can be mined by creating a solution of brine but solar evaporation is not viable, artificial heat is used to recover the salt. In days gone by salt was boiled to a concentrate over open fires. You can read about these methods in the chapter 'Salt Throughout History', but nowadays multiple-effect vacuum evaporators and open crystallisers are widely used.

GRAINER OR OPEN CRYSTALLISATION METHOD
The first stage is to pump the brine, whether natural or

man-made, into settling tanks, and calcium, sulphate and magnesium compounds are removed with chemical treatment using lime and sodium hydroxide. The brine is fed into a long open trough called a grainer which is heated by steam coils at a temperature slightly below that of the brine already in the grainer. The brine residue, or bitterns, is then removed on a regular basis, or continuously in very big operations. Evaporation happens at the surface of the solution and the crystals remain held there by surface tension, as they continue to grow at the top edges in what look like upside-down, hollow pyramids called hoppers. These eventually sink and stop growing, and when they are recovered they are like flakes. This type of salt is used by many consumers in the food industry.

MULTIPLE-EFFECT VACUUM EVAPORATORS
Most of the salt produced in colder climates comes from rock salt and most of this is produced by using multiple-effect vacuum evaporators. In these evaporators a series of chambers is used, each with a greater level of vacuum or 'effect'. The brine boils off through the action of the vacuum. This method is much more efficient and uses a lot less energy than open pans. It also produces very pure salt. Early evaporator vessels were made of cast iron, were not suitable for the pressures necessary and were limited to three effects. For the last half-century or so, steel has been used, allowing for up to six effects.

ALBERGER PROCESS
This is a combination of the grain and vacuum methods. It produces cubic crystals by the graining method and then uses a partial vacuum to create a cross between flakes and seed crystals. The salt is removed by centrifugal force and dried. The energy used for this method amounts to just over twice that for the vacuum method but only a quarter of that used by the open pan grainer method.

SALT IN THE UK
Salt can be extracted from great depths. Water is forced down a shaft which dissolves the salt. The brine is then pumped to the surface. Mined rock salt can also be

extracted in huge lumps, which are crushed and brought to the surface for processing or transporting. The purity of rock salt, or halite, depends on the extent of the thickness of the mudstone it is found with. In the UK salty rocks do not occur on the surface because groundwater dissolves the salt. Sometimes it is easier to extract as brine by pumping. Where the brine or halite has been taken away, large underground cavities are left behind. These provide ideal conditions for storing gas and have, in the past, been used for storing oil.

The UK is a large producer, with 95% coming from England and the rest from Northern Ireland. Of the UK output about 70% is extracted as brine and the rest as halite. Salt is now only produced commercially in Cheshire and in the North York Moors National Park, where it is mined alongside potash. Rock salt is usually in greater demand during bad weather, when it is used for de-icing. About 2 million tons of halite are produced each year. Britain is self sufficient in salt, although some exporting and importing goes on. White salt production is about 1 million tons per year, and UK consumption is declining overall, from 7 million tons in 1980 to about 5.5 million tons in 2004.

MINING IN THE UK

Salt mining began at Winsford Minen in 1844, but the mine was closed between the 1890s and 1928. The salt is taken from galleries about 8 by 20 metres (26 by 65 feet), with 20 metre (65 feet) pillars being left behind. Drilling and blasting used to be the main methods for extraction, but now a continuous mining machine, introduced in 2002, is used as well. The rock is crushed underground and no waste is generated.

Solution mining recovers about a quarter of the salt reserve and is just as it sounds. Once the salt deposit is located, water is forced under pressure into a cavity which forms in the underground salt bed, as the salt dissolves. These cavities, designed to maintain the overlying rocks, can be 145 metres (475 feet) across and up to 200 metres (656 feet) high. The final size and shape of the cavity can be controlled by the positioning of water injection tubes and a compressed air blanket, which prevents dissolution upwards. The whole process is monitored by sonar. Mudstone falls to the base of the cavity and when these holes are no longer required they are left filled with brine.

All of this seems like very small fry, compared with the USA, where about 29 million tons of dry salt are produced each year. Unsurprisingly, the USA is the world's leading producer.

GRADES OF SALT

REFINED SALT
About 7% of refined salt is used as a flavour enhancer and food additive. The rest is used in paper, textile, soap and detergent manufacture. During the drying process anti-caking agents are usually added. These absorb humidity and stop the crystals sticking together.

TABLE SALT
Table salt is 95% sodium chloride and usually contains minute quantities of sugar, as well as an anti-caking agent. The sugar stops the salt turning yellow in sunlight and prevents loss of iodine, which has been added as a trace dietary supplement since 1924. Table salt is usually used for cooking or adding at the table. In 1911 magnesium carbonate was first added.

OTHER ADDITIVES
In some countries, where fluoride is not added to drinking water, brands of salt are available with added fluoride. Folic acid (Vitamin B) is also added to some brands, especially important for women in pregnancy.

COMMON SALT
This is a technical term for salt that is neither fine nor coarse. In days gone by, the texture, volume and moisture content of salt was determined by an experienced worker, simply by holding it in the hand. Nowadays, this is all controlled by machines.

FINE SALT

Fine salt is produced at higher temperatures and the crystals are smaller than common salt. This was used to make block salt in the past, by putting it into a mould for baking over flues in a hothouse.

COARSE OR FISHERY SALT

This is a washed grade used in the stock feed, hide curing, poultry feed and pet food industries, as well as for salting fish. It was often called 14-day salt, that being the time taken to evaporate the brine to form crystals. It requires slow simmering over a cool heat.

SUPERFINE SALT

This is a high quality salt used in bread, processed meats, biscuits, soap manufacture, and chemical applications.

LOW SODIUM SALT

Reduced-sodium alternatives contain less sodium than standard salt but taste similar. Sodium is the part of salt that can lead to high blood pressure, but salt substitutes are not suitable for some people. Low salts use potassium instead of purely sodium.

UNREFINED OR SEA SALT

This salt is sometimes called *fleur de sel* and has distinctive flavours, depending on the region it comes from. A lot of people prefer this for cooking or as a condiment, but others advocate the refined salt in case a deficiency of iodine occurs. It's all a matter of taste, really. See the chapter 'Salt Kill or Cure' for the effects of too much or too little salt in the diet. Sea salt is also used in cosmetics and as a hair product.

KOSHER SALT

Salt used to prepare Jewish food has larger flakes or crystals and a more open granular structure. Today kosher, or koshering, salt is commonly used in commercial kitchens as it does not contain additives. Because kosher salt grains are larger than ordinary table salt it does not dissolve readily. Salt remains on the surface of the meat longer, allowing fluids to leach out of the meat. This type of salt is not recommended for baking, where little liquid is used.

BLACK SALT
Black salt is an unrefined mineral salt that is really pinkish grey. It has a strong sulphuric flavour. Black salt is mined in India. It is used extensively in Indian cuisine and is considered a cooling spice in Hindu medicine, where it is used as a laxative and an aid to digestion. It is also believed to relieve intestinal gas and heartburn. It is sometimes used by people with high blood pressure or on low-salt diets because of its lower sodium content. Chemically, black salt is almost pure sodium chloride, with iron and trace minerals.

PRAGUE SALT
Road grit salt.

Salt
Throughout
History

For centuries salt has been used as a commodity as well as for flavouring and preserving food. It has been argued that the ability to preserve food has greatly contributed to the development of societies and civilisations as we know them today. As well as a saver of lives, salt had been used as a bartering tool, payment for work, a taxable item and has contributed to the cause of wars and economic embargoes.

Man cannot survive without salt but it was a long time before it was consumed directly as a mineral. We all need sodium and chlorine in our bodies, but before salt became a trading commodity early man got all the salt he needed through eating fish, shellfish and meat. It is believed that salt eating developed when humans started to keep animals and grow crops, that is, when they became farmers rather than hunter gatherers. Relying on hunting for meat wasn't exactly a sound choice unless you could outrun the local wildlife. So from about 10,000 BC the proportion of meat and fish in the diet declined. People had to find salt for their domesticated animals as well as themselves, especially if they moved away from the coast to areas where shellfish were not easily available.

First records of salt use date back to 4000 BC, unsurprisingly in Egypt. Clearly the presence of salt helped such civilisations, near desert climates and close to the sea, to develop. We know that the ancient Egyptians used salt and other sodium minerals to preserve food and embalm their dead. Egyptian art and hieroglyphs show salt-making taking place around 1450 BC. Salt was available as exposed rock outcrops in arid regions and as dried deposits on the shores of seas and salt lakes. By 2000 BC people elsewhere had discovered that salt preserved food and stopped it rotting. It was used to preserve meat, fish and vegetables. Salt also made a contribution to the development of society, when people began to come together to trade this valuable commodity and to share expertise. Practices such as salting olives added variation to the diet. Salt was expensive because of the hard work involved in extracting it, collecting it and carrying it across land and water.

PHOENICIAN TRADING

The Phoenicians were great traders and began harvesting salt from the sea and exporting it to other countries. They flooded the plains along coastal areas with sea water and left it to dry in the sun. After the water had evaporated the collected salt could be sold. Of course, this meant that the value of salt gradually decreased in real terms because there a constant supply available. Trading helped to spread techniques and ideas to other coastal areas, where people could also exploit their own salt.

TRAVEL

The availability of salt meant that food which was seasonal could be kept fresh for longer thanks to brine solution or a sprinkling of salt. This also meant that people could travel greater distances before their food supplies ran out or were spoiled by hot weather. People were no longer limited in their travel and trading by seasonal variations.

It wasn't only sea salt that changed the nature of trading and travelling, however. Salt had been mined since the Iron Age, although production was very small and local to the communities it supported. But warmer and dryer climates made evaporation of brines a much easier process than having to excavate rocks to reach small deposits. The European production of sea salt centred around the Mediterranean Sea, where the brine had a high salt content and the sun shone regularly. Even so, overall it wasn't a particularly easy process and was governed by the solar evaporation rates. Changes in sea level in the Mediterranean prevented some civilisations from obtaining consistent salt supplies. This in turn made people migrate and conquer or stay and take the consequences of being overrun by others. Salt remained essential but expensive because of transport costs up rivers, across seas and overland. It was in the interests of the traders to make sure that costs stayed high so that they could become very rich. It wasn't long before someone had the bright idea of taxing salt.

CHINESE SALT

In China around 2200 BC, the Emperor Hsia Yu levied one of the first known taxes in the world, on salt. As early as 2700 BC a work called *Peng Tzao Kan Mu* was known. It contained medical knowledge and observations on 40 kinds of salt. It explained a system for extraction very similar to the open pan system known today. Much later, during the Late T'ang Dynasty (AD 755–907) in China, tax and labour services were disrupted by a breakdown in authority and by huge movements of population. This was brought under control by a new government monopoly on salt. By 780 this salt monopoly was producing a large percentage of the state's revenue. The state salt commission gradually took over the financial administration of southern and central China. Salt rules!

ROMAN TIMES

The Romans valued salt so highly that they controlled the price of it. They increased the cost to raise money for wars against their less civilised or less well organised neighbours, in order to expand their empire. They also lowered it to make sure that poorer citizens could afford to buy it. Maybe that's why Roman soldiers were paid at certain times with salt. That's where we get the word 'salary' from – see the literary section for more details. *Salarium Argentum* was the name for the salt rations given to soldiers. This was a pretty shrewd move really, considering that the soldiers were expected to walk for days on end, often in unpleasantly hot conditions, and arrive fit and healthy, ready for a good fight! The salt would have been essential for their continued health.

The Romans were great engineers and road builders. This meant that the soldiers could march quickly and directly and also that salt could be easily moved around as Rome developed. The Via Salaria was a road that led from Rome to the Adriatic Sea where the shallow depth of water meant that there was a high salt content. Evaporation produced much more salt than the Tyrrhenian Sea, which was much closer to Rome.

At the beginning of the Roman period the sea level was a good 2 metres (6 feet) below the present level. Salt-making was well established on the coasts of western Europe and the Mediterranean, until the vast, flat coastal areas ideal for making salt were gradually submerged. By about AD 400 the traditional Roman salt flats of Ostia and Aquilea had been irreparably flooded. Osia was the port of Rome and was moved inland three times. Rome needed to find more supplies of salt, or lose its empire.

WHAT'S IT WORTH?

In ancient Greece slave traders often bartered salt for slaves. A slave who failed to come up to the expectations of his master was said to be 'not worth his salt'.

In Tibet, the explorer Marco Polo wrote about salt as if it was as precious as gold, which it probably was. Gold was formed into thin rods and cut to certain lengths as currency. He noted that for smaller amounts of currency, cakes of salt were produced from brine springs by boiling to evaporate the water. After about an hour the salt could be pressed with symbols of the Grand Khan, dried and used as coins. Only officers of the Grand Khan could make this money. The salt coins appear to have increased in value the further they were carried from the towns into remote areas. This is not the only use of salt for actual money. Salt is still used as currency among the nomads of the Danakil Plains in Ethiopia.

POWER IN TIMBUKTU

By the 8th century Islam was spreading to West Africa and had travelled to Ghana and its empire. Mediterranean countries badly wanted gold but all they had to offer was a load of salt. In contrast, West African countries had plenty of gold but needed salt to survive. The Mali Empire was founded and trade in gold and salt prospered. In the Mali Empire the city of Timbuktu was the gateway to the Sahara and a prestigious seat of learning and civilisation. It developed as a huge salt market, giving it power and wealth previously unimagined. Supplies of salt in an arid region provided the power to control life and death.

Between the 8th and 16th centuries trade between countries around the Mediterranean and West Africa thrived. The Sahara Desert stood in the path of the lucrative trade which was conducted by caravans of camels. The animals would be fattened up before setting off in their thousands. Guided by Berber tribesmen, safe passage was ensured. Runners were sent ahead to oases, to carry back essential supplies of water, enabling the huge distances to be covered safely. The camels could last weeks without food or water, but people could not. The merchants of the 12th century valued salt so highly that they reportedly paid for it by its weight in gold. Legends abounded that Timbuktu was very rich indeed and news of its wealth fuelled stories in Europe from countries who were importing the mineral. There are reports of up to 12,000 camels trekking 644 kilometres (400 miles) across the Sahara Desert with cargoes of salt, some of which was exchanged for another valuable asset in the form of slaves.

THE SILENT TREATMENT
When language was a barrier to trade, silent trade or dumb barter was used, similar to methods known in the silk trade.

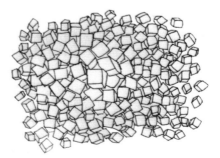

When merchants reached a settlement or trade area they beat great drums to summon the natives, who would not appear in the presence of the strangers. An alternative method was for the locals to beat a drum, light a fire or use some other form of signalling to attract the merchants. The merchants arranged their salt in piles, signalled and then withdrew. The local people then appeared and examined the goods, left a heap of gold beside each pile and retired. If the merchants were satisfied, they took the gold, beating their drums to signal completion of the deal. If the local people did not agree to the barter, they, in theory at least, had the option of removing some of their gold. I can't help wondering how much gold was traded for a lump of life-giving salt.

According to one Moorish proverb, 'The price of a negro is salt'.

ANCIENT SALT WORKS

Archaeologists know that there were many early attempts to quarry and mine salt. Salt tunnels containing stone hammers and axes have been found at numerous sites in Asia Minor, Armenia, South and North America. The Hallstadt salt mines in the Austrian Alps and the Italian mines were important in supporting prehistoric communities. Similar tools were used across all continents.

The earliest coastal salt manufacture depended on wide, flat coastal areas and in making use of natural depressions or lagoons. Later, man-made salt works were formed, called salterns (see below). These were 15-20 centimetres (6-9 inches) deep and had to be created at mid-tide level so that they would fill from the sea.

The Chinese developed the idea of drilling into a salt deposit with at least two holes. One was used to flood fresh water into the salt deposit while the second hole allowed the water to well up after dissolving the salt. They used bamboo pipes to reach brine at depths of up to 1,000 metres (3,281 feet). This was then collected in the evaporation pans, where it could be concentrated again. Very old solar pans are still in operation in the salt water swamps that lie in the bend of the Yellow River. Similar operations provided salt in Iran.

SALT ROUTES

During the later years of the Roman Empire and into the Middle Ages, salt continued to play a big part in economic development. Salt routes, such as the Old Salt Route in northern Germany, allowed towns like Lübeck and the trading company the Hanseatic League to be powerful forces in the Middle Ages. Salt was mined near Luneburg, associated with salt for 1,000 years, and called 'white gold'. From Luneburg, known as the City of Salt, the salt route led to Lübeck from where cartloads of salt were sent by ship to various places around the Baltic. At its destination it was used to preserve fish caught by fishing boats across the Baltic Sea. The fish were then exported to other parts of Europe. After 1398 the salt could be transported by water along the Stecknitz Canal, one of the oldest canals in Europe. The journey didn't get any shorter, however, lasting about 20 days, either by canal or cart.

NO EASY SOLUTION

For evaporation methods to work properly it would take an estimated 50,000 cubic metres of sea water spread over 100,000 square miles of solar evaporation area. All this would produce only 1,000 tons of salt a year. Not such an easy proposition! You also needed a hot sun with a warm breeze and a steady sea level. This made the Mediterranean, where the tide fluctuates by only a few centimetres, ideal, whereas other major seas and oceans have tides of several metres. When the sea was a metre or two below its present level there were plenty of areas to choose from, but as climates changed and sea levels rose, the right land became less easy to find.

Deltas of rivers like the Nile, Rhône and the Euphrates also changed and the establishment of new ponds became more difficult. Brine production from one level of concentration to the next could take months or even years. A change in climate conditions, or even a minor fluctuation in ocean levels, could have a serious effect on coastal salt-making. Mining salt from the ground or collecting from inland salt springs or brine lakes like the Dead Sea became the only alternative in some areas. Evidence still exists along the shores of the Dead Sea, where you can find solar pans that were used by ancient salt-makers.

SOUTH AMERICA

Before the 1500s the main applications of salt in Mexico and South America related to rituals, staying alive and preserving fish. The Mayans enjoyed a good living until the Spanish conquest, when the Spanish took over numerous salt sources. Before long they had taken control of a major part of the continent. A process developed in Mexico whereby silver was leached from ore with a sodium solution. This process became a major industry, and the demand for salt increased. The vast Yucatan resources of evaporated salt met most of the needs.

SALT IN THE UK

EARLY SALT WORKS IN BRITAIN

About 250 million years ago salt was laid down in what is now Britain, but what was, at the time, a shallow inland sea close to the equator. Continental drift accounted for the migration of land masses northwards. Some of the former inland seas, now salt beds, were left exposed and dissolved away but others lay buried as rock salts, waiting to be discovered. Britain has few sites where rock salt can be extracted but in Cheshire the deposits are fairly close to the surface at about 50 metres (150 feet). This didn't stop people 2,000 years ago from discovering that the water draining into the ground dissolved the rock salt into brine and created salty springs. What could be more convenient for the exploitation of the salt?

IRON AGE SALT

The earliest examples of salt works date back to prehistoric times. Archaeologists have found the remains of rough pottery and supporting pillars, known as briquetage, which were used for salt-making. These Iron Age remains have been found along the east coast, in East Anglia and Essex, as well as Lincolnshire. Clay pans were used which were 60 centimetres (24 inches) wide, 120 centimetres (48 inches) long and 12 millimetres (½ inch) thick. These were supported on pillars and brine was evaporated in smaller vessels which were broken to get out the lump of salt produced. In Cheshire, Wales and western England the finished salt was sold or given out in the vessels it was made in.

SALTERNS

The word saltern on a map denotes the existence of medieval salt works. A saltern was often a clay hut used for salt production and could be set up wherever conditions were favourable, but was more commonly found in conjunction with other industries or with farming. Salterns were often to be found near tanning works in areas of pastoral farming. This meant that there was a supply of salt for curing hides and skins close to the supply of animals. Salterns also needed to be near a market, where the salt could be sold. Then all you needed was a gently sloping coastline, a tidal river or a salt marsh, and a reliable fuel for evaporating the salt.

The huts had a hole in the roof to allow smoke to escape. Large fires were lit beneath clay troughs of brine, rather than sea water, to evaporate water, leaving salt crystals. The brine was produced by passing fresh water over salt-rich sand or mud collected from beneath the sea and packed into clay troughs.

IT'LL ALL COME OUT IN THE WASH

During both Roman and medieval times the area around the Wash in eastern England fitted the bill perfectly. The tide brought in the salt water, the saltings gave plenty of pasture areas for animal grazing and the Fens provided peat for fuel. The brine was evaporated by the sun into a slurry-like mess of salt, sand and silt. This was then cleaned with sea water so that the sand and silt settled. The brine was then taken off the top and poured into shallow pans made from the local clay. These were set on clay pillars over peat fires to finish the evaporation process. Dried salt could then be removed and sold. Other salterns existed wherever the land was low enough and the conditions were right. Some certainly existed in the south on the Pevensey Levels in Sussex, close to the now inland site of Pevensey Castle, originally built by the Romans on the coast, and at the Great Salterns near Southsea, where the inlet of Langthwaite Harbour provided the right conditions. Much of the salt collected here went straight to Portsmouth for naval use.

SUPPLY AND DEMAND

Both Roman and medieval salt pans have been discovered in Cheshire. These were made of lead and were about 1 metre square (1 square yard) in area. The names of some of the Roman salt makers are written on the lead pans, so we know that Viventius and Veluvius worked there. Middlewich was called Salinae at the time, demonstrating salt's importance even back then. British salt making was already established along the coasts, but the Roman conquest brought new needs and demands.

The nearly saturated brine at inland spring sites needed much less fuel to evaporate the liquid than the weaker sea water. By AD 60 military camps were established at Chester and Middlewich. The Chester site acted as a supply port and control station for Wales's lead and silver mines and Middlewich commanded the River Dane. Here, the Romans created their own salt works.

DOMESDAY

Salt-making continued after the Roman occupation through to Anglo Saxon times and later attracted the attention of the Vikings, although there were few changes in methods of production except that the lead pans increased in size after the Norman conquest. Salt works are mentioned in the Domesday Book of 1086, which also included information on which manors owned coastal salt works. The number was considerable and these were mainly concentrated along the east and south coasts, where solar evaporation was harnessed on a seasonal basis. This meant that less fuel was needed for final evaporation. Before 1066 Droitwich in Worcestershire seems to have been much more important than other inland sites and produced more than the whole of Cheshire. A total of 318 salt houses were recorded in the Domesday Book.

Lead remained in use until the end of medieval times, when iron pans were found to be more effective, and when coal replaced wood as a fuel for heating brine. With this new, better fuel the size of the pans increased steadily until they reached about 6 by 9 metres (20 by 30 feet). This meant that production could be stepped up considerably. Pan houses have been excavated at Nantwich in Cheshire and Droitwich.

PRESERVATION

Up until the Industrial Revolution the main use for salt was the preservation of food, so obviously as the population of Britain grew the demand for salt increased as well. Between 1066 and the Black Death in the mid-14th century the population doubled. Coastal salt works traded with the continent and salt was also imported from the Bay of Biscay area, along with wine from Gascony. Henry II married Eleanor of Aquitaine in 1152 and much of south-west France belonged to the English crown. Trade was prosperous and the salt merchants formed a Fraternity of Salters.

PLAGUE

With the Black Death the demand for salt dwindled, along with the population, which was reduced by a half. Coupled with rising sea levels this virtually saw off the exports from Fenland ports and instead coastal salt-makers started to import grey Bay salt to refine. This grey salt was re-crystallised from sea water to give white salt for home consumption as well as for re-exporting for a profit.

In Cheshire the plague meant there was a drop in demand as well. Middlewich and Northwich belonged to the crown and taxes were levied on making, selling and buying fuel for processing. In Nantwich, where ownership remained with the gentry or with monasteries, the pattern was different. By the mid-14th century salt houses had spread to both sides of the river and 'walling land' was designated to prevent further expansion. By the mid-1600s there were 216 lands of ancient inheritance, each with six lead pans. Strict rules governed shares of the brine pit and a rota was set up stating the days when each owner could access the brine. This was called 'walling the kale'.

RECOVERY

By Tudor times the population had recovered to the level before the Black Death. Supplies still came from coastal areas and from France, but now also from Scotland. By now, coal was available as fuel and iron pans had replaced the lead ones, thankfully. I can't help wondering how many people died of lead poisoning during the previous centuries of salt production. Queen Elizabeth I gave a patent to Tyneside producers to try to make Britain self-sufficient in salt, but this proved unsuccessful.

WHERE'S MY PAN GONE?

The use of coal instead of wood as fuel forced a change from lead to iron pans, as the coal actually melted the lead pans. The aim with coal was to boil and evaporate quickly, which didn't fit well with the Nantwich walling rules of having your days for working fixed, making it essential to keep the fires stoked and burning intensively. In the early 17th century a method of distributing the brine in overhead wooden channels was developed and the flow was measured. A common cistern was installed and the fires under the pans were only allowed to burn for set times. Ingenious! Gradually lead pans were replaced with iron ones, although, of course, iron rusts and corrodes through constant contact with salt and water. The rust also stained the salt. Lead was much easier to work and recycle, although, obviously, with the benefit of hindsight, not a healthier option. Nantwich was slower to change than other salt works, and the standard-sized six lead pans were each replaced with four iron ones by 1650.

SALT ROCKS

In 1670 deep rock salt reserves were discovered in Cheshire. This led to some drilling for commercial exploitation through brine production, either by dissolving the rock salt or by developing the existing brine springs. Some of the mined salt was used to strengthen the content of weaker brines. Shallow mines flooded as a result and pumping of the brine water caused the roof pillars to collapse. Many of these now form lakes throughout the area. This led to damaging subsidence on the surface, often at some distance from the point of extraction, surprising many people at the time. This subsidence finally stopped modern extraction in Worcestershire in 1971 and Staffordshire in 1970. Lancashire ceased to produce brine in 1993.

Eventually smaller salt works couldn't keep up with the cheaper production costs at the Cheshire sites and larger producers took over. Conditions in the salt works were appalling, with whole families employed to look after the pans in hot, steamy and smoky conditions. Sixteen-hour shifts were not unheard of.

A LION AMONG SALT WORKS

The Thompson family, long associated with the salt industry from the 18th century, created a vast range of industries associated with the mining of rock salt, including evaporating brine, running a brick works and a boatyard. They also had interests in a colliery and imported timber, making raw materials for mining easily available. The Lion Salt Works at Northwich continued to expand and adapt to market changes.

By 1900 fuel and labour costs were reduced by the introduction of the vacuum evaporation system. This didn't make the required grade of salt that the old, open pan methods had provided, but gradually the cheaper salt vacuum crystals were accepted. People became ever more concerned about the subsidence caused and by the poor air quality around the old open pan salt works. The Lion Works continued to operate until, in 1960, it was the only open pan salt works in operation. It closed in 1986, when Nigeria, a major purchaser of the salt produced, was engaged in civil war, resulting in a collapse of the market. A museum now re-enacts the methods used at Northwich.

LOCAL SALT FOR LOCAL PEOPLE

At first the salt produced from Cheshire brine was only for local use and had little impact on London markets. The main form of transport was packhorse and trails spread from the salt towns to the surrounding area. After the industrial revolution, when coal was available, river transport increased and the construction of canals expanded. The Weaver Navigation was completed in 1710 and the Trent and Mersey Canal opened in 1777. The railway system started to develop and Cheshire had a big advantage over the small brine producers along the coast.

TECHNOLOGICAL IMPROVEMENTS

During the 18th century pumping technology improved and allowed for deeper brine shafts. Horse gins or water wheels were used to raise the brine. The first steam engine to drive a brine pump was used in 1777 and was based on Watt's 1775 model. Edward Salmon's new Lawton Salt Works used the new canal network to reach Liverpool and eastwards to the Potteries. By 1790 the canal network had expanded and Lawton salt could be shipped to Hull. Lawton Salt Works was the first company to use hessian bags for salt instead of the traditional wicker baskets.

As a result of improvements in the salt-based chemical industry, changes were afoot elsewhere. The major uses of salt had been the preservation of food and flavouring, although the meat aspect had widened to include leather curing and tanning. Salt was also used to embalm the dead. In the 1770s salt was first used with sulphuric acid to make hydrochloric acid for bleaching. The textile and soap industries had previously been dependent on importing alkali in the form of potash, but in the 1760s salt was used as a raw material for making alkali. The invention of the Leblanc process in 1783 provided a cheaper alternative. You can read more about this in the section on industrial uses. Production also needed sulphur, coal and limestone, all available on Tyneside and in Glasgow. By the close of the 18th century salt was well and truly established as an industrial chemical and salt tax was abolished in order to promote this industry. This coincided with the end of the Napoleonic wars and renewed prosperity in Britain.

19TH CENTURY DEVELOPMENTS

During Victorian times salt was important for the development of the chemical industries. It became easier to mine salt in the second half of the 19th century, so it was more easily available in large quantities for industrial use and didn't rely on evaporating sea water or extraction of brine alone. Salt also became much cheaper. It has been suggested that the port of Liverpool expanded in the 1800s as a result of the salt dug from the Cheshire mines, which became a major world supplier during the 19th century. Liverpool certainly exported vast quantities of salt as well as coal and manufactured goods at this time.

After the repeal of salt tax (see below), in 1824, Merseyside grew as an alkali-producing area due to its proximity to the Cheshire salt deposits. Salt could be transported via the Weaver Navigation and the demand for salt from the home market and for export led to the development of a huge site at Winsford and another along the Trent and Mersey Canal. Salt works grew up elsewhere and soon there was a problem of overcapacity. This led to a merger in 1888 to form the Salt Union and standardised method and measures.

QUALITY AND GRADES

For many years the Cheshire salt had been considered unsuitable by the fishing industry as it was too fine. The coarser sea salt (Bay salt) was preferred for salting fish and continued to be imported from France, even when Britain was at war with the French in the 1740s. In 1748 Thomas Lowndes advocated an open pan method, involving slow evaporation in larger pans, which became the standard method. Alum was also added to produce clear, harder crystals. This produced the pyramidal hopper crystals seen in coarser salts and didn't need to be dried in a hothouse. Other additives were also tried in addition to alum, egg white, blood and ale, including glue and soft soap. The glue increased the surface tension and the soap decreased it. Crystal size obviously affected density of the product. Where the product was sold by volume rather than weight, size of crystal could be a critical factor in profit margins. Different markets required a range of crystal size, for example butter- and cheese-makers needed finer salt. Too much glue could make for a continuous crust of salt, which wasn't always desirable.

Pans were 7–7.5 metres (24–25 feet) wide to allow for 3.5 metres (12 foot) long rakes to draw salt from the centre of the pans. For fine pans, the length was about 12 metres (40 feet). Fast fires heated and boiled the brine while also heating hothouses where the salt was dried over the course of about two weeks, before being crushed and processed into fine crystalline salt for dairy use. Common pans were about twice the length of fine pans and were kept at simmering temperature to produce large crystals. Salt for alkali-making formed after a day or two, but salt crystals for fisheries or tanneries might take two or three weeks to form. Drained salt was then transported directly, without drying.

20TH-CENTURY PRODUCTION

Vacuum evaporation, as described in the previous chapter, was a process developed from sugar refining. It was first applied to salt in the USA in the 1880s but the first commercial use for salt production in the UK was in 1901 in Middlewich. The Winsford Vacuum Plant of 1905 quickly followed and a much larger model was built six years later alongside the Manchester Ship Canal, at Runcorn. Vacuum works didn't replace open pans until later, but by the end of the 1930s it was apparent that they were taking over. Also, by this time, refrigeration was taking over many of the food preserving functions that salt had provided. In 1937 the Salt Union was taken over by ICI and cleaner, more efficient vacuum evaporators were developed. The Winsford open pans were closed down in the 1950s and all open pans in Middlewich had closed by 1970, leaving only the Lion Salt Works, providing specialised products for Nigeria until 1986. British Salt was formed in 1969.

Like most industries, the open pan method had its share of specialist vocabulary and unusual terms.

From Anglo Saxon times to around 1890 cone-shaped baskets called *barrows* were woven from hazel, in which the salt was placed. From the turn of the century *peg top* tubs were made by coopers, or barrel-makers, from elm wood. Later models called tubs were made in tapered wooden moulds of varying size. A popular size was 80s, which weighed between 11 and 12 kilograms (28 pounds). Workers had to *lump* the salt into the moulds. Their job, therefore, was known as *lumping*. These lumps had to be crushed before the salt could be used, but were often transported as lumps. *Lumpmen* stood on woven hurdles which created walkways between the ancient salt pans. The salt was put on hurdles in a wall of salt. *Wallers*, often women, raked the salt.

During the 16th century protein, in the form of blood, egg white or ale, was added to the brine to form a froth in which to trap suspended solids. This was called *froth flotation* and is still used in some mineral processing.

SALT DOME

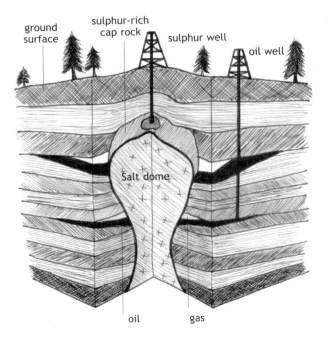

SALT TAXES

Salt has probably been one of the most taxed commodities of all times. From early times people have appreciated the need for salt and have cashed in accordingly.

ENGLISH SALT TAX

The Stuarts raised tax on salt, wine and tobacco in 1644 but after the Restoration Charles II sensibly chose not to tax salt. In 1693 William III reintroduced a salt tax, but luckily for the English poor, the tax was levied on the manufacturers instead of the consumers. Perhaps the French monarchy should have followed suit, thereby possibly avoiding losing both their throne and their heads. George III used salt tax in 1767 to pay for the American War of Independence.

The salt tax was collected by a whole host of officials and supervisors, weighers, watchmen and salt officers, who, despite their numbers, failed miserably to stop smuggling. Originally there were two collection groups, a Board of Customs for foreign trade and a Board of Excise for home trade. Home-produced salt was taxed at several times its market value and tax on imported salt was twice as much. There were cheaper rates for fishery salt, however, and for rock salt. The relatively heavy taxation on salt made it a favourite cargo for smuggling from Ireland to Wales at the end of the 17th century, and there seems to have been little enthusiasm on the part of the collectors to enforce the law. It is doubtful that the expense of collecting the tax justified the revenue it raised.

Exports of rock salt to Ireland were free of duty during most of the following century and so Ireland developed quite a large salt-refining industry along the coast. Imports lasted until the Cheshire rock salt industry took off. Another spin-off was that salt production along the west coast declined because the smuggling of refined salt back into England and Wales made salt-making unprofitable.

Meanwhile, in Ireland salt refining developed into a major industry, with exports to Russia, Scandinavia and America.

The untaxed white salt helped to develop the butter industry until Ireland became a world leader in butter exports. The salt was also used for preserving fish, beef and pork. The fish came from Scotland and Sweden for processing before being barrelled and sent to the West Indies.

SALT TAXES IN FRANCE

Charles of Anjou levied a salt tax in 1259 to help pay for a war on the Kingdom of Naples. The *Gabelle*, or salt tax, was introduced across France in 1286 by Philip IV as a temporary source of revenue and was not finally seen off until the French Revolution in 1790, when it had become one of the most hated taxes in the country.

France had always produced salt along the Mediterranean and Atlantic coasts but was not one of the major trading nations, so salt became an important commodity. The government controlled a state monopoly and then made everyone over the age of eight buy a weekly minimum amount of salt at a fixed price. The price varied in different parts of France and six distinct regions each had their own salt granaries, dating from 1342. All producers were obliged to take their salt to the *greniers a sel* or risk having their entire supply confiscated. Of course, the *greniers* then sold the salt at a much higher price. As you can imagine, a lot of smuggling and tax evasion took place. A fairly sophisticated method of buying salt in a region where the price was cheaper and selling it 'under the counter' at a higher price, but still cheaper than the official price, was rife. Smugglers like these risked being sent to the galleys if caught unarmed, or sentenced to death if found armed. Imagine having a large family and being forced to buy salt per head on a regular basis. Obviously nobody knew that too much salt is bad for you, especially for children!

From 1630 to 1710 the tax had increased tenfold. In 1675 a group in Brittany, known as the red bonnets, rebelled against the *Gabelle* and wrote down their grievances in the Peasant Code. As conditions went from bad to worse over the following decades and a series of bad harvests led to crop failure, the price of bread rose as well. Bread was the staple diet of the poorest peasants and starvation increased. By 1789 the price of bread had rocketed. The salt tax was hated by all and the towns and cities were full of hungry, angry peasants. The bread riots that followed turned into a main cause of the French Revolution.

While average taxes were higher in Britain, it was the poorer people in France who suffered more than the rich. The collection of the *Gabelle* was contracted out to a few chosen people who were allowed to charge even more for the salt than the government requested, allowing unequal tariffs to exist. When Louis XVI was deposed by the mob, the tax was repealed. Interestingly enough, it was re-introduced early in the 19th century and stayed until after the end of World War II, in 1946.

SALT AND INDEPENDENCE IN INDIA

A high salt tax imposed by the British in India provoked a 322 kilometres (200 mile) march led by Mahatma Gandhi in 1930. Gandhi decided to make the tax on salt high profile in a non-violent protest.

Although salt was acknowledged as a basic necessity, it had been taxed in India even before the era of British rule, although not to the same extent. The local rulers had a variable tax imposed, dependent on the religion of the traders. Those who were Muslim paid 2.5%, whereas Hindus were charged 5%. The traders were taxed as they travelled up the River Ganges.

Tax increased under the umbrella of the East India Company, who had a monopoly and doubled the price of salt. This only encouraged illegal trading, so an inland customs line was set up between the 1840s and 1880s, stretching 3,701 kilometres (2,300 miles). This line was guarded and patrolled by a staggering 12,000 men. The barrier was really a hedge of thorny trees and bushes with walls and ditches. It was almost impossible to cross without being stopped or incurring injuries. It has been suggested that many thousands of Indian subjects suffered salt deprivation as a result. Even after the Great Hedge was dismantled and forgotten, the tax remained.

Gandhi used the salt tax as an expression of disapproval of British colonial rule. The monopoly on salt continued and it was stated that the sale or production of salt by anyone other than the British was a punishable offence. Although salt was readily available along the coast, locals were not allowed to collect it for themselves, but had instead to buy it from the government. Gandhi devised a means of protest that brought together people across class, religion and regions, as the tax impacted on the whole of India, and he created a popular following.

Gandhi first wrote to the Viceroy, Lord Irwin, informing him that he was about to disregard the salt laws. This was reported in newspapers and when Irwin failed to reply Gandhi and about 80 followers set off from Sabarmati Ashram on 12 March, 1930 for the coastal village of Dandi, over 322 kilometres (200 miles) away. Thousands joined him along the wayside and the British were powerless to stop the protest because Gandhi had not asked anyone to join him. The event was covered by the press and on arrival in Dandi on 5 April, Gandhi was interviewed and able to make a powerful statement before collecting some muddy salt which he boiled in sea water to produce salt, saying 'With this, I am shaking the foundations of the British Empire'. He encouraged others to copy him, wherever and whenever they wished, rather than purchasing salt from the British.

This symbolic gesture started a non-violent programme of civil disobedience which spread across the country. Along with a boycott on British-made goods, salt was made and sold illegally along the coastal areas and the British government had locked up over 60 000 people by the end of the month. Gandhi was arrested under a law passed in 1827, but the world had heard about the protest. After his release he continued to work for Indian independence, which was finally achieved in August 1947.

SALT TAX IN ITALY

Until 1975, salt tax was collected through monopolies and the imposition of import customs. The state had a monopoly on the manufacture and sale of salt, and fixed the final market price, which included the tax rate of about 70%. Discount prices were fixed on salt for agricultural and industrial uses and production was tax-free in Sicily, Sardinia and in a few towns.

A BRIEF SUMMARY OF SALT HISTORY IN THE USA

The first Europeans to reach America noted native groups harvesting salt from the sea and it is thought that they had been producing salt for at least 500 years before that. The Hopi people in the south-west had ceremonial salt mines. The USA has massive reserves of salt available, although there have been times in its history when a shortage of salt caused major upheaval.

During the 15th century Portuguese and Spanish fleets used a method of salting fish on board ship, whereas the French and British fleets took their catch ashore to dry and salt on racks. This is how Britain and France became the first white settlers in Newfoundland since the Vikings.

SOME DITCH!
The Erie Canal, connecting the Great Lakes to New York's Hudson River in 1825, was hailed as an engineering marvel, although nicknamed 'the ditch that salt built'. Salt tax revenues paid for half the cost of construction of the canal and salt was the main cargo to use the waterway.

STRATEGY WHICH DIDN'T WORK
Part of the British strategy during the American War of Independence (1763–1789) was to deny salt to the rebels, so Americans had to learn to make their own salt. The Iroquois had a treaty with the State of New York to provide salt reservations. Reports from 1654 show that

Onondaga Indians were making salt by boiling brine from springs, as were the native people of West Virginia in 1755. Larger-scale production was under way by 1800 and drilling for concentrated brine soon followed. Solar salt works survived without the ideal climate for evaporation by means of movable sheds over evaporating pans. Sites on San Francisco Bay, California in 1770 and later at Great Salt Lake in Utah, in 1847, were important to the economy.

AMERICAN CIVIL WAR

Full-scale production from open pits began in 1862, during the Civil War, and underground mining started in 1869. Confederate salt production facilities in Saltville, Virginia and Louisiana, were early targets of the Union Army. In 1864 the North fought for 36 hours to capture Saltville, where the salt works were considered crucial to the Rebel army. This was the last important salt processing works in the hands of the Confederates and essential to the army. Confederate President Jefferson Davis was so concerned about salt supplies that he offered to waive military service in return for tending coastal salt kettles to supply the South's war effort. The salt was needed to tan leather, dye cloth for uniforms and to preserve meat. The lack of salt was lowering morale considerably among the population as well.

SALT IN RUSSIA

Salt production has influenced all spheres of life in Russia and is the oldest branch of Russian industry. The struggle for supremacy over salt resources led to bloody wars and to uprisings like the 1648 Moscow salt riot, when the masses revolted against overburdening salt taxes.

At the end of the 16th century many salteries owned by associations of townspeople, peasants or by monasteries, were taken over by force. Monasteries, granted exemption from tax by the Tsar, made a good business out of salt, which was expensive to buy. The technology was quite sophisticated, with wells being drilled to a depth of 180 metres (590 feet). Another means of making salt was to dig a canal from an existing lake to an artificial lake for extraction. Brine was then transported by pipe to salt works in the towns.

SALT STROGANOV

In the mid-16th century, Ivan the Terrible granted the Stroganovs, who were merchants, a charter that entitled them to a vast, uninhabited area extending 250 kilometres (155 miles) along the banks of the River Kama. Mass settlement followed and they became the 'salt kings of Russia' owning, by the end of the 17th century, 233 salteries along the Kama around Perm. Until the middle of the 17th century, the main area of salt production in Russia was the northern region of Belomorye, but it was superseded by the Perm region as the main supplier of salt to the Russian State.

The name of Solikamsk means Salts of Kama and is well known throughout Russia as the 'salt cellar of Russia'. The industry was at its peak in the 17th century. After the state ownership was declared there was a decline until the 1870s. However, in 1887, the Ustj-Borovskoy salt factory was built and Solikamsk once again became the main salt producer of Russia.

SIBERIAN SALT MINES

Little information seems to be available about the Siberian salt mines, although they are referred to frequently because of the extremely harsh conditions and forced labour. The building of the Trans-Siberian Railway, completed in 1914, opened up the area for exploitation of massive mineral reserves, but before it was built convicts had to walk for three months to cover the 1,609 kilometres (1,000 miles) over the Ural Mountains to the salt mines and labour camps around Irkutsk. By 1900, over one million people had been exiled and had made the long journey to the so-called salt mines, where they were in fact often mining gold, silver and copper, rather than salt. After the discovery of the mineral deposits within Siberia the use of exiled 'criminals' was the obvious answer.

The Industrial Uses of Salt

A BRIEF SUMMARY OF THE EARLY HISTORY OF CHEMICAL SALT

Only a small percentage of salt produced is for domestic use. The vast majority produced worldwide since the late 18th and early 19th centuries has been used in chemical industries. These industries grew out of the previous work of alchemists who changed substances with water, mixed them together or studied the effects of heat on them.

Initially salt didn't seem to be very exciting, until someone discovered how to make hydrochloric acid from sulphuric acid and salt. Sulphuric acid and hydrochloric acid were used instead of buttermilk to provide a souring agent in the bleaching of textiles. In 1772 or 1773 a Swedish chemist called Carl Scheele managed to react hydrochloric acid with manganese dioxide to make chlorine. Chlorine was able to bleach products derived from vegetable matter, such as cotton. In 1785 a French chemist, Berthollet, used a solution of chlorine in alkali to make an industrial bleach. James Watt, who was a chemist before he got more interested in steam power, had been researching the production of alkali from the reaction of salt with lime and coal.

Early production of chlorine meant that you needed salt, sulphuric acid and manganese dioxide altogether at the point where you wanted to use the chlorine, which was not always convenient, but in 1790 Charles Tennant introduced ready-made bleaching powder in Glasgow. What was really still needed for the industry to develop further, however, was the production of alkali from salt. But salt tax was still in place and the government was unwilling to reduce this tax on the raw material for anything, even the advancement of science. They needed the money for the Napoleonic Wars. Watt and friends tried to change the government's mind, but to no avail. James Kier tried to get round the problem by using potassium and sodium sulphate with nitric acid and lime to make soap. Although this avoided the salt tax, it was slow and gave a poor yield. Another attempt was made by Fordyce, a doctor and chemist, but was thwarted by the Board of Customs, as potash was involved and that was also taxed. The supplies of ash had declined and Europe was being deforested. Potash had to be imported from North America, Russia and Scandinavia.

THE LEBLANC PROCESS

The breakthrough came from France. Scheele's discovery had provided the first step in the race to make alkali. Louis XVI in France offered a prize for a method of producing alkali from sea salt. In 1791 Leblanc found the second step in the process by adding crushed limestone and coal to sodium sulphate. The coal (carbon) was oxidised to form carbon dioxide and the sulphate became sulphide, leaving the sodium carbonate and calcium sulphide, or black ash. By 1800 soda ash was being produced at the rate of 10,000 to 15,000 tons per year. Because sodium carbonate dissolves in water the soda ash was separated from the black ash by washing. This water was then evaporated to leave the sodium carbonate.

The end of the Napoleonic Wars brought stability. After a repeal of a tax on salt in Britain in 1824 the development was unstoppable and by 1870 the output of soda ash from Britain had reached 200,000 tons a year, more than all other countries put together. The price was environmental devastation. Sulphuric acid released hydrochloric acid gas into the atmosphere. For every 8 tons of soda ash produced, 7 tons of calcium sulphide waste hung around on the ground, smelling of rotten eggs. The surrounding land was scorched and fields and gardens produced little that was not spoiled. The people who worked in these factories or who lived close by must have suffered greatly. Luckily another process was invented without the major disadvantages. This was the Solvay process.

THE SOLVAY PROCESS

Ernest Solvay developed a method of bubbling carbon dioxide through brine mixed with ammonia to make sodium bicarbonate (baking soda). This could then be converted to soda ash by drying in a kiln. This was much cleaner and more efficient. The Leblanc process needed a large supply of white salt, whereas the Solvay process used brine, which saved a lot of production costs and evaporation processes.

ELECTROLYSIS OF BRINE

Over the years, soda and potash were defined as both natural and artificial products and as vegetable and mineral. Sir Humphry Davy decomposed both alkalies and called them sodium and potassium, which are really Latinised versions of soda and potash. The two metals cannot be isolated by normal chemical processes and were only prepared after the discovery of the electric current in 1800, when the electrolytic processes were developed. Davy's method was modified and called the Castner process. This produced chlorine, caustic soda and hydrogen on an industrial scale in the 1870s and was used to prepare sodium for a long time. Most is now prepared by the Down's process which produces chlorine as well as sodium.

DOWN'S PROCESS

This uses a carbon anode and iron cathode. The electrolyte sodium chloride has been fused to a liquid by heating. Sodium chloride is a poor conductor of electricity, but fusing it mobilises the sodium and chloride ions, which then allow conduction of electric current. Some calcium chloride and sodium carbonate is added to reduce the temperature and to keep the electrolyte liquid at around 600°C.

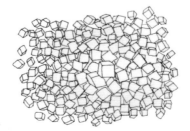

INDUSTRIAL USES TODAY

Passing an electrical current through a strong solution of salt in water causes electrolysis. Three products are formed:

- chlorine (Cl_2)
- hydrogen (H_2)
- sodium hydroxide (NaOH)

Hydrogen and chlorine gases are explosive when mixed so they must be separated. All three chemicals are important useful products which can be combined to make a whole array of other chemicals and products.

CHEMICALS MADE FROM SODIUM CHLORIDE

CHLORINE
This is used primarily in producing polymers in the manufacture of plastics, synthetic fibres and synthetic rubber. It is also used in crude oil refining, for making pesticides and in household bleach, water and sewage treatment.

Demand for salt to produce chlorine chemicals is falling. Much of the decreased demand for chlorine has been attributed to environmental concerns about dioxins.

CHLORINE DIOXIDE
This form of chlorine is used for bleaching wood pulp and flour and for disinfecting water. Chlorine dioxide is used in many industrial water treatment applications including cooling towers, food processing and the control of the legionnaire bacteria.

SODIUM HYDROXIDE
More commonly known as caustic soda or lye, this is a main constituent of a range of more complex chemicals and used as a strong chemical base in laboratories and in the manufacture of pulp and paper, textiles, drinking water, soaps and detergents.

Sodium hydroxide is used domestically for unblocking drains. The chemical converts grease to a form of soap, producing a water-soluble form which can be dissolved by flushing. Strong drain cleaners are highly caustic and should be handled with care.

In the early 20th century it was used to relax or straighten the hair of people of African ethnicity, but because of the high incidence of chemical burns, chemical relaxer manufacturers started to use other alkaline chemicals.

Sodium hydroxide is used as a catalyst in the manufacture of biodiesel, a liquid fuel source largely compatible with petroleum-based diesel fuel. It replaces glycerol with a short chain alcohol such as methanol or ethanol. Waste vegetable oils can even be used, so the process is very 'green', generating a valuable fuel to combat pollution by carbon fuels.

Given the caustic nature of sodium hydroxide it is slightly surprising to note that food uses of lye include washing or chemical peeling of fruits and vegetables. It is also used in chocolate and cocoa processing, caramel colour production, poultry scalding, soft drink processing, and for thickening ice cream. Pretzels are glazed with it to make them brown and olives are often soaked in lye to soften them, while German lye rolls are glazed with a lye solution before baking to make them crisp.

SODIUM HYPOCHLORITE

Sodium hydroxide and chlorine combine to form sodium hypochlorite solution. When concentrated it is a strong oxidiser so is highly corrosive. It is used in dilute form of 3 to 6% as domestic bleach. Commercially it is used in the dairy industry as a disinfectant. It is also used to chlorinate water.

SODIUM CHLORATE

Under different reaction conditions, sodium hydroxide and chlorine will react to form sodium chlorate. This is mostly used for bleaching paper and pulp and as a herbicide. Pretty nasty stuff, the white crystals can be highly explosive or inflammable if mixed with organic matter. Weedkillers contain about 53% sodium chlorate. Poor plants!

HYDROGEN CHLORIDE
As we have already seen, when chlorine gas is burned in hydrogen, the two gases react to form hydrogen chloride. This dissolves in water to form hydrochloric acid. Made in this way it is very pure, and can be used safely in the food and pharmaceutical industries.

CALCIUM HYPOCHLORITE
Calcium hypochlorite, known as bleaching powder, is widely used for water treatment and as a bleaching agent for cotton and linen. This chemical is relatively stable and has greater chlorine available than sodium hypochlorite, which is liquid bleach. Calcium hypochlorite is used for the disinfection of drinking water or swimming pool water. It is also used in the manufacture of chloroform.

SODIUM SULPHATE (Glauber's salts)
Sodium sulphate has several important industrial uses. It is produced from naturally occurring sodium-sulphate-bearing brines or crystalline evaporite deposits and as a by-product from different chemical processes. Examples of these are the production of ascorbic acid, boric acid, cellulose, chromium chemicals, lithium carbonate, rayon, silica pigments, and battery acid recycling. Sodium sulphate is considered to be a waste product but has several important and useful applications in various products, such as in pulp and paper, soaps and detergents, and textiles.

Sodium sulphate summary:

- Batteries
- Cellulose
- Ceramics
- Detergents
- Dyes
- Explosives
- Fertilisers
- Metal fluxes
- Paper
- Pharmaceuticals

- Pharmaceuticals
- Photography
- Pigments
- Plating salts
- Rayon
- Rubber
- Soap
- Textiles

SODIUM PERCHLORATE

Perchlorate salts act as oxidisers in propellants such as rocket boosters. Sodium perchlorate is used in some pyrotechnics but is hygroscopic. It is made from sodium chloride with platinum anodes, or sometimes other metals are involved.

SODIUM BICARBONATE (bicarbonate of soda)

This common substance is used in textile manufacturing, processing leather, making soap and glass. It is also used for leavening food when baking and is the main constituent of baking powder. It is used for neutralising acids and odours, and for cleaning. It should be part of anyone's store cupboard because it is so versatile. In fact there are so many uses, I have written a separate book on it!

SODIUM CARBONATE

More commonly known as soda ash or washing soda, this chemical is used in the manufacture of glass, pulp, paper and rayon. Its most important use is in the chemical make-up of glass. In chemistry it is often used as an electrolyte, as it acts as a very good conductor in the process of electrolysis. Sodium carbonate is widely used in photographic processes as a pH regulator for developing agents. In brick-making it is used as a wetting agent, and is used in some swimming pools to neutralise the acidic effects of chlorine and raise pH.

Domestically it is used to soften water during laundry and reduces the amount of detergent needed. It effectively removes oil, grease and alcohol stains, and is used as a de-scaling agent in boilers.

Here is a summary list of uses of sodium carbonate:

- Abrasives
- Adhesives
- Batteries
- Ceramics
- Cleansers
- Cosmetics
- De-scaler
- Degreasers
- Detergents
- Dyes
- Explosives
- Fats and oils
- Fertilisers
- Fire extinguishers
- Insecticides
- Leather
- Metal fluxes
- Ore refining
- Paint removers
- Paper
- Petroleum
- Pigments
- Soap
- Textiles
- Water softeners
- Wetting agent

SODIUM PEROXIDE

This is an oxidising agent for bleaching paper, cloth, wood, ivory and for purifying the air in confined spaces such as submarines or aeroplanes.

HYDROCHLORIC ACID

This has been an important fundamental chemical since the Industrial Revolution. Applications include vinyl chloride, for PVC plastic, polyurethane, synthetic rubber and the cleaning of gas and oil wells. It is an element used in making glass, rayon, polyester and other synthetic fibres, leather processing, plastics, soaps and detergents. Other uses include household cleaning, many pharmaceutical products, and building construction. Oil production is sometimes stimulated by injecting hydrochloric acid into rock formations to dissolve rock. Nice!

Another slightly surprising application, to a novice like me, is its use in the food industry, such as in the production of gelatin and other food ingredients. Perhaps it helps to know that hydrochloric acid forms the majority of the human digestive fluid, gastric acid. Many chemical reactions involving hydrochloric acid are used in food additives such as fructose, citric acid, lysine and aspartame, my most feared additive. Yet another good reason for getting away from processed foods.

SODIUM NITRATE (Chile saltpetre)

This is an ingredient in fertilisers, rocket propellants and explosives. It was used extensively for the making of gunpowder towards the end of the 19th century. It also finds uses in the glass and pottery enamel industries.

Sodium nitrate is used as a food preservative and is found naturally in leafy green vegetables. It is believed to have health benefits by increasing oxygen supply to blood, as well as known health side effects at high doses. It is used in the curing of bacon and is found as an additive in hot dogs.

LIQUID SODIUM

This is used as a coolant, or heat exchanger, and is an essential element in the nuclear process. It is prepared by electrolysis of dry-fused sodium chloride. Liquid sodium is also used in medicine, agriculture and photography, in street lights, batteries and glass.

METALLIC SODIUM

In its metallic form sodium can be used to refine some reactive metals, such as zirconium and potassium, and is used in making brass, bronze and case-hardened steel. It is also used for fumigating materials and in indigo and other synthetic dyes. The largest use was once in leaded petrol and high-performance internal combustion engines. It is used as a heat transfer fluid in some types of nuclear reactors.

Sodium vapour lamps are an efficient means of producing light from electricity, often used for street lighting. Low-pressure sodium lamps give a distinctive yellow-orange light and high-pressure lamps give a more natural peach-coloured light.

Summary of sodium uses:

- Bactericides
- Case hardening
- Cosmetics
- Detergents
- Dyes and fixation
- Flour conditioning
- Fumigation
- Heat transfer

- Ore refining
- Organic synthesis
- Paints
- Pharmaceuticals
- Photography
- Pigments
- Plating salts
- Pulp bleaching
- Starch conversion
- Tetraethyl lead
- Textile bleaching
- Titanium metal
- Zirconium metal

SOAP MANUFACTURE

The most common early soaps were made from potash and pearl ash. Early references to the use of soap include the Babylonians, about 2800 BC, and the Phoenicians, c.600 BC. The Egyptians used natron, and the Spaniards and other Mediterranean people, were using burned seaweed to provide the alkali they needed. Early uses included the cleaning of wool and cotton fibre prior to spinning and weaving.

Soap is basically a reaction between fatty acids and an alkali. When fats or oils are mixed with a strong alkali the fats are split into fatty acids and glycerine. The sodium or potassium in the alkali joins with the fatty acid as the basis of soap.

The three main stages of early soap-making were:
- making a wood ash solution called lye
- cleaning the fats
- boiling the fats with the lye to make soap.

Early manufacturers obtained the lye from putting potash into a bottomless barrel over a stone slab, resting on rocks. Straw or sticks were put in the bottom as a sort of sieve. By slowly pouring water over the ashes you could produce the lye, a brown liquid dripping down into a container below. This could then be used with the rendered-down fat to produce soap. When wood supplies dwindled towards the end of the 18th century, pearl ash manufacturing started to decline, making way for more commercial methods. The Leblanc process changed soap-making for ever. Sodium alkalis made harder, better soap without the necessity to add salt.

SOAP AND GLYCERINE MANUFACTURE

Fats and oils are heated with caustic soda to produce soap and glycerine. The continuous process, developed in about 1940, means, as the name suggests, that production can continue without making batches. Soap takes about six hours to make nowadays. Previously, by the 'kettle process', it took 4 to 11 days to complete a batch.

Soap and glycerine are produced as the fat reacts with alkali after boiling. To separate the soap and glycerine, salt is added, causing the soap to rise to the top and the glycerine to settle to the bottom. A second step to remove small amounts of fat that have not turned to soap may involve the use of caustic soda (which is also made from salt), followed by a second salt treatment.

Glycerine is used to make hand lotion, drugs and nitro-glycerine, the main component of explosives such as dynamite.

Sodium sulphate is used to make soaps and detergents. It is an especially important ingredient in powdered soaps, although not as much is needed to make liquid soaps.

GLASS-MAKING

The most important chemical activity was the making of alkali. When mixed with lime and sand it could be used to make glass. Worldwide, synthetic production of alkali is about 22 million metric tons, about twice that of natural production. Most of this soda ash is used to make chemicals and glass.

NATRON AND GLASS-MAKING

Glass-makers didn't wait for the invention of the Leblanc process. People had been making glass since before 2200 BC in Iran and the Egyptians were able to make coloured glass. Roman technology used glass for more practical purposes than just for decoration and used semi-precious stones to give different colours. For example, turquoise gave a pale blue glass, and fluorite a purple hue. It was manufactured by melting alkali (potash or sodium) with silica such as quartz or sand.

During the next several hundred years, glass developed in different ways in various parts of the world, and was based on either soda or potash. The soda was found in Mediterranean regions in the ashes of plants in salty sea marshes and in seaweed. Germany and Bohemia used potash from beechwood and France used bracken as a source. The quality of the glass depended on the preparation of the soda.

Lead glass or flint glass was invented in the 17th century, in the days of William and Mary of Orange, in the Netherlands. This could be cut to enhance designs and show off its sheen. After this, there were still more changes and refinements to glass and its production; for example, large amounts of lead were used with potash and Venetian glass was produced with soda. Flint glass was made from three parts sand, two parts red lead and one part potash or pearl ash from Canada or Russia.

The Leblanc process made alkali easier and cheaper to make and therefore glass-making developed at a faster rate. Europe seemed to have the monopoly on expensive and decorative blown glassware until an unknown carpenter in Massachusetts, USA, invented a new method of pressed glass in 1827. Then, in 1864 in Western Virginia, William Leighton brought about a revolution in the process of making glass at a fraction of the price of the lead and flint varieties. His pressed glass was of equally good clarity and could be produced thinly by being pressed into a mould. The major difference, though, was the use of sodium bicarbonate and lime instead of lead. All this and manufactured at a third of the price, because the bicarbonate of soda was readily available in large quantities.

SODA-LIME GLASS
Nowadays, 90% of commercial glass is produced in this, the least expensive way of making glass. Soda-lime glass is primarily used for bottles, jars, everyday drinking

glasses and window glass. It contains approximately:
- 60-75% silica
- 12-18% soda
- 5-12% lime

Soda-lime glass is not resistant to high temperatures, sudden thermal changes, or to corrosive chemicals

Using bicarbonate of soda for commercial production of glass has several benefits. It is effective at high temperatures of around +400°C. During manufacture the glass gives off acid fumes and dust. Bicarbonate of soda neutralises acid components of gases so that they can be discharged into the atmosphere. The residual chemicals of sodium sulphate are recycled in the furnace, also using bicarbonate of soda.

LEATHER CURING AND TANNING

If you are vegetarian you'll probably want to skip this section and move on. I wouldn't blame you!

The processing of animal hides for making leather has changed little since primitive man started to use it. Unless they were treated, the skins used for clothes, footwear, water carrying and many other things would have rotted. Drying skins preserved them, but resulted in a very hard, uncomfortable material.

Curing protected and softened the skins and made them waterproof. Several methods have evolved.

DRYING
Chilling or refrigeration requires no chemical additions, but before this was available skins were laid out on stones in the sun to dry. This method is the oldest form of curing, but there is very little control on speed of drying and it is liable to cause problems later on during the tanning process. Stretching the skins on frames and drying in the shade was a better method, but not as good as brining.

BRINING

Washed skins or hides are put into a salt solution and kept moving constantly, until the brine penetrates the skins. The concentration of salt is kept high, by continually adding salt to the brine solution and a disinfectant. The skins are then taken out and dried ready for shipping or further processing. This is a good but expensive method for preserving skins. It is more common than wet-salting, as it's considered a faster, easier method. It takes 10-16 hours before the skins are completely cured and ready to move on to the next stage.

WET-SALTING

Skins are placed in a pile with salt sprinkled on top of each addition to the pile, until there are about 50 skins. The salt absorbs the moisture from the skins and the resulting brine penetrates the skins, killing off the bacteria. Once the hides are in this state, they will keep for a very long time, as long as temperature and humidity are controlled.

DRY-SALTING

This involves wet-salting as a first stage before the hides are hung up to dry. Dry-salting reduces the chance of heat damage and brings down transport costs.

PICKLING

This is a method most commonly used with sheepskins. The skins are kept damp and cool (below 20°C, 68°F) in a salt and acid solution.

THE START OF THE TANNING PROCESS

If you are still reading this section, well done! Having researched this topic, I know why I never considered the medical world as a career. I'm not normally squeamish and I do wear leather shoes, but there is a limit. You don't really need to know some of the details, so I've only included the first stages of tanning, where salt products are used.

SOAKING

The first operation is to soak the skins. This is done to reverse the curing process and to remove dirt and nasty bits. Soaking takes place in big drums, firstly with water and then with detergent, salt and a biocide (usually chlorine-based) being added. The process continues until the water remains clean and the skins have been rehydrated. This may take from 18 to 72 hours.

LIMING

The cleaned skins still have their hair on which must be removed completely with the root hairs and epidermis. Sodium sulphide or sodium hydrosulphide is added to the soaked skins for about an hour until they do their job. Let's leave it there. Salt doesn't feature in the remainder of the process.

PULP AND PAPERMAKING

In papermaking, caustic soda is used to process wood fibres. Chlorine is used to bleach the pulp, but sodium chlorate, also made from salt, is replacing chlorine as the primary chemical for bleaching pulp.

The following chemicals derived from salt are used in pulp and paper production:

- Sodium sulphate (salt cake), for recovering other chemicals
- Sodium carbonate (soda ash), as above
- Sodium hydrosulphite, for bleaching
- Sodium silicate, for deinting, i.e. cleaning waste paper for recycling
- Sodium hydroxide, for pulping
- Chlorine dioxide, for pulp bleaching
- Chlorine, for water treatment

Emulsified sulphur and sodium hydroxide can be used in place of sodium sulphate in paper production.

FOOD INDUSTRIES

FARMING

Rock salt is sometimes scattered on grass to make it more appetising for beef cattle. They eat more and gain weight. In sugar beet production rock salt is used to fertilise the soil with sodium. This makes sugar beet yield more sugar.

CURING FISH

Methods of curing fish by drying, salting, smoking or pickling have been employed since ancient times. Before the days of refrigeration, fishing boats used brine or dry salt to keep fish from rotting. Salting and drying made the fish very hard so it would keep for a long time. Sometimes fish was packed fresh in barrels of salt.

The swifter boats of today and the use of refrigeration mean that most fish are now brought ashore unsalted. Fish to be cured are usually first cleaned and scaled before being packed between layers of salt or immersed in brine. The most commonly salted fish are cod, herring, mackerel and haddock. Kippers are split herring, and bloaters are whole, salted, smoked herring.
Sardines, pilchards and anchovies are all fish of the herring family, often salted and smoked before they are preserved in oil. Fish are dried under controlled conditions of temperature, humidity and air velocity.

In Norway, there used to be five different grades of salt cod. The best grade was called superior extra. Superior klippfisk is salted fresh, whereas the cheaper grades might be frozen first. Lower grades are salted by injecting a salt-water solution into the fish. The superior grade is dried twice, much like Parma ham (see below). Between the two drying sessions, the fish rests and the flavour matures.

You can find some recipes and methods of curing fish in the recipe section.

MEAT CURING

Ham

The word *prosciutto* means 'thoroughly dried' although it means ham in Italian. Raw ham is cured ham which has not been cooked. Making cured ham can take from nine to eighteen months, depending on the size of the ham, which is first cleaned, salted with sea salt and left for a couple of months. During this time it is squeezed in a press to drain out any blood left in the meat. Next it is washed several times to remove the salt, after which it is hung in a cool, airy place. In some places the ham is smoked by burning different types of wood to give a special flavour. The ham is then left to dry for a varying amount of time, depending on the weight and the climate.

Prosciutto is never cured with sodium nitrate or potassium nitrate, which are normally used in other hams to produce a rosy pink colour. Prosciutto's characteristic pigmentation seems to be produced by certain bacteria, rather than a direct chemical reaction.

Bacon

Bacon is made from fresh pork which has been preserved with salt so that it will keep for longer. There are two main methods of curing:

Dry Curing

From Saxon times pigs were fattened on acorns in oak forests during autumn and the meat cured to provide food for the family in winter months. Bacon formed part of the rations for long distance sea journeys.

Wet Curing

This method immerses the meat in a liquid solution of salt and saltpetre, containing useful salt-tolerant bacteria, for three to four days. This provides a milder form of curing in the brine under refrigeration. As meat keeps fresh longer at lower temperatures it does not require so much salt. This was developed in the 1840s in Wiltshire. As there were no refrigerators back then the roof was packed with winter ice to lower the temperature.

Nowadays curing is usually carried out by dissolving salt to form a strong brine to act as a pickle. In many cases the pickle is pumped into the meat to speed up the process, as in the case of bacon and ham. Yield is increased by the addition of water. The salt for these purposes is refined and of high quality.

See the recipe section for some methods and ideas.

BREAD AND PASTRY

Salt is used to give added flavour to bread and pastry. Salt performs a function in controlling the rate at which the yeast works in the dough, giving a better texture. It is almost impossible to make bread without adding salt.

CANNING OF MEAT AND VEGETABLES

Salt is added to the products during processing. Many vegetable products are packed in brine, which should be washed out before reheating.

CHEESE MANUFACTURE

Salting is a vital part of the cheese-making process and serves four purposes:

- To slow down the development of bacteria at the beginning of the cheese-making process. These bacteria aid the formation of the curds and whey. Unchecked they would cause the cheese to spoil very quickly.
- Salt acts as a preservative in the cheese-making process. This is important in making hard cheese that will keep a long time, like Cheddar.
- It slows down the growth of undesirable bacteria.
- Salt acts as a flavour enhancer. If the cheese does not have salt it cannot mature and would quickly become inedible.

Most cheese today is made on automatic machines and salting must be carried out in a continuous process. The salt used must be extremely dry at all times. I remember visiting a cheese farm in Normandy some years ago, producing Neufchatel cheese. I was amazed to see the half-ready cheese being rolled in salt before being left in a cool room for the bacterial moulds (or 'mushrooms', as they were translated) to finish the process.

Again, you can find out more about cheese and salt in the recipe and health sections.

OTHER INDUSTRIES AND USES OF SALT

TEXTILE INDUSTRIES
Salt is used to standardise dye batches. Salt is added to the dye baths during the process to make the dyes fast. Flossy salt is the grade most commonly used in this process. Sodium sulphate is also used in the textile industry.

METAL PROCESSING
Salt is used in metal processing and secondary aluminium, making to remove impurities. Salt is used as a flux. The salt sits on top of the molten aluminium in molten form, removing iron and other metals and leaving pure metal.

RUBBER
Rubber manufacturers use salt to separate rubber from latex. Synthetic rubber is produced in the form of white latex to which salt is added as an emulsifier. Medium quality, unrefined salt is used for this purpose.

CERAMICS
Salt is used to vitrify or fire the surface of heated clays. Ceramics are formed at temperatures above 800°C. This process is called vitrification.

Salt is used to form the very smooth glaze on clay tiles or pottery ware. After a kiln of tiles reaches a white heat, salt is fed onto the fire. The salt vaporises and passes on to the surface of the tile, forming a glass film.

OIL AND GAS DRILLING
Drillers working on muds use salt to prevent fermentation,

increase density and to stabilise drilling in rock salt formations. Salt is used to mix with boring mud (yes, mud is boring isn't it?) which is pumped down bore holes. This forms a wall when drilling through gravel or sandy material, which would otherwise not stand up on its own.

DRY CLEANING
Salt is used in dry-detergent processes.

WATER SOFTENING
Salt is used in both industrial and home water-softening units. Salt for this purpose is usually a washed or refined grade. A similar type of salt is used for making a brine for brine cooling systems.

FREEZING POINT DEPRESSANT
Salt finds its way into making coal antifreeze, highway de-icing, ice manufacture, iron ore antifreeze, refrigerating brines and refrigerating cars.

DE-ICING ROADS
Salt is the major de-icer used around the world. Some other salts, such as calcium chloride and potassium chloride, can be used but these options are more expensive than salt. Due to the limitless supply available, salt is not likely to be replaced in most of its industrial and domestic uses. We'll just have to put up with the damage to metal and road surfaces caused by the salt, in exchange for its ability to melt ice.

LENSES AND PRISMS
Sodium chloride is used for windows, lenses and prisms. Because of its low absorption, sodium chloride is being used in high-power laser systems. It can be used at temperatures up to $400°C$.

RENEWABLE ENERGY
Salt domes produce heat which may be used as a source of renewable energy, either by developing and using this energy directly or by making electricity from the heat.

Molten salt solar energy production

Systems using molten salt as thermal media have been proposed for solar thermal power generation and for synthetic fuel production. Research is progressing in California and in Japan.

Salt gradient solar ponds

Solar ponds are an inexhaustible source of renewable energy, given the right conditions. A salt gradient solar pond operates using layers of different concentrations of salinity to trap heat so it can be recovered. There are three distinct layers of water in the pond. The top layer has a low salt content whereas the bottom layer has a high salt content. The middle layer acts as an insulation that prevents heat exchange. A solar pond can be used for various applications, such as process heating, sea water desalination, refrigeration, drying and generating solar power. There are many ponds operating throughout the world, largely in developing countries, where large collectors can be set up with clay or plastic pond liners at low cost.

MOLTEN SALT WASTE INCINERATION

This is a way of dealing with unwanted 'energetic' materials that cannot be easily recycled. Open burning, detonation and incineration have been the most commonly used in the past but this method may provide a more environmentally friendly means of destroying materials from conventional and nuclear weapons. The process involves a crucible of molten salt in which high explosives and propellants are reduced to carbon dioxide, nitrogen and water.

SALT-BATH FURNACE

This is a liquid-bath furnace in which the heating medium is a molten salt material. Salt-bath furnaces are used for heat treating, brazing, and tempering steel.

Salt: Kill or Cure?

PHYSIOLOGICAL NEED FOR SALT

Sodium chloride is a vital constituent in all living creatures. It is essential for the functions and processes of all animals, including human beings. All of our tissues and body fluids contain salt. Tears are salty and when you sweat, or gently perspire if you are a genteel person, you are losing salt through the pores of your skin, as your body cools down. Salt helps to regulate the water content of the body and is replaced by natural or added salt in your food and also when you add it as a condiment at the table. A normal body contains about a third of the quantity of salt there is in sea water. It has been suggested that the need for salt has come from the days when animal life first emerged from the oceans, which reminds me of a memorable beer advertisement that retraced the steps of mankind from shore to pub.

As we saw earlier, when early man was a hunter he got all the salt he needed from animals, if he managed to catch any, that is. The alternatives were shellfish and other aquatic sources, like fish. As more pastoral activities like farming took over and omnivorous humans learned to love grains and plants to eat, there was a greater need for salt, both for humans themselves and for their animals.

LOW SALT DIETS
It is interesting to note that among isolated groups of people discovered around the world over the course of time, required intake of salt is low, if not non-existent. Sodium and chlorine, the two components of salt, are both necessary for survival, but that doesn't mean to say we need to eat them together as salt. Many parts of equatorial Africa do not have huge salt reserves because of the igneous rocks that dominate and the only salt is to be found in rain or dust. Here, plants and insects exist that are able to capitalise on minute quantities of chlorides and concentrate them. People have, in the past, survived by drinking the blood and urine of animals that have collected and concentrated the salt in their blood by feeding on large quantities of plants.

The Yanomami Indians, who live in the Amazon in South America, are hunters, fishermen and cultivators of plantains and cassava in forest clearings. The people eat a diet that is very low in salt. They have the lowest blood pressure readings measured and there is no obesity or consumption of alcohol. Studies of the Yanomami have provided scientists with valuable insights into the link between hypertension and consumption of sodium. Their blood pressure does not increase with age, unlike in most countries.

Indigenous hunters in Greenland did not eat salt until they were introduced to it in the 17th century by Europeans, who were whaling. Like our ancestors, Lapps, Samoyeds, Bedouin, Masai and Zulus used to consume all the sodium they needed from the animals and fish they ate. There is no doubt that early settlements grew up around brine springs. These were probably discovered by following animals to their salt licks.

SALT DEFICIENCY
Tribes like the Masai believe that cattle are too precious and valuable to kill, so daily nourishment is received by bleeding live cattle by opening a vein on the neck or flank with the point of an arrow. The blood is collected and often mixed with fresh or curdled milk and in this way salt is included in the daily diet.

Salt deprivation has its problems for health and well-being and it has been suggested that, just as salt-starved animals eat part of their litter in order to stay alive, extreme salt hunger is one of the causes of cannibalism. Women of the Suya people in the Amazon collect water hyacinth or pond lilies, dry them in the sun and burn their leaves. The ash is then passed through a kind of grass filter to obtain a potassium chloride salt, or potash. This is not the same as sodium chloride and is too rich in potassium to make a good salt, but it avoids salt deficiency.

Aborigines in New Guinea have been observed making secret expeditions to the sea coast to put sea water into hollow bamboos which are carried back to their tribe. A long walk for a little salt, but if you don't have a lot of salt in your diet, you don't miss it.

SODIUM AND CHLORINE

As we have seen, sodium is a component of salt. In 2.5 grams of salt there is 1 gram of sodium. Sodium is a component of other ingredients, as described previously. Sodium bicarbonate used in baking and monosodium glutamate used as a flavour enhancer are two examples, but we'll come back to the latter one shortly. Too much sodium in the diet can lead to health problems, such as high blood pressure (hypertension). This in turn substantially increases the risk of developing heart disease or stroke.

FUNCTIONS OF SODIUM

Sodium is a must in our diet and is an element the body cannot manufacture itself. Many functions are regulated by sodium which is contained in body fluids transporting oxygen and nutrients. Sodium also regulates the balance of fluids in the body that deliver the nutrients, the fluid volume and the balance of acids. The average salinity of blood and other body fluids is 0.9%. An adult human body contains about 250 grams of salt. Any excess is automatically disposed of.

In addition to controlling fluids, sodium facilitates the transmission of nerve impulses. Like potassium, calcium and magnesium, sodium is an electrolyte, regulating the electrical charges moving around cells in the body.

Sodium controls some of the senses, which would otherwise be dulled. For example, it is necessary for signals to reach and return from the brain. It regulates taste, smell and touch processes. Sodium ions are essential for the contraction of muscles. Of course, the biggest muscle of all and the most vital of these is the heart. So, you might think, a little extra salt can only do you good if we need it to function properly, but that's where we go wrong.

FUNCTIONS OF CHLORIDE

Like sodium, chloride is essential to good health as well. It is a must in the digestion process, where it preserves the acid-base balance in the body. Chloride helps the body to absorb potassium. It supplies the basis of the hydrochloric acid in the stomach's gastric juices. These help to break down and digest the food we eat, and control levels of bacteria in the stomach. Another function of chloride is to help the blood carry carbon dioxide back from tissues to the lungs.

KEEPING THE BALANCE

A little is good, but too much is bad. The balance needs to be upheld. This is why patients who are dehydrated by vomiting or extreme diarrhoea are given saline drips. These are a weak solution of salt and liquid nutrients fed into the body via a blood vessel, when the patient is too ill to eat or drink normally. People suffering from drought and starvation in Third World countries, or after disasters, are given salt and sugar solutions to help rehydration.

Living in a hot climate means you sweat more, so you lose more salt through loss of fluid. In the same way, a good workout in the gym or on an athletics track will get your heart pumping and your sweat glands working overtime to cool you down. Some athletes take salt tablets to relieve the effects of muscle cramps, brought on by the loss of fluids and salt, but these are not normally necessary for everyday life. Sodium requirements are linked closely to water needs. If you drink more water you will replace the losses without the need for extra salt. One exception to this were coalminers, who were given salt tablets to take in the extremely hot conditions tolerated daily when working underground under great physical stress. These salt tablets were added to the miners' metal water carriers, known in some mining areas including the Kent coalfield, as Dudleys.

People who suffer from kidney problems and very young children can't take high levels of sodium because the kidneys can't excrete the excess. It is very important, therefore, that salt is never added to baby food.

HEALTH PROBLEMS

HIGH BLOOD PRESSURE

The link to high blood pressure or hypertension has already been referred to, although consuming high levels of sodium is not the only cause of high blood pressure. There are often no symptoms of hypertension, but over-consumption increases the risk of heart disease and stroke. It is recommended that the most effective diet to prevent or treat high blood pressure is one which is low in fat and sodium, and includes low fat dairy products and plenty of fresh fruit and vegetables. Other factors, such as keeping physically active, not smoking and maintaining a healthy body weight, are also important in preventing hypertension. You can't do much if it is genetic, other than maintain a healthy and active lifestyle.

It has been estimated that about 18 million people in the UK have high blood pressure. The risk of developing heart disease or having a stroke is three times higher than for people with normal blood pressure. Nearly 238,000 people die each year from heart disease in the UK and around 50,000 people a year die from stroke. Lowering salt consumption seems to be, therefore, an important priority. There are variations. Statistically, among people of Afro-Caribbean origin living in the UK, up to 50% over the age of 40 are likely to have high blood pressure compared to other ethnic groups. Stroke is also more common in Afro-Caribbean people. People of Pakistani, Bangladeshi and Chinese origin appear to have a lower risk.

A diet that is healthy doesn't have to be restricted to a particular need or symptom, especially when there might not be any outward symptoms for several years, before a condition is diagnosed. In any event, it makes sense to eat healthily, and without salt to cover up other flavouring in food you can identify other, more subtle flavours. In my experience, when you give up eating lots of salt, you find that processed food begins to taste even more salty, almost to the point of being inedible.

KIDNEY PROBLEMS

Our kidneys filter and clean the blood and get rid of waste products by making urine. They also regulate the amount of fluid we have in our bodies and the sodium levels and other salts. If these levels are too low, a hormone is released and this increases the amount of sodium held in the body by reducing the amount lost in urine. Regulation of fluid helps to regulate blood pressure as well. If the kidneys don't work properly, there will be changes in blood pressure and in the fluid balance of the body, leading to swelling, especially in the feet and ankles. More severe kidney problems will lead to a build-up of waste products in the blood, which the body cannot get rid of. It is very important to identify kidney disease at an early stage, especially among people with heart disease, hypertension or diabetes, and that is why these conditions are closely monitored, once identified. Treatment may be through a limited diet, to cut out high levels of potassium, sodium or phosphate and high protein foods and so limit the build-up of waste products.

CARDIAC ENLARGEMENT

Left ventricular hypertrophy is the thickening of the muscle of the left ventricle of the heart. It is frequently seen as a symptom of heart disease, although it can occur naturally as a reaction to aerobic exercise and strength training. High blood pressure can also be a cause.

STOMACH CANCER

A study a few years ago suggested that people who eat a high salt diet have a higher risk of stomach cancer. Research was carried out in Japan, where consumption of salt is high. Highly salted pickled food is popular and rates of stomach cancer are high. Nearly 40,000 men and women between 40 and 59 were followed over an 11-year period, measuring their daily salt intake. Researchers found that men who ate less than 6 grams of salt a day had a risk of 1 in 1,000 of developing stomach cancer. This risk went up to 1 in 500 for men eating 12-15 grams a day. Women faired a little better: those who ate less than 6 grams of salt a day had a risk factor of 1 in 2,000, but the risk rose to 1 in 1,300 for those who ate 12-15 grams a day. Eating high levels of salt is thought to waste the stomach lining.

In the UK the rate of stomach cancer has been falling over the last 70 years or so, making it the sixth most common cancer. One theory for this fall is that people in Britain have been eating less salted, smoked and pickled foods, as refrigeration has become the main way of preserving food. Cancer of the stomach is more common Nine out of ten people diagnosed with stomach cancer are over the age of 55.

OSTEOPOROSIS

Oh, the joys of getting older. Osteoporosis is a bone-wasting disease costing the NHS millions of pounds and causing disability in the elderly, especially women. The greatest risk factors for osteoporosis are poor diet in childhood and adolescence, when the bones are being formed. Also, the rate of bone loss in later life can be affected by other changes, such as hormone imbalances, speeding up the loss of calcium. Researchers now believe that eating too much salt can raise the blood pressure and that this also speeds up the body's loss of calcium. Measurements of over 3,600 women over three and a half years led the researchers to conclude that post-menopausal women with higher blood pressure had greater and faster loss of bone minerals than those with lower blood pressure. Smoking also increased the bone loss.

Bone loss over many years can lead to osteoporosis. Research shows hypertensive people excrete higher amounts of calcium in their urine than those with low blood pressure. Potassium helps to reduce calcium loss, whereas sodium speeds up the process, so, yet again, a low salt diet may save you from pain and suffering later in life. It is interesting to note that our diet today tends to be low in potassium and high in sodium. Potassium lowers blood pressure as well. Food processing tends to lower the potassium levels in many foods while increasing the sodium content, so, by cutting out a lot of the processed foods and eating potassium-rich fruit and vegetables, we can all do ourselves no end of good by lowering the blood pressure and delaying the onset of osteoporosis. By the way, men suffer from this disease as well. Many people seem to think it is only little old ladies who suffer.

OEDEMA

Oedema, or fluid retention, can be caused by eating highly salted food, and is more likely to occur when you get older. Cutting down your salt intake will help to reduce fluid retention, and patients who already have heart, kidney or liver problems will particularly benefit from cutting salt intake.

MENIERE'S DISEASE

This is a condition associated with vertigo, fluctuating hearing loss and tinnitus. Studies have shown in patients suffering from frequent attacks of vertigo that a change to a very low salt diet will lessen the frequency and severity of attacks measured over the period of a fortnight.

RECOMMENDED DAILY INTAKE OF SALT

Nowadays, most people eat more salt than they should. The recommended maximum amount for an adult is 6 grams of salt a day. This is the equivalent of taking 2.5 grams of sodium a day. It has been estimated that the average adult intake of salt is nearer to 9.5 grams a day, equivalent to about two teaspoonfuls of salt, or 3.7 grams of sodium. Children need less, but with the popularity of salty snack foods over the past couple of decades the amount of salt consumed by younger people has certainly not decreased.

Recommended salt intake per age group:

Age	Grams per day
Adult (over 15 years)	6
7-14 years	5
1-6 years	2
7 12 months	1
0-6 months	Less than 1 gram

UNDERSTANDING LABELS

First of all you have to understand the terms sodium and salt on food labels. Manufacturers don't have to give information unless a claim is made for nutritional value, but most manufacturers do so. If nutritional information is given, it has to be as sodium, not as salt. This is because it is the sodium that matters and because other additives contain sodium, apart from salt. These include monosodium glutamate, my personal horror 'flavour enhancer' additive, sodium saccharin (a sweetener), sodium ascorbate (an antioxidant) and sodium bicarbonate. Sodium is also found in some medicinal products, e.g. antacids. Chemical preservatives, such as sodium nitrite, sodium benzoate, sodium propionate, sodium citrate and sodium phosphate, contain small amounts of salt.

Read the labels

I've been reading food labels for a long time. I'd been aware of the salt and sugar added to baby foods and other foods when my children were growing up in the 1980s. One of the best interactive homework activities I ever set was for my class of primary pupils to go home and look at the baked beans in their cupboards. The sheer variety of products was astonishing, and the nutritional information most informative. We studied comparisons of contents in terms of food groups, energy and value for money. Some of the brands, usually but not always the cheapest, contained very high salt levels. It was a good exercise for all of us, adults and children. Tinned soups provide another eye-opener.

In the last few years I've developed high blood pressure and Type 2 diabetes, despite the fact that I've always watched our salt and sugar intake and I'm not obese. Nowadays, nearly all the food we eat at home is unprocessed or home grown. Having the odd treat of a meal out or a takeaway can send my body into a feeling I can only describe as like suffering from a mild hangover, even though I haven't overindulged. A tin of soup or a piece of blue cheese in isolation is okay, but the dreaded monosodium glutamate of a Chinese meal will give me the whole hangover feeling, even without any alcohol. Many people associate diabetes with only being about sugar intake, but there's a lot more to it than that. As a list of processed food containing sodium shows, there's a great deal of it about, so not adding salt to food at the table is only the tip of the iceberg. It's all the salt in the food already bought which causes the problems. High sodium foods don't always taste salty!

As well as reading labels you have the choice of reduced salt or low salt products and there is a big difference between the two.

REDUCED SALT PRODUCTS
Food labelled as 'reduced salt or sodium' may indicate a lower salt content but it is still important to check food labels. Guidelines suggest that products labelled 'reduced salt' or 'reduced sodium' should contain at least 25% less than the standard product. The baked beans I've been buying for the last 25 years are a reduced sugar and reduced salt type. The label information gives the following:

COMPARISON TABLE

Standard beans per 100 g	*Reduced salt / sugar beans*
Sugars 5.2 g	Sugars 3.2 g
Sodium 0.4 g	Sodium 0.2 g

Fine, that's within the 25% reduction, but that's only per 100, about half a portion per ½ can, i.e. one serving.

Carbohydrates	26.5 g
Of which sugars	6.7 g
Of which starch	19.8 g
Salt	1.0 g
Of which sodium	0.4 g

So, I'm still eating a whole gram of salt in one healthy helping of high fibre (6.7 grams), protein filled (9.5 grams) portion, when only 49% of the product is beans. Slightly confusing and surprising, isn't it? I'm going for the low salt in future.

LOW SALT PRODUCTS
Food labelled as low salt or low sodium needs to have no more than 40 milligrams sodium per 100 grams or 100 millilitres.

SALT-FREE PRODUCTS
Salt or sodium free products must have no more than 5 milligrams sodium per 100 grams or 100 millilitres.

LOW SODIUM ALTERNATIVES TO SALT
There are many products around these days that are labelled as low in sodium, so you might think that the answer is just to use one of these in the same quantities as before, liberally sprinkling your fish and chips or whatever. Just remember that most of the salt you are going to eat is already there, in the batter, in the ketchup or other sauce and possibly the chip coating as well.

Salt substitutes vary in their composition, but their main ingredient is always potassium chloride. As I said earlier, potassium is an alternative, but shouldn't be used by some people on various medications or by those suffering from kidney problems. Even where the main ingredient is potassium chloride, there will still be between 20% and 33% sodium chloride in the low salt brand, plus an anti-caking agent, such as magnesium carbonate.

CALCULATING THE SALT

To convert sodium to salt intake on packages, if only the sodium content is shown, you need to do a quick calculation. Salt is about 40% sodium, so if you multiply the content figure by 2.5 you will be able to work out the salt content. Also, remember that the figure will probably be given per 100 grams, so you need to consider the size of the portion as well.

Example: sodium content 0.8 g x 2.5 = 2 g of salt

The Food Standards Agency suggests the following categories for ready-made or processed food:

'a lot of' = 0.5 grams of sodium or more
per 100 grams of food
'a little' = 0.1 grams or less per 100 grams

TRAFFIC LIGHT LABELS

The newer food labels used by some supermarkets and manufacturers have 'traffic light' colours on the front of the pack. I find these very useful as they show you, at a glance, if a food is high (red), medium (amber) or low (green) in salt, sugar, fat and saturated fat. This is much easier to my mind than reaching for the reading glasses in the middle of the supermarket and reading the small print.

High or **red** means that you can eat small amounts, or just occasionally.

Medium or **amber** means that it is OK most of the time.

Low or **green** means a healthier choice.

This is fine unless you have a particularly strict diet or need to avoid a particular ingredient altogether.

SOME SURPRISING, HIDDEN SALT

On average, 75% of the salt in our diet comes from processed foods, although people eating more processed foods have even more. A further 10–15% comes from salt added when cooking. Salt found naturally in foods represents the remaining 10%. Such foods are whole grains, meat and dairy products which contain traces of sodium.

As well as being used as a flavour enhancer and preservative in processed food, salt has also been used as a binder, a fermentation control agent in breadmaking, as a colour enhancer and to add texture. The following processed foods all contain plenty of salt:

- biscuits
- bread
- butter and spreads
- cakes
- canned and packet soups
- canned vegetables and baked beans
- cheese
- crisps, salted nuts and snack foods
- ham, sausages, bacon and other meat products
- olives
- pastries
- pizza
- pork pies
- ready meals
- smoked fish
- some breakfast cereals

Some foods contain higher amounts of salt than you might expect.

Soup

A recent survey of nearly 600 brands of soup showed that almost half had more than the recommended levels of salt (0.6 grams per 100 grams). The average was 1.6 grams per serving. 20% had over 2 grams of salt, which is a third of the recommended daily intake for an adult. Hmm, that doesn't seem to make soup a healthy option, unless you read labels carefully or make your own.

Sandwiches
A jam sandwich has only 30% less salt than a vegemite or marmite sandwich. Most of the salt comes from the bread.

Cereals
A bowl of cornflakes may have about the same salt content as a small packet of plain crisps.

Biscuits
Some sweet biscuits contain as much or more salt than savoury biscuits, although they don't taste very salty because the sugar masks the taste.

Other salts
Sea salt, onion, celery or garlic salts are not low sodium substitutes.

Fatty spreads
Ordinary mayonnaise has the most salt (240 mg/100 g), followed by margarine (140 mg), butter (130 mg) and cream cheese (85 mg)

Soft drinks and mineral water
Salt is sometimes used to cover up a metallic or chemical aftertaste in soft drinks. Some mineral waters contain sodium and the amount they contain can vary quite a lot. This depends on the mix of mineral and the source of the water. There are no limits on the amount of sodium a mineral water can contain, so you need to read the labels. Spring water and table water are controlled, however, by a limit on sodium content of 200 milligrams per litre, which makes them low in sodium, like tap water.

Smoked foods
Smoked foods can contain up to 50 times more salt than the same, unsmoked foods. Fresh mackerel contains 0.15 g salt per 100 g, but smoked mackerel has 1.9 g salt per 100 g when smoked. Fresh salmon contains 0.1 g salt per 100 g, but smoked salmon has 4.7 g salt per 100 g. Luckily, we don't eat smoked salmon every day!

WAYS TO REDUCE YOUR SALT INTAKE

Here are 20 ways of avoiding hidden salt:

- Reduce the amount of salt used when cooking. Do this gradually and probably no one in the family will notice. Start with boiled vegetables first.
- If using canned vegetables, look for no added salt varieties.
- Rinse vegetables canned in brine through a sieve before heating up in ordinary water.
- Look for low salt or reduced salt alternatives of products like baked beans, ketchup, crisps, biscuits, butter, margarine, soups and gravy granules.
- Choose tinned fish, such as tuna, prepared in mineral water rather than brine.
- Read the labels and avoid monosodium glutamate.
- Offer low sodium salt at the table, unless you have kidney problems.
- Lessen the amount of salt added through stock cubes. I cut them in halves or quarters. Use the rest very soon, or throw it away. Better still, read below:
- Use herbs, garlic, spices, wine or lemon juice to add flavour.
- Avoid soy sauce, or use very occasionally.
- Avoid white bread, which tends to have more salt added. Choose reduced salt bread instead, or granary.
- Choose reduced salt breakfast cereal.
- Watch out for the bowls of salted nuts, olives and crisps at parties. There are unsalted varieties available, and at reasonable prices.
- Eat five portions of fruit and vegetables a day, unsalted of course.
- Eat bacon and sausages less frequently.
- Cut down on takeaways and ready meals. Avoid dehydrated pasta meals.
- Go for less salty cheeses, like ricotta, cottage, mozzarella and Swiss cheeses.
- Cut down on mayonnaise, which has a high salt content.
- Avoid processed foods for at least certain days of the week.
- Make your own soup; much tastier, cheap and less salty.

THE HEALTH BENEFITS OF SALT

Well, after all the doom and gloom of the problems associated with salt, it is good to know that some people get benefits from it, even though these are mostly topical.

SALT BATHS

After delivering my first child I was told to take a bath with a cup of salt dissolved in it. I thought that, since I was in a military hospital and the midwives were all unmarried and childless, this was one of their ways of getting back at you if you went over time in the delivery suite. (I did, by several hours.) Some of them also went for the dry shave before delivery, just to make it more uncomfortable as well. But, the salt bath is a great way of cleaning and preventing infection.

You can find a salt bath recipe in the rituals and customs section, if you fancy it.

SALT GARGLES FOR SORE THROAT

The age-old remedy for a sore throat is to gargle with a salt water solution. Since you don't swallow the salt (yuck!) it can be soothing and it allows salt to use its properties of cleaning and disinfecting. I remember several years ago being surprised when I visited our GP with a sore throat. I was expecting the usual antibiotics, but was sent packing with instructions to gargle twice a day for a few days instead. Half the time a sore throat will not be cured by antibiotics anyway.

MOUTH ULCERS

Gargling with salt water stings, but only in the same way that if you have a sore mouth you want to eat something salty to make it hurt, if you know what I mean. It does work!

THE DEAD SEA

The mineral content of the Dead Sea, combined with the lack of pollen and other allergens, has great benefits to some patients with respiratory problems. Reduced ultraviolet solar radiation and higher atmospheric pressure also benefit some people.

People suffering from cystic fibrosis apparently benefit from the atmosphere here, where oxygen levels are higher.

People suffering from skin disorders also benefit, in two different ways. Firstly, the reduction in harmful rays means that they can expose their skin to the sun for longer periods and secondly, the salts in the water have been shown to help psoriasis patients.

Year round sun, dry air and low levels of pollution all help.

Some popular therapies are:

- Climatotherapy and heliotherapy – that's your sunbathing, taking the air, etc.
- Thalassotherapy, or bathing in Dead Sea water.
- Balneotherapy, or treatment with black mineral mud.

Salt in Customs, Religions and Rituals

SALT IN CUSTOMS, RELIGIONS AND RITUALS

Salt has played an important role in many diverse religious and cultural customs for thousands of years. In both Islam and Judaism, salt is used to seal a bargain, because it is unchangeable. Even when it is dissolved it is still salt and can be returned to its original state. The ancient Egyptians, Greeks and Romans all included salt in sacrifices and offerings, and they called upon deities and gods using salt and water. It has been suggested that this may be the origin of Christian holy water.

Add to these ancient beliefs an array of other rituals and superstitions and you have a rich source of material. This section is intended to give a very brief summary of various beliefs, customs and rituals.

> *'Salt is born of the purest of parents:*
> *the sun and the sea.'*
> PYTHAGORAS (580-500 BC)

ANCIENT CIVILISATIONS
The Druids used salt in their rituals at Stonehenge. It is thought that this was as a symbol of the life-giving fruits of the earth. Salt is associated with life and health, and is used in rites of passage ceremonies in some cultures. It is also associated with good and has been used to counteract the effects of evil. Homer called salt divine and Plato termed it a 'substance dear to the Gods'. Since salt was so valuable — indeed, life depends on salt — it is hardly surprising that it found its way into the religious beliefs and practices of the worshippers.

Greek worshippers consecrated salt in their rituals and most ancient civilisations were accompanied by myths, religious and magic rites involving salt. The ancient Greeks and the Hebrews used salt during sacrifices.

GOOD TRIUMPHING OVER EVIL
The widespread notion that spilling salt will reap evil consequences is probably a relic of the sacred character of salt in early times. Anyone unfortunate enough to spill

salt is supposed to incur the anger of all good spirits. As a child I remember various older members of the family throwing salt over their shoulders (was it left or right?) if some was spilled. I also remember someone younger, pointing out that from a scientific point of view, salt would damage the floor covering. Another superstition I recall was not offering to dispense salt for anyone else, in the days when salt was always sprinkled on food, even before tasting it. Someone would invariably shout 'Help you to salt, help you to sorrow', if this happened. Perhaps the response should have been to throw some over the shoulder to recompense in some way. Still, worse things happen at sea (on the briny?).

HATCHES, MATCHES AND DISPATCHES

Similarities exist across continents and cultures. A range of traditions and rituals spans the human life cycle events of birth, marriage and death. Throughout the ages, there has been a belief in the sacred properties of salt.

BIRTH RITUALS
- The practice in Europe of protecting newborn babies, either by putting salt on their tongues or by submerging them in salt water, pre-dates Christian baptism. In Roman times a baby was rubbed with salt on the eighth day after birth, to keep away the demons and evil spirits. Until the practice was abolished in 1408 in France, children were salted until they were baptised.

- The Book of Ezekiel mentions rubbing newborn infants with salt to protect them from evil.

- In Holland, the practice was modified to placing salt in the cradle with the child.

- In the Catholic Church, salt has been used in a variety of purifying rituals, one of which was to place a small taste of salt on a baby's lip at the baptism with the words *accipe sal sapiente* ('receive enlightening salt'), meaning that wisdom should flavour man's entire life.

MARRIAGE

- In the Pyrenees, bridal couples went to church with salt in their left pockets to guard against impotence.

- In some parts of France, only one partner carried salt, either the groom or the bride. This is also the country that still conducts processions around the local area with the effigy of the groom on a gallows. Nice touch — what kind of taste does that leave in the mouth, I wonder?

- In Germany, in the past, the bride's shoes were sprinkled with salt.

- It is customary in some countries to greet newly-weds with gifts of salt and bread, instead of throwing confetti.

DEATH

- In the Buddhist tradition, salt repels evil spirits. Apparently, it is customary to throw salt over your shoulder before entering the house after a funeral, in order to scare off any evil spirits that may be clinging to your back.

- In 1933, the Dalai Lama was buried sitting up in a bed of salt. This was a common practice among some ancient groups of people. The dying person was encouraged to sit before death to make the process easier.

- In Wales there was a tradition of putting a plate of bread and salt on the coffin. A local professional sin-eater would arrive to eat the salt before burial of the deceased.

- A popular custom still in use in a number of countries requires that a handful of salt be thrown in the coffin of a dead person before the burial.

OTHER TRADITIONS

JAPANESE
- In Japan, where salt is obtained only from the sea, a salt culture has developed that can be traced in the rituals of everyday life, including meal preparation, sports and ceremony. Shinto religion uses salt to purify. Before sumo wrestlers enter the ring for a match, a handful of salt is thrown into the centre to drive off malevolent spirits.

- Before each performance in Japanese theatres, salt was sprinkled onto the stage to prevent evil spirits from casting spells and spoiling plays.

SCOTLAND
- In Scotland, salt was held in high repute as a charm. The salt box was the first object to be moved into a new dwelling. Robert Burns recalled in 1789 that on moving house he was escorted there by a procession of relatives carrying a bowl of salt.

- Also in Scotland, in ancient times, it was the tradition to add salt when brewing beer, to prevent ruination by witches and evil spirits. Mind you, adding salt to yeast prevents excess fermentation, so maybe there was more to it than superstition.

INDIA
- A gift of salt in India shows good wishes and recalls Gandhi's salt walk, which you can read about in the history section.

- Nagin women were sacred prostitutes known as 'wives of the snake god' in India. From time to time they would give up salt and go begging, giving half of the proceeds to priests for buying salt for the villagers.

- Indian troops pledged their loyalty to the British with salt.

GREECE

- In Greece salt is considered to have great powers as a purifying force. It can be used to ward off demons and evil spirits by being thrown over your left shoulder.

- A new house can be purified by sprinkling it with salt to remove any demons or lurking evil spirits.

- You can remove an unwanted guest or someone who has overstayed their welcome by sprinkling salt where the person will sit or by throwing it behind them. This is not as effective if the person sees you. It'll probably have the desired effect though, if they think you've gone potty!

- Salt should be covered up at night because if the moon or stars see the salt the carrier of the salt will develop warts or a rash. So if you are eating an open bag of chips in Greece, watch out!

GOOD OR BAD LUCK?

- Hamburg, in Germany, renews its good luck every year by parading a bread loaf covered in chocolate and a marzipan salt cellar filled with bread through the streets. This presumably recalls the great wealth brought from the salt trade in the Middle Ages and the famous Lübeck marzipan as well.

- In the past, Germans took oaths of allegiance with their hand sunk in it.

- In medieval times, salt was never touched at the table by hands but only with the point of a knife for the sake of purity and manners.

- Sailors in days gone by would not mention salt while at sea. Salt was never thrown overboard.

- Anglo-Saxon farmers included salt in the magic ingredients placed in a hole in the plough, as they ensured good harvests.

- In Borneo, when tribesmen returned from killing, they gave up salt and sex for a period of time. This also happened among some Native American tribes.

- Salt in Arab countries was used to seal a bargain and as a sign of friendship. It also served as a sort of insurance: if you ate another man's salt in his house you could not harm him and he could not hurt you.

- The Hopi people had a legend that angry warrior twins punished mankind by placing salt deposits far away from civilisation, just to make it hard and dangerous to harvest the precious mineral.

- A 16th century book of Jewish Law explains the only safe way of handling salt: with the middle two fingers. If the thumb was used, a man's children would die; use of the little finger would bring poverty and use of his index finger may make him become a murderer. No good throwing a pinch over your shoulder there, then.

- Bringing bread and salt to a new home is a Jewish tradition dating back to the Middle Ages.

- Salt is believed to be able to drive off demons. Apparently, you won't find salt served at a witches' sabbath or in any pagan religious offering. This also applies to some African and Caribbean ceremonies, where spirits are summoned and the salt might keep them away.

- In Haiti it is said that the only way to break a spell and bring a zombie back to life is with salt.

- In parts of Africa and the Caribbean, many people believed that evil spirits were disguised as women who shed their skin at night. They travelled in the dark as balls of fire. To destroy these spirits their skin had to be found and salted, so that they could not return to it in the morning.

- In Cervia, in Italy, the rite of the Virgin of the Fire dates from the 18th century. In February, a parade of salt workers carry a huge crucifix, rejected by the sea, to Forli. The mystery of how it got there gave rise to its use as a symbol of protection for the workers against illness and disaster, as well as for a good salt harvest. Locals believe that if you keep Cervian salt in your house, you and your family will live a long and healthy life.

- You should never pass salt directly to someone. Always put the salt cellar down on the table, otherwise it means passing on sorrow. This can also be averted by passing the salt and pepper together. It's also, apparently, good etiquette to pass both together.

ROMAN RELIGION AND SALT

Roman religion and mythology, although based on the Greek model, underwent several changes and other influences, making it a more complex mix of traditions, with separate cults as well.

SACRIFICIAL LAMBS

During Roman times, sacrifices of animals were used to please various gods. Sacrificial millstones were prepared by first rubbing them with salt. Domestic sacrifices were practised for different occasions and were often followed by a banquet in which most of the sacrifice was eaten. The first act of *Ritus Romanus* was the consecration of the victim, where the sacrificer, usually the head of the household, consecrated the victim by the *mola salsa*. This was roasted wheat flour with added salt, associated with the fire of Vesta, goddess of the hearth. In order to do this, the sacrificer powdered the back of the animal with the *mola salsa* and poured a little wine on its forehead. Some say that if the salt fell from the head of the sacrifice's chosen victim, it was a sign of bad luck.

Salt made other appearances during sacrifice in the form of offerings. *Penates*, the household gods, protected the household's food supply, and were worshipped or appeased so that the family would not go hungry or be unable to offer hospitality. Most families would keep a salt cellar and first fruits of the season on the family dining table for the *Penates*.

For general offerings to the *Penates*, wine and cakes were used. A two-month-old piglet might be offered, but it wasn't considered a good omen to make such an offering on your birthday. Fair enough: I think sharing a cake with your family and friends is a much nicer idea.

For funerals, when a ewe, pig or lamb would be slaughtered, boiled salted wheat was offered. For offerings to *Manes*, in honour of deceased loved ones, milk, wine and salted corn were added, along with the blood of a ewe, pig or bull calf. *Ceres*, goddess of crops and harvests (from whom we have the word 'cereal'), was honoured with bread, salt, incense and the first harvest goods.

During the second and third centuries AD, the worship of the Iranian god of the sun, justice, war and contract grew into a cult among Roman soldiers. The god was called *Mithra* by the Romans, and its following took the form of a secret cult, very Dan Brown style, complete with initiation ceremonies and seven levels of enlightenment. *Mithraism* was the way in which subjects honoured this deity by loyalty to the emperor. Worship involved the sacrifice of a bull in one of many underground caves in which a well or spring was present. The soldiers possibly used some of their *salarium* or payment to acquire the salted meat consumed.

The Roman goddess of health, safety and welfare, called *Salus*, was identified with the Greek *Hygieia*, presumably where we get the word hygiene from. Her temple was the scene of an annual sacrifice, in August.

Februa were purifying elements or instruments which the Romans believed averted evils resulting from contact with forbidden objects. Salt was used as a talisman here, along with water, fire, wool and laurel. Evils, whether physical or spiritual, could be washed or burned away by the use of these objects.

MUMMIFICATION AND PRESERVATION

EGYPTIAN MUMMIFICATION

The earliest Egyptian mummies date back to around 3200 BC. The process of mummification was described by the Greek historian, Herodotus. This involved laying the body in a bath of natron, the sodium mineral used by the Egyptians for brining, for at least 70 days. Sodium salt solution has a desiccating effect of attracting water from the tissues, since the salt solution water pressure is considerably lower than the tissue liquids. For mummification to occur, all water must be removed from the body and there must be little or no decomposition from bacterial action. Understandably, most mummies have been discovered in desert environments, although remains discovered in acidic peat bogs and glacial regions have also been preserved.

The process developed refinements over the years, but initially the body was treated with natron and then wrapped in bandages that had been soaked in a sort of resin.

Later, by around 1500 BC, morticians would first remove the brain and vital organs and pack the cavities with natron, sawdust or sand and immerse the body for about six weeks. After this time, the body was washed, treated with spices and more natron and wrapped in bandages for a further 30 days or so. These remains have given scientists and archaeologists plenty of information about diet and health of the time. The many artefacts discovered buried with the mummies included food, tools, clothing and jewellery. Sometimes pets were buried with their masters.

SACRIFICE AND PRESERVATION

The process for preserving meat from slaughtered animals by dehydration was similar to that used for burials. The result was to dehydrate the meat to a point where no bacteria could grow and cause decomposition. This method has been found in many cultures and religions.

Following the animal slaughter the carcass was drained of blood by slinging the animal up in a hanging position and letting gravity do most of the rest. The last of the blood and body fluids was drawn off by dehydrating the carcass. This was achieved by soaking in brine or by placing it in a bed of salt crystals. Other methods involved broiling with vinegar or using oils and spices.

The process of dehydration was well known to most ancient civilisations, and was the most efficient method of preserving meat when salt was easily available, although the method was not used by all communities.

FROM ABATTOIR TO TEMPLE
Preparing the concentrated brine needed an advanced water and drainage system. One such example was the hydraulic system in the Temple of Solomon in Jerusalem, or the First Temple, utilising freshwater springs and a reservoir. The water was directed through the Temple by gravity, where baths were available for salting meat.

The Temple was a religious focal point and the ritual of sacrifice and salting became part of a covenant for the Jewish religion. It was completed in the 10th century BC by Solomon, the son of King David, but destroyed in 586 BC by the Babylonians. The concentration of religious ritual at the Temple made Jerusalem a place of pilgrimage and an important commercial centre.

SOLOMON'S TEMPLE
A laver was the sacred wash-bowl of the tabernacle and a basin for the water used by the priests in their ablutions. The one originally used in the tabernacle was of brass. The inner court of the priests contained the altar of burnt offering, the Brazen Sea and ten lavers used for sacrifice. The lavers, each of which held the equivalent of 40 baths, rested on portable holders made of bronze, provided with wheels and ornamented with figures of lions and palm-trees.

The Brazen or Molten Sea was a laver measuring an impressive 5 metres (16 feet) wide, 2.5 metres (8 feet) deep and with a circumference of 15 metres (49 feet), resting on the backs of 12 oxen. The capacity is said to have been 2,000 baths, or 80,000 litres (21,133 gallons). The priests used this laver when they washed their hands and feet on entering the tabernacle. It stood in the court between the altar and the door.

Many other religions and religious traditions developed as a result. People worshipping at temples also used baths for washing hands and feet before entering. The design is said to have been based on an area the Babylonians used in their temple rituals. Such a pity they had to destroy the original!

The reconstructed temple in Jerusalem, which stood between 516 BC and AD 70, was the Second Temple, rebuilt and expanded by King Herod. This reworking sat nicely with his harbour at Caesarea, inaugurated in 9 BC. His monopoly of the salt supply from the Dead Sea mountain provided the Temple with a highly profitable source of income. The port was the ideal way of exporting the salt to Rome, which was having trouble with supplies by then due to rises in sea level. This was at a time when salt supplies were unavailable from the Mediterranean because of flooding.

JEWISH FOOD LAWS

The word kosher or *kashrut*, is translated as 'fitting' or 'correct'. Kosher or koshering salt is a form of salt that has irregularly shaped crystals. The crystals make it suitable for preparing meat in accordance with *kashrut* law because the increased surface area of the crystals absorbs blood more effectively. Kosher laws ensured the hygienic processing of meat by dehydration. All liquids had to be removed. The requirement in ancient times is carried on today, and aims to prevent the meat from deteriorating. In this way it can be consumed long after the animal has been slaughtered. Given that butter needs a 2% salt solution, meat 6% and fish 20%, this could lead to up to 100 grams of salt being consumed per day. This law for preparing meat is a theme in many other religions.

Kosher slaughter requires all animals and birds to be slaughtered by a trained person using a special method. Blood must be thoroughly removed from all meat, using one of several methods such as soaking and salting, or broiling. Any utensils, or whole kitchens, which are used with non-kosher foods, are generally considered to make otherwise kosher food non-kosher.

STAR OF DAVID
During times when Jewish slaves were held by Egyptians along the Nile, they made salt briquettes from straw left in brine. Like the formations made today for tourism and artefacts (see Fascinating Facts chapter), strong geometric shapes such as crosses, squares and stars (formed from two equilateral triangles) were used and planted vertically in the brine pans to allow crystallisation to occur. It has been suggested that the Star of David as a symbol of Judaism may have evolved from these straw stars.

As described above, Jewish Temple offerings included salt. On Friday evenings, the start of the Jewish Sabbath, Jews still dip their bread in salt as a remembrance of those sacrifices. Bread is the symbol of food and salt preserves this food.

BIBLE REFERENCES

Covenants in both the Old and New Testaments were sealed with salt. Hebrew salt was the symbol of the eternal nature of God's covenant with Israel. In the Book of Numbers, it says, 'It is a covenant of salt forever, before the Lord', and in Chronicles, 'The Lord God of Israel gave the kingdom over Israel to David forever, even to him, and to his sons, by a covenant of salt.'

The importance of salt in ancient times is apparent through the numerous references to it in the Bible. For example, the Book of Job, in the Old Testament, raises the question: 'Can nothing which is unsavoury be eaten without salt?'

The most well-known reference is probably that which tells of Lot's wife. Lot, a nephew of Abraham, lived with his wife and two daughters in Sodom. Just before the city was destroyed for its acts of sin, two angels came to Lot and warned him to escape. They told him and his family not to look back once they had left. Lot's wife, however, couldn't resist turning to look back at the burning city and as punishment she was turned into a pillar of salt.

It is thought that the colour of brine, which can take on a red appearance in some circumstances, was responsible for the Moabites' interpretation of water 'as red as blood'. Red brine not only looks like blood but also tastes like it and leaves a deep and disturbing impression. It has been suggested that the red salt pans at Sodom, at the southern end of the Dead Sea, may be derived from the Hebrew words for field and red.

When Elisha sweetened the waters of Jericho, he cast salt into them to illustrate its purifying power. Since the earliest times salt has been associated with value and worthiness. The Bible reference, 'Witness, we are the salt of the earth,' is also echoed by Jesus who called his disciples the 'salt of the earth'. This is said to show them as men who were able to keep others from corruption and sin.

A primary source of salt was the shore of the Dead Sea or the Salt Sea as it is called many times in the Bible. Jesus is said to have told his followers: 'You are the salt of the earth, but if the salt has lost its taste, it is good for nothing except to be thrown out and trodden under the foot of men.'

In the New Testament salt is represented in a great number of metaphors or in parables as a symbol of wisdom, incorruptibility, eternity and alliance between God and man. This may account for Leonardo da Vinci's depiction in *The Last Supper* of Judas Iscariot with an upturned salt cellar in front of him. This symbol is thought to represent the covenant of friendship and love broken by Judas in his betrayal of Jesus.

A HINDU STORY

Hinduism is not one religion but a family of religions. It is a whole complex of beliefs and institutions that have appeared from the time of the ancient and most sacred scriptures.

The Upanishads, composed during the period 800 to 600 BC, convey the idea of secret teaching. The following story teaches about the commonality of divine essence: the self of the whole world, Brahman.

A father told his son to put a piece of salt in a container of water and come back the next day. The son did as he was told. The next day the father told the son to bring him the piece of salt. He groped for it but could not find it, as it had dissolved completely. 'Take a sip from this corner,' said the father 'how does it taste?'
'Salty' was the reply.
'Take a sip from the centre — how does it taste?'
'Salty.'
'Take a sip from that corner — how does it taste?'
'Salty.'
'Look for the salt again,' said the father.
The son said 'I cannot see the salt. I only see water.'
The father told him, 'You, of course, did not see it there, yet it was always right there. In the same way, you cannot see the spirit, but in truth he is there.' An invisible and subtle essence is the spirit of the whole universe. It is the essence of Hinduism that there are many different ways of looking at a single object, none of which will give the whole view, but each of which is entirely valid in its own right.

OTHER BELIEFS

The fact that salt is a natural preservative and antiseptic means it has long been used as a purifying agent in folk magic and traditions. Many Wiccan traditions recommend ritual bathing before any major spell can work. Ritual bathing allows participants to wash away the mundane world, as they prepare for the spiritual. By taking a ritual bath and using the items saved only for magical purposes, many people believe they begin to put themselves in a spiritual mindset. On occasions when participants must travel to the ritual site after the bath has been taken, they may need to refresh themselves by taking a spray bottle full of pure water and a tablespoon or two of special ritual salts or some sea salt and sage. This spritz is said to refresh you and revitalise the feelings of the ritual bath, making it easier for you to get into a spiritual frame of mind.

Salt has a long history of use in rituals of purification, magical protection and blessing. Among spell-casters working in the European tradition, it is commonplace to lay down a pinch of salt in each corner of a room before performing a spell. This has carried over into contemporary African-American voodoo practice as well.

When the intention of a spell is protective, salt may be used alone or combined with ingredients like saltpetre and black pepper. For more aggressive spells against enemies, salt may be added to red pepper, sulphur and bluestone. Ritual cleaning is an important facet of African folk magic and salt is a common ingredient in protection spells.

Cooking
With Salt

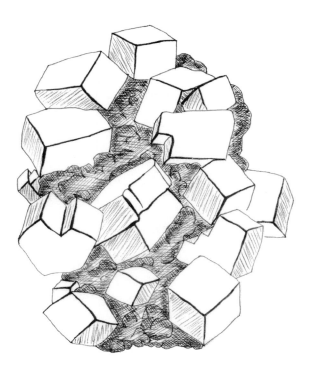

COOKING WITH SALT

The normal procedure for this series of books would require this section to be all about using the foodstuff in many recipes over as wide a range of dishes and courses as possible. Salt is the exception because it mustn't be eaten in vast quantities. After putting the case for eating less salt it would be contradictory, to say the least. There are, however, some dishes that need salt to taste right and complete an important part of the process, such as bread-making and other procedures outlined below. Some, such as porridge-making, may appear to need salt, too, although, not being a Scot, I find I can eat porridge without it.

Because we shouldn't eat too much salt it doesn't mean that we can't indulge on occasions, or use salt to prepare a dish. The methods described here, therefore, are included because this is a book about the uses of salt. The recipes have been chosen because they need salt in the preparation, or because they are so bizarre, interesting or unusual, I just had to share them. As always, I leave it to you to decide what to do with them.

THE USES OF SALT IN COOKING

THERMAL PROPERTIES, HOT AND COLD

You may have been surprised to read in an earlier section that salt is used in ice cream making. This is not only for flavouring, but also to use its thermal properties. Rock salt dissolving in ice water pulls heat from its surroundings. Ice cream makers sit the salt-and-ice mixture in an insulated container, and inside that is placed a highly conductive container of the cream mixture, which freezes rapidly.

Salt can be used to cook food as well. Large amounts of rock salt are heated in an oven to temperatures around 200°C (400°F). Once the salt gets hot, the food is placed in the salt and another layer of preheated salt is poured on top. This method is an extremely fast way to get heat into food and means cooking times can be shortened. You can follow some recipes for this style of cooking later in this chapter.

Adding salt to boiling water apparently raises the temperature very slightly as well as flavouring the food. The amount of salt should vary according to the amount of water and quite a lot is usually used. On reflection, I think I'll stick to not salting the potatoes or pasta and cook them for a minute longer.

REMOVING BITTERNESS
Some foods respond well to salting before cooking, to remove liquid or bitterness and to alter the texture, such as the aubergine. Another technique is to sweat onions or garlic over a low heat to draw out their moisture and soften them.

ENHANCING SWEETNESS
Salt also tends to enhance our perception of other flavours, particularly that of sweetness. This explains its use in ice cream, for example, or kettle corn. Most confectionery recipes have a small amount of salt which, though it cannot be directly detected, has a noticeable effect on the final result.

BINDING AND TEXTURISING AGENT
Salt acts as a binder, as it helps to extract the proteins in processed and formed meats, binding the meat together and reducing cooking losses. It strengthens gluten in bread dough, providing uniform grain, texture and strength. Salt allows the dough to expand without tearing. It also helps to harden rind and develop an even consistency in cheese.

COLOURING
Salt gives processed meats, such as ham, bacon and hot dogs, more colour when used with sugar and nitrate. It also enhances the golden colour in bread crust by increasing the caramelisation process.

FERMENTATION CONTROL
In baked products such as bread and some cakes, salt controls fermentation by retarding the growth of bacteria, yeast and moulds. It has also been used in brewing to prevent excess fermentation.

PRESERVATION AND PROCESSING

Salting is one of the oldest food preservation methods. Before refrigeration and freezing it was about the only method used in the home. Even since the development of refrigeration, salt preserving has remained an important aid to food hygiene. Sodium chloride helps prevent spoiling, by drawing water out of the food and depriving bacteria of the moisture needed for them to thrive. As an antibacterial agent, salt performs well at killing some of the bacteria that would cause spoiling. Today there are many other methods used commercially, including pasteurisation, dehydration and freeze-drying, irradiation and the use of chemical preservatives, as described earlier. Each of the newer processes is good news in terms of the reduction of salt intake as an ingredient.

Some cultural traditions use a lot more salt than others, so preparing food in the oriental or Indian style will suggest more salt or the inclusion of salty sauces, such as soy sauce. If you prepare your own food you have the choice of leaving a lot (or all) of the salt out. It doesn't help though if you prepare all your stir-fry ingredients and then buy a jar of sauce which is highly salted.

Other foods such as smoked meat or fish have more salt than you might think. Some are very high in salt, so eating them less often would be a sensible option

SMOKED AND CURED MEAT

The smoking process includes adding salt to preserve the meat, fish or other food. Prepared food is salted or soaked in brine and placed in an oven and smoked for up to two days. Unsmoked bacon will also be high in salt, as it has been prepared with salt.

PORK BELLY TO BACON

I have never tried this myself, so include it for those who might be interested in reading about the theory of how to produce home-made bacon.

Choice of meat

Use the belly meat closest to the loin, the meatiest part of the belly. Begin with fresh bellies that have been properly chilled. If you are using a whole side of belly pork, cut it into three pieces for ease of handling.

BRINED OR WET-CURED BACON

This is a much milder form of curing, and the meat is cured in the brine under refrigeration. As meat keeps fresh longer at lower temperatures, it does not require so much salt.

The ingredients of brine for curing are salt and sugar. The sugar helps to keep the meat moist and soft as it ages and takes away some of the harshness of the salt. The salt in the brine is used to pull moisture out of the meat and preserve it from bacteria. Brining also prepares the meat for smoking, which brings a lot of flavour, aroma and perhaps colour to the bacon, depending on what you use. Nitrates and nitrites are often included as antibacterial agents and to ensure a pink hue on the meat, but they don't have to be used. Commercially prepared brines are available, but not necessary. If you are going to all the trouble of making your own bacon, why use a commercial product? Make enough brine to fill a non-metallic container that allows you to completely submerse your pork bellies.

BRINE RECIPES

BRINE I
For each 2 litres (3¼ pints) of chilled water, add
300 g (10½ oz) pickling salt
100 g (3½ oz) soft brown sugar

Optional
2 teaspoons black pepper
4 bay leaves
4 cloves of garlic
12 juniper berries

12 allspice berries
2 cinnamon sticks
1 giant shallot
sprigs of sage

BRINE II

For each 3.6 litres (1 gallon) of water, add
750 g (about 1½ lb) salt
1 kg (2.2 lb) brown sugar

To prepare the brine

1 Heat up the brine in a pot, steep it with fresh herb sprigs, shallots, garlic, juniper berries, etc., until the solids have dissolved.
2 Cool it down, strain and cool it again.
3 Submerge the belly pork and let it sit for two to four days, depending on the size of the belly.

Curing method

This assumes you have a BIG fridge which should be between 2°C and 4°C (about 38°F).

Place the container with the submerged pork bellies in a fridge for four days. Use plates to weigh down the bellies if they float to the top. Turn the meat.

Preparation for smoking

1 Rinse the pork bellies with fresh water, and dry thoroughly. Before smoking the bellies, they must be left to dry further so that a pellicle forms on the outside of the meat. This forms as a result of water-soluble proteins being brought to the surface. When dry, these proteins form a sticky coating over the meat, which will absorb the smoke much better. The meat won't take smoke anyway until the surface is dry. If the meat is smoked when still damp, it will be inferior in taste and colour.
2 Elevate the meat on cooling racks and set up a fan to blow over it for about 30 minutes each side and speed up the drying process. Turn the meat over halfway through. The meat takes on a surface sheen when the pellicle has formed.

Source of wood for smoke

Only hardwood sawdust or chips should be used for smoking. Don't use pine. Apple and cherry woods both give a mild, slightly sweet, fruity smoke. Hickory and oak give a strong, more robust flavour.

Maple gives sweet smoke: good for bacon with pancakes.

Cold smoking
This ensures smoking and penetration over a low temperature for a long period.

1 Hang the pork bellies on bacon hangers in a smoker.
2 Try to keep the temperature of the smoker between 27-38°C (80-100°F). Smoke the meat for about 8 hours.

DRY-CURED BACON

This is the oldest method. From Saxon times pigs were fattened on acorns (mast) in the autumn before slaughtering in November. The meat would keep the family going through the winter. Each farmhouse would have its own recipe and a slab of bacon would be kept above the fireplace. Heavily salted bacon would be part of the rations for long sea journeys and would make it very tough and dry.

This recipe produces a salty, streaky bacon. It can be added to stews, soups and sauces. The amount of dry cure may vary, but the proportions should be as follows:

Dry cure I
    750 g (about 1½ lb) salt
    250 g (9 oz) soft brown sugar
    25 g (1 oz) freshly ground black pepper

Optional ingredients
    Bay leaves
    20 juniper berries, lightly crushed
    25 g (1 oz) coriander seeds, crushed

Dry cure II
Use in the following proportions:
    50 g (2 oz) salt
    60 g (3 oz) brown sugar
    40 g (1½ oz) ground peppercorns

Method

1 Mix the salt, sugar and pepper in a non-metallic bowl. Add any optional spices.
2 Take one piece of belly at a time and prepare on a clean surface by rubbing all over with the dry cure mix.
3 Place in a clean, non-metallic tray (plastic is ideal), and repeat with the other pieces.
4 Pile the pieces on top of each other and leave, covered, in a cool place for 24 hours. Use a cover to keep any flies away if this is not a fridge. Keep any leftover cure. When the meat has leached the liquid, drain this off and use the rest of the salt to rub over the meat. Restack the meat with the top piece in the middle and the bottom piece on top.
5 Continue for at least four days, reordering the pile each day. You can leave the pork for up to ten days.
6 Rinse off the salt, dry off the meat and wrap in clean muslin. Hang in a well-ventilated place and use as required by cutting off slices or chunks and rewrapping. If you are not going to use all of the meat within a month, consider freezing some of it.

Meat that has been salted for long periods will be very salty, so you may need to soak in clean water for some time to reduce the salinity, in the same way that ham needs to be soaked before boiling or roasting.

HOME-CURED BACON WITH LENTILS

Here is a recipe to celebrate the use of your home-cured bacon. If very salty, soak it first for an hour or so in cold water.

Ingredients   Serves 4
    4 thick slices home cured bacon with the rind on
    1 onion
    2 carrots
    2 celery sticks
    1 bayleaf
    4 tablespoons lentils

Method

1 Chop the vegetables roughly and put in a pan with the pork.
2 Bring to the boil, and simmer very gently for 1½ hours, until tender.
3 Remove the vegetables with a slotted spoon and put in the lentils. Simmer for about 20 minutes.
4 Serve bacon on a bed of lentils and pour over a little of the liquid from the pan.

MILD BRINE FOR CURING MEAT

This is a simple, quick, all-purpose mild brine for beef, chicken, turkey and pork. It can be used when grilling chicken pieces and the meat will never be dry.

For 1 litre (2 pints water) add
60 g (2 oz) salt
30 g (1 oz) sugar

1 Mix cold water, salt and sugar and stir to dissolve.
2 In a non-metallic container, immerse food (not frozen) in brine, seal and refrigerate for an hour per 500 g (1 lb) of meat. Don't leave for more than 8 hours.

SPICED AND SALTED BEEF

This takes a lot of planning ahead, but the result is truly delicious: a real Christmas special.

Ingredients   Serves 12

3 kg (7 lb) beef brisket, on the bone
175 g (6 oz) coarse salt
4 tablespoons soft brown sugar
1 tablespoon black peppercorns, crushed
1 tablespoon ground allspice
6 juniper berries, crushed (optional)
1 teaspoon saltpetre
1 teaspoon ground mace
1 teaspoon ground cloves
1 teaspoon fresh nutmeg, grated

Method

1 Place the beef in a ceramic or plastic bowl. Rub the salt well into the beef, cover and refrigerate for 12–24 hours.

2 Remove the meat, drain the liquid off and return the beef to the bowl.

3 Mix all of the other ingredients together and rub into the meat, ensuring good coverage. Cover with foil or cling film and return to the fridge for 10-12 days, turning the meat daily and basting with the juices that collect.

4 To cook, put the meat and juices in a large pan and cover with cold water. Bring to the boil and then simmer for 3-3½ hours. Leave to cool in the pan for another hour.

5 When cool enough, remove the bone and press the meat between two plates with a weight on top. Chill overnight before slicing.

CORNED BEEF

This name for preserved beef dates from the 1600s. The word 'corn' comes from an Anglo-Saxon word for granule and refers to the grains of salt used to make the brine in which the beef soaked. When Europeans went to the Americas, the term corn stuck as the name for any grain. In the New World, the most common grain was the maize the natives grew and what we now call maize. Corned beef is really salted beef, but modern refrigeration has meant that milder brines have been used to create what we know as corned beef.

BOILED SALT BEEF WITH DUMPLINGS

You can buy your beef already salted and cook at home.

Ingredients   Serves 6

1.5 kg (3½ lb) salted silverside or brisket beef
2 large onions, whole
6 cloves, stuck into the onions
½ teaspoon ground mace
½ teaspoon grated nutmeg
12 crushed black peppercorns

For the dumplings
> 110 g (4 oz) self-raising flour
> 55 g (2 oz) suet
> salt and black pepper
> 2 tablespoons chopped parsley
> 1 tablespoon horseradish sauce

Method
1 Put the beef into a pan with the onions and cloves. Add the spices and pepper and just cover with cold water.
2 Bring to the boil then simmer gently for 3½ hours, uncovered.
3 Remove the meat to a serving dish and keep warm. Keep half of the liquid in the pan and reduce to thicken the rest in another saucepan while you make the dumplings.
4 Sieve flour and add the suet, herbs and seasoning. Add the horseradish and a little water to make a sticky dough that will gather in a ball. Lightly flour your hands and make small dumplings.
5 Poach the dumplings in the remaining liquid from the meat until just cooked. Serve the beef and dumplings hot with mashed potatoes and carrots.

SMOKED AND CURED FISH

Smoking has been used as a means of preserving fish for a long time. Carp, buffalo catfish, salmon, trout and chubs may be successfully smoked. Certain steps in the process require careful attention. As with brined and smoked bacon, there are four steps to smoking fish:

- Brining or salting
- Curing
- Drying to form a pellicle
- Smoking

You can read about some other forms of smoked and preserved fish in the chapter on fascinating facts.

Brining

To tell if you have used enough salt, float an egg in the mixture. As long as the egg floats you have enough salt (about 80%).

SMOKED SALMON

Ingredients

22–44 kg (10-20 lb) salmon fillets
1.5 kg (3½ lb) brown sugar
3 kg (7 lb) salt
22 litres (5 gallons) water

Method

1 Cut fillets into even-sized pieces. Mix the salt, sugar and water. Mix enough brine to completely immerse the fish in the solution.

2 Cover the fish in brine and place the container(s) in a refrigerator for two hours

3 Remove fish from the brine and rinse under cold running water.

4 Place brined portions onto a greased smoking rack. Keep adequate space around each piece to allow the smoke to filter around the fish from all sides. Place racked fish into refrigeration for a minimum of 12 hours to allow the fish to cure and form a pellicle.

5 To smoke, start out as cool as possible and gradually increase temperature to 65°C (150°F) for 30 minutes. Remove rack from smoker and allow product to cool

6 The fish is now ready to be vacuum sealed or consumed. If vacuum sealed it must be kept refrigerated until you are ready to use it.

Now I know why I buy small packets of smoked salmon from a supermarket. It's much cheaper to buy in France, where we normally eat it, than in England.

GRAVLAX

This is a traditional Swedish method of curing fish. Don't be tempted to add more alcohol, as the fish might go rubbery. Use within one week of preparation.

Ingredients
    125 g (4½ oz) coarse sea salt
    150 g (5 oz) cup chopped fresh dill
    3 tablespoons fresh grated orange zest
    1 tablespoon fresh coarse ground black pepper
    80 ml (3 fl oz) vodka
    125 g (4½ oz) sugar
    1.4 kg (3 lb) tuna steaks, salmon or other fish fillets or steaks

Method
1 If using fillets leave the skin on and wrap in pairs with the skin side out. Wrap steaks individually.
2 In a non-metallic mixing bowl, combine all the ingredients except the fish.
3 Lay out several large pieces of plastic wrap. Rub the fish all over with the curing mix and cover with another plastic sheet.
4 Wrap tightly in several layers of plastic, packing the mix into the fish. Place this packet on a deep plate or baking dish and cover with another plate to weigh the fish down. The plastic will leak liquid, so be prepared. Add more weights on top and refrigerate for between one and four days to infuse.
5 When completed, unwrap, rinse in cold water to remove all of the cure. Pat dry and slice thinly with a sharp knife.

TRADITIONAL ALASKAN SALMON

This is a traditional way to preserve or dry salmon for the winter. The native people of Alaska still dry salmon on large wooden racks for use during the winter. This process remains in the realms of theory for me and is for interest only.

Method

1 Slice the fillets lengthwise into 1.27 cm (½-in) wide strips. You can freeze them first to make cutting easier.
2 Make your brine.
3 Brine the strips for 10 minutes and then rinse under a cold tap.
4 Spray a rack with cooking oil. Hang the strips on the rack or tie strings from the strips to hang in the smokehouse.
5 Smoke at 27°C (80°F) for 24 hours. The strips should be dry to the touch but raw in the middle.
6 Remove for drying with a strong fan for two days or so.
7 Freeze the salmon. This will kill any parasites and prevent over-drying.

ITALIAN SARDINE FILLETS IN SALT

Method

1 Cut off the head and take the innards out of the sardines.
2 Put the fillets on a plate in layers and cover each layer generously with salt.
3 After two hours rub the salt from the fish and add some olive oil.
4 Grill until cooked.

SOUSED HERRINGS I

This is an easy recipe and can be used for mackerel as well.

Ingredients   Serves 4

    2 herrings per person
    2 bay leaves
    1 large sliced onion
    1 teaspoon pickling spice
    Malt vinegar and water to cover
    2 tablespoons salt
    Pepper

Method

1 Preheat the oven to 170°C (325°F, gas mark 3).
2 Clean the fish and remove the heads and tails. You don't need to fillet them.
3 Rub salt into the skin and lay them in an ovenproof dish. Add the bay leaves, pickling spice, onion and pepper.
4 Just cover the fish with a mixture of vinegar and water. Cover with foil or a lid and bake for 30 to 40 minutes.
5 Serve hot or cold, with a little of the liquid poured over.

SOUSED HERRINGS II

This is a faster recipe which doesn't need an oven, just a hot plate.

Ingredients   Serves 2

 6 fresh herring fillets
 1 tablespoon salt
 1 teaspoon ground pepper
 Pinch of allspice
 2 small onions, finely chopped
 50 g (2½ oz) white sugar
 3 bay leaves
 2 tablespoons water
 275 ml (10 fl oz) white wine vinegar

Method

1 Sprinkle the fillets with salt, pepper and allspice. Add the onions and roll up the fillets, securing each with a toothpick.
2 Put the fish into a saucepan with the rest of the ingredients. Bring to the boil and simmer for 3-4 minutes.
3 Allow to cool in the pan. Serve cold.

COOKING IN SALT CRUSTS

This method of cooking uses salt to keep food moist and to seal in flavour. The instructions may look a little unorthodox, and the method is certainly not one you can use to knock up a quick meal.

CHICKEN IN A SALT CRUST WITH HAY

This dish has a lot of preparation, starting with a visit to the pet shop, unless you live on a farm or keep horses. You need a carrier bag of hay, not straw, to start with. Your own chickens would be advisable too, for the eggs.

Ingredients   Serves 4

1 medium-sized chicken	Black pepper
1 lemon	Bunch of thyme

For the salt crust pastry

50 g (2 oz) thyme, chopped	700 g (1 lb 7 oz) salt
50 g (2 oz) rosemary, chopped	12 egg whites
1.6 kg (3½ lb) strong plain flour	370 g (13 oz) water

Method
1 Soak the hay overnight and squeeze to dry.
2 Mix all the dry ingredients for the pastry together with the eggs whites and herbs. Use enough water to form a dough which is not too wet.
3 Knead for 10 minutes, then cover and leave to rest in the fridge for a couple of hours. (You'll probably need a rest too by now!)
4 Preheat the oven to 220°C (425°F, gas mark 7)
5 Roll out the dough onto a floured surface to about 25cm (10 in) in diameter. Put a portion of damp hay in the centre.
6 Season the chicken inside and out with pepper and stuff the lemon and the thyme inside. Put it upside down on the hay and cover with more hay. Wrap the dough around the bird to seal it in, making sure there are no holes in the pastry to let steam out.
7 Put the whole thing in a large ovenproof dish and cook for about 40 minutes. The pastry should be brown and dry.

8 Remove the chicken from the oven and leave it untouched for another 40 minutes. Carefully open the crust, keeping out of the way of hot steam escaping. Throw away the pastry and the hay.

9 Check that the chicken is thoroughly cooked before serving.

SALT-ENCRUSTED WHOLE FISH

As for the chicken recipe, the purpose of the salt is to cook the fish evenly without it drying out. The result is a very moist fish. Bass works well, but you can use any whole fish. You need to use sea salt, kosher salt or very coarse salt to prevent the fish from absorbing the salt. The amount of salt will vary, depending on the type and the size of the fish, but you will need at least as much salt as weight of fish.

Ingredients   Serves 2

1 whole bass, about 700 g (1.5 lb), gutted and
    scaled but not skinned
1 bunch of mixed herbs
1 sliced lemon

Method

1 Preheat oven to 240°C (475°F, gas mark 9) and line a baking tray with foil.

2 Rinse the fish in cold water and dry. Stuff with lemon slices and herbs. The herbs should keep the salt out of the fish, so be generous.

3 Pour salt to make a thick layer over the middle third of the lined pan. Place the fish on top. Pour more salt on top of the fish, leaving the head and tail uncovered. Push the aluminium foil towards the fish. Splash the top salt layer lightly with water to help form a crust when it bakes and seal the parcel carefully.

4 Bake for 20 minutes then let the fish rest for 10 minutes before removing the salt.

5 Crack the salt crust gently with a knife. Remove the top layer of salt. Gently remove the fish to a plate, being careful not to break the skin. Remove the herbs, lemon and any salt remaining on the fish.

WHOLE SALMON COOKED IN SALT

The only problem with big fish like whole salmon is that you might have trouble fitting it into the oven, although baking a whole salmon is the best way to cook it any day. If you want, you can use egg whites, as in the following recipe for whole salmon.

Ingredients

    1 small to medium salmon, about 2.25 kg (5 lb), cleaned

    6 egg whites

    8 tablespoons cold water

    3 kg (7 lb) kosher or coarse salt

    2 tablespoons oil

Method

1 Preheat the oven to 200°C (400°F, gas mark 6).
2 Whisk together the egg whites and enough water to combine with the salt in a large mixing bowl. The salt mixture should hold together when you press it between your hands.
3 Proceed as for the recipe above, using the oil to prepare the foil.
4 Bake for 40 minutes and then rest to continue cooking out of the oven for another 20 minutes.
5 Complete as for the previous recipe.

SALTED COD WITH CREAM

I've often wondered what people do with salted fish I see them buying at the supermarket and local produce market in France where we spend a lot of our time. If you buy salted fish you normally need to soak it in cold water for 12 hours, changing the water every few hours to remove the salt. This recipe may provide the answer, although I still prefer fresh fish, or smoked salmon. Freezing has all but stopped the need for salting, but each to their own.

Ingredients   Serves 2-3

    500 g (about 1 lb) salt cod   1 tablespoon flour

    150 ml (5 fl oz) water   25 g (1 oz) butter

    150 ml (5 fl oz) milk   Black pepper

Method

1 Divide the fish into small fillets, put into a pan with the water and salt, and simmer for about 10-15 minutes. Take the fish out with a slotted spoon and keep warm.

2 Make a roux with the flour and butter and add to the liquid, stirring all the time. Add pepper and serve with the fish.

SALT AND CHEESE-MAKING

Salt is an integral part of the cheese-making process and has served four distinct purposes for centuries.

- It slows down the development of bacteria at the beginning of the process.
- Bacteria help to form the curds and whey and the salt speeds up the expulsion of whey from the curd.
- It prevents the growth of harmful bacteria by preserving it, especially while cheese is maturing.
- It acts as a flavour enhancer. Cheese without salt wouldn't taste very nice and would quickly become unfit to eat.

The salt content is normally shown on the nutritional labelling of most cheeses but is labelled as sodium, as described earlier. This is the sodium content in grams or milligrams per 100 grams of cheese. With over 400 varieties of British cheese and many hundreds of other cheeses around the world, there is obviously a great range of types and a wide range of salt content. Soft and fresh cheeses contain less salt and a higher moisture content, so have a shorter shelf life. Many continental hard cheeses use brine baths to add the salt and have a higher salt content. I recently bought some hard goat cheese from our supermarket, thinking that as we don't eat a lot of cheese it would keep longer than the softer rolls of goat cheese we eat in France. The shelf life or best before date was three months away and the salt content considerably higher than expected at 1.5 grams per 100 grams of cheese. With so many factors regarding salt content as well as fat content to consider, my only option seems to be to abstain more often!

Comparison of salt content in some typical cheeses
These are given as examples only and the salt content will vary between brands and fat content. There is a surprising variation:

Type of cheese	Mg of salt per 100 g cheese
Low fat fromage frais	36
Full fat cream cheese	288
Low fat cream cheese	438
Cottage cheese	300
Wensleydale/ Lancashire type	500
Brie	556
Red Leicester	630
Cheddar type	723
Parmesan	756
Stilton (blue)	788
Feta	1440
Roquefort	1670

I was interested to note, while researching, that processed cheese slices are only just behind feta in their salt content. Considering that these form a large part of some children's packed lunches in my experience, there's a lot of salt being consumed by some young people, even without a packet of crisps every day. The recommended daily intake is lower for children than adults, at 2 grams per day for children up to 6 years and 5 grams per day for 7–14-year-olds.

MAKING CHEESE

Home-made cheeses have a shelf life of about a week, if you want to try, and you can decrease the salt content that way. You can, apparently, use a microwave to save the need for a double boiler. You need ten times as much milk as you will make cheese.

SOFT CHEESE

Ingredients
3.6 l (1 gal) pasteurised milk
1 rennet tablet
50 ml (2 fl oz) cold water
125 ml (4½ fl oz) unsalted buttermilk or
50 ml (2 fl oz) plain yoghurt
3 teaspoons salt

Method
1 Put the milk into the upper part of a double boiler with enough water in the bottom to prevent the milk from burning or scorching. Stir in buttermilk or yoghurt and warm slowly to 34°C (92° to 94°F). Keep the milk at this temperature for the following steps.

2 Add the rennet tablet dissolved in cold water. Stir into the milk for 2 to 3 minutes. Allow the milk to rest undisturbed for about 30 minutes, until a firm gel forms.

3 To test for curd formation, cut a slit in the curd with a metal spatula and lift it slightly. If the cut in the curd breaks clean, it is ready for the next stage.

4 Cut the curd into cubes. Stir gently and continuously for 20 to 30 minutes to help firm curds whilst keeping the temperature constant.

5 Pour off the whey (liquid) and allow the curds to settle. Add 1 teaspoon salt and mix gently at 5-minute intervals until all the salt is used.

6 Divide the curds into two batches and put into muslin bags or a colander lined with cheesecloth. Squeeze the cheese over the sink to allow excess whey to drain.
If you prefer, put the cheese into containers to form a regular shape, still in the cheesecloth and press. Leave a weight on top and leave for 3 or 4 hours.

7 Remove the formed cheese and the cloth. Rewrap tightly in plastic or waxed paper and store in a refrigerator. Use within a week.

MAKING PIZZA CHEESE

You can use half whole milk and half skimmed, or all semi-skimmed for this recipe. I include this for the process as much as anything. I can't think why people buy

cheese these days when you can make it so simply!
(I gave up on yoghurt, making some years ago because of the time it took to get the milk right.)

Ingredients

3.6 l (1 gal) pasteurised milk
50 ml (2 fl oz) fresh, plain yoghurt
1 rennet tablet
125 ml (4½ fl oz) cold water
1 kg (2 lb) salt dissolved in 3.6 l (1 gal) water

Method

1 Heat the milk to 32°C (90°F) in a double pan and add the yoghurt. Stir slowly for 15 minutes while maintaining this constant temperature.

2 Dissolve the rennet in the water and add to the pan, stirring for 3 to 5 minutes.

3 Cover, maintaining the temperature. Allow to stand until coagulated, which will take about 30 minutes.

4 Cut the curd into small cubes. Allow to stand for 15 minutes with occasional stirring.

5 Slowly increase the temperature to 48°C (118°F) over a period of 45 minutes. Hold this temperature for another 15 minutes.

6 Allow the curds and whey to separate. Remove the whey and transfer the curd to a flat pan that can be kept warm. Turn it over every 15 minutes for a 2-hour period without breaking.

7 Cut the curd into long strips, 2-5 cm (1-2 in) wide. Put in hot water at 80°C (180°F). Using wooden spoons, tumble and stretch it underwater until it becomes elastic. This will take about 15 minutes.

8 Remove the curd from hot water and shape it by hand into a ball or a loaf. Place in cold water for about an hour.

9 Remove the cheese from the water and put into the cold salt solution in a plastic bucket or bowl and leave for 24 hours.

10 Remove the cheese from the brine and let it dry for several hours. Wrap in plastic film and refrigerate.

That's all there is to it, apart from making the pizza, that is!

Black salt is an unrefined mineral salt that is actually pinkish grey and has a strong sulphuric flavour. Black salt is mined in India and is used extensively in Indian cuisine as a condiment or added to chaats, chutneys, raitas and many other savoury Indian snacks. Chaat masala, an Indian spice blend, is dependent upon black salt for its characteristic aroma and flavour. Chemically, black salt is almost pure sodium chloride, with iron and trace minerals.

SAUCES AND SEASONINGS

Some cultures don't salt their meals directly but use salty sauces to flavour the dishes. Sodium levels are therefore quite high in foods that include large quantities of soy sauce or other oriental sauces. Our own Worcestershire sauce contains a lot of salt, although there is no indication on the bottle of quantity, and trying to read the amounts on other ketchup and brown sauce bottles isn't easy unless you have a magnifying glass as well as reading glasses!

SOY SAUCE

Soy sauces are made from whole soybeans and wheat, rice or barley grains, but many cheaper brands are made from hydrolysed soy protein. These latter sauces do not have the natural colour of authentic soy sauces and contain caramel colouring. Traditionally, soy sauces were fermented naturally, in giant urns and under the sun. Nowadays, most of the commercially-produced sauces are fermented under factory conditions. Nearly all soy sauce has some alcohol added during bottling to act as a preservative. It should always be kept refrigerated and out of direct sunlight, otherwise it may become bitter.

Soy sauce originated in ancient China and has since been integrated into the traditional cuisines of many East Asian and South-East Asian cultures. Soy sauces produced in different cultures are very different in taste, consistency, fragrance and saltiness. Like olive oils, the quality of the sauce depends on the pressing of the beans. There are two main Chinese varieties:

- Light/fresh soy sauce is thin, opaque and dark brown. It is the main soy sauce used for seasoning, since it is saltier, but it also adds flavour without colouring the food.
- Dark/old soy sauce is slightly thicker, aged longer and contains added molasses to give a distinctive appearance. This type is mainly used during cooking since its flavour develops under heating. It has a richer, slightly sweeter and less salty flavour than light soy sauce.

Thick soy sauce has been thickened with starch and sugar and may also contain monosodium glutamate. You may be interested to know that Worcestershire sauce, made from anchovies, onions and garlic is called 'foreigners' soy sauce' in parts of China and Malaysia.

Japanese soy sauces include wheat as a primary ingredient, and this tends to give them a slightly sweeter, alcoholic, sherry-like taste. Low-salt sauces also exist, but you cannot make soy sauce without salt. On a positive note, a recent study showed that Chinese dark soy sauce contains ten times the antioxidants of red wine. Unfortunately is doesn't contain the benefits of other soy products such as tofu and the salt content may rule it out of the diet anyway. Tests have found that nearly a quarter of soy sauces made from hydrolysed soy protein contain chemicals with the potential to cause cancer. It is becoming a food allergen for many people, so maybe I'm not the only one with whom it doesn't agree. I'll stick to using balsamic vinegar in my stir-fries, with a drop of sherry if available.

VIETNAMESE COOKING

Fish prepared in a variety of ways is the most common protein in the Vietnamese diet. The most common condiment for steamed, sautéed or fried fish is *nuoc mam* – a fish sauce made from salted and fermented anchovies. The Vietnamese diet can be high in sodium, with its reliance on fish sauce, and low in fibre with its lack of whole grains.

PORRIDGE RECIPES

Having previously prepared a whole book on the benefits of porridge I felt obliged to include some recipes that include salt.

TRADITIONAL SCOTTISH PORRIDGE RECIPE I

Ingredients

1 cup of oatmeal
3 cups of water
1½ cups of milk

knob of butter
½ teaspoon of salt

Method

1 Put oatmeal, water and milk in a pan, stirring all the time.
2 Bring to the boil, add butter and salt.
3 Keep stirring until it thickens.

TRADITIONAL SCOTTISH PORRIDGE RECIPE II

Ingredients

110 g (4 oz) oatmeal
150 ml (¼ pt) milk
575 ml (1 pt) boiling water
1 teaspoon salt

Method

1 Mix the oatmeal and milk together to form a paste, then add the boiling water.
2 Heat and simmer for 15 minutes, stirring occasionally.
3 Stir in the salt and serve.

BREAD-MAKING

Bread-making is another process that needs salt to control the action of yeast. Making bread in a machine leads to over-rising of the dough if you don't use salt at all and a disappointing end product. You can cut the amount of salt, but don't leave it out altogether. If you use bicarbonate of soda as a raising agent instead of yeast you are still using a fair amount of sodium. Here are some fairly healthy bread recipes. Being home made, at least you'll have the satisfaction of knowing exactly what's in it.

WHOLEMEAL BREAD

You don't have to invest in a bread-maker or a lot of equipment to enjoy home-made bread. I used to make a lot of it and often used cake tins to make round dome-shaped loaves.

Ingredients
1.5 kg (3 lb) wholemeal flour
1 tablespoon salt
25 g (1 oz) fresh yeast or
  1 sachet dried yeast and
  2 tablespoons warm water

50 g (2 oz) fine oatmeal
1 l (35 fl oz) warm water
2 tablespoons malt extract
2 tablespoons oil

Method
1 Mix together the flour, oatmeal and salt in a large bowl.
2 Mix the yeast with some of the water and leave to froth.
3 Add the flour and the rest of the water, malt and oil. Mix to a smooth dough.
4 Knead on a floured board for about 10 minutes until elastic. Put into a clean bowl, cover and leave in a warm place for a couple of hours, until it has doubled in size.
5 Preheat the oven to 220°C (425°F, gas mark 5) and grease four x 500 g (1 lb) loaf tins. Alternatively, use cake tins and make round loaves.
6 Turn the dough onto a floured board again. Knead a little then divide into four. Shape and place in the tins,

sprinkling a few oats or sesame or poppy seeds on top (optional). Leave for about 20 minutes and bake for 15 minutes. Lower the temperature to 190°C (375°F, gas mark 5) and bake for a further 20-25 minutes. When done, the loaves should sound hollow when tapped.

7 Cool on a wire rack.

OAT ROLLS

Ingredients

25 g (1 oz) fresh yeast or
1 sachet dried yeast and
  2 tablespoons warm water
1 tablespoon honey

425 ml (¾ pt) skimmed milk
225 g (8 oz) oatmeal
450 g (1 lb) wholemeal or plain flour
1 teaspoon salt

Method

1 Mix the yeast with the honey. Warm the milk and stir in the oatmeal. Add the yeast to the oats and leave to stand for an hour.

2 Stir in the flour and salt and knead to form a dough. It should be soft but not too dry. Leave to rest for 30 minutes.

3 Knead again for a couple of minutes. Don't be heavy handed.

4 Divide into 12 portions and make into balls. Make a dent in the centre of each one.

5 Leave to rise for another 30 minutes on a greased baking tray and preheat the oven to 220°C (425°F, gas mark 7).

6 Bake for 15-20 minutes until the rolls sound hollow when knocked. Cool on a rack.

SODA BREAD

This is the easiest bread to make. It uses buttermilk which gives a distinctive flavour. If, like me, you have trouble getting hold of buttermilk, you can make the milk sour with the addition of lemon juice.

Ingredients

    250 g (9 oz) plain flour
    250 g (9 oz) wholemeal flour
    2 teaspoons bicarbonate of soda
    ½ teaspoon salt

25 g (1 oz) butter, cut in pieces
450ml (16 fl oz) buttermilk or semi skimmed milk
Juice of a lemon (if using milk)

Method
1 Preheat the oven to 220°C (425°F, gas mark 7) and dust a baking sheet with flour.
2 If using milk, pour it into a jug and add the lemon juice. Leave to stand for 15 minutes.
3 Sift the white flour, salt and bicarbonate of soda into a large bowl and add the wholemeal flour.
4 Rub in the butter. Make a well in the centre and gradually pour in the buttermilk or the milk. Combine from the centre with a wooden spoon or your fingers, handling it gently. The dough should be soft but not sloppy. If it gets too wet add a little more flour.
5 Turn onto a floured board and shape it into a flat, round loaf, about 5cm (2in) thick.
6 Put the loaf onto the baking sheet and score a deep cross in the top with a floured knife. Bake for 20-25 minutes until the bottom of the loaf sounds hollow when tapped. Reduce the heat to 190°C (375°F, gas mark 5) and cook for a further 25 minutes, or until the crust is browned.
7 Transfer to a wire rack and eat while still warm.

PRESERVED FRUIT AND VEGETABLES

In Victorian times salt was still used widely to preserve food, along with copious amounts of sugar, vinegar and ice saved from winter weather, if Mrs Beeton is anything to go by. I've just seen a recipe for mango chutney, using 50 green mangoes and a pound of salt, 3 pounds of sugar and 6 pints of vinegar, but I'm giving it a wide berth. What about cockles, covered in vinegar, peppercorns and salt? Not for me, thanks.

Here are just a few common and/or quirky ways to preserve with salt. I'll leave you to decide.

I remember how, when first married and with a garden of runner beans, I decided to salt some of them. We didn't have a freezer back in the dark ages, 30-odd years ago. I spent ages stringing and slicing them to pack into a wine maker's demi-john (I was into the whole thing, including elderberry wine). The result was a disappointing, grey, salty mass of beans which wouldn't come out of the jar very easily. We got a freezer soon after that!

PRESERVED CUCUMBERS

Ingredients

 Salt and cucumbers

Method

1 Peel and thinly slice the cucumbers. Sprinkle liberally with salt and leave for 24 hours.
2 Drain off the liquid and pack into clean jars, sprinkling each layer with more salt. Cover with a non-metallic lid.
3 To use, wash well in cold water. Drain and dress with pepper, vinegar and oil. Obviously, no salt needed!

SALTED ALMONDS

Ingredients

 225 g (8 oz) blanched, whole almonds
 150 ml (5 fl oz) vegetable oil
 1 tablespoon celery salt
 ¼ teaspoon cayenne pepper

Method

1 Fry the almonds in the oil until brown. Drain on kitchen paper.
2 Toss in the celery salt and pepper. Serve in small fancy paper cases.

SALTED PEANUTS

You may be interested to know that peanuts can be salted in their shells simply by soaking them in brine before drying them by roasting. This leaves a salt residue behind on the nut in the shell. Sometimes a vacuum is used to remove air from the batch before the brine is introduced.

PRESERVED LEMONS

This Middle Eastern method of preserving lemons can be used with a variety of dishes such as stews and rice dishes, added at the end of the cooking.

Ingredients
8 unwaxed lemons
4 tablespoons coarse sea salt

Method
1 Cut four of the lemons into quarters. Smother in sea salt and squash into a preserving jar. Cover and leave for two or three days.
2 Juice the remaining lemons and add to the jar. Leave for four weeks.
3 To use, scoop out the flesh and add the peel to the dish.

SALT AND ALCOHOL

PEPPER AND VODKA-SOAKED CHERRY TOMATOES

There's nothing like something salty to eat with a drink before dinner. This could dispense with the need for the drink and save time as an all-in-one treat!

Ingredients   Serves 6
250 g (9 oz) baby plum or cherry tomatoes, stalks removed
200 ml (7 fl oz) vodka
1 tablespoon sherry
1 tablespoon Worcestershire sauce
Drops of Tabasco sauce
½ teaspoon celery salt

For the dip
1 teaspoon celery salt
¼ teaspoon cayenne pepper
2 tablespoons sea salt

Method

1 Score a cross in each tomato base, as if you are preparing brussels sprouts.

2 Mix together the vodka, sherry, Worcestershire sauce and celery salt. Add a few drops of Tabasco. Pour over the tomatoes and leave to marinate for at least 24 hours, covered, in the fridge.

3 Drain the tomatoes and serve at room temperature. Keep the marinade for other batches, or dispose of how you wish . . .

4 Mix the dipping spices together. Arrange the tomatoes around the dip and enjoy. Cheers.

TEQUILA SHOTS

The Mexican drink known as tequila derives from a fermented drink the Aztec people made from the agave plant, long before the Spanish conquistadors arrived in 1521. When the Spanish ran out of brandy, they began to distill this agave drink.

One, two three, floor!

The modern way to drink tequila is a communal event, with everyone downing their drink together. A single shot of tequila is often served with a pinch of salt and a slice of lemon or lime. This is called 'tequila cruda'. The drinker licks the back of their hand below the index finger and pours on the salt. The salt is licked off the hand, tequila is drunk and the fruit slice is quickly bitten. What fun! The salt lessens the burn of the tequila and the citrus juice is said to enhance the flavour. Mexican people have long known that a little salt on the tongue can help to mollify the fiery flavour of much of their food, for instance, chilli peppers. By the same token, citrus juices of various kinds have long been used to kill the aftertaste of more potent forms of alcohol. Try this for a chaser.

SANGRITA CHASER

This a spicy and refreshing non-alcoholic chaser made of fresh orange juice, grenadine and chilli piquín or a mix of different chillies. Sangrita owes its name to the Spanish diminutive for 'blood'. Commercially bottled brands are available, but you can make your own.

Ingredients
　　1 l (35 fl oz)freshly squeezed orange juice
　　150-300 ml (5-10 fl oz) fresh lime juice
　　1 tablespoon of grenadine syrup
　　1 tablespoon salt
　　¼ tablespoon Chilli piquín (optional) or few drops
　　　Tabasco sauce

If you want really red sangrita you can add tomato juice as well.

Method
1　Mix all of the ingredients together and drink a shot of tequila, followed by a glass of sangrita.

GOLDEN HONEY MARGARITA

If you are too old for the whole tequila shot business, like me, you might prefer this drink.

Ingredients per drink
　　1 part tequila
　　½ shot Triple Sec/Cointreau
　　1 part honey syrup
　　2 parts lemon juice
　　Salt

Method
1　Shake all the ingredients together except the salt, with ice.
2　Strain into a large cocktail glass with a salted rim.

SWEET AND SALTY FOOD

Whilst at an asparagus festival in France recently, I noticed, among the local produce, a number of pots of jam, preserves and some caramel spread made with sea salt. I declined the offer to purchase some, but was not that surprised to see salt included in a sweet spread. As proof that a number of sweet recipes contain salt, here is a biscuit recipe guaranteed to contain 7% salt: not to be recommended on health grounds. I even found one aptly called 'Cookies of death'.

CHOC CHIP AND SALT COOKIES

Ingredients
    120 g (4 oz) soft butter
    200 g (7 oz) brown sugar
    2 tablespoons white sugar
    1 egg, beaten
    1 teaspoon vanilla extract
    1½ teaspoons instant coffee
    225 g (8 oz) flour
    ½ teaspoon bicarbonate of soda
    ½ teaspoon baking powder
    ½ teaspoon salt
    200 g (7 oz) chocolate chips
    50 g (2 oz) chopped nuts

Method
1 Preheat oven to 140°C (275°F, gas mark 1).
2 Cream together the butter and sugars. Add the egg, vanilla and coffee. Beat well.
3 Fold in the flour, salt, baking powder and bicarbonate of soda. Add the choc chips and nuts, mixing gently.
4 Form into balls of the desired size. Place on greased baking sheets with room to spread.
5 Bake for 20-25 minutes and allow to cool for 10 minutes before taking them off the sheets, when they will harden.

Hints
and Tips

There are many ways in which salt can be used around the home. Don't just look upon salt as a seasoning that should be used sparingly. Here are a few suggestions for helping with some tough domestic jobs. Many of these may look slightly familiar, especially if you have read a book on the benefits of bicarbonate of soda recently. I have tried not to overlap too much, although bicarbonate of soda can be used to perhaps greater effect in many cases. You may, of course, as always, take some of them with a pinch of . . . sodium chloride

FOOD RELATED USES

DESCALING FISH
Soak fish in salt water before removing the scales, which will come off more easily.

FISHY NIFFS
Can you still smell the fish? Dip a lemon wedge in salt and rub the item (hands, cutting board, or work surface) before rinsing with water.

FREE-FLOWING SALT
Add a few grains of rice to the salt cellar to keep the salt flowing freely.

CLEANING LETTUCE
Adding salt to the water will get rid of unwanted insects and slugs. If it doesn't get rid of them all, at least they'll be dead.

TEST FOR FRESHNESS OF EGGS
Put an egg into a cup of salt water. If it floats, ditch it.

CRACKING EGGS!
If you want to boil a cracked egg, or prevent one from spoiling if it cracks in the water, add some salt to the pan to keep the egg in the shell.

FLUFFY EGG WHITES
Adding a pinch of salt to egg whites helps to make them fluffier when beating.

CRACKING NUTS
Soak whole, unshelled nuts in brine overnight. They will crack out of their shells whole when you tap the end with a hammer.

PREVENT FOOD FROM STICKING
Rub salt onto a griddle to prevent food from sticking.

REVIVING JADED APPLES
I hope they don't do this in shops. Wrinkled apples can be soaked in mild salt solution to perk them up. Fruits put in mildly salted water after peeling will not discolour. The same applies to lemon juice. On the other hand, if you use too much salt you could end up with a mummified apple. See the chapter on fascinating facts.

Salt is also said to improve the taste of cooking apples.

REDUCING SALT CONTENT
Add raw potatoes to stews and soups that are too salty. Don't eat them, of course.

SETTING GELATINE
Gelatine sets more quickly when a dash of salt is added to it.

MOPPING UP IN THE OVEN
If something bubbles over in your oven, put a handful of salt on top of the spilled juice. The mess won't smell and will bake into a dry, light crust which you can wipe off easily when the oven has cooled.

You can also sprinkle salt into milk-scorched pans to remove the odour.

CLEANING A COFFEE POT OR JUG
Use salt to clean your discoloured coffee pot or jug.

CLEANING USES

These tips are passed on in good faith. If in doubt about cleaning a particular item, please refer to expert advice.

BATH AND TOILET CLEANER
Some people must have very grubby baths, or very grubby bodies. Mixing salt with turpentine whitens your bathtub and toilet bowl, apparently. Not recommended for smokers!

REMOVING GREASE
To remove grease stains on clothing, mix one part salt to four parts alcohol. If it works on the bath, it will work on the clothes.

PRESERVING BRUSHES
Soak new brushes in warm, salty water before you first use them. They will apparently last longer.

DISCOLOURED GLASS
Soak discoloured glass in a salt and vinegar solution to remove stains.

STOCKINGS OR TIGHTS
If you have odd stockings or tights of different colours try boiling them in salty water and they will come out matched, and hopefully without holes.

HANDKERCHIEF STAIN REMOVAL
If you are the type who still prefers to use real handkerchiefs, especially when you have a cold (they don't seem to hurt the tender bits when you have a very runny nose), soak them in salt water before washing. You can then rinse them before washing alongside other clothes in the washing machine.

BLOODSTAINS
Nosebleed? Cut finger? Soak clothing in a bucket of salty water as soon as possible to prevent staining.

PRESERVING CLOTHES PINS
Boiling clothes pins in salt water before using them may

make them last longer, apparently. They'll need careful drying, however.

METAL CLEANER
Clean brass, copper and pewter with a paste made from salt and vinegar, thickened with flour. Bicarbonate of soda works better I think, and without the flour.

NEW LAMPS FOR OLD
Polish your old kerosene lamp with salt for a brighter look. You never know what genie you may find!

REMOVING INK FROM A CARPET
To remove an ink spot from a carpet, pour salt onto the stain and let it soak up the liquid before brushing up the salt. As with all stain removal, try on an inconspicuous bit of carpet first.

REMOVING RED WINE FROM A TABLECLOTH
Since you can't usually whip off the tablecloth if a guest spills red wine on your best cloth, just pour a little salt onto the splash immediately. This will soak up the wine and then you can soak the cloth at the end of the meal and brush up any salt that has escaped the cloth.

REFRESHING WHITES
Restore yellowed cottons or linens to their original white by boiling the items for one hour in a salt and bicarbonate of soda solution. Perspiration stains may be removed by adding four tablespoons of salt to a litre (2 pints) of hot water. If you can't soak the item, sponge the fabric with the solution until the stains disappear.

TO CLEAN AN IRON
Rub some salt onto a damp cloth and apply to a warm, but not hot, iron. Switch off the iron first, of course.

CLEANING THE PIANO
I'm not brave enough to subject our ancient piano keys to this one, I'm afraid. Perhaps it is better for newer models rather than ivory. The suggestion is to mix lemon juice with salt to clean the keys.

GETTING RID OF SOAP SUDS
Rinsing clothes with a little salt in the water can get rid of excess soap. This is also said to allow fabrics to hold their colour.

CLOTHES LINES
This is a bit tricky with a rotary clothes line, but soaking your clothes line in salt water will prevent your clothes from freezing to the line. Alternatively, use salt in your final rinse to prevent the clothes from freezing. Better still, dry them indoors.

CLEANING PANS
Soak enamelled pans in salt water overnight and boil them with salty water the next day to remove burned-on stains. Don't soak chipped pans or metal ones.

WICKER FURNITURE
Rub any wicker furniture you may have with salt water to prevent yellowing.

CLEANING CLOTHS AND SPONGES
Freshen sponges and cloths by soaking them in salt water.

RINGS ON FURNITURE
Remove white rings left on tables caused by wet or hot dishes and glasses. Rub a thin paste of salad oil and salt onto the spot and let the mixture stand for an hour or two before removing. As always, try out the technique first on a less conspicuous mark if possible. Complete the process by polishing the whole item of furniture.

PEST PREVENTION

ANT DETERRENT
Sprinkle salt onto your shelves to keep ants away. I don't recommend this where you may have any damp getting in, or where the salt is likely to spill onto a floor.

WEEDS AND SLUGS
Use salt for killing weeds in your lawn or slugs and snails in the garden.

WEED-FREE PATHS
Sprinkle salt between bricks or paving slabs where you don't want grass (or any other plants) to grow.

MISCELLANEOUS

FLOWERS
Add a pinch of salt to the water in the vase your cut flowers will stand in. They will last longer.

VASES
Clean the grot and nasty smell out of vases after the flowers are dead by rubbing the inside with salt water.

CANDLES
Soak new candles in a strong salt solution for a few hours and then dry to reduce dripping wax.

WINDOWS
To keep single-glazed windows from freezing outside, rub the inside of the window with a sponge dipped in a salt water solution and wipe dry.

PERSONAL CARE

SORE MOUTHS
Mild salt water makes an effective mouthwash. Use it hot for a sore throat gargle.

BRUSHING TEETH
Use equal parts of salt and bicarbonate of soda for brushing your teeth. Dry salt sprinkled on your toothbrush makes a good tooth polisher. Ouch!

CUTS AND SCRATCHES
A mild salt solution is a good way to clean small cuts and scratches, using the antibacterial qualities of salt.

REMOVING A SPLINTER
To remove a splinter from a finger easily, soak the area in warm salty water for a few minutes. If this doesn't work, mix a little water with half a teaspoon of bicarbonate of

soda to form a paste. Apply this to a splinter and cover it with a plaster for a couple of hours. The soda should draw out the splinter, which can then be easily removed, along with any toxins, and solve the problem.

FACIAL
For a stimulating facial, mix equal parts of sea salt and olive oil. Gently massage in with long upward strokes. Remove and wash with mild soap and warm water.

HAIR RINSE
Mix one part bicarbonate of soda to two parts water to form a paste. Massage into the scalp and it will cleanse your hair of shampoo and product build-up. Rinse well with warm water.

BATH TREATMENTS

Bath treatments can be used to help a wide range of ailments and to help you relax. If you can't run away to a spa or afford a pricey treatment, try one of these. Don't fill the bath too full so you can add more hot water when required. If you can't run to a whole bath try soaking your feet instead. It will revive you in no time.

BATH SOAK
Sea salt can be used for a hot soak. Try adding a cup of sea salt to a bath and soaking for at least ten minutes. You will feel soothed and clean. Add a few drops of your favourite scented oils to soften the skin.

BATH DETOX
Use one part (3 tablespoons) bicarbonate of soda to one part sea salt in a hot bath. Lie back and relax for 20 minutes. Rinse off or shower to remove the salt. For a more luxurious soak, add a tablespoon of citric acid and a few drops of essential oil to the salt and bicarbonate of soda.

You can mix up a jarful and add food colouring as well for a gift idea.

SPORT RELIEF SOAK
Mmm, smell that wintergreen . . .

1 cup coarse sea salt
2 drops of wintergreen essential oil
2 drops of eucalyptus essential oil
1 drop of peppermint essential oil

Just add all the ingredients together and mix well.

BODY SCRUB
Very thorough, for real toughies.

½ cup coarse sea salt
¼ cup rosemary oil

Put some oil on a loofah then dip it into the salt. Using circular movements, rub over the skin. Give extra attention to rough areas. Continue to do this until your body is covered. Rinse with a warm water shower and pat dry. Follow up with moisturiser.

COFFEE AND GRAPEFRUIT THIGH SCRUB
This makes two applications, if you can bare it! It will keep in an airtight container until you forget what it was like the first time. Coffee stimulates fatty congestion and grapefruit stimulates the lymphatic system, removing toxins from the body.

½ cup sea salt   10 drops peppermint oil
¼ cup clay   15 drops grapefruit essential oil
1 teaspoon ground coffee   15 drops orange essential oil
1 teaspoon cinnamon

Directions
Combine all the ingredients together, breaking up any clumps. To use mix 2 tablespoons with enough water or milk to form a smooth paste. Massage into the thigh and buttock areas. Rinse off in the shower.

Fascinating
Facts

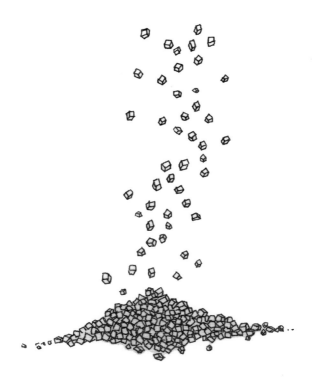

THE LANGUAGE OF SALT

SALTY WORDS
Roman soldiers were paid for some of their service in salt. This is where we get the word salary from. Also from Roman times we get the word salacious. Gossip of a salty kind is today referred to as 'appealing to or stimulating sexual desire, lascivious'. The Romans liked a good gossip over affairs of the heart, apparently, as much as the next man or woman.

WORTH HIS SALT?
There is more than one possible derivation of this phrase. Some say that it refers to the days when salt was a very precious commodity. Since Roman soldiers were paid partly in salt, it became equated with wages. A person not worth his salt did not, therefore, give value for money. Others would have it that the phrase originated in ancient Greece, where slaves were traded for salt. An unruly slave was not worth his salt.

PINCH OF SALT, ANYONE?
The phrase today suggests scepticism, caution or incredulity. One suggestion is that salt makes things more flavoursome, so easier to swallow. The Roman phrase *cum grano salis*, meaning 'with a grain of salt', seems to come from the Roman historian Pliny the Elder, who wrote that the general Pompey had discovered an antidote for poison that was to be taken *cum grano salis*. This was apparently to make the antidote more effective. Other etymologists believe that Pliny had been sceptical about the antidote and, therefore, took the phrase to mean 'with a dose of scepticism'. Believe what you will.

SALTY ADDITIVES
Sauce, salami, salad, sausage and salsa also come from the word for salt, because they all require salt in their making or preparation to give a unique flavour.

EATING SALT TOGETHER
In Greek, Roman and Semitic cultures, 'eating or taking salt' with a person forged a sacred bond of hospitality. Salt has been used in rituals since ancient times. The devil

is said to hate salt, which is why it has been used in holy water and placed on the tongues of infants at baptism.

SYMBOL OF PURITY
Salt is a symbol of purity and incorruptibility. In Numbers 18:19, 'a covenant of salt' means a covenant that cannot be broken. Jesus says to his followers, in Matthew 5:13, 'Ye are the salt of the earth'.

ABOVE OR BELOW THE SALT
In the days of knights and banquet halls your position at the table was shown by the proximity of the 'saler' or salt cellar (see below) and signified a place of esteem if you sat 'above the salt'. This meant that you were in a position of honour, close to the head of the household. Equally, it meant that you sat, as a visiting noble, with the grown-up members of the family and other important members of the household. Minor officials, subordinates and others sat below. All a bit 'upstairs downstairs', really.

HELLO SALER
The 'cellar' part of salt cellar comes from the Norman *saler*, itself from the Latin *sal*, meaning 'salt'. Early in the 13th century, the word *celer* meant 'a container for salt'. The original, between salt and *celer*, was forgotten and the word became *salte-seler* in the 15th century, i.e. a salt cellar for salt. The Latin *cellarium*, meaning a 'seat of cells' or a receptacle for food, later replaced *celer*, so that's why a salt receptacle is called a salt cellar. Sounds a bit like 'Call my Bluff', doesn't it?

OLD SALT
This term refers to a sailor, presumably because of his weather-beaten appearance after being exposed to salt, sun, wind and rain over many voyages. Still, better an old salt than a jack tar, gob or a sea dog, which are other endearing names for sailors.

SALTY DOG
A Salty Dog is a cocktail of vodka or gin and grapefruit juice, served in a glass with a salted rim. The salt makes the difference. A Greyhound is the same drink without the salt rim.

FASCINATING FACTS ABOUT SAL

WHAT'S IN A NAME?
You can tell a lot about a place by its name. Place names with Hall, Halle or Sal in them probably developed because of salt deposits or brine springs nearby.

SALZBURG
Salzburg means salt town. The nearby Dürnberg mine was originally worked by the Celts over 2,500 years ago. Salt beds range from a metre to hundreds of metres thick. Salt brought riches to Salzburg, in Austria, in a time when salt was still 'white gold'. Today you can visit the mines and experience them via a cross between a museum and an amusement fair.

THE HALLSTATT 'MAN IN SALT'
The prehistoric 'Man in Salt' was discovered in an old salt mine in Hallstatt, Austria, in 1734. The corpse was discovered preserved in salt 'pressed flat and tightly grown into the rock', with strange clothing and tools. Hallstatt enjoys the title of 'World's oldest salt mine', dating back 7,000 years.

THE ROYAL SALTWORKS OF CHAUX
These salt works at Chaux, in France, constitute a historical monument of worldwide heritage, recognised by UNESCO. Over the last 60 years they have been restored as a testimony to neoclassical architecture. What is more surprising is that the design was applied to industrial buildings, dating from the Age of Enlightenment. Built between 1775 and 1779, the Royal Saltworks used the wood from the Forest of Chaux as firewood, to extract the salt from the water. The water was carried in from the old salt mine of Salins les Bains. Designed by Claude-Nicolas Ledoux, it included 11 buildings in a semi-circle, five of which were workshops and workers' living quarters. Unfortunately for Ledoux, he was imprisoned during the French Revolution and his big plan for a whole 'Ideal City' was never built. The Royal Saltworks closed in 1895 and fell into ruins.

HOW SALTY IS THE SEA?

Sodium chloride is by far the greatest solid present in sea water. Each gallon (4 litres) contains, on average, 105 grams (0.23 pounds) of salt. Some scientists have estimated that if all the oceans in the world dried up they would produce 14½ times the bulk of the continent of Europe. How would anybody be able to tell if they were right? Should we take this with a mountain of salt?

HALITE

1. Hopper crystals

Although most crystals of salt are arranged in isometric form, with three axes of symmetry, halite crystals called 'hopper crystals' are sometimes found. These look like skeleton cubes, with the edges extending outward, leaving hollow, stair-step faces between these edges. They form in this way due to different growing rates of the edges and faces from the centres. Some entrepreneurial spirits have started growing these crystals, which form quickly, by putting sticks, animal skulls and other artefacts into lakes for crystals to form. They can then be retrieved, covered in crystals, for sale.

2. Veined crystals

Purple fibrous halite is found in France. These crystalline specimens can be impressive. The colours reflect the bacterial debris trapped in evaporated lakes. They are highly prized by collectors.

3. Flowers

Halite flowers are rare stalactites found growing down from the roofs of arid caves under the Nullarbor Plain, in Australia. Halite stalactites have also been found in Michigan. Halite rock is usually 95-99% pure, but is found with gypsum, dolomite, quartz, anhydrite and pyrite.

DEAD BUOYANT

The Dead Sea has such a high concentration of salts that objects which are not usually able to float are buoyant in it. It is impossible to swim on your front in the Dead Sea or to dive without weights. All you need to do is float on your back.

JACK TAR OR BLACK SEA?

One of the most unusual properties of the Dead Sea is the way it discharges asphalt. The Dead Sea constantly spits up small pebbles of the black substance from deep below the water. After earthquakes, chunks as large as houses have been produced.

SALTY REMAINS IN IRAN

In 1993 miners discovered human remains at a salt mine in north-west Iran. The body was buried under a 2-ton rock. Several items, such as a leather sack full of salt, a clay tallow burner, two pairs of leather shoes and two cow horns, were discovered nearby. This was the third set of remains to have been discovered. The items were in considerably good shape, unlike the crushed skeleton.

The second discovery, in 2004, which came to be known as The Salt Man, was the body of a miner preserved by the salt. He lived around 1,700 years ago, but was mummified naturally where he died, complete with long white hair and beard. Aged about 35 years, no mean age in those days, he was wearing leather boots and had some tools and a walnut with him when found. He now resides in the National Museum in Tehran.

Since these discoveries, there seems to have been a lot of activity in 2005, resulting in still more finds. While bulldozing salt into trucks, the Twin Salt Man was unearthed, complete with hair and nails. Some pieces of clothing and a hand-woven thatch rug with a unique texture were discovered with the man, who was 180-185 cm (71-73 in) tall and also aged between 35 and 40.

Another, younger man was found and said to be the most intact of all four found so far. Experts found an iron dagger and scabbard attached to his waist and two ceramic jugs with oil inside: probably used as a lantern. He wore a long quilted item of clothing and gaiters as well as two earrings of indistinguishable material.
The fifth salt man to be found was discovered in Chehr-Ābād Mine in Zanjan City. It now seems likely that a large number of men were buried there. The mine was in use

from about 400 BC to AD 650. These salt men are among rare discoveries around the world, mummified as a result of natural conditions. Most of their tissues are well preserved and the conditions in the mines mitigated the effects of micro-organisms.

SALT MINES AND STORAGE
During World War IIo the Third Reich stored paintings, art works and huge amounts of money in salt mines. Today, old salt mines provide storage for petroleum, chemical waste and nuclear waste.

TOO LITTLE SALT
During Napoleon's retreat from Moscow thousands of troops died due to inadequate wound healing and lowered resistance to disease. This was because they were suffering from salt deficiency.

WHAT A WASTE
In January 2007, a competition was held by a radio station in Sacramento, to see who could drink the most water without needing to go to the loo. A Nintendo Wii was the prize, obviously considered a very funny line by the station, until one of the contestants, a 28-year-old mother of three, died from water intoxication. Known as hyponatremia, the condition is usually seen among athletes who consume too much water quickly, causing a critical loss of sodium.

NOW YOU SEA IT!
The Salton Sea is a relative newcomer to southern California and was created by accident 100 years ago, when flooding on the Colorado River allowed water to crash through canal barriers. For the next 18 months the entire flow of the Colorado River rushed downhill into the Salton Trough. Previously this had been the bottom of a dry lake. During earlier geological periods a large body of water had occupied the basin. By the time engineers were finally able to stop the breaching water in 1907, the Salton Sea had been born. Now 72 kilometres (45 miles) long and 32 kilometres (20 miles) wide, this 932 square-kilometres (360 square-mile) basin is a popular site for

boaters, water-skiers and anglers. Kayakers, birdwatchers and visitors enjoy the site's many recreation opportunities. Thanks to the sea's low altitude (69 metres/227 feet below sea level), atmospheric pressure improves speed and ski boat engine performance, which is nice . . . unless you're an angler or a swimmer.

WIELICZKA SALT MINE

The Wieliczka Salt Mine is situated outside Krakow and has been worked for 900 years. In medieval times it was one of the world's biggest and most profitable industrial sites, when common salt was the commercial equivalent of oil. Today it is a major tourist attraction with 200 kilometres (124 miles) of passageways and over 2,000 caverns. You can walk underground for about 2,000 metres (6,561 feet) in the oldest part of the salt mine and see its subterranean museum, the biggest mining museum in the world.

At a depth of 210 metres (689 feet) there is a sanatorium for those suffering from asthma and allergy. Concerts and other events take place in the mine's biggest chambers and the mine has been a UNESCO World Heritage Site since 1978. Beneath the mine there are a number of chapels and churches. Near the entrance is the chapel of Saint Antonius, but, due to the location, the moist air has destroyed the chapel figures. One late 19th-century American traveller described these in amusing terms:

> Here was the chapel of St. Anthony, the oldest in the mines — a Byzantine excavation, supported by columns with altar, crucifix, and life-size statues of saints, apparently in black marble, but all as salt as Lot's wife, as I discovered by putting my tongue to the nose of John the Baptist. The humid air of this upper story of the mines has damaged some of the saints: Francis, especially, is running away like a dip candle, and all of his head is gone except his chin. The limbs of Joseph are dropping off as if he had the Norwegian leprosy, and Lawrence has deeper scars than his gridiron could have made, running up and down his back. A Bengal light, burnt at the altar, brought into sudden life this strange temple, which presently vanished into utter darkness, as if it had never been.

Today they have been described as either more like modern art, or prehistoric sculptures. Other churches, like the cathedral, are well preserved. Here, even the chandeliers are made of salt. The walls are covered with sculptures of saints and scenes from the Bible. Here, the temperature stays at a uniform 15°C (59°F) throughout the year.

One well-travelled Frenchman observed in the 18th century that the Wieliczka Salt Mine was no less magnificent than the Egyptian pyramids. Another described a hall carved like a Greek theatre. There was also a large salt ballroom:

> . . . *with well-executed statues of Vulcan and Neptune. Six large chandeliers, apparently of cut-glass, but really of salt, illuminate it on festive occasions, and hundreds of dancers perspire themselves into a pretty pickle. I purchased a salt-cellar, which has the property of furnishing salt when it is empty. But it seemed to me that I should not need to use it for some days. I felt myself so thoroughly impregnated with salt, that I conceived the idea of seasoning my soup by stirring it with my fingers, and half-expected that the fresh roast would turn to corned beef in my mouth.*
>
> *Eva March Tappan*

THE SALT CATHEDRAL OF ZIPAQUIRÁ

Underground salt cathedrals are not confined to Europe. This cathedral, near the town of Zipaquirá, in Colombia, South America, was built inside a mountain after exploitation of the salt mines, long before the Spanish conquests. The salt deposits formed 200 million years ago and were raised above sea level when the Andes Mountains were formed in the late Tertiary period.

The miners had carved an earlier sanctuary, but the construction of a modern, subterranean, Roman Catholic church began in the 1950s. Because it was carved into an existing mine, structural problems developed and it was shut down in 1990.

The current cathedral was started in 1991, 61 metres

(200 feet) below the old one, and was dedicated in 1995. It has 14 small chapels representing the stations of the cross, depicting Jesus's last journey, and the bottom section has three sections, representing the birth, life and death of Jesus.

INCA SALT MINES, MARAS
Visitors to Peru can visit salt works where local people still work the grey-green salt pools layering the hillside, as they have since the days of the Inca kingdom. Every year the rainy season dissolves the hillside and the entire labyrinth of salt pans needs to be rebuilt. For centuries people have directed the brine coming out of the ground to evaporation pools. This salt is then treated and sold in the local market. The sight of the group of about 3,000 pools has been described by tourists as spectacular. Local people show their ancient techniques to the visitors and allow them to participate in the collecting as well as in Andean rites and celebrations. It's a pity they have to do it for tourists.

THE PATIO PROCESS
No, this isn't about using salt to lay slabs on, but about Spanish silver miners in the mid-16th century. It was used to extract silver from silver sulphide ores. Developed in Mexico in 1557, it was the first process to use mercury to recover silver from ore. Silver ores were crushed to a fine slime which was mixed with salt, water, copper sulphate and mercury. It was then spread in a thick layer in a shallow-walled, open enclosure, or patio. Horses were driven around on it to mix it further. After weeks of mixing and soaking in the sun, a reaction converted the silver to metal, which amalgamated with the mercury and was then recovered.

I didn't find out what happened to the horses, but I suspect they needed replacing quite often. But never mind, the patio process solved a crisis in the silver-mining districts of the Spanish colonies. So the colonials were able to keep up the exploitation and continued silver mining for centuries in Mexico, Peru and Bolivia.

Science and The Past

To all of our colleagues, past and present

Alexander Scott DSc, ScD, FRS. The British Museum's first scientist, he was Director of Scientific Research from 1920 to 1938.

SCIENCE
and
THE PAST

Edited by Sheridan Bowman

Published for the Trustees of the British Museum
by British Museum Press

© 1991 The Trustees of the British Museum
Published by British Museum Press
A division of British Museum Publications Ltd
46 Bloomsbury Street, London WC1B 3QQ

British Library Cataloguing in Publication Data
Science and the past.
  1. Archaeology. Use of Science
  I. Bowman, Sheridan
  930.1028

ISBN 0-7141-2071-5

Designed by Carla Turchini

Set in 10/12pt Photina and printed and bound in Great
Britain by Butler & Tanner Ltd, Frome and London

Jacket illustration Three scanning electron microscope X-ray
maps showing element distributions (*from upper left*) of
silver, copper and sulphur on a detail (*lower right*) of a
Japanese *tsuba* (sword guard). The concentration of each
element is colour-coded: white and red are high, yellow and
green are medium, and blue and purple are low.

Illustrations have been provided by the British Museum
Photographic Service (particular thanks go to Tony Milton
and John Heffron) or by the authors unless otherwise stated
in the captions.

The contribution of JEOL (UK) Ltd to the cost of producing
this book is gratefully acknowledged.

Contents

Sir David Wilson   Foreword   7

Sheridan Bowman   Preface   9

List of Colour Plates   10

Paul Craddock   1. The Emergence of Scientific Inquiry
into the Past   11

Andrew Middleton   2. Ceramics: Materials for all reasons   16

Ian Freestone   3. Looking into Glass   37

Paul Craddock   4. Mining and Smelting in Antiquity   57

Michael Cowell &   5. Metalwork: Artifice and artistry   74
Susan La Niece

Michael Hughes   6. Tracing to Source   99

Sheridan Bowman   7. Questions of Chronology   117

Paul Craddock &   8. Spotting the Fakes   141
Sheridan Bowman

Peter Main   9. Computing and Mathematics: Putting two
and two together   158

Lea Jones   10. Computerising the Collections: The art of
successful flea handling   172

Glossary   182

Index   188

Foreword

Sir David Wilson FBA
Director of the British Museum

The collections of the British Museum are rich and diverse; their origins are global and extend from the earliest stone tools to twentieth-century prints and drawings. It has long been recognised that the scholarly investigation of such an important and vast range of material depends on a number of disciplines, and among our staff we include archaeologists, art historians and numismatists. Perhaps less apparent to the public have been our scientific staff, but the Museum has maintained a scientific laboratory for most of this century. The Department of Scientific Research, although not the first laboratory established by an antiquities museum, is the longest surviving, being over seventy years old.

A research laboratory was first established in 1920 to advise on the conservation of the collections. From an early stage, however, it played a leading role in the application of the methods of physical science to the understanding of the cultures of the past. Quick to adopt computerised approaches to the storage and manipulation of information, it was the natural home for the collections documentation programme. It is now a department with forty-five staff which, in addition to its scientific work, is responsible for the provision of computer services throughout the Museum. Meanwhile conservation itself has grown, and the Museum's conservators and conservation scientists now form the Department of Conservation.

Rarely is the Museum's scientific work brought to the attention of the four or five million visitors who pass through its doors each year. This book provides an insight into a fascinating area of our activities which normally remains entirely 'behind the scenes'.

Preface

Sheridan Bowman
Keeper, Department of Scientific Research, British Museum

The contribution of scientists to the study of the past has a long and productive history. Over the past few decades, however, there has been a veritable information explosion, resulting from a proliferation of scientific techniques and subdisciplines which have been focused on archaeological problems. Some of this work is undertaken as a sideline by interested scientists whose main research is in other fields such as medicine, materials science and nuclear chemistry. However, the majority is carried out by institutions specifically dedicated to the investigation of early cultures and these laboratories provide the continuum of understanding and expertise upon which the effectiveness of the new science of archaeometry depends. This volume highlights the work of one such laboratory, the British Museum's Department of Scientific Research.

The staff of the Department (formerly known as the Research Laboratory) include physicists, chemists, metallurgists, geologists, statisticians and computer scientists. They provide evidence of the date, composition and technique of manufacture of the objects in the Museum's collections. The Department also includes a sizeable team of curatorial staff who advise on the storage and treatment of information relating to the collections, and are responsible for the entry of this information on to a computer. Their task is complex and somewhat daunting; it involves data on some six million objects recorded in different ways and in varying detail over the Museum's 238-year history.

This book is concerned only with the application of the physical and computer sciences to the understanding of the past from the perspective of a single laboratory. Its coverage is therefore far from comprehensive, and it is not intended as a textbook. The book has been written primarily to provide the non-specialist with some insight into this field of research, and for anyone interested in an introduction to the subject. Hopefully it also conveys just a little of the excitement experienced upon attaining some new understanding, and gives an indication of the wealth of information about the past that can be unlocked by science.

Although the number of authors is of necessity limited, the book draws heavily upon the work and experience of the other members of the Department, many of whom have helped most generously with its production. Speaking on behalf of all of the authors, we also wish to thank our colleagues in other departments of the Museum, for without their expertise in fields such as photography, conservation and administration our work would be the poorer; in particular, we owe a debt to the staff of the curatorial departments, who respond to queries with fortitude and provide a stimulating collaborative framework for our scientific endeavours.

List of Colour Plates

The illustrations listed below appear between pages 80 and 81. Plate numbers refer to the chapters in which the photographs are discussed.

Plate 2.1
The Prunay Vase (Morel Collection, ML 2734). Height *c.* 310 mm.

Plate 2.2
Egyptian faience shabti and sistrum, 25th–26th Dynasty (EA 34095 and 26975). The height of the shabti figure is *c.* 155 mm.

Plate 3.1
Fragment of mosaic from San Marco, Venice (MLA 1882.11–1.11). Width *c.* 250 mm.

Plate 3.2
The Lycurgus Cup (MLA 1958.12–2.1): (**a**) in transmitted light and (**b**) in reflected light. Height 165 mm.

Plate 5.1
The Sutton Hoo purse lid (MLA INV. 2) with the associated gold coins, coin blanks and ingots. This piece is typical of the high quality of the Sutton Hoo goldwork. It is decorated with inlaid garnets and millefiori glass, the garnets backed with patterned gold foil to enhance their colour. Length 190 mm.

Plate 5.2
Japanese shakudo alloy sword guard, with gold, silver and brass inlays (OA 1952.2–11.28). 80 × 60 mm.

Plate 6.1
Petrographic thin sections of Iron Age pottery sherds from Hengistbury Head, Dorset (on loan from the Society of Antiquaries): (**a**) locally made Durotrigian ware with very sand-rich fabric. Width of field *c.* 4 mm; (**b**) cordoned ware, imported from northern Brittany, containing amphibolite rock. Width of field *c.* 1 mm.

Plate 8.1
Contemporary paintings can give us an indication of the original appearance of ancient metalwork, as in this Roman wall painting from Pompeii (from A. de Franciscis, 1963, *Il Museo Nazionale di Napoli*, Naples, Di Mauro). The bronze statues shown in this street scene are not patinated green or black, but are apparently bronze coloured.

Plate 8.2
The fake patina on this Chinese bronze sleeve weight (OA 1894.1–8.8) was put on when the piece was made in the twelfth century AD. China has a long tradition of quite sophisticated faking methods designed to fool the scholar and collector. Diameter 60 mm.

Plate 8.3
These two bronzes are both quite genuine Roman pieces. However, the symbolic hand (GR 1824. 4–41.1) on the left was given a false patina by the great collector Richard Payne Knight in order to give it the appearance he felt it would have had originally. Length 146 mm. The statuette on the right (GR 1920.2–18.1), shown for comparison, has a natural patination. Height 140 mm.

CHAPTER 1

The Emergence of Scientific Inquiry into the Past

Paul Craddock

From the beginning of the serious academic study of antiquities in Renaissance Italy, science had a part to play. Scholars and collectors were impressed by the beautiful colour and texture of Classical bronzes, and set out to determine their composition, incidentally giving us the word bronze (from the Italian *bronzo*) to describe the alloy of copper and tin used by the ancients. Such famous antiquities as the Horses of San Marco were analysed, and by the eighteenth century interest had extended to prehistoric antiquities; thus in 1774, for example, King George III's assay master, Mr Alchorn, analysed two Bronze Age swords from Cullen in Ireland.[1] Antiquities began to attract the attention of famous scientists, such as Martin Klaproth, the 'Father of Analytical Chemistry', who analysed items including Roman bronze mirrors and glass.[2]

Slightly later, in the early nineteenth century, an Italian scholar, Fabroni, published a prescient paper on the composition of metalwork found in Etruscan graves, noting that the jewellery from the poorer graves tended to be of brass rather than of bronze, in imitation of the colour of the gold jewellery found in the rich graves.[3] This was the first occasion on which comments about social significance had been drawn from purely scientific examination of archaeological material. In 1815 Sir Humphry Davy published his work on the nature and manufacture of ancient pigments, both natural and synthetic.[4] Davy showed that the blue colours encountered in the plaster from many Classical buildings was made up of a blue pigment mixed with varying amounts of lime to produce the required shade. He correctly identified the pigment with that described by the ancients as being produced in Egypt, now known as Egyptian Blue, which was made from copper, silica and the naturally occurring alkali natron. This was the first detailed technical study of ancient synthetic materials.

Throughout the nineteenth century scientists retained their interest in the past. One is struck by the historical perspective of such works as Percy's *Metallurgy*,[5] which is still a prime source of information about early and traditional processes. Other eminent metallurgists had similar interests. Gowland, for example, studied traditional smelting and metalworking techniques in Japan and applied this experience to his many studies of ancient materials, including his work on smelting and silver-refining debris recovered from the excavations then in progress at the Romano-British cities of Silchester, Wroxeter and Caerwent.[6]

The burgeoning collections of Europe's museums in the nineteenth century included excavated material, much of it in a highly corroded state, creating the need for a scientific approach to conservation.[7] This interest began in Scandinavia and Germany, and the first laboratory devoted to scientific conservation and examination of antiquities was opened in 1888 at the Königliche Museum in Berlin.[8] With the work and publications of the laboratory's founder, H.O.W. Olshausen, and of its first chemist, F.W. Rathgen, scientific conservation can be said to have become established.

Unhappily, the Königliche Laboratory did not survive the First World War. However, the British Museum Research Laboratory was born out of that conflict and is now the oldest surviving laboratory attached to a museum. After the commencement of hostilities in 1914 much of the British Museum's collections was shipped off to underground quarries for safe-keeping. When the objects returned in 1919, many were found to have deteriorated quite badly in the damp conditions in which they had been stored. The Museum Trustees requested an eminent chemist, Dr A. Scott, to investigate the problems and recommend suitable treatments. This was to have been a short-term advisory position, but during that time the general applicability and usefulness of the work was appreciated, and the establishment of a laboratory was sanctioned in 1920, with Dr Scott in charge of a small team. In the early days much of the work was concerned with conservation, especially on complex or difficult pieces, and with the development of new methods which in turn led to the first standard textbooks on scientific conservation.[9,10,11] Inevitably the conservation work led to analysis and technical examination: the Laboratory was able to carry out considerable research on the material from the tomb of Tutankhamen shortly after its excavation in the 1920s, and on material excavated at Ur by Woolley during the 1930s.

The first major scientific impact on archaeology itself was made by the life sciences, and scientists in Scandinavia seem to have been the first to become aware of the potential. Thus, for example, prospection methods for locating sites of early human occupation from the phosphate content of the soil were pioneered in Sweden following soil surveys carried out to assess agricultural potential.[12] Palaeobotanists and geologists studying the rapid changes at the end of the last Ice Age and the beginning of the present interglacial period, which were particularly evident in southern Scandinavia, were quick to realise that they could re-create the environment experienced by the first hunter-gatherers, and detect the influence of man on the early landscape, especially the arrival of the first farmers. Of equal importance was the development of geological dating methods[13] which, together with related botanical techniques, gave some indication for the first time of the antiquity of prehistoric man in Europe. For later prehistory, archaeologists still had to rely on the chronologies derived by comparison with the historic civilisations of the Middle East.

The environmental and life sciences continue to play an important role in archaeology and this is now a recognised discipline in its own right. The physical sciences only began to develop systematically within the practice of archaeology in the 1920s and 30s. Analysis and scientific examination using newly developed techniques such as the emission spectrograph (see glossary) were found to be especially useful for giving a rigorous physical description of artefacts. This in turn led to questions of source and provenance of materials based on composition. In both Britain and Germany, the first major analytical programmes to locate sources of metals used in antiquity from the characteristic trace elements in the contemporary artefacts were in progress in the 1930s.[14,15] Independently, the study of early technology, especially of ceramic, glass and metal production, became another area of research in which the physical sciences proved useful. The serious archaeological investigation of pottery and iron production sites was often accompanied by experimental replication.

After the Second World War the advent of radiocarbon dating had a major and continuing impact on archaeology – the first physical scientific method to do so. Radiocarbon dating was developed by Libby in the late 1940s, and created great interest amongst archaeologists everywhere.[16] It also earned Libby acclaim in the scientific community, and he was awarded the Nobel Prize in 1960. To meet the demand for radiocarbon dates both in archaeology and other disciplines, laboratories were established all over the world, and the British Museum set up such a dating facility in the early 1950s. Radiocarbon dating was followed by thermoluminescence dating, developed at Oxford in the late 1960s. This technique is particularly applicable to ceramics,[17] but has now been applied successfully to other materials as well.

At the same time, physical prospection techniques to locate and plan archaeological features buried beneath the soil were introduced in Britain and elsewhere, utilising changes in the electrical resitivity of the soil, or in the local magnetic intensity.[18,19]

New analytical methods and ever improving apparatus meant that more accurate results could be obtained more quickly, and on smaller samples – an important consideration where antiquities are concerned. This in turn meant that a much wider range of analytical projects became feasible, some involving hundreds if not thousands of samples. Projects were designed to find out more about past technologies and also to link characteristic compositions to particular sources and thus to provenance ancient material.[20,21]

Provenance studies on metals and ceramics became much more sophisticated. New methods such as stable isotope analysis for metals and neutron activation analysis of ceramics (see glossary), coupled with advanced statistical treatments of the data, allowed attributions of source for a variety of materials to be made with much greater confidence than had been possible before. Petrological studies on both ceramics and rocks have been of enormous value. Careful petrological identification of the numerous sources of hard rock used in the British Neolithic era for stone axes has meant that the source of these artefacts can now be routinely identified.[22] At last, after several false starts, provenance studies began making a real contribution to our understanding of trade and distribution patterns in the past. Similarly, the general introduction of the scanning electron microscope (see glossary) revolutionised the examination of antiquities, elucidating hitherto obscure details of structure.

This ever-increasing data bank of information on the materials and methods of all periods has become an invaluable aid in exposing fakes.

Combined with research on the typical products of corrosion, and using the standard dating methods, this means that scientific authentication is now routinely possible.[23]

The new scientific techniques are applicable to the study of early technology, especially those which left behind a good deal of material waste, such as the production of ceramics or metals. Materials such as furnace fragments and slags, which had previously been regarded as of little consequence, could now be studied scientifically to reveal many of the basic parameters of the processes involved. This extension into the investigation of early technology has meant that scientists are now often actively involved in the excavation and interpretation of production sites.[24]

Perhaps the most far-reaching recent development in this field, and in museum studies generally, has been brought about by the rapid advances in mathematics and computer science. Not only has this revolutionised the handling of scientific data, but computerisation has extended into all areas of the actual curation of museum collections and of excavation finds and records. Computer registration is now greatly facilitating the use of these often large bodies of material. For collections as large, complex and diverse as those of the British Museum, designing appropriate computer software has been very challenging; the task of actually entering the collections data is enormous and will take many years to complete. Nevertheless, information that only a few years ago would have been impossible to contemplate bringing together can now be summoned up in seconds.

As the range of scientific apparatus and methods applied to archaeological problems has grown, so more and more of the world's major museums and galleries have established their own laboratories, often in association with their conservation laboratories. The subject has now entered the regular curriculum of many universities. For example, it was at Oxford, where the Research Laboratory for Archaeology and the History of Art was founded in 1955, that the word 'archaeometry' was coined by Professor Hawkes to describe the new discipline of the physical sciences applied to the study of the past. Methods of physical dating, prospecting and methods of scientific examination now regularly form part of undergraduate archaeology courses, as also does environmental science.

As the subject of archaeometry becomes more established and defined and as the number of specialists and specialist institutions continue to grow, there is the danger (common to all specialities) of isolation, that archaeometrists will speak mainly to other archaeometrists rather than to the world of archaeology and history in general. The British Museum Laboratory, attached to and serving one of the major museums in the world, is perhaps in less danger of this, because the staff are in daily contact with the archaeologists, art historians and specialists from other disciplines who make up the diverse talents of the Museum. But we are still very conscious of the need to communicate both with our professional colleagues in other subjects and to the interested layman. Much of our work necessarily appears as internal reports or in very specialised publications, and the aim of this book is to bring some of this work before a wider audience.

References

1. These analyses were published in *Archaeologia* III (First Series). Other early analyses of British and Irish material are given in J.W. Mallet, 1852. *Account of a Chemical Examination of the Celtic Antiquities in the Collection of the Royal Irish Academy, Dublin*. Dublin, University Press.

2. M.H. Klaproth, 1798. *Memoires de l'academie royale des sciences et belles-lettres, Berlin, Classe de philosophie experimentale*, pp. 97–113, etc, and also scattered throughout the six volumes of his collected analytical work, *Beitrage zur chemischen Kenntniss der Mineralkorper*, published between 1795 and 1815. Berlin and Posen.

3. G. Fabroni, 1810. 'Il bronzo ed altre leghe conosciute in antico'. *Academia Italiana di Scienze, Lettere ed Arti*. Livorno. Also discussed in Grassini, R., 1931. 'L' Oricalco e gli Ettruschi'. *Studi Etruschi VII*, pp. 331–4.

4. H. Davy, 1815. 'Some Experimental Observations on the colours used in painting by the ancients'. In *Philosophical Transactions*, CV, pp. 97–124.

5. J. Percy, *Metallurgy*. Pt. 1 (1861) *Fuel, Fire-clays, Copper Zinc and Brass*. Pt. 2 (1864) *Iron, Steel*. Pt. 3 (1870) *Lead*. Pt. 4 (1870) *Silver, Gold*. London, Macmillan.

6. W. Gowland, 1899. 'The Early Metallurgy of Copper, Tin and Iron in Europe as Illustrated by Ancient remains and the Primitive Processes surviving in Japan'. *Archaeologia* 56, 2, pp. 267–322. 1918. 'Silver in Roman and Earlier Times'. *Archaeologia* 69, pp. 121–60.

7. V. Daniels (ed.), 1988. *Early Advances in Conservation*. London, British Museum.

8. H. Otto. 1979. Das chemische Laboratium der koniglichen Museen in Berlin. *Berliner Bietrage zur Archaometrie* 4.

9. A. Scott, 1926. *The Cleaning and Restoration of Museum Exhibits*. London, Department of Scientific and Industrial Research.

10. H.J. Plenderleith, 1956. *The Conservation of Antiquities and Works of Art*. Oxford, Oxford University Press.

11. A.E.A. Werner, and H.J.Plenderleith, 1971. *The Conservation of Antiquities and Works of Art*, 2nd edition. Oxford, Oxford University Press.

12. O. Arrhenius, Fosfathalten i Skanska Jordar. *Sveriges Geologiska Undersokning*. Ser. C, no. 383, Arsbok 28, No. 3. A good survey of early work in phosphate prospection is given in S.F. Cook and R.F. Heizer, 1965. *Studies on the Chemical Analysis of Archaeological Sites*. Berkeley and Los Angeles, University of California Press.

13. F.E. Zeuner, 1946. *Dating the Past*. London, Methuen.

14. Reports of the Sumerian Copper Committee published annually in the *British Association for the Advancement of Science Reports*, between 1928 and 1938.

15. H. Otto and W. Witter, 1952. *Handbuch der altesten vorgeschichtlichen metallurgie in Mitteleuropa*. Leipzig.

16. W.F. Libby, 1946. *Physics Review* 69, p. 671, and more generally W.F. Libby, 1955. *Radiocarbon Dating*. Chicago, Chicago University Press.

17. M.J. Aitken, 1985. *Thermoluminescence Dating*. London, Academic Press.

18. M.J. Aitken, 1974. *Physics and Archaeology*. Oxford, Clarendon Press.

19. R.J.C. Atkinson, 1953. *Field Archaeology*. London, Methuen.

20. S. Junghans, E. Sangmeister, and M. Schroder, 1960, 1968 and 1974. *Kupfer und Bronze in der fruhen Metallzeit Europas*. Berlin, Mann Verlag.

21. J.F.S. Stone and L.C. Thomas, 1957. 'The use and distribution of Faience in the Ancient East and Prehistoric Europe'. *Proceedings of the Prehistoric Society* 22, pp. 37–84.

22. T.H. McK. Clough and W.A. Cummins (eds.), 1979. *Stone Axe Studies*, Report 23. Council for British Archaeological Research, London.

23. Jones, M. (ed.), 1990. *Fake? The Art of Deception*. London, British Museum Publications.

24. P.T. Craddock, 1989. 'The Scientific Investigation of Early Mining and Smelting'. In *Scientific Analysis in Archaeology*, ed. J. Henderson. OUCA Monograph, Oxford, pp. 178–212.

CHAPTER 2

Ceramics: Materials for all reasons

Andrew Middleton

Ceramic artefacts figure amongst the most ancient of manufactured products; they range from rather mundane but useful everyday objects through to exquisitely beautiful works of art produced to delight the observer. The earliest known examples of burnt (or fired) clay objects, the female figurines from Dolni Věstonice in Czechoslovakia, are about 25 000 years old, whilst bricks and domestic ceramic vessels were produced as long as 10 000 years ago. These earliest examples of ceramic art and technology already illustrate three of the fundamental properties of ceramic materials: moist clay is plastic and can thus be moulded into quite complex shapes; after firing at a high temperature the clay is transformed into a rigid material which can be used to bear loads or to contain loose materials such as grain or even to hold liquids; and, finally, ceramics are durable, as demonstrated by the preservation of pottery, often in considerable quantities, on many archaeological sites. The abundance of pottery fragments illustrates another feature of fired clay objects – that they are relatively easily broken. Although examples do exist of ancient vessels which have been repaired and of sherds re-used for other purposes, once broken they are of little use or value. Unlike metals, fired clay cannot easily be melted and 'recycled' on a large scale.

Early examples of ceramic artefacts also demonstrate the division (often blurred) between 'practical' applications and those which might be termed 'aesthetic', and already we can begin to appreciate the versatility of ceramic materials which is so apparent in the modern world. Indeed, this prompts the question, what is a ceramic? A modern materials scientist's definition of 'ceramics'[1] would include many other materials in addition to the fired clay products discussed above, from concrete foundations through bricks and mortar to terracotta chimney pots; household objects from ovenproof stoneware casseroles through everyday tablewares to fine porcelain figures, and from elegant glazed tiles to window glass and fine-cut crystal glass. Also included would be industrial materials such as the furnace linings essential for high-temperature metallurgical and glass-making processes, electrical insulators for power transmission lines, and glass fibres for thermal insulation and for making reinforced plastics; as well as 'hightech' ceramics for replacement limb joints, engineering components, and the heat-resisting tiles on the space shuttle, among other applications.

Narrower definitions of 'ceramics' have been proposed. Some restrict usage of the term to the history and art of pottery-making or even to the study of high-quality glazed wares with vitrified, or glassy, bodies (ceramics), as opposed to lower-fired vessels (pottery). In this chapter, however, the aim is to explore how scientific analysis can illuminate the way in which man has exploited the natural versatility of ceramic materials in their broadest sense throughout history. Discussion of glass will be taken up in the next chapter since it represents a specialised and well-defined aspect of ceramic art and science.

Scientific study of ancient ceramic materials can tell us a great deal. It can contribute to our understanding of the raw materials that were used, the particular technological or decorative properties that may have led to their selection, and the manner in which those raw materials were modified during the manufacturing process. Scientific study can also tell us something about how well the products performed in use, especially those used for 'technical' applications such as ancient metallurgical processes. Thus we can achieve a better appreciation both of the objects themselves and of their makers' skill in manufacturing products to meet particular aesthetic and technological demands. As will become apparent, there is an extensive array of techniques which can be used to determine the properties of a ceramic object, but xeroradiography, X-ray diffraction, optical microscopy (thin-section petrography) and examination in the scanning electron microscope are particularly useful (see glossary for all these terms).

By comparing the composition of ceramic objects with those of possible raw materials or with objects of known origin (e.g. from excavated production sites such as kilns) scientific analysis can also sometimes reveal where they were manufactured, but these aspects of ceramic studies are discussed in Chapter 6.

Ancient building materials

Even apparently mundane items, such as bricks and tiles, water pipes, plasters and concrete, can yield useful information, and scientific analysis can help to elucidate both the organisation of manufacture and the technical expertise of the people who made these essential everyday products.

Bricks and tiles

The provision of suitable building materials has been essential to civilisations throughout the ages, and mud and clay, the raw materials of brick and tile, are used for building to this day. Earth may be used in a raw, unfired state as turves dug straight from the ground, or after mixing with water and other ingredients, such as chopped straw, sand or chalk, in the form of daub or as sun-dried bricks. In recent years the use of such materials has become fashionable in the affluent society of California, whilst at the other end of the economic spectrum, in the poorer countries of the world, a return to traditional methods of building with mud brick may help to ease problems of homelessness. Daub and mud brick are vulnerable to erosion by wind and rain, but burning the clay greatly increases its weather-resistance and the use of burnt brick extends back to some of the earliest civilisations. Some of the finest examples come from

Mesopotamia – from the palace of Nimrud and from the city of Babylon, rebuilt in burnt brick by Nebuchadnezzar II in the seventh century BC. Similarly, the use of burnt or fired clay for roofing tiles extends back into antiquity, with some early examples from Olympia dating to about the same period as Nebuchadnezzar's rebuilding of Babylon.

The production of tiles, in particular flue tiles, by the Romans in southern England during the first and second centuries AD provides an interesting example of the contribution of scientific investigation to the study of ancient fired clay building materials. Hollow box-flue tiles or *tubuli* (fig. 2.1) were essential to the construction of the 'central heating systems' of Roman villas. They were used to carry hot air through the walls and even over arches by means of wedge-shaped box tiles known as *tubuli cuneati*. Some of these flue tiles are distinguished by impressed designs, which range from fairly simple geometric chevron patterns to more complex curvilinear designs and even include a fine pictorial design depicting a dog and stag. The patterns were impressed into the soft clay surface, before firing, using wooden roller-dies, but despite their decorative nature they were intended simply to act as a key so that the coating of plaster would adhere to their surface.

The complex design of the flue systems implies that the production and installation of the flue tiles was a specialist job, and it seems that the distinctive relief patterns could have been some form of trademark, applied to identify the products of a particular team or firm of tile-makers. The observation, first made more than forty years ago,[2] that there were a limited number of dies and that examples of tiles with identical patterns, produced by the same die, can be found at locations as far apart as London and Leicester (a distance of about 160 km), raises a fundamental question about the organisation of the tile-making 'industry'. Were the tiles made at a limited number of production centres and then transported to the 'consumer sites', or did the tile-makers travel about the country, taking their roller-dies with them, and make the tiles close to where they were to be used?

The application of thin-section petrography and chemical neutron activation analysis (see glossary) is beginning to provide an answer. Petrographic work carried out some years ago on tiles from northern Oxfordshire[3] suggested that a tile kiln at Long Hanborough produced relief-patterned tiles which were used for villas in the surrounding area, up to a distance of about 23 km away. A similar picture of centralised production has emerged from a combined petrographic/chemical analysis study of relief-patterned flue tiles and also roofing tiles (*tegulae*) from two sites south of London, Ashtead and Beddington.[4] The evidence suggests that tiles were produced from the local, silty clays at Ashtead; some tiles were used there whilst others were transported to Beddington, a distance of about 15 km.

Thus both studies suggest that flue tiles were produced at central locations and then transported up to about 25 km to the consumer sites. However, it seems unlikely that it would generally have been worth transporting such heavy and bulky yet fragile objects as tiles over much greater distances. The tilers would therefore probably have set up new

2.1 Romano-British box flue tile (PRB 1973.4–3.144). Length *c.* 407 mm.

production centres in order to supply more distant markets, and there is evidence to support this view. Petrographic analysis of two tiles with similar patterns (one from Oxfordshire, the other from Essex) showed that they had been made from different clays, and the investigators concluded that they were probably produced by the same team of tile-makers but at different tileries.

From these studies, we can deduce something about where the tiles were produced and we can also begin to make some tentative suggestions about the way this Roman 'central heating industry' was organised. The production of the flue tiles was apparently concentrated in a number of production centres, each of which supplied its own surrounding area. Particular groups of tilers may have operated a number of such centres in order to supply customers in widespread parts of the country, rather like the regional distribution depots used by many modern-day suppliers.

Mortars and concrete

Plasters, mortars and concrete constitute another group of building materials, widely used in the modern world but which have antecedents in some of the earliest civilisations: for example, the first lime plaster, the precursor of modern calcium silicate cements, was probably produced in the Middle East around 12 000 BC. Its uses are manifold and apart from straightforward application as a protective coating or as a ground for subsequent painting it has been used for architectural mouldings, beads, containers, sculptural figures, mortars and concretes, and even as an adhesive.[5]

The production of lime involves heating a relatively pure, lime-rich rock such as limestone or marble at a temperature of at least 800–900°C, to produce calcium oxide or quicklime. This is then slaked with water to form calcium hydroxide, a smooth, creamy lime putty. On exposure to carbon dioxide in the atmosphere the calcium hydroxide re-carbonates to form fine-grained calcium carbonate, which can often be distinguished by its texture from unburned limestone (fig. 2.2).

Scientific examination[6] of material from the linings of ancient lime kilns has shown that during the firing process peak temperatures in the region of 1100°C may have been achieved and that these were maintained for about a day, although the overall cycle of loading, heating, cooling and unloading the kiln would have been longer, perhaps in the region of a week or more.

Timber would have been the fuel normally used to fire the kiln, and examination of charcoal from a kiln in Northamptonshire[7] showed that a mixture of woods including beech, oak and poplar had been used. This tells us something about the locally available woodland but it also seems likely that these particular woods may have been deliberately chosen – poplar for its rapid burning and high heat production, and oak for its slower-burning properties. Very large quantities of fuel would have been required to raise and maintain the temperature of the kiln; figures given in the last century refer to the use of about 1400 kg of oak or 1900 kg of fir to produce about 1000 kg of lime.[8]

Because the provision of fuel on this scale is expensive, there has always been an incentive to extend building mortars by adding cheap 'fillers' such as sand, crushed stone, crushed tile or ashes. In addition, such material may help to reduce cracking and enhance the strength of the mortar. However, the proper selection of sand for use in mortars was (and still is) important, something which was clearly recognised by the Roman architect Vitruvius, writing in the first century BC. For instance, he commented on the need for clean, well-graded material and was aware that the use of sea sand would cause problems of slow setting and salt deposits rising to

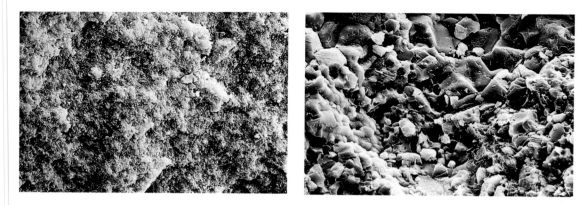

2.2 Scanning electron microscope photomicrographs of fractured surfaces of a first millennium BC Syrian cylinder seal, made by working plaster *left* on a core of limestone *right*. Note the very fine-grained nature of the plaster in the first micrograph. Width of field *c.* 0.1 mm in each case.

the surface. Furthermore, Vitruvius was aware that some additions, in particular *pulvis puteolaris* (a volcanic ash deposit from the Bay of Naples area), produce a very durable mortar which will set underwater. This material was quarried near Puteoli, modern Pozzuoli, from which *pozzolana*, the modern term for such additions, is derived.

Scientific study has shown that these pozzolanic additions, whilst not in themselves useful as cement, react with the lime to form strong mortars. This high strength is due to the formation of calcium silicates and aluminates during the setting process; these compounds act as bonding agents, giving the mixture its high set strength. Modern cements contain rather similar compounds but they are produced by firing mixtures of limestone and clay at high temperatures (in the region of 1400°C). Artificial materials such as burnt clay and crushed tile or potsherd also have pozzolanic properties, and many Roman mortars and concretes contain crushed ceramic materials.

The Roman development of these strong mortars, building upon techniques used by the Greeks, opened the way to the production of concrete, which revolutionised Roman architecture. No longer were architects constrained to think in terms of roofs supported on beams; instead the plasticity of concrete enabled them to construct lofty vaults and domes, of which the ultimate example is perhaps the dome of the Pantheon in Rome, erected early in the second century AD.[9, 10]

Household ceramics

Cooking pots

Some ceramics may have to withstand exposure to high temperatures; indeed, the refractories used to line furnaces for metal extraction and glass production must be capable of withstanding extremely high temperatures, up to around 1600°C. (The definition of refractory materials used in the ancient world is discussed more fully below.) However, the inability of many ceramic vessels to withstand sudden changes in temperature is a familiar shortcoming even of modern materials, and this problem of thermal shock has been the subject of extensive study in relation to both modern and archaeological ceramic materials. The problem would perhaps have been most acute in the use of ceramic vessels as cooking pots. Nevertheless the tradition of using fired clay vessels as cooking pots is almost as ancient as the history of ceramics. Petrographic examination of ancient cooking vessels has indicated the way in which the ancient potter, perhaps unwittingly, overcame this technological problem.

Here we will consider two examples of ancient cooking wares, both of Roman date; the first is from recent excavations at Cherchel in North Africa, the other is the well-known black-burnished wares which form one of the more common types of Romano-British pottery from about AD 120 until the end of the Roman occupation.

The cooking wares from Cherchel were hand-made rather than thrown on a wheel and petrographic examination has shown that the clay fabric

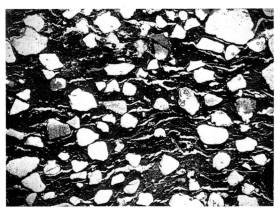

2.3 *left* Black-burnished ware cooking pot (PRB 1883.12–13.436). Height *c.* 200 mm.

2.4 *above* Photomicrograph of thin section of a sherd from a black-burnished type cooking pot; note the abundant sand grains and numerous elongate voids. Width of field *c.* 7 mm.

contains abundant coarse, angular rock fragments.[11] These inclusions, or temper, appear to have been added deliberately by the potter and were in fact essential to the successful firing and use of these wares. Unlike modern pottery, these pots were probably fired in an open bonfire rather than a kiln. It is difficult to exert much control over a bonfire firing and experiments have shown a characteristic rapid rise and fall of temperature during such firings. Maximum temperatures in the range 650 to 900°C are rapidly attained and the total duration of the firing is frequently less than thirty minutes. Experience suggests that unless the clay fabric contains a sufficient proportion of coarse temper (or 'opening material') it is liable to explode during the early stages of firing when water is being expelled as vapour from the clay. Thus the most severe thermal shock was likely to occur during the initial firing, and pots which survived the firing were likely to be suitable for cooking over an open fire.[12,13]

The production of Romano-British, black-burnished cooking pots (fig. 2.3) appears to have originated from an earlier, Iron Age tradition, but it evolved into a major industry during the Roman occupation. Examining thin sections of black-burnished wares originating from Dorset, using a petrographic microscope, it can be seen that the fabric of the pots is packed with grains of quartz sand, apparently deliberately added by the potter (fig. 2.4). However, in order to minimise the effects of thermal shock, the theory is that inclusions should not be of quartz but of materials such as grog (crushed ceramic), calcite or feldspar, which expand to a similar degree as the fired clay when they are heated. In fact, quartz expands significantly more than the clay on heating. One would therefore expect it to cause the object to crack and fall apart as it was heated during use in cooking. The explanation for the unexpected success of such fabrics seems to lie in the presence of numerous voids formed when the damp clay shrinks away from the opening materials during the initial firing (see fig. 2.4); these spaces allow the fabric to accommodate the changing size of the quartz grains during the heating and cooling cycles of cooking.

Thus, although the Roman potters of Cherchel and the Iron Age and Romano-British potters may not have understood the technical reasons for their success, it would seem that accumulated experience had taught them that it was necessary to use a fabric with ample opening material. The nature of the opening material was not critical. What was important was that there be enough of it; if the clay did not contain this naturally then it was added using locally available material such as sand, crushed flint or rock or grog. Having produced a vessel which could withstand the rigours of a bonfire firing it was likely that it would also stand use as a cooking pot.

Tablewares

Pottery intended for use simply as tableware undergoes much less rigorous treatment than vessels which are to be used for cooking; dishes and plates will not have to withstand particularly high temperatures, nor will they suffer rapid changes in temperature. However, such wares may have to satisfy other, aesthetic demands: they should look attractive and provide a pleasing surface from which to eat food. These requirements are admirably fulfilled by two of the best-known Roman pottery types, Arretine and its successor, samian ware (*terra sigillata*) (fig. 2.5). Both these wares were mass-produced on a huge scale and they were widely distributed across the Roman Empire to places as far apart as England and India. The Arretine industry was centred on the town of Arezzo (Roman Arretium) in western central Italy, and flourished from about 50 BC until AD 50 when production declined, to be replaced by samian wares. These were manufactured at a number of centres (the products of which have been characterised by elemental analysis of the clay fabrics[14]), especially in Gaul but also in Spain, North Africa and Britain.[15]

Both Arretine and samian wares are characterised by their bright red, glossy finishes and it is perhaps remarkable that such consistency of production was achieved in the ancient world. Scientific analysis, using X-ray diffraction (XRD) and examination in a scanning electron microscope (SEM) equipped with an energy-dispersive X-ray analyser (EDXA) (see

2.5 A samian bowl from London, first century AD (PRB 1915.12–8.51). Diameter *c.* 229 mm.

23

glossary) for chemical analysis of samples in the microscope, has shown how the glossy red finish was obtained and also demonstrated that the selection and preparation of clays for these wares were carefully controlled.

The mineral responsible for the bright red colour of samian pottery has been identified as hematite (iron oxide, Fe_2O_3) by X-ray diffraction, and examination of a polished section in the SEM shows that the glossy finish was produced by a fine slip (a thin layer of fine clay applied to the surface of the vessel before firing). Throughout the slip there are very fine (less than a thousandth of a millimetre in diameter) bright particles which were found to be iron oxide when analysed by EDXA. These are particles of the hematite detected in the XRD analyses.

More general EDX analyses of large areas of the slip layer showed that its composition differs from that of the body clay (see Table 2.1). In particular, the slip contains more iron oxide and potash (potassium oxide) and has a higher ratio of alumina (aluminium oxide) to silica (silicon dioxide). It is also noticeable that the slip contains almost no coarse inclusions and the slip clay was apparently carefully prepared, perhaps by sedimentation of the original body clay. The resulting clay contains a high proportion of platy particles of illite, a mineral rather like mica; these, aligned parallel to the walls of the pot, give rise to the high-quality glossy finish.

As well as being a key element in producing the red glossy finish, choice of clay was also important to the stability and reproducibility of the clay bodies of samian wares. The clays used were calcareous (rich in lime), and experimental studies[16] have shown that when such clays are fired they develop a stable vitrified (glassy) texture in the temperature range 850° to 1050°C. Thus precise firing temperature was not critical. So long as the samian pottery was fired somewhere within this range, a good-quality standardised fabric would be produced, and so long as a plentiful supply of air was maintained, a high-quality glossy red finish would be achieved.

The potters responsible for producing the early Arretine wares may have stumbled by accident upon a finely calcareous, illitic clay containing fine-grained iron oxide particles. However, those who established the later centres of production for samian wares must have had sufficient empirical understanding of the technical properties required of the body and slip clays to select localities where suitable clays were readily available.[17]

Oxide	Body of sherd	Red glossy surface
	(weight per cent)	
Silica (SiO_2)	51.0	43.5
Alumina (Al_2O_3)	21.0	32.9
Iron oxide (FeO)	5.9	12.4
Magnesia (MgO)	2.4	0.8
Lime (CaO)	17.2	2.3
Soda (Na_2O)	0.8	0.3
Potash (K_2O)	1.4	6.9

Table 2.1 Analyses of clay in body and surface finish of samian sherd.[17]

Decorative pottery

Thus far we have looked at essentially practical ceramics, used for fairly mundane, everyday activities. Even amongst these examples, however, there has been an indication of another aspect of ceramics – their decorative nature. The Arretine and samian wares discussed above were presumably popular because they were both useful and attractive. The tradition of decorating ceramic vessels, whether by impressing designs into the soft clay before firing, by scratching on designs after firing or by applying mineral pigments, clay slips and glazes, is almost as ancient as the art of making ceramics itself.

Funerary vessels

The practice of interring the dead extends back almost to the beginnings of mankind; the oldest known burial in Britain is the so-called 'Red Lady' of Paviland, of Upper Palaeolithic date. The skeleton, which was found in 1823 in the Paviland Cave in south Wales, is in fact that of a young man, and had been sprinkled with red ochre. It was accompanied by a selection of objects, including mammoth ivory and shells, indicating the existence of some sort of burial ritual, including the interment of 'grave goods' with the body, even at this early date. In Britain graves of Neolithic date are generally rather poor in grave goods, but the Beaker culture of the Early Bronze Age takes its name from the characteristic ceramic cup or beaker which was placed in the grave. Sometimes other finely made objects, including some of the earliest metalwork excavated in Britain, were interred along with the beaker.

Despite (or perhaps because of) the fact that many of these grave goods were apparently produced specially for the burial ritual, they are sometimes highly decorative and very skilfully made. Here we will consider the production of some fine pottery found in the rich La Tène burials of about the fourth century BC in the Champagne region of France. These vessels appear to have been produced primarily for ritual purposes since they are found almost exclusively in burials rather than on domestic, occupation sites. Not all the vessels were decorated but they are all inherently elegant in form, and some were painted in beautiful bichrome designs. The Prunay vase (plate 2.1), an outstanding example of Celtic ceramic art, is one such vessel and was included in the group examined.

This particular study prompts a comment upon one of the inevitable problems common to much scientific analysis of antiquities – the need to remove samples, albeit small ones, and the limitations that this may place upon the techniques which can be used and the vessels which can be sampled. Some techniques, such as radiography, XRD and XRF, can be essentially non-destructive but others, such as thin-section petrography and to a lesser extent SEM and NAA, require the removal of small but noticeable amounts of material. Because of the high quality and completeness of many of the vessels in the present study, sampling had to be restricted and carried out in an opportunistic fashion over a period of years. For instance, samples would be taken during the conservation or restoration of objects.

Simple examination with the naked eye can often tell us which vessels were entirely handmade, entirely wheel-thrown or handmade with wheel-thrown rims, although on narrow-necked complete vessels such distinctions become less obvious. Examination of the 'Prunay group' suggested that these vessels had been wheel-thrown and this was confirmed by xeroradiography. Petrographic examination of thin sections from vessels in the Prunay group showed that a high proportion of sand temper (opening material) had been added to the clay, implying that the potters were firing their work in open bonfires (see p. 22). This inference is consistent with the degree of vitrification of the clay, observed in the SEM, which suggested that the vessels were fired at around 800°C or less (see p. 30), and this accords with archaeological evidence which suggests that kilns were not introduced into north-west Europe until the second century BC.

The vessels studied have very rich, deep red coatings which are distinctly less orange in colour than the Roman Arretine and samian wares; the explanation for this lies in the raw materials used and the manner in which they were applied. As for the samian wares, XRD analysis indicated that the red coloration was due to hematite. In the case of the Prunay group, however, the coating is much richer in hematite, and SEM examination revealed that it consists almost entirely of particles of crushed iron oxide (fig. 2.6). Comparison with modern replica red finishes prepared by Ann Woods at the University of Leicester suggested that the Prunay potters were using a different technique from the samian potters. Instead of applying a thin, ferruginous clay slip, it appears that they burnished powdered iron oxide (in the form of hematite or ochre – a less pure, hydrated iron oxide) into the surface of the dried, leather-hard pots, prior to firing. Oxidising conditions would have been necessary to ensure that the coating fired red, and experimental bonfire firings suggest that this may well have been achieved by allowing the fire to burn down around the pots, thus exposing them to the air whilst still at a high temperature.

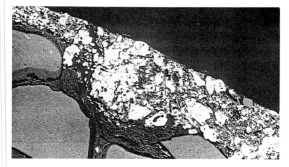

2.6 *above* Scanning electron microscope photomicrograph of cross-section through the red finish of a pedestal vase from the Champagne region of France. Note the thick coating formed from particles of iron oxide (white in the micrograph). Width of field *c.* 0.3 mm.

The elegant black designs on the decorated vessels are more enigmatic. Examination using a low-power binocular microscope showed that the black 'paint layer' is very thin, with no relief or 'barbotine' effect which would have been expected if the decoration had been trailed on to the surface of the pot. Analytical techniques such as XRD, XRF and EDXA in the SEM failed to detect any compound which could account for the black colour, suggesting that the coating consists of amorphous carbon black (or soot), which would be undetectable by any of these analytical techniques. But how was the coating applied?

The main design on the Prunay vase was created by negative painting (probably the most familiar example of this is batik, in which wax is used as a resist to create designs on cloth). On the basis of replication experiments it seems that a similar technique may have been used by the Prunay potters. Wax would have been applied to the red surface of the already-fired pot to protect the areas intended to be red in the final design. An 'organic paint' such as fruit juice or vegetable water would then have been applied to the background, and the wax resist would have prevented this 'paint' from 'taking' on the reserved area. Finally, the pot would be gently heated in the embers of the dying fire to char and blacken the organic paint, the wax would melt and run off or vaporise.[18]

The scientific evidence thus provides some indication of the skills employed by the Prunay potters in their selection of raw materials and in their techniques for forming, firing and decorating their products. In the Prunay workshop we can perhaps see the beginnings of a new and innovative tradition which, starting with the introduction of the potter's wheel, was to lead eventually to the highly organised Gallo-Roman pottery industry with its large-scale production and extensive trading network.[19]

Chinese porcelain

The pottery of China, especially its porcelain, is admired around the world and for a millennium attempts have been made to emulate its combination of pleasing appearance and excellent material properties (fig. 2.7). The name porcelain derives from the Portuguese word *porcellana* (shell), which is said to have been applied by Marco Polo to these high-quality ceramics because of their delicate translucency. The white body of porcelain, together with its translucency and impermeability – arising from its vitrified (glassy) nature – and its finely glazed surface, distinguish it from other ceramics. In China porcelain was manufactured on a large scale and was exported, first to the Near East and later to Europe.

From the ninth through until the fifteenth century AD Islamic potters responded to influxes of high-quality Chinese imports with what might be termed essentially 'cosmetic' solutions, producing vessels that had the appearance but not the technical properties of porcelain.[20] For example, in the ninth century conventional red-firing clay bodies were covered by opaque white glaze coatings in imitation of Tang dynasty whitewares, while later, in the twelfth century, late Sung dynasty *yingqing* porcelains were imitated by decorating less sophisticated vessels using transparent

2.7 *left* Chinese underglaze-blue porcelain dish, mid-fourteenth century AD, Yuan dynasty (OA 1968.4–22.26). Diameter *c*. 470 mm.

glazes, applied over the painted design (underglaze decoration), and also opaque glazes which formed a ground on which the design could be painted (overglaze decoration).

By about the fourteenth century Chinese porcelain was finding its way in significant quantities to Europe, and from the sixteenth century it was imported on a large scale by Portuguese, English and Dutch traders. The technological problems in replicating it were, however, considerable. It was not until the late sixteenth century that the first partially successful Medici porcelain was produced and not until the early eighteenth century that the first hard-paste porcelain was made at Meissen. Microscopical examination and analysis in the SEM of examples of various European attempts to imitate porcelain has shown why some attempts were more successful than others and has highlighted some of the technical problems that had to be overcome; in particular, the difficulty that pure white clays could not be vitrified, whilst those clays which could be vitrified were impure, so that they did not fire to the required pure white colour.[21]

Jingdezhen in southern China was the acknowledged centre of the Chinese porcelain industry and production continues there to this day. The availability of suitable clays and fluxes in this area was one of the factors which accounted for the precociousness of the Chinese ceramic industry, and scientific analysis, particularly SEM examination, has provided some insight into the nature of these raw materials.[22] Observation of the microstructure, combined with chemical analysis of *yingqing* porcelain, has shown that the microstructure of Chinese porcelain (fig. 2.8) can be related to four minerals, quartz, mica, kaolin and feldspar, which make up a naturally occurring kaolinised porcelain stone. This stone, found near Jingdezhen, contains all the ingredients necessary to produce a high-quality white vitrified ceramic body when fired at around 1250°C. Of particular significance is the mica, which was the main source of alkali flux, essential to the vitrification (partial melting) of the white-firing, kaolinitic clay. In addition to its fluxing properties the mica would also have improved the plasticity of the clay, thus increasing the range of forms which could be produced.

The presence of a high-quality glaze is another feature which distinguishes Chinese porcelain. A glaze is a glassy coating applied to a ceramic body to enhance its appearance or to improve its technological

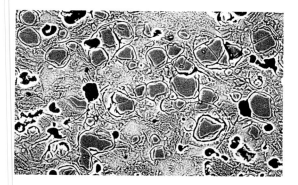

2.8 Scanning electron microscope photomicrograph of underglaze-blue porcelain showing the microstructure of the vitrified body. The grey rounded grains are quartz. Width of field *c.* 0.25 mm.

properties: for instance, to reduce abrasion of the surface or to render the surface less porous. It differs from a clay slip (as used in Roman samian pottery) in being essentially glassy in nature. Glazes may be colourless and transparent (e.g. when applied over underglaze painting); they may be transparent but coloured by the presence of small amounts of particular elements; or they may be rendered opaque, for example by the addition of a component such as tin oxide, calcium or lead antimonate, which precipitates as very fine crystals in the glaze layer, thus reducing its transparency (see Chapter 3 for discussion of colorants and opacifiers). The essential glassy nature of glazes is achieved by the incorporation of fluxes into the glazing mixture. In the earliest glazes the fluxes were soda (sodium oxide) and/or potash (potassium oxide) derived from natron (a naturally occurring sodium carbonate mineral) or from various plant ashes.

The glazes on Chinese porcelain were prepared by adding 'glaze-ash' (lime) to the clay used to make the clay bodies. Analyses have shown that the precise composition of the glaze mixtures used for different types of porcelain was sometimes carefully controlled. For instance, the glazes used on porcelains with underglaze blue decoration have a composition which would have given the optimum properties with respect to transparency and the absence of crazing, so that the underglaze decoration would have been displayed to best effect.

Thus the Chinese potters produced wares so far in advance of other civilisations partly because of the potters' ingenuity (in particular their highly developed kiln technology, which allowed very high firing temperatures to be attained), but also because of the availability of a suitable raw material – the kaolinised porcelain stone. As we have already seen, the lack of such an ideal raw material was the major problem faced by the European imitators.

Ceramics for metallurgy

Ceramic materials are indispensable to the modern metallurgical industry and on ancient metal smelting and metal working sites there is often abundant ceramic debris such as furnace linings and tuyeres (the clay tubes used to supply air to the furnaces; see also Chapter 4) from the smelting process, crucibles for subsequent refining or re-melting and sometimes ceramic moulds for casting metal artefacts. The ceramics used for such purposes must be refractory (able to withstand exceptionally high temperatures without melting). Analysis and laboratory experiment have shown that in general these ancient refractories were not, by modern standards, truly refractory. They were, however, required to withstand more extreme conditions than those of a normal domestic hearth and using the term refractory for these archaeological materials is therefore justified.[23] Normally, locally available raw materials were used, but the evidence suggests that there was careful selection and, if necessary, modification so as to achieve the particular properties of strength (e.g. in a crucible), dimensional stability (e.g. in a mould) or resistance to high temperature (e.g. in a furnace wall).

Estimation of furnace operating conditions

As well as providing information on the selection of raw materials, the examination of ceramic debris from ancient metallurgical operations can shed light upon the operation of the furnace: at what temperature was the process carried out and how long did it take? Ceramic materials generally melt gradually as the temperature is raised. Examination of a ceramic material subjected to successively higher temperatures shows that its texture changes in a predictable manner. Such changes can be seen in the SEM; Figure 2.9a is an SEM photomicrograph of a low-fired (*c*. 800°C), poorly refined clay, taken from the outer (cool) portion of the wall of one of the zinc distillation furnaces at Zawar, India (see Chapter 4). In this sample the individual mineral grains are clearly visible, but at the higher temperatures encountered towards the inner (hot) face of the furnace wall the ceramic had started to melt and was partially vitrified (fig. 2.9b; T = 1000–1050°C). Close to the hot face itself the temperature was in the region of 1150°C and it can be seen (fig. 2.9c) that further melting occurred, leaving rounded grains of quartz in a glassy matrix. The expansion of hot gases trapped in isolated pores within the melting material resulted in the development of rounded bloating pores, and these can also be seen in the micrograph.

The temperatures at which these changes in the melting texture occur depend upon the composition of the original clay; clays with higher amounts of soda and potash (i.e. fluxes) are less refractory and begin to melt at lower temperatures. By firing test pieces of known composition in the laboratory it is possible to determine the temperatures at which clays of different composition will melt, so that the changes in texture observed in the SEM can be used to estimate the temperatures attained in the ancient furnaces.

During the operation of the furnace, heat will penetrate into the furnace wall and, as the process continues, this has the effect of steadily reducing the thermal gradient (the rate at which the temperature decreases away from the hot face). Thus the longer the process lasts, the lower will be the gradient. By taking a series of samples from known positions through the furnace wall, from the hot inner surface to the cool outer surface,

 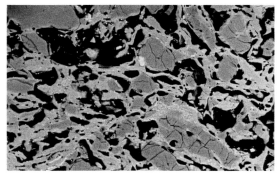

and estimating the temperature reached at each point, it is possible to reconstruct the thermal gradient; from this the approximate duration of the process can be estimated.

Chinese bronze moulds

Very demanding technical properties can be required of materials used for casting metal – for instance, a high resistance to thermal shock, chemical resistance to hot metal, mechanical and dimensional stability, and sufficient porosity to allow the escape of hot gases. One of the most exceptional ceramic moulding materials must be loess, which made possible the casting of the very fine detail on ancient Chinese bronzes (fig. 2.10). Loess is a natural sedimentary deposit formed from fine, wind-borne dust; it occurs as an extensive blanket covering the earth's surface in many parts of the world. Although it may be loose and crumbly in a hand specimen, it has sufficient strength when dry to form vertical cliffs. In China, where it is known as *huangtu* and where its relationship to wind-blown dust was recognised at least two thousand years ago, thick deposits of loess cover more than 250 000 square km.

In thin sections (examined using a petrographic microscope) or in the SEM the ceramic moulds can be seen to consist largely of extremely fine, angular particles of quartz and feldspar with very little clay between the particles. They had high porosity and a very low clay content which would have resulted in excellent dimensional stability, making this an almost ideal casting medium for bronze.

The loess deposits of northern China, where the bronze moulds were made, are quite varied in character and it is clear that the artisans of the Shang dynasty were aware of the technical properties required and selected their loess carefully, or perhaps refined the raw loess to remove any fine clay and coarser particles.[24]

Ceramics for the plastic arts

We have already seen that the earliest known application of fired clay was not for a utilitarian purpose but rather Palaeolithic man exploited the plastic properties of ceramic materials to make clay figurines. The moulding

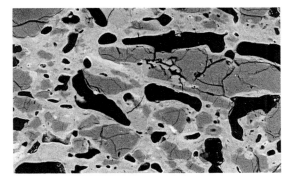

2.9 Scanning electron microscope photomicrographs of sections through fragments from a zinc distillation furnace at Zawar, India. Samples were taken from the cool outer zone **(a)** *far left*, within the thickness of the wall **(b)** *centre* and at the hot inner face of the furnace **(c)** *left*. Note the successive changes in vitrification texture. Width of field *c.* 0.3 mm in each case.

of ceramic materials into relatively complex shapes extends from the oldest through to modern ceramics and encompasses the whole range of ceramic materials: from coarse earthenware clays to fine porcelain, from the use of concrete to produce plastic architectural forms to the production of plaster-based stucco sculpture figures.

Egyptian faience has been produced in Egypt and Mesopotamia from about 4000 BC until modern times, and in this final section we shall consider how scientific analysis has revealed the skill and ingenuity which went into producing what has been termed 'the first high-tech ceramic'.[25] Faience was used to make a variety of objects such as scarabs, seals, beads and amulets, as well as bowls, cups and other small vessels. Several colours – including black, red, pink, yellow and green – are known, but the most common was the bright turquoise variety. This was probably made in imitation of the natural mineral lapis lazuli which is very rare and which is thought to have been available in antiquity from a single source, Badakshan in Afghanistan, said to have been visited by Marco Polo in the thirteenth century. Indeed, this appears to have been the sole supply until the nineteenth century and in medieval Italy the blue pigment ultramarine, derived from lapis, was valued more highly than gold. One of the advantages of faience was that it could be mass-produced (like samian tablewares) and it was widely used for personal ornament and for funerary equipment, including the well-known *shabti* figures (plate 2.2).

Faience consists of a ground quartz body covered by a layer of glaze. SEM analysis of polished sections through small fragments of turquoise faience objects has shown that the glaze is of the alkaline type with sodium as the main flux; the blue colour was achieved by the addition of a few per cent of copper. The application of such a glaze to a conventional earthenware body would not have been at all successful, partly because the underlying colour of the ceramic body would have interfered with the bright blue transparent glaze, but also because alkaline glazes do not adhere well to earthenware bodies; it was not until the introduction of lead glazes that such bodies could be successfully glazed. The development by the pre-Dynastic Egyptians of an alternative body for faience was therefore essential.

X-ray diffraction analysis and SEM examination have shown that the faience body consists of angular particles of crushed quartz set in a more

2.10 *left* Shang dynasty ritual bronze food vessel from Henan province, Anyang, China (OA 1957.2–21.1). Height *c.* 153 mm. *right* Fragments of bronze-casting moulds. (OA 1937.5–19.3,4 and 5). The smallest fragment is *c.* 40 mm across.

or less glassy matrix (fig. 2.11). Modern production of faience donkey beads at Qom in Iran has been observed by Hans Wulff and, based upon his reports and also on replication experiments in the laboratory, it has been shown that the variations in the amount and distribution of the glassy phase reflect the use of three distinct glazing techniques.[26]

The glazing mixture would have consisted of crushed quartz, a source of alkali (natron or plant ash), and a source of copper (copper filings or malachite, a natural copper carbonate mineral); a small amount of lime is usually found in the analyses but this is thought to have been introduced as an impurity in the raw materials. In one method of glazing this mixture was fritted by heating, crushed and applied directly to the surface of a pre-formed, crushed quartz body. It was then fired at about 800 to 900°C to give a thick, well-defined glaze layer with little if any glass in the core of the object (fig. 2.11a).

Alternatively, in the so-called cementation method (used in modern bead production at Qom), the object was buried in the glazing mixture and fired. Again, a well-defined but often thinner glaze layer was formed, with no development of glass in the core of the object. In the third method, known as the efflorescence technique, the glazing components were mixed with the moistened crushed quartz body and allowed to dry. Evaporation brought some of the soluble alkali to the surface so that on firing a thick glaze layer formed. Because some of the alkali flux remained in the core, faience produced by the efflorescence technique had a diffuse boundary between the glaze layer and the core and there was extensive development of glass in the core of the object (fig. 2.11b).

The introduction of a special crushed quartz core was thus the key to allowing the use of alkaline glazing mixtures, which had already been used to glaze stone objects, especially steatite. Although the quartz body would have been more difficult to work than an earthenware clay, it nevertheless opened the way to the production of more plastic forms than could be achieved using stone carving techniques. In particular it permitted the production of attractive and desirable objects in large quantities from cheap and readily available raw materials.

 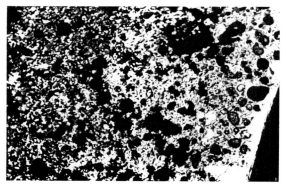

2.11 Scanning electron microscope photomicrographs of sections through faience produced by **(a)** *left* the direct application of fritted and crushed glaze mixture, and **(b)** *right* the efflorescence technique. Note the different textures, in particular the distribution of the glassy phase (white). Width of field *c.* 1.2 mm in each case.

Conclusion

Within the context of the diversity of ceramic materials and the multitude of ways in which they have been employed throughout history, the aim of this chapter has been to illustrate how scientific analysis of ancient ceramic artefacts can increase our understanding of the practical skills of the people who made them. Analysis can tell us about the raw materials that were selected, the manner in which those raw materials were processed and transformed into useful or attractive objects, and sometimes even something about how well those objects performed in use. Although the theoretical reasons underlying success or failure may not have been understood in antiquity, analysis of artefacts from the ancient world frequently demonstrates that the artisans of the time had a remarkable practical understanding of the materials and processes they were using.

Further reading

The list of publications below is not intended to be in any way comprehensive but it is hoped that it will, in conjunction with the references which follow, provide the interested reader with further information on the topics covered in the text and also a 'way in' to the extensive literature on scientific examination and analysis of ceramic materials.

G. Brodribb, 1987. *Roman Brick and Tile*. Gloucester, Alan Sutton.

N. Davey, 1961. *A History of Building Materials*. London, Phoenix House.

R.W. Grimshaw, 1971. *The Chemistry and Physics of Clays and Allied Ceramic Materials*. 4th edition. London, Benn.

A. Kaczmarczyk and R.E.M. Hedges, 1983. *Ancient Egyptian Faience*. Warminster, Aris and Phillips.

W.D. Kingery, H.K. Bowen and D.R. Uhlmann, 1976. *Introduction to Ceramics*. 2nd edition. New York, Wiley.

W.D. Kingery and P.B. Vandiver, 1986. *Ceramic Masterpieces: Art, Structure and Technology*. New York, Free Press.

F.R. Matson (ed.), 1966. *Ceramics and Man*. London, Methuen.

J.S. Olin and A.D. Franklin (eds.), 1982. *Archaeological Ceramics*. Washington DC, Smithsonian Institution Press.

D.P.S. Peacock, 1982. *Pottery in the Roman World*. Harlow, Longman.

P.M. Rice, 1987. *Pottery Analysis: A Sourcebook*. Chicago, University of Chicago Press.

O.S. Rye, 1981. *Pottery Technology: Principles and Reconstruction*. Washington DC, Taraxacum.

A.O. Shepard, 1976. *Ceramics for the Archaeologist*. Washington DC, Carnegie Institution of Washington.

T.A. Wertime and S.F. Wertime (eds.), 1982. *Early Pyrotechnology: The Evolution of the First Fire-Using Industries*. Washington DC, Smithsonian Institution Press.

In addition to the volumes listed above, numerous contributions of interest will be found in the *Ceramics and Civilisation* series (Series Editor W.D. Kingery) published by the American Ceramic Society (Westerville, Ohio): I, 1985. *Ancient Technology to Modern Science*; II, 1986. *Technology and Style*; III, 1986. *High-Technology Ceramics*; IV, 1989. *Cross-Craft and Cross-Cultural Interactions in Ceramics*; V, 1990. *The Changing Role of Ceramics in Society*. Papers will also be found in the Proceedings of the International Archaeometry Symposia (see for example Y. Maniatis (ed.), 1989. *Archaeometry: Proceedings of the 25th International Symposium*. Amsterdam, Elsevier) and in journals such as *Archaeometry* (Oxford Research Laboratory for Archaeology, Oxford University) and *Journal of Archaeological Science* (London, Academic Press).

References

1. W.D. Kingery, H.K. Bowen and D.R. Uhlmann, 1976. *Introduction to Ceramics.* 2nd ed. New York, Wiley.

2. A.W.G. Lowther, 1948. 'A study of the patterns in Roman flue tiles and their distribution'. *Research Papers of the Surrey Archaeological Society,* No. 1, pp. 1–35.

3. D. Johnston and D. Williams, 1979. 'Relief patterned tiles: a reappraisal'. In *Roman Brick and Tile,* ed. A. McWhirr, pp. 375–93. Oxford, British Archaeological Reports, International Series 68.

4. A.P. Middleton, M.N. Leese and M.R. Cowell, 1991. 'Computer-assisted approaches to the grouping of ceramic fabrics'. In *Recent Advances in Ceramic Petrology,* eds. A. P. Middleton and I. C. Freestone. London, British Museum Occasional Paper 81.

5. W.D. Kingery, P.B. Vandiver and M. Prickett, 1988. 'The Beginnings of Pyrotechnology, Part II: Production and Use of Lime and Gypsum Plaster in the Pre-Pottery Neolithic Near East'. *Journal of Field Archaeology* 15, pp. 219–44.

6. A.P. Middleton and M.S. Tite, 1989. 'Report on the Examination of some Fired Materials Associated with the Lime Kiln in Trench B11 and of a Fragment of the Plaster Bedding of the Dromos from Trench B9'. In *Excavations at El-Ashmunein, II: The Temple Area,* A.J. Spencer, pp. 80–81. London, British Museum Publications.

7. D.A. Jackson, L. Biek and B.F. Dix, 1973. 'A Roman Lime Kiln at Weekley, Northants.' *Journal of Roman Studies* 4, pp. 128–40.

8. G.R. Burnell, 1856. *Limes, Cements, Mortars and Concretes,* Weales' Rudimentary Series, 2nd edn., Crosby Lockwood; quoted by N. Davey, 1961, in *A History of Building Materials,* London, Phoenix House.

9. H.N. Lechtmann and L.W. Hobbs, 1986. 'Roman Concrete and the Roman Architectural Revolution'. In *Ceramics and Civilisation III: High-Technology Ceramics,* ed. W.D. Kingery, pp. 81–128. Westerville, Ohio, American Ceramic Society.

10. T.W. Potter, 1987. *Roman Italy.* London, British Museum Publications.

11. I.C. Freestone, forthcoming. 'Petrology of pottery from Cherchel, Algeria'.

12. A. Woods, 1982. 'Smoke gets in your eyes: patterns, variables and temperature measurement in open firings'. *Bulletin of the Experimental Firing Group* 1, pp. 11–25.

13. A. Woods, 1986. 'Form, Fabric, and Function: Some Observations on the Cooking Pot in Antiquity'. In *Ceramics and Civilisation II: Technology and Style,* ed. W.D. Kingery, pp. 157–72. Westerville, Ohio, American Ceramics Society.

14. F.A. Hart, J.M.V. Storey, S.J. Adams, R.P. Symonds and N.J. Walsh, 1987. 'An Analytical Study, Using Inductively Coupled Plasma (ICP) Spectrometry, of Samian and Colour-Coated Wares from the Roman Town at Colchester together with Related Continental Samian Wares'. *Journal of Archaeological Science* 14, pp. 577–98.

15. C. Johns, 1977. *Arretine and Samian Pottery.* London, British Museum Publications.

16. Y. Maniatis and M.S. Tite, 1981. 'Technological Examination of Neolithic-Bronze Age Pottery from Central and Southeast Europe and from the Near East'. *Journal of Archaeological Science* 8, pp. 59–76.

17. M.S. Tite, M. Bimson and I.C. Freestone, 1982. 'An Examination of the High Gloss Surface Finishes on Greek Attic and Roman Samian Wares'. *Archaeometry* 24, pp. 117–26.

18. L. Cheetham, 1985. 'Pre-Columbian Negative Painted Pottery; Some Notes and Observations'. *Bulletin of the Experimental Firing Group* 3, pp. 34–41.

19. V. Rigby, A.P. Middleton and I.C. Freestone, 1989. 'The Prunay Workshop: Technical Examination of La Tène Bichrome Painted Pottery from Champagne'. *World Archaeology* 21, pp. 1–16.

20. M.S. Tite, 1988. 'Inter-Relationship Between Chinese and Islamic Ceramics from 9th to 16th Century AD'. In *Proceedings of the 26th International Archaeometry Symposium,* eds. R.M. Farquhar, R.G.U. Hancock and L.A. Pavlish, pp. 30–34. Toronto, University of Toronto.

21. W.D. Kingery, 1986. 'The Development of European Porcelain'. In *Ceramics and Civilisation III: High-Technology Ceramics,* ed. W.D. Kingery, pp. 153–80. Westerville, Ohio, American Ceramic Society.

22. M.S. Tite, I.C. Freestone and M. Bimson, 1984. 'A Technological Study of Chinese Porcelain of the Yuan Dynasty'. *Archaeometry* 26, pp. 139–54.

23. I.C. Freestone and M.S. Tite, 1986. 'Refractories in the Ancient and Preindustrial World'. In *Ceramics and Civilisation III: High-Technology Ceramics*, ed. W.D. Kingery, pp. 35–63. Westerville, Ohio, American Ceramic Society.

24. I.C. Freestone, N. Wood and J. Rawson, 1989. 'Shang Dynasty Casting Moulds from North China'. In *Ceramics and Civilisation IV: Cross-Craft and Cross-Cultural Interactions in Ceramics*, eds. P.E. McGovern and M.D. Notis, pp. 253–73. Westerville, Ohio, American Ceramic Society.

25. P.B. Vandiver and W.D. Kingery, 1986. 'Egyptian Faience: The First High-Tech Ceramic'. In *Ceramics and Civilisation III: High-Technology Ceramics*, ed. W.D. Kingery, pp. 19–34. Westerville, Ohio, American Ceramic Society.

26. M.S. Tite and M. Bimson, 1986. 'Faience: An Investigation of the Microstructures Associated with the Different Methods of Glazing'. *Archaeometry* 28, pp. 69–78.

CHAPTER 3

Looking into Glass

Ian Freestone

In the modern world, glass is ubiquitous. We use it in our windows, televisions, containers and spectacles. If asked to name those characteristics which are particularly special to glass, it is probable that at the top of our list would come transparency and colourlessness. Close behind would inevitably come fragility.

To members of early glass-using societies, the foregoing description would have been unrecognisable. Before the Roman period, glass was a rare, luxury material, almost invariably coloured and often opaque. It was predominantly decorative rather than utilitarian and appears to have been strongly associated with semi-precious stones in the minds of its users. Pale blue glass was associated with turquoise and purple glass with fluorite, while the rare colourless pieces were equated with rock crystal. Mesopotamian cuneiform recipes for glass-making refer to glass as 'artificial lapis lazuli', emphasising its equivalence to the valued gemstone from Afghanistan.[1] In Han China, glass plates were used as a substitute for precious jade in the funerary suits of the dead. This tradition of using glass as a substitute for precious and semi-precious stones continues in jewellery of the present day.

The origins of glass

Glass was traditionally made by melting a mixture of two materials, silica (sand or quartz pebbles) and an alkali (potash or soda). The Roman author Pliny recounts that glass was discovered by a group of traders who, having put in to the beach near the mouth of the river Belus (near Haifa, modern Israel), supported their cooking pots over the fire with cakes of soda. The soda reacted with the sand of the beach to form 'a strange translucent liquid [that] flowed forth in streams'.[2] On cooling, this strange liquid would have formed glass. Unfortunately, Pliny wrote some 2000 years after the production of the earliest recorded glass objects, so we must regard this rather satisfying tale as apocryphal, owing more to the reputation of the Belus as a source of good glass-making sand in Roman times than to historical fact.

Current thinking is that glass-making originated in two older pyrotechnologies: the production of faience and of metals.[3] Faience is a ceramic body composed predominantly of crushed quartz and covered with an alkaline glaze (see Chapter 2). Failures in the production of faience are likely to have resulted in the accidental formation of glass. A glassy material familiar in the Bronze Age was the slaggy by-product of met-allurgical processes, and recent work suggests that some very early glassy beads may have a significant metallurgical component.[4]

Small glass beads and pendants that date back as far as the middle of the third millennium BC have been reported from sites in the Near East, but these finds are far from common. Furthermore, the objects were generally cut and ground in the cold state using lapidary techniques and did not make use of the special high-temperature properties of glass which allow it to be drawn, wound and moulded. Such widely spaced, somewhat enigmatic finds of glass occur over about a millennium; the establishment of a true glass industry did not occur until the sixteenth century BC, when the production of glass vessels began on a significant scale.

The earliest vessels were produced by trailing molten glass on to cores made from a mixture of clay and dung; the cores were removed when the vessels had cooled and hardened. An extensive palette of glass colours had been developed and a range of brightly coloured polychrome vessels was produced, initially in Mesopotamia and, it is believed, somewhat later in Egypt (fig. 3.1). At about the same time, glazed pottery was also introduced, an innovation thought to be related to that of glass-working.[5]

Some colourless glass was produced in the early period, as shown by the analysis of a colourless glass bead in the British Museum's collection, dated by inscription to the reign of the Egyptian Queen Hatshepsut (1473–1458 BC),[6] but colourless pieces were rare. It was only following the discovery of glass-blowing, somewhere in the coastal region of Syria in the first century BC, and the explosion of glass-making activity which occurred somewhat later throughout the Roman world, that vessels made of thin-walled, transparent and colourless glass became common.[7]

The nature and properties of glass

If glass cannot be defined in terms of its colour and transparency, then what is it? As with all materials, scientists define glass on the basis of its atomic structure. Although a piece of glass is hard to the touch, the arrangement of its atoms is the same as that of a liquid.[8]

In the melting pot, glass is viscous or treacle-like; its stiffness, relative to more familiar liquids such as water, originates in the very strong chemical bonds which hold its atoms together. This stiffness allows the molten glass to be blown, coiled or moulded. When it is cooled this sluggish material fails to adjust to the new conditions and the glass retains the atomic arrangement of the molten state although it is a solid.

Most solids are crystalline. Their atoms are arranged in very regular, ordered arrays and this order is reflected in their properties. For example, they tend to break in certain preferred directions which are parallel to layers of atoms. A crystalline solid cannot accommodate atoms which are too big or too small in its rigid structure, so that its chemical composition may not be readily modified. In a liquid, on the other hand, the atoms occur in a disordered, random fashion. The liquid structure of glass is responsible for many of its special characteristics.

3.1   Core-formed Egyptian vessel dating to the New Kingdom. Deep blue glass trailed with yellow, white and turquoise bands (EA 37.7–14.155). Height 101 mm.

Unconstrained by the crystal planes that dictate the cutting of most natural gems, glass may be cut and ground into any shape required, limited primarily by the skill and the imagination of the craftsman. Furthermore, its accommodating liquid structure allows it to incorporate components which modify its colour, transparency, brilliance and hardness. The flexibility imparted by the special nature of glass was well recognised in the ancient world for, as Pliny states, '... indeed, glass exists in any colour. There is no other material that is more pliable or more adaptable, even to painting'.[9]

Composition of ancient glass

Table 3.1 gives some examples of glass compositions, showing the main types used in Europe and the Near East from the second millennium BC through to the medieval period, along with a modern glass. The main chemical constituent of glass is silicon dioxide or silica, given in the top row of the Table. It is the most common component of the earth's crust and is familiar as the quartz sand on the beach, white quartz pebbles and flint. It typically makes up 50–70 per cent by weight of ancient glass. However, glass could not be made from quartz alone. To melt a crushed quartz pebble, extremely high temperatures, which were beyond those of early technologies such as pottery kilns or metallurgical furnaces, would have been required. A flux was mixed with the silica in order to lower the temperature at which it melted and thus allow the production of glass. Additions of about 20 per cent of such a flux could reduce the melting temperature of quartz from 1700° to well under 1000°C.

The fluxes most commonly used in the ancient world, particularly in Europe and the Near East, were the alkalis, soda (sodium oxide) or potash (potassium oxide). The alkalis were obtained either as naturally occurring minerals, or as the ashes formed by burning plant material or wood. Glasses formed from a simple mixture of silica and pure soda or potash would not be particularly successful, however. Such glasses are not stable and corrode in relatively short periods. An additional component to reduce the solubility of the glass is required and this is known as a stabiliser. In ancient glass the stabiliser was generally lime (calcium oxide). The lime was probably not added intentionally, however. It is believed that it was usually added incidentally, either with the silica or with the alkali, and was not recognised as a separate component by the glass-makers.[10] In addition to lime, its close chemical relation, magnesia, is given at the bottom of the Table.

Looking along the horizontal rows of Table 3.1 we notice that, with the exception of the medieval European glass, the ancient glasses are all quite similar in composition, and similar to the modern glass. These are soda-lime-silica glasses; soda is the flux and lime the stabiliser. It appears that by the time the earliest glass vessels were made in the middle of the second millennium BC, a glass formulation relatively close to that of a successful modern glass had already been attained.

The medieval European glass differs from the others in its higher potash and lime contents which result in a low silica content. This difference is due to the use of a different source of alkali flux. The medieval glass-makers north of the Alps used the potash-rich ashes from inland plants such as burnt wood or fern for their glass, as opposed to the soda-rich ash which was used in the Mediterranean area and in earlier periods. According to Theophilus, a monk who wrote in the early part of the twelfth century, the ash of the beech was preferred.[11] The workshops producing glass in the medieval period were commonly situated in wooded areas, sources of both raw material and fuel, so that it is sometimes termed 'forest glass'.

	Egyptian 15th cen. BC	Roman 1st cen. AD	European 13th cen. AD	Syrian 14th cen. AD	Modern
Silica, SiO_2	65	68	53	70	73
Soda, Na_2O	20	16	3	12	16
Potash, K_2O	2	0.5	17	2	0.5
Lime, CaO	4	8	12	10	5
Magnesia, MgO	4	0.5	7	3	3
Batch Materials	plant ash quartz	natron sand	wood ash sand/quartz	plant ash sand/quartz	synthetic components
Glass Category	High Magnesia	Low Magnesia	Forest Glass	High Magnesia	

Table 3.1. Typical composition of some glasses. The components are given in weight per cent. In addition to those listed, the ancient glasses would also have contained up to one per cent iron oxide and up to three per cent aluminium oxide, in addition to any colorants and opacifiers.

The change in composition brought about by the introduction of wood ash to produce forest glass in the medieval period is very pronounced, but other categories of glass are also readily recognised, although based on somewhat more subtle distinctions. The oxides of magnesium and potassium (Table 3.1) are very useful in helping us recognise these. Most early soda-lime-silica glasses, such as the Egyptian example in Table 3.1, are characterised by the presence of several per cent of both potash and magnesia. These are believed to have been introduced with the ash used to flux the glass, which was produced by burning saline plants found in the desert and around the marshy areas of the Mediterranean and the Near East.[12]

In about the seventh century BC, a second type of glass was introduced which became dominant in the Mediterranean world in the Roman period. This is so-called 'low-magnesia' glass, in which the magnesia and potash contents are typically less than about 1 per cent (Table 3.1). The elevated magnesia and potash contents of the earlier glasses are inherited from the plant ash itself, which never approaches pure soda in composition. The Roman glass-makers, however, used high-quality mineral soda or natron, producing a final product low in these impurities.[13] The main deposit of natron in the Mediterranean area is the Wadi Natrun, in the western desert of Egypt, and this is generally assumed to have been a major source in Roman times, implying extensive trade in raw materials. It appears that the old plant ash recipe did not die out completely in the Roman period, but continued to be used in Mesopotamia and other areas to the East.[14] In the middle of the ninth century AD, however, the use of natron appears to have ceased even in Egypt itself; the Islamic world reverted to the use of plant ash as a flux.[15] It is unlikely to be a coincidence that forest glass began to displace natron-based glass at about the same time in northern Europe.[16] Changes in supply and demand of glass and its raw materials, as yet not fully understood, resulted in the adoption of the new formulations.

Colour and opacity

Given the frequent use of glass in luxury items, the craftsman's ability to control and manipulate its colour and opacity was critical. An understanding of the ways in which these properties were manipulated provides us with much more than just an insight into the skills of the glass-maker. As standard practice varied so much with time and place, information on dating, provenance and authenticity may also be revealed.

Ancient glass often contains impurities of iron at levels which would have imparted an incidental coloration; the rarity of early colourless, transparent glass is likely to be at least partly due to this effect. In order to minimise the problem, raw materials had to be carefully selected. Quartz pebbles could be eliminated as a source of silica if they deviated far from a pure white colour, suggesting the incorporation of iron compounds, while the Belus sand favoured by the Romans has been shown by analysis to have low concentrations of iron.[17] In addition, from around the middle of the first millennium BC, substances were added which tended to neutralise the colorant effects of the iron. Before the Roman period antimony was the main decolorant, while from the second century BC manganese became important.[18] In northern Europe in the medieval period, a virtue was made of necessity; the wood ash glasses often contained such high concentrations of iron and manganese oxides that they were quite strongly coloured. By modifying conditions in the furnace, a wide range of colours could be produced from a single glass composition, from blues and greens through yellows and browns to violet. Incidental colours such as these were widely used in the so-called 'stained glass' ecclesiastical windows, and Professor R.G. Newton has recently estimated that less than 10 per cent of 200 pieces of analysed window glass from York Minster contained colorants that were deliberately added, most being coloured by components that were naturally present in the raw materials.[19]

For many purposes a strongly coloured glass of a particular colour was required and the craftsmen deliberately manipulated the composition of the glass to achieve the desired result. From a very early stage in the history of glass, a number of additives were utilised to impart a desired colour. The simplest were those which merely dissolved in the glass base to produce a strongly tinted transparent or translucent glass. These included copper, which resulted in a turquoise to green glass, cobalt, which gave a

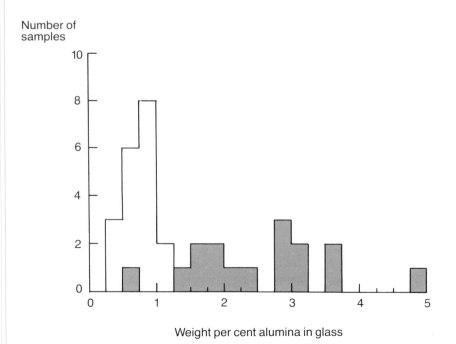

3.2 Histogram showing the aluminium oxide contents of thirty-five Egyptian glasses of the New Kingdom. The number of glass samples which have a particular alumina content is indicated by the vertical scale. The dark blue glasses (shaded) have higher alumina contents than the other colours.

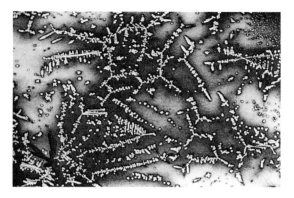

3.3 Opaque red glass from Nimrud, Iraq (eighth century BC) seen in the scanning electron microscope. The branching structure is composed of crystals of copper oxide or cuprite, which are red in ordinary light. Field of view *c.* 0.5 mm across.

deep blue, and manganese, responsible for shades of violet. While these colorants would sometimes have been added as natural minerals – for example malachite or copper carbonate – in others they were added as a simple synthetic product, such as copper oxide produced by heating bronze in air.

The form in which the colorant was added may in some cases be inferred by analysis. Thus, if bronze was used as a source of copper to produce a turquoise blue glass, then the glass has a high concentration of tin, which is an essential constituent of bronze. Sources of cobalt are particularly characteristic. Cobalt blue glasses from Egypt dating to the New Kingdom period (1560–1080 BC) have elevated aluminium oxide contents relative to associated glasses in other colours, as shown in the histogram in Figure 3.2. This implies that the source of the cobalt was rich in alumina and such deposits are unusual. It appears that the sources of the cobalt were cobalt-bearing alum minerals from the western oases of Egypt.[20] The use of these deposits as a source of cobalt appears to have been limited to the time of the New Kingdom. Furthermore, Mycenaean blue glasses of around the same date show very similar compositional characteristics, suggesting that Bronze Age Greece obtained its cobalt pigment, or perhaps its raw glass, from Egypt.[21]

To produce an opaque glass it was necessary to introduce a dispersion of particles within the glass which did not transmit light. Such opacifiers could be mixed directly with the glass, or alternatively the glass composition could be modified so that opacifying particles crystallised from the glass as it was held at some temperature below the melting temperature. Opacifiers were of two types. Those which were white or neutral in colour served simply to opacify a transparent glass, which might have its own colour, to produce, for example, an opaque blue. Some opacifiers, on the other hand, imparted their own colour.[22] An example of the latter is the red cuprous oxide or cuprite which is present in many opaque red glasses and which may display intricate growth patterns under the microscope (fig. 3.3). Such a delicate structure could not have been produced by crushing and mixing the cuprite with the glass. It was formed by crystallisation from the glass itself as it was cooled, or as a result of heat-treating the glass, that is, deliberately holding it in a temperature range favourable to the growth of the cuprite. The formation of cuprite in the glass required careful control of both the glass composition and of the furnace atmosphere; too little or too much air in the furnace would have caused the colour to fail. Because of the stringent conditions required for the production of cuprite red glass it is regarded as one of the most technically demanding glasses of antiquity.[23]

Roman luxury glass: the Portland Vase

Examination and analysis of ancient glass can enable us to answer questions about specific objects of particular art historical or archaeological interest. The example of the Portland Vase shows how scientific analysis can contribute to our understanding of an object's history. The vase (fig. 3.4) is one of the British Museum's most valued objects and is arguably the most famous piece of glass in the world. It is a cameo formed by dipping a gather of blue glass on the end of a blowing iron into a pot of hot white glass, then blowing a vase with a layer of white glass overlying a blue body. The cameo design was then produced by cutting and grinding away the white layer to reveal the blue. At some stage in its history the base of the vase was broken and replaced with a disc of cameo glass (fig. 3.4). Later damage was caused in 1845, when a visitor to the Museum, one William Lloyd, smashed the vase with a 'Persepolitan monument of basalt' which was on display nearby. Subsequent restorations have left a number of glass fragments so tiny that they cannot be reincorporated, and several of these have been made available for scientific work.

3.4 **(a)** *left* The Portland Vase. White cameo on a very deep blue background (GR 1945.9–27.1). Height 245 mm.
(b) *above* The base disc of the Portland Vase (GR 1945.9–27.2). Diameter 122 mm.

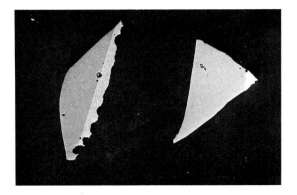

3.5 Samples of the Portland Vase *right* and its base disc *left* seen in the scanning electron microscope. The blue glasses appear dark grey, while the white overlying glasses are represented by the thin pale layers on the right-hand side of each sample. The photograph is about 4.5 mm across.

3.6 Detail of the boundary between the blue and white cameo glasses (fig. 3.5) at high magnification in scanning electron microscope. The numerous particles in the white glass *lower right* are of calcium antimonate, and render it opaque. Field of view *c.* 0.4 mm across.

In addition to the technical questions concerning the origins of the colour of the vase and its opacity, information was sought on a number of other problems. The relationship between the vase and the base disc was unclear and it was of interest to determine whether it might have been a repair carried out in response to damage inflicted when the vase was made. Surprisingly, there remained some question as to the date of manufacture. Roman cameo glasses were made in the period 50 BC to AD 50. Although the vase was generally accepted as of Roman date, some had suggested, due to the circumstances of its discovery, that it might be a Renaissance copy of a Roman form, perhaps made in a Venetian workshop. Scientific evidence to back up the conviction of most scholars that the vase was Roman might put this suggestion to rest once and for all.

Two tiny fragments, one of the vase and the other of the disc, were mounted in a block of epoxy resin and polished until completely flat cross-sections of the fragments were exposed. These were then examined in the scanning electron microscope (see glossary) and elemental compositions determined with the X-ray spectrometer (see glossary) attachment. Fragments of a number of other Roman cameo glasses were also examined for comparative purposes.[24]

Figure 3.5 shows the images of the fragment of the vase (on the right) and the base disc (on the left). This demonstrates the very small size of the samples required for such studies, only about one millimetre across. On the left of each sample is the blue cameo background, appearing grey, and on the right the white glass. Analysis shows that the dark blue colour is due to the presence of just one-tenth of 1 per cent of cobalt oxide dissolved in the glass. No opacifying particles are present in the blue glasses, so that the almost opaque appearance of the cameo background is due to the very powerful blue coloration imparted by the small quantity of cobalt. Figure 3.6 shows the boundary between the blue and the white glasses at a higher magnification. The boundary is very sharp, being only a few micrometres (thousandths of a millimetre) across. A number of gas bubbles occur close to it. The white glass contains numerous small, bright particles which are responsible for its opaque appearance. These are crystals of calcium antimonate, a standard opacifier of the Roman and pre-Roman periods.

Returning to Figure 3.5, one is struck by the difference in brightness between the white of the base disc and the white of the vase itself. The brightness of the white of the vase is due to a high concentration of lead oxide. A high lead concentration is unusual in Roman glass, but is known from a number of other cameo glasses. The addition of lead would have made the glass softer and easier to cut. The base disc, however, contains no lead. It seems unlikely that a workshop, having discovered the advantage of lead to the cameo cutter, would have used it in some pieces and not in others. This, coupled with other analytical differences, led to the conclusion that the vase and its base were indeed products of different craftsmen, brought together some time after they were made rather than produced in the same workshop.

It soon became apparent that the vase was not a product of the Renaissance. Documentary evidence indicates that Venetian glasses of the Renaissance period were made using ash derived from plants – either the barilla from marine plants of the Alicante region of Spain, or ash from desert plants from the Near East. Analyses of Venetian glasses confirm this; they have the characteristic elevated potash and magnesia contents of plant ash glasses.[25] However, the Portland Vase, along with other Roman cameo glasses and Roman glass in general, has low potash and magnesia, as shown in Figure 3.7.

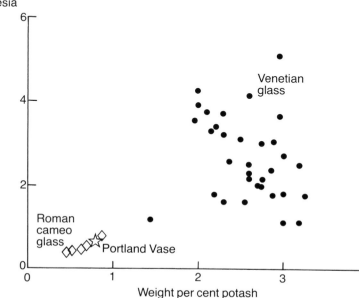

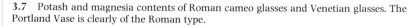

3.7 Potash and magnesia contents of Roman cameo glasses and Venetian glasses. The Portland Vase is clearly of the Roman type.

Byzantine mosaics

Opaque and coloured glasses were widely used as tesserae (small cuboid building blocks) in the wall mosaics of the Roman and Byzantine worlds. The tesserae were broken from flat sheets of glass which are likely to have been cast specifically for use in mosaics. Examination of glass tesserae gives us some insight into the way the mosaicists obtained their glass and the constraints placed by the availability of certain materials upon the final appearance of the mosaic.

The fragment of mosaic shown in Plate 3.1 is from San Marco, Venice, and dates to between the eleventh and thirteenth centuries AD. It is known from documentary evidence that Byzantine mosaicists were employed at San Marco during this period. It was also possible to examine tesserae from Shikmona in Israel, dating to the fifth century, and the monastery of Hosios Loukas, in northern Greece, dating to the tenth century. For the examination, small pieces of glass were removed from the backs of tesserae representing each shade of colour.

Most of the colorants are typical of ancient glass in general. Blues are due to dissolved copper or cobalt, purples due to manganese and greens due to copper or iron, while the reds are opaque due to fine copper-rich particles, either of cuprite or possibly metallic copper itself. Opacifiers in the greens and yellow-greens from Shikmona and San Marco are lead stannate or 'lead-tin yellow', while the blues from San Marco contain many fine particles of tin oxide. In the Mediterranean world by the fourth century AD, opacifiers based on compounds of tin had begun to replace those based upon compounds of antimony (such as the calcium antimonate in the white of the Portland Vase). As the millennium progressed, tin opacifiers became more common and eventually became dominant. However, no significant concentrations of either tin or antimony are present in the tenth-century tesserae from Hosios Loukas. Instead, an attempt has been made to opacify some of the glasses by mixing crushed quartz grains with the glass (fig. 3.8). This technique produces a glass which is not transparent but neither is it fully opaque; the tesserae have a characteristic sugary or saccharoidal appearance. Of particular interest is the technique used to produce the gold tesserae seen in Plate 3.1. A

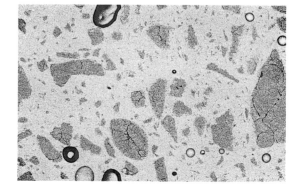

3.8 Glass mosaic tessera from Hosios Loukas. It contains abundant fragments of crushed quartz, which appear dark in this scanning electron microscope image. Field of view *c.* 1 mm across.

sheet of very fine gold leaf was laid over a sheet of glass and covered with a thin layer of transparent glass, which was then melted to produce a 'sandwich', giving a brilliant gold appearance.

The base compositions of the glasses correspond well with our understanding of the evolution of glass technologies in the period under consideration. Thus the glasses from Shikmona are of the low magnesia, low potash type, reflecting the use of natron as a flux in the fifth century AD (fig. 3.9). Most of the glasses from Hosios Loukas are of the high magnesia type, while San Marco yielded a range rich in potash, paralleling the widespread introduction of potash-rich glasses in the medieval period in northern Europe. Figure 3.9 shows the existence of a core group of glass analyses for each of these sites, but each also has a number of outliers, i.e. analyses which do not group with the others. Thus certain of the San Marco tesserae show characteristics which are more typical of earlier glass groups and therefore group with them in the graph.

The nature of the compositional outliers is of considerable interest. It appears that, to exploit the full range of colours, it was necessary to obtain glass from more than one source. At San Marco the gold tesserae are compositionally distinct, while at Shikmona the opaque reds differ from the other colours in their base composition. These are technically demanding glasses, probably produced by workshops which specialised in these colours and therefore more expensive. At Hosios Loukas, however, the blue glasses are the outliers, suggesting that either the mosaicists or the merchants who supplied them had to 'shop around' for even the relatively common glass colours. Furthermore, the range of effects due to tin-based opacifiers does not appear to have been available to the mosaicists of Hosios Loukas; the absence of tin from this assemblage suggests that the use of crushed quartz to produce a translucent, as opposed to an opaque glass, may have

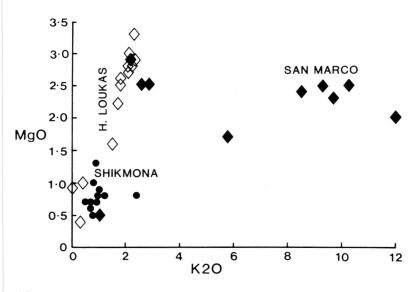

3.9 Potash and magnesia contents of Byzantine mosaic tesserae. There is a core group from each of the three sites examined, with a number of outliers.

been due to necessity rather than choice. It is likely that tin-opacified glass was not available, or was too costly.

These features imply that the colours used in Byzantine mosaics were at least in part determined by the ability of the mosaicists to obtain certain colours. The final appearance of the superb designs which we can see today may therefore partly reflect the practical availability of certain glass types to the craftsmen.

Medieval enamels

The technique of enamelling – where glass was fused to a metal substrate to decorate an object of copper alloy, silver or gold – was highly developed in the medieval period. Cells to enclose the glass were formed by attaching fine wire to the substrate (the cloisonné technique) or alternatively by gouging out the metal (the champlevé technique). Powdered glass was placed in the cell or recess and the object heated in a furnace to melt the glass. When cool, the fused glass was ground and polished down to give a smooth, even surface.

Enamels such as that shown in Figure 3.10 pose a number of questions which might be answered by analysis of the glass. Of particular interest is the technology and source of the glass and whether such information will allow us to identify the products of different workshops of enamellers according to the composition of the glass they used. The example considered here relates to the enamels produced in the twelfth century in the Mosan workshops, located in the region of Liège and Cologne in the valley

3.10 Mosan enamel plaque, twelfth century AD (MLA 1913.12–20.1). Enamelling in opaque white, blue, turquoise, red, green and yellow glasses on a copper substrate. Width *c.* 60 mm.

of the River Meuse. Some of these enamels had been damaged or corroded due to age so that minute fragments of glass could be removed for examination without causing additional visible damage to the object.

Microscopy and analysis of the enamels revealed a number of features which were quite surprising for glasses dating to the medieval period. Firstly, the opacifiers in the white, turquoise and blue enamels were based upon compounds of antimony. As we have seen, antimony was the typical opacifier of the Roman period. The opacifiers used in the Byzantine and Islamic glasses of the medieval period were typically tin-based. Furthermore, of the twenty or so glasses analysed, only two were of the medieval potash-rich type; the remainder were soda-lime-silica glasses. Glasses of the soda-lime type could have been obtained from the Mediterranean area, but this is unlikely in the present case because the glasses also have low magnesia and potash contents and are therefore of the old Roman formulation. Thus, on the basis of their bulk composition and the opacifiers used, these glasses were technologically anachronistic.

Might there have been a continuation of the Roman tradition of glass-making into the medieval period in the region of the Meuse? This is most improbable, not only because the raw materials were not locally available but also because medieval-type potash glass is represented among the enamels, suggesting that glass of the standard type was available to the enamellers and presumably made in the region. Rather, the explanation for the Roman compositions of the glasses may be found in the writings of the twelfth-century monk Theophilus, who comments that, 'Different kinds of glass, namely, white, black, green, yellow, blue, red, and purple, are found in mosaic work in ancient pagan [i.e. Roman] buildings. These are not transparent but are opaque like marble, like little square stones, and enamel work is made from them . . .'.[26]

Thus the enamellers obtained their glass from the mosaics in old Roman buildings and the analytical study confirms the account of Theophilus. This is not the complete story, however, for some contemporary glass is present in the enamels. Interestingly, this medieval glass is opaque red which, as has already been noted, was difficult to produce and likely to be relatively rare and expensive. It would also have been difficult to use in enamel work, as it would have tended to spoil easily for the same reasons that made it difficult to manufacture. A shortage of opaque red glass from the ancient mosaics is likely to have made it necessary to obtain such glass from contemporary glass-makers and, indeed, may have been responsible for the production of such glass in the first instance.

The investigation of the Mosan enamels has provided a graphic confirmation of the behaviour described in the writings of Theophilus, our most important documentary account of medieval enamelling techniques. Unfortunately, however, it has not proved helpful in identifying the products of different workshops, as was originally hoped. The re-use of old Roman glass means that the products of a particular enamelling workshop will not be characterised by glass of distinctive composition, but will reflect the rather diverse sources from which the glasses were obtained.

3.11 *right* The Aldrevandini Beaker, thirteenth century AD (MLA 76.11–4.3). Colourless glass, enamelled in red, yellow, white, blue, green and black. Height 130 mm.

Enamelled glass

Powdered glass may be melted on to glass objects for decorative purposes, just as it has been used upon metals. Magnificent examples of enamelled glass were produced in Syria in the thirteenth and fourteenth centuries but the evidence for the production of enamelled glass in Europe during this period is not strong. However, a small group of glasses dating to the later part of the thirteenth century, with decoration incorporating Latin inscriptions and heraldic coats-of-arms, has been found on a number of European sites, notably in Germany and in London. These glasses are sometimes termed the 'Aldrevandini Group', after the British Museum's Aldrevandini Beaker (fig. 3.11). They have been attributed to a workshop in Syria, but current scholarly opinion appears to favour a European origin, perhaps in Venice, which was to become the centre of European glass-making. Although it was not possible to sample the glass of the beaker, as it is intact, analysis of some closely related fragments from recent excavations, now in the Museum of London, has allowed investigation of the technology and comparison with enamelled Islamic glass.

The enamelled designs were painted on to the vessels, which were then placed in a furnace and fired to fuse the enamel. Microscopy allows us to determine the way in which the pigments were produced. Figure 3.12 shows a fragment of colourless vessel glass and the red enamel which has been painted and fused upon it. The enamel layer is only about one-tenth of a millimetre thick. Note the numerous small white particles in this layer. These are the particles of red iron oxide, or hematite, which are responsible for the colour. Examination of the micrograph suggests that the hematite particles are not evenly distributed: they occur in strings which outline areas of glass free from the pigment. These clear areas represent the original particles of glass which were crushed to make the enamel. They were then

3.12 *below* Layer of red enamel on the Aldrevandini Beaker, running diagonally, with the colourless glass at bottom right. The enamel contains numerous small particles of iron oxide, which themselves outline dark 'ghosts' of the original glass particles painted on to the vessel. Scanning electron microscope. Field of view *c.* 0.3 mm across.

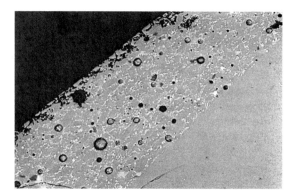

mixed with very finely divided hematite (probably an artist's pigment), which adhered to the surface of the grains. When the enamel was fired, the glass was sufficiently softened to cause the particles to fuse together, but the duration was not long enough to cause the hematite to dissolve. One can therefore still see the somewhat distorted outlines of the original particles. It appears that the particles of glass were of the order of 10 micrometres, that is one-hundredth of a millimetre, in size.

Analysis shows that the glass used to produce the red enamel has a soda-lime-silica composition typical of the glass used to produce the vessels themselves. A few per cent of cobalt pigment was added to a similar glass to produce the blue enamel. The yellow and green enamels, however, are basically lead glasses with lead-tin yellow as a colorant and opacifier, combined with copper to produce the green. To obtain their colours, the craftsmen made use of a much wider range of formulae or recipes than those we have seen in any other well-defined group of glass objects, reflecting the considerable technical knowledge required to produce enamelled glass.

Analysis of the colourless body glass and comparison with contemporary Near Eastern material reveals no significant technical differences. However, glass from Venice, dated to before the middle of the fourteenth century, is of a similar type. Similarly, the cobalt pigment used for the blue enamel is a particular zinc-rich variety, but essentially the same pigment is present in both Syrian ceramics and Venetian glass. This similarity between the Syrian and Venetian materials is not surprising: Venice occupied an important position in the Mediterranean trade network and the importing of Near Eastern materials would be expected. Furthermore, documentary evidence suggests that, at least from time to time, the raw materials for glass-making were imported into Venice from the Near East. Comparison of the enamels on the Aldrevandini group with those on Islamic glass suggests the use of an almost identical technology. The enamel compositions are so complex that it is most unlikely that they were developed independently in Europe. A substantial input of Syrian technical knowledge was probably required, wherever the vessels were made.

A unique glass: the Lycurgus Cup

The Lycurgus Cup (plates 3.2a and 3.2b) is an outstanding example of a late Roman cage cup. It has been cut and ground from a blown blank to produce a frieze in openwork, showing scenes from the myth of King Lycurgus. The cup is not only renowned for the outstanding workmanship of its decoration, but also for its unusual colour effects. When light is reflected back from the surface of the glass it appears pea green, but when light passes through it, it appears wine red. So unusual are the effects that in the 1950s, when the cup was first shown to Professor W.E.S. Turner, a leading glass scientist and doyen of the study of early glass technology, he doubted that it was glass and it was referred to the Natural History Museum in case it was mineral. More recent work has confirmed that the cup is indeed glass.

A number of other examples of Roman glass showing similar dichroic (two-colour) effects have come to light but less than ten are known, they are fragmentary and the dichroism is not always as well developed. In order to investigate the origin of the extraordinary colour effects shown by the Lycurgus Cup, a small sample was required. As it happened, the base of the cup had been broken at some time in the past and it had been replaced in the nineteenth century by a metal mount. Removal of the mount when the cup was acquired by the British Museum in 1958 revealed a number of minute fragments of glass which had become detached from the broken surface; these were saved for analytical work.

Investigations over several decades have revealed that the colour of the cup is due to the presence of small amounts of silver and gold, at levels of 300 parts per million (ppm) silver and 40 ppm gold. These have precipitated in the glass to give very small particles or colloids of silver-gold alloy such as that shown in Figure 3.13. The particles are typically 70 nanometres (millionths of a millimetre) in diameter and are very widely spaced. In order to obtain images such as that shown in Figure 3.13, it was necessary to use a modern transmission electron microscope in the University of Essex,[27] for the particles are too fine to be seen by more routine techniques.

The physics behind the colour effect is complex and lends itself more to mathematical equations than to a conceptual explanation. Briefly, the colour in transmitted light is due to the very fine size of the particles, which are of a similar size to the wavelength of light. They scatter the blue end of the spectrum more effectively than the red, resulting in the red transmission. In the Lycurgus Cup, the metal particles are just coarse enough to reflect back a certain amount of the light without eliminating the transmission. The green colour seen in reflection is likely to be due mainly to the silver which makes up two-thirds of the alloy.

The ruby coloration imparted to glass by the incorporation of minute amounts of gold was exploited in Europe following its discovery in the seventeenth century. The secret was to obtain a solution of the gold in the form of chlorides, the so-called 'Purple of Cassius'. However, the production of the Lycurgus Cup and related dichroic glasses, along with a small group

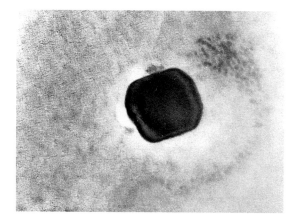

3.13 Particle of silver-gold alloy in the glass of the Lycurgus Cup, seen in the transmission electron microscope. The particle is approximately 70 nanometres across (photograph by Professor David Barber, University of Essex).

of flesh-coloured glasses of around the same date,[28] indicates that at least one Roman workshop was able to produce glass of a technically similar type some 1200 years earlier. Just how the Roman craftsmen produced this glass remains to be determined.

Looking to the future

The analysis of ancient glass objects tells us a good deal about how, when and where they were made. The examples outlined above concern relatively small, well-defined groups of material. However, there are whole regions and periods represented by only a handful of published analyses. For example, it has recently been demonstrated that, although glass from the Mediterranean world was imported into ancient India, China and north-western Europe, these areas also developed their own indigenous glass technologies with their preferred raw materials and compositions.[29] With such broad geographical distinctions just being recognised, the scientific study of ancient glass is clearly at a relatively early stage in its development. The sample of glass which has been examined to date remains very small, but as we gain a deeper understanding of the temporal and geographical variations in technology and composition, we can expect many more interesting and, in some cases, exciting discoveries to be made.

Further reading

A brief and well-illustrated history of glass is given by Chloe Zerwick, *A Short History of Glass* (1980, Corning Museum of Glass; distributed in the UK by Dover). A more comprehensive account is given by Hugh Tait (ed.), *Five Thousand Years of Glass* (1991, London, British Museum Press). *Glass and Glassmaking* by Roger Dodsworth (1982, Shire Publications) provides an excellent introduction to traditional glass technology as practised in the post-medieval period. General publications on the scientific analysis of glass are sparse. 'Ancient Glass' by Robert Brill (1963, *Scientific American*, pp. 120–30) is still a very good introduction, while the reader is directed to the bibliography of the present chapter for more detailed and up-to-date coverage. Papers dealing with technical aspects of early glass are frequently published in *Journal of Glass Studies* and *Archaeometry*, and sometimes in materials science journals, notably *Glass Technology* and *Glastechnische Berichte*.

References

1. A.L. Oppenheim, R.H. Brill, D. Barag and A. von Saldern, 1970. *Glass and glassmaking in ancient Mesopotamia*. New York, Corning Museum of Glass.

2. D.E. Eichholz, 1962. *Pliny, Natural History*, volume 10, book 36, p. 65. London, William Heinemann.

3. E.J. Peltenburg, 1987. 'Early faience: recent studies, origins and relations with glass'. In *Early Vitreous Materials*, eds. M. Bimson and I.C. Freestone, London. British Museum Occasional Paper 56, pp. 5–29.

4. Work in progress by Dr. P.B. Vandiver, Smithsonian Institution, Washington DC.

5. Peltenburg, *op.cit.*

6. M. Bimson and I.C. Freestone, 1988. 'Some Egyptian glasses dated by royal inscriptions'. In *Journal of Glass Studies* 30, pp. 11–15.

7. For the development of the Roman glass industry, see D.F. Grose, 1986. 'Innovation and change in ancient technologies: the anomalous case of the Roman glass industry'. In *Ceramics and Civilisation III: High Technology Ceramics, Past, Present and Future*, ed. W.D. Kingery, pp. 65–79. Westerville, Ohio, American Ceramic Society.

8. For a more extensive discussion of the nature of glass intended for the non-scientist, see R.H. Brill, 1962. 'A note on the scientists' definition of glass'. In *Journal of Glass Studies* IV, pp. 127–38.

9. Eichholz, *op.cit.*

10. W.E.S. Turner, 1956. 'Studies in ancient glasses and glass-making processes. Part V: raw materials and melting processes'. In *Journal of the Society of Glass Technology* 40, 277T–300T.
R.H. Brill, 1970. 'The chemical interpretation of the texts'. In Oppenheim *et al.*, *op.cit*, pp. 105–28.
R.G. Newton, 1980. 'Recent views on ancient glass'. In *Glass Technology* 21, pp. 173–83.

11. J.G. Hawthorne and C.S. Smith, 1979. *Theophilus: On Divers Arts*. New York, Dover Publications.

12. Turner, *op.cit.*, Brill, 1970, *op.cit.*

13. E.V. Sayre and R.W. Smith, 1967. 'Some materials of glass manufacturing in antiquity'. In *Archaeological Chemistry, A Symposium*, ed. M. Levey, pp. 279–311. Philadelphia.
J. Henderson, 1985. 'The raw materials of early glass production'. In *Oxford Journal of Archaeology* 4, pp. 267–91.

14. R.W. Smith, 1963. 'Archaeological evaluation of analyses of ancient glass'. In *Advances in Glass Technology, Part 2*, eds. F.R. Matson and G.E. Rindone, pp. 283–90. New York, Plenum Press.

15. E.V. Sayre and R.W. Smith, 1974. 'Analytical Studies of Ancient Egyptian Glass'. In *Recent Advances in the Science and Technology of Materials*, volume 3, ed. A. Bishay, pp. 47–70. New York, Plenum Press.

16. J.R. Hunter, 1981. 'The medieval glass industry'. In *Medieval Industry*, ed. D.W. Crossley, pp. 143–50. London, Council for British Archaeology, Research Report 40.

17. Turner, *op.cit.*

18. E.V. Sayre and R.W. Smith, 1961. 'Compositional categories of ancient glass'. In *Science* 133, pp. 1824–6.
E.V. Sayre, 1963. 'The intentional use of antimony and manganese in ancient glasses'. In *Advances in Glass Technology, Part 2*, eds. F.R. Matson and G.E. Rindone, pp. 263–82. New York, Plenum Press.

19. R.G. Newton, 1978. 'Colouring agents used by medieval glassmakers'. In *Glass Technology* 19, pp. 59–60.

20. A. Kaczmarczyk, 1986. 'The source of cobalt in ancient Egyptian pigments'. In *Proceedings of the 24th International Archaeometry Symposium*, eds. J.S. Olin and M.J. Blackman, pp. 369–76. Washington DC, Smithsonian Institution Press.

21. E.V. Sayre, 1964. *Some Ancient Glass Specimens with Compositions of Particular Archaeological Significance*. New York, Brookhaven National Laboratory Report BNL 879.

22. W.E.S. Turner and H.P. Rooksby, 1959. 'A study of the opalizing agents in ancient opal glasses throughout three thousand four hundred years'. In *Glastechnische Berichte* Special Supplement, 5th International Glass Congress, Part 8, pp. 17–28.
W.E.S. Turner and H.P. Rooksby, 1961. 'Further historical studies based on X-ray diffraction methods of the reagents employed in making opal and opaque glasses'. In *Jahrbuch des Romisch-Germanischen Zentralmuseums* Mainz VIII, pp. 1–6.
H.P. Rooksby, 1962. 'Opacifiers in opal glass through the ages'. In *G.E.C. Journal* 29, pp. 20–26.

23. I.C. Freestone, 1987. 'Composition and microstructure of early opaque red glass'. In *Early Vitreous Materials*, eds. M. Bimson and I.C. Freestone, pp. 173–91. British Museum Occasional Paper 56, London.
     R.H. Brill and N.D. Cahill, 1988. 'A red opaque glass from Sardis and some thoughts on red opaques in general'. In *Journal of Glass Studies* 30, pp. 16–27.

24. M. Bimson and I.C. Freestone, 1983. 'An analytical study of the relationship between the Portland Vase and other Roman Cameo glasses'. In *Journal of Glass Studies* 25, pp. 55–64.

25. R.H. Brill, 1973. 'Analysis of some finds from the Gnallic wreck'. In *Journal of Glass Studies* 15, pp. 93–7.
     M. Verita, 1985. 'L' Invenzione del cristallo muranese: una verfica analitica delle fonti storiche'. In *Rivista della Stazione Sperimentale del Vetro* 1, pp. 17–36.

26. J.G. Hawthorne and C.S. Smith, *op.cit.*

27. D. Barber and I.C. Freestone, 1990. 'An investigation of the origin of the colour of the Lycurgus Cup by analytical transmission electron microscopy'. In *Archaeometry* 32, pp. 33–45.

28. R.H. Brill and D. Whitehouse, 1989. 'The Thomas Panel'. In *Journal of Glass Studies* 31, pp. 34–50.

29. R.H. Brill, 1987. 'Chemical analyses of some early Indian glasses'. In *Archaeometry of Glass*, ed. H.C. Bhardwaj, pp. 1–25. Calcutta, Indian Ceramic Society.
     Zhang, Fukang, 1987. 'Origin and development of early Chinese glasses'. *Ibid.*, pp. 25–8.
     Shi Meiguang, He Ouli and Zhou Fuzheng, 1989. 'Chemical composition of ancient glasses unearthed in China'. In *Proceedings of XVth International Congress on Glass: Archaeometry*, ed. O.V. Mazurin, pp. 7–12. Leningrad.
     J. Henderson, 1988. 'Glass production and Bronze Age Europe'. In *Antiquity* 62, pp. 435–51.
     An Jiayao, 1984. *Early Chinese Glassware*. Oriental Ceramic Society Translations 12 (1987). London, Oriental Ceramic Society.

CHAPTER 4

Mining and Smelting in Antiquity

Paul Craddock

The mining and smelting of metals has always been one of the most technically demanding and arduous of human activities. A wide-ranging practical if not theoretical knowledge of geology, mechanics, chemistry and physics was required. Indeed the development of these technologies into true academic sciences may well have been spurred on by the insatiable demand for metals, creating the need for ever deeper mines and more sophisticated smelting processes. As with the influence of steam on science in the Industrial Revolution, science in antiquity owed more to mining than mining owed to science. Thus the study of early metallurgy is important to our general understanding of man's technical development.

Until very recently this study was largely confined to ancient literary sources or the contemporary metalwork itself, with early mines and smelting places receiving little attention. This was partly because it was believed that later activity would have destroyed or masked any ancient workings. Where ancient remains were suspected, the sprawling heaps of apparently featureless and undatable mine spoil and slag were a daunting prospect. It was difficult to see what could be gained from their excavation, and thus the few investigations on Roman mine sites, for example, tended to concentrate on the cemeteries, the inevitable bath house, and even the amphitheatre in one instance, rather than tackle the more crucial question of how the metal was produced.

In reality it is very rare for later workings to obliterate the ancient workings totally. Thus even at Rio Tinto in southern Spain, where there are enormous modern opencast mines, enough survives of the old workings to reconstruct their technical history. Where early workings have been cut by later workings, physical dating techniques such as radiocarbon can resolve them into periods, and the surviving heaps of production debris (made up of furnace fragments, crucibles and other refractories, all in the ubiquitous slag) encapsulate all the parameters of the processes of which they were once a part. Detailed scientific examination of carefully excavated material can then elucidate the nature of these processes.[1]

This chapter follows some of the principal developments in metal production, from its inception through to the beginnings of the scientific age, using a number of early mining and smelting sites as examples.

The earliest use of metal

The first use of metal stretches back to the first farming communities in the Middle East, some ten thousand years ago.[2] The surviving metal objects tend to be small pins and trinkets, all of native copper, rather than gold. (Contrary to the common assumption, goldworking in fact came rather late in the development of metallurgy, except in exceptional areas such as South America.[3]) The native copper used to make these small copper trinkets forms part of a class of luxury exotic decorative materials including brightly coloured minerals such as lapis lazuli and metal ores.

Native copper tends to be formed in nature by the reduction of copper-rich minerals in the upper exposed sections of an ore deposit. Thus small nuggets and stringers (thin threads of metal) will have been found at the surface of eroding deposits or in adjacent stream beds.[4] The archaeological evidence for the discovery of melting and smelting metal is tenuous – little survives beyond the few small metal artefacts themselves – but we can speculate on how it may have developed. The brightly coloured copper ores and the native metal itself were collected, and their proximity in the ground would itself have been suggestive. Both metal and ore are dense and burn with a distinctive green flame; when artefacts of native copper were left in the open they would go green; and both the metal and the ore would go black when heated strongly in a fire. It must eventually have been appreciated that the metal and ore were in some way linked and that it could be possible to turn the ore into metal.

It would have been possible to shape the native copper by hammering, but it would soon have developed cracks unless periodically subjected to annealing by strong heating during the working. Inevitably the metal would have occasionally overheated and melted (1084°C), thereby leading to the discovery of casting. This stage was apparently not reached until several thousands of years after the first use of metal in the Middle East, but the discovery of smelting metals from their ores seems to have followed on from melting fairly swiftly. Reducing ores to metal is essentially fairly simple. A good charcoal fire with a strong controlled air supply will raise the ore to the required temperature and reduce it to metal. Of course we can only speculate about the circumstances of the first smelting, but it could have come about quite accidentally. When melting lumps of native copper, still mixed with fragments of their ore matrix, in a crucible under charcoal it would have been noted that the ore had largely disappeared but the quantity of metal had increased. It is perhaps significant that the crucible smelting of copper does seem to be the earliest process recognisable at a number of sites around the world.[5]

Locating the ore

The layout of any mine is largely determined by the ore body. Most deposits originated in hot aqueous solutions containing metals which came up from the underlying magma and penetrated faults and cracks in the rocks deep underground. These solutions slowly cooled and precipitated the dissolved material, filling the fissures with vein rocks, typically quartz, pyrites etc, together with minerals of any non-ferrous metals which were present. Early miners followed the veins closely and tended to take out as little as possible apart from the ore, often creating complex and tortuous systems of galleries.

The first miners attacked the ore where it outcropped at the surface. The ores of non-ferrous metals, such as the copper ores malachite and azurite, tend to be brightly coloured and the iron minerals with which they are usually associated oxidise at the surface to give a very distinctive red 'gossan' or 'iron hat', which has always attracted the attention of prospectors. In heavily glaciated areas such as Britain most if not all the gossans and oxidised minerals will have been planed off by the ice and the ground surface now tends to be covered by dense vegetation. Here prospecting would have been confined to stream and river beds, but a knowledge of the local flora could have helped to locate hidden ore deposits. Most plants are intolerant of even small quantities of heavy metals in the soil, but just a few, such as the aptly named lead wort (*minuartia vernal*), are more amenable and can flourish where other plants would perish; they have thus been a valuable indicator to prospectors.

Early mining techniques

Having located the ore, how was it mined? The prehistoric copper mines in the British Isles serve well as an example.[6] The mine sites currently known are concentrated in the south-west of Ireland and in central and north Wales, but with important outliers such as Alderley Edge in Cheshire. All these mines have large numbers of crude stone hammers in the old workings and spoil tips. These hammers are cobbles of locally available hard rock, collected from stream beds or beaches. They are often slightly worked to aid hafting, with handles of either wood or twisted withy (fig. 4.1).[7] Tools of wood, bone and antler would also have been used, but the soil conditions in the vicinity of the mines are very acidic and little bone or antler could have survived. However, in the mine at Great Orme's Head, Llandudno, on the north Welsh coast, the conditions are much more alkaline and an enormous number of bone scoops and wedges have been preserved. These would have been useful for scraping out the soft clayey ore that filled small crevices in the workings. More rarely, remains of antler picks have been found.[8]

The rock face would normally have been too hard to attack directly with stone tools, and at all the British and Irish mines investigated so far there is abundant evidence of firesetting, in which fire was used to shatter the rock prior to mining. Experiments have recently been carried out to test the efficacy of the old miners' methods at the early mine of Cwmystwyth, in central Wales, adjacent to the ancient workings.[9] About three quarters of a tonne of dry logs were used to make a good fire against the rock face and it was soon cracking quite explosively, with rock fragments flying in all directions (fig. 4.2). After the fire had burnt itself out overnight, the shattered rock face was attacked with replicas of ancient hafted stone hammers and antler picks which both proved very effective (fig. 4.3), and one person was able to mine about one and a half tonnes of rock in a morning.

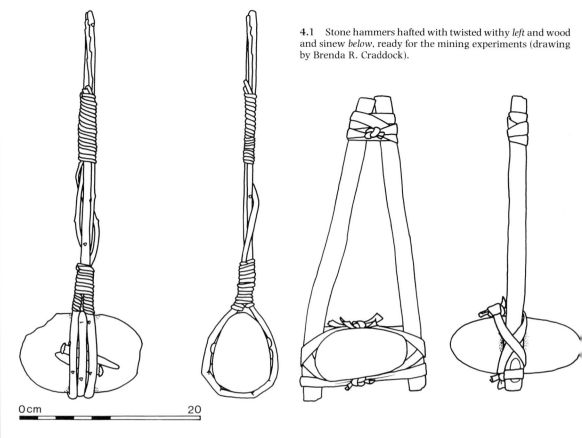

4.1 Stone hammers hafted with twisted withy *left* and wood and sinew *below*, ready for the mining experiments (drawing by Brenda R. Craddock).

0 cm   20

Samples of charcoal from the remains of ancient firesetting excavated at Cwmystwyth, Great Orme's Head and at other sites with stone hammers suggest they were worked during the second millennium BC, that is, the Early and Middle Bronze Age.[10] Most of these mines seem to have been little more than small surface trenches or pits. The mine at Cwmystwyth seems to have been confined to a single large quarry on top of a vein running down the steep hillside[11] (fig. 4.4). The quarry is about 50 by 20 m and is partly filled with rock debris. Excavations into this have uncovered a small gallery, bearing very clear marks of stone hammer work.

At Great Orme's Head there are the well-preserved remains of a much more extensive underground mining system,[8] similar to the well-known system at the Mitterberg in Austria.[12] The copper ore was followed from where it outcropped at the surface, apparently for several hundred metres into the hillside, through a myriad of small chambers and galleries. These are choked with ancient mining waste which is now cemented with travertine deposited from the calcareous waters which have percolated through it for over three thousand years. The dates from the mine so far suggest a much longer period of use than at the other British mines, from the Early Bronze Age at the surface to the end of the Middle Bronze Age deep underground, a span of over half a millennium.

4.2 Fire-setting experiment in progress at Cwmystwyth in central Wales. About three-quarters of a tonne of dry logs were left to burn *above* against the rock face.

4.3 After the rock face had been shattered and weakened *right*, it could be easily mined with the stone hammers shown here and with antler picks.

4.4 At Cwmystwyth *above* copper ore was mined from this opencast working in the second millennium BC.

Early smelting techniques in Western Europe

Although abundant remains of the mines and their spoil tips survive in Britain and Western Europe, there is very little evidence of how the metal was smelted. The more sophisticated furnaces used elsewhere and described in the following section left copious heaps of slag and other debris, usually in the immediate vicinity of the mines. The absence of slag from the British and other primitive mines is difficult to explain unless, of course, it never existed. The implications of this hypothesis, if correct, are far-reaching. If the metalsmiths of Western Europe were indeed using a much more primitive process than had been used for over a thousand years previously in the eastern Mediterranean and Middle East, then this strongly suggests that metallurgy developed completely independently in Europe, without any help from putative prospectors or settlers from more advanced cultures.

The evidence from the mines suggests that all the available ore was taken and used. First it would be beneficiated (crushed and concentrated) by removing as much as possible of the gangue (waste rock). This would either be done by swirling the crushed material in water and letting the denser ore separate out or by simply picking out the richest mineral manually. The enriched ore would then have been smelted, either in a

61

crude clay crucible covered with charcoal or in a simple clay furnace. Some recent smelting experiments using small clay shaft furnaces, rather like large inverted flower pots with the bottoms missing, successfully produced copper from high-grade ore after smelting for one or two hours. The conditions in the furnace were not very reducing and no slag was produced. Significantly, all trace of the experimental furnaces had disappeared within days of the operation. If a similar simple but rather inefficient process was used in Western Europe, this could explain why no archaeological evidence for the smelting process has yet been found.

Metal production in the developed Bronze Age

In the Middle East mining and smelting technology developed early to meet the demands of the precocious empires of Egypt and Mesopotamia, and even within the Bronze Age metal production was a highly organised operation often run directly by the state. For example, the major mining and smelting operation at Timna, way out in the deserts of the Negev, now in southern Israel, seems to have been under the direct control of the pharaohs.[13] These copper mines are of very ancient origin but seem to have been at peak production in the later part of the second millennium BC, and the cartouche of pharaohs such as Ramesses II found carved on rocks at the mine attest state control. The logistical problems must have been formidable: the mines were hundreds of kilometres out in the desert; the presence of hostile tribes necessitated defended camps; and virtually all food and other supplies must have been brought in to the hundreds if not thousands of workers.

The mine workings at Timna are made up of a prodigious number of small shafts rarely more than a few metres apart, linked by a maze of small galleries at a depth typically between 5 and 20 m underground. Metal chisels were in use, but the large number of closely linked shafts suggests that underground ventilation was an unsolved problem. The principal development from the early simple processes, still being practised in Bronze Age Wales at that date, was in the smelting process.

Copper smelting at Timna

After mining and sorting, the ore would be smelted to produce metal. During the Bronze Age the basic procedures of metal smelting evolved to such a pitch of efficiency that the form of the furnaces and their mode of operation were to remain substantially unchanged through several millennia until the Industrial Revolution.[14]

To smelt the metal, the ore would first have been roasted to make it more friable and to convert any sulphides or chlorides to oxides. The furnaces were normally built of clay, or stone mortared with clay; those at Timna were built of the local sandy clay sometimes tempered with crushed slag. They were built in the form of a shaft or a steep-sided cone. Air was supplied by manually operated bellows fed into the furnace through clay tubes known as tuyeres (fig. 4.5). These entered the furnace

4.5 A nineteenth-century drawing of a copper smelting furnace in India, typical of the traditional form of smelting furnaces from the Bronze Age onwards (from Ball's *Economic Geology of India*, 1881).

at regular intervals; three would often be spaced regularly at 120° around the furnace.

The furnaces were always necessarily quite small: typical dimensions would be about 1 m tall with an internal diameter of about 30 cm. Archaeologists always seem rather surprised, if not disappointed, by the small size of the individual furnaces, but there are good technical reasons for this. Air supply was one of the major constraints; if the furnace volume had been any larger then it would have been impossible to supply enough air manually to maintain the necessary temperatures. When, much later, bellows driven by waterwheels were introduced to blow the air into medieval European iron smelting furnaces, the size of the furnaces began to grow rapidly. This expansion continued until the next constraint was reached: the limited ability of the fuel, usually charcoal, to support the weight of the furnace charge above it. The introduction of coke in the early eighteenth century removed this barrier and paved the way for the enormous blast furnaces of today.

In antiquity charcoal was both the fuel and the source of the carbon monoxide used to reduce the ore to metal. At Timna, acacia was the main source of the charcoal, and obtaining the necessary supplies of wood in the desert must have been a major problem, necessitating ever longer expeditions in search of fuel. Indeed, exhaustion of fuel rather than of ore may have led to the mines' closure.

A fire would be lit in the furnace and charcoal added to bring the temperature up to about 1000°C. This would take about an hour, after which the first charge of roasted ore and charcoal could be added. In the reducing conditions of the furnace the charcoal would burn to form the intensely reducing gas, carbon monoxide. Permeating through the ore at high temperature, the carbon monoxide would reduce it to molten metal, which would slowly sink to the bottom of the furnace. The remaining

63

carbon monoxide would burn at the furnace mouth, indicating to the smith that the conditions were correct.

Scientific study of the burnt furnace fragments excavated from the slag heaps can tell us a great deal. The temperature of the process can be estimated by studying the degree of vitrification (melting) of the clay wall. Put very simply, the hotter the furnace the greater the degree of vitrification. Most clays begin to vitrify around 900°C and have sub-stantially melted by 1400°C. The longer the furnace wall was subjected to the maximum temperature, the deeper the vitrification penetrated into the clay, thus providing a good indicator of the duration of the process. Once again, this can be quantified by controlled refiring, and more details of these methods are given in Chapter 2.

However, this is not the whole story of metal smelting, for no matter how carefully the ore was beneficiated inevitably some gangue would still be present when the ore was charged into the furnace. Unless this waste rock could be removed, the furnace would rapidly choke up and the process come to a halt. The great advance of Bronze Age smelting was the introduction of slagging, whereby the gangue material was reacted with a suitable flux so that it could be liquefied and tapped from the furnace. Usually the ore contained either quartz (silica) or iron minerals as the gangue, and quite often both. These two would react together to produce a liquid slag of iron silicates. It would be rare for the iron and silica to be present in just the right proportions, so if the ore was rich in silica then iron oxide minerals would be added as the flux; conversely, if the ore was rich in iron then crushed quartz would be added as the silicate flux. The liquid slag would slowly build up in the lower part of the furnace, absorbing all the gangue and ash; when it reached tuyere level the smith would hear air bubbling into it and know that it was time to drain it by knocking a hole in the furnace side. The tapped slag quickly solidified, forming an excellent permanent record of the conditions within the furnace only seconds before, literally frozen within it (fig. 4.6).

Although the slags appear amorphous and uninformative, they are in fact complex interacting systems of various crystalline minerals and glassy phases. Many of the minerals only form under quite specific conditions, and their identification and analysis, principally by scanning electron

4.6   Photomicrograph of a section through a Roman silver smelting slag from Rio Tinto. The complex mixture of minerals is a good record of conditions within the furnace.

microscope and X-ray diffraction (see glossary), can reveal much of the temperature and reducing conditions within the furnace. The bulk analysis of the slags, together with the identification of the minerals present, enable the chemistry, thermodynamics and efficiency of the process to be reconstructed. Taken together with the temperature and duration data from the study of the vitrified furnace wall, this information enables us to establish the principal parameters of the process.

The process at Timna was so reducing that some of the iron minerals added as a flux were themselves reduced to metallic iron. Indeed, by omitting the copper ore and increasing the iron flux, iron could be smelted in the furnace, and it is possible that iron smelting developed from these copper smelting furnaces. However, in copper smelting iron was just a nuisance because it was dissolved by molten copper as it drained through the slag. Thus the raw copper, as found at Timna, often contained several per cent of iron and had to be refined before it could be alloyed with tin and used to make artefacts. It was refined by re-melting in an open crucible and allowing the iron, which floated to the surface, to oxidise. Even so, the iron content of copper made in slagging furnaces is typically much higher than that made in the very primitive furnaces used in Western Europe, and the very low iron content in most Bronze Age metalwork from Western Europe is a further indication of the generally low level of smelting technology there.[15]

Thus careful excavation and scientific study of the production debris (slags, refractories, etc), coupled with scientific study of the contemporary metalwork, enables us to reconstruct the smelting process with much greater precision than has hitherto been possible.

Metal production in the Iron Age

During the first millennium BC there was a great increase in intellectual activity throughout the Old World, and the application, at least empirically, of scientific and engineering knowledge is very evident in mines across the world, from those of the Greeks and Romans in the Mediterranean, through the Mauryeans of northern India to the Han Chinese. Before this, mine galleries had not penetrated far away from the shafts and had stopped altogether when the water table was reached. Now, with a practical understanding of mechanics, pneumatics and hydraulics, it was possible to ventilate galleries hundreds of metres from the shaft and to keep workings tolerably drained well below the water table.

During this period some of the great mines of antiquity were at the peak of their productivity: mines such as the Chinese copper mine at Tonglushan in Hunan;[16] the Mauryean silver mines at Agucha, Dariba and Zawar, in Rajasthan, India;[17] the Greek silver mine at Laurion in Attica;[18] and the Roman silver and copper mine at Rio Tinto in the south of Spain.[19] Indeed, the demand for silver, following the introduction of coinage, seems to have stimulated technical development everywhere. The excavations at the Indian mines have shown that production expanded dramatically during the fourth century BC to reach a peak in the third and second centuries BC, before falling away in the first century BC, almost exactly matching the rise and fall of both the Mauryean Empire and the production of the punch-marked silver coins of India.

Iron Age mining

Using firesetting, deep shafts and galleries were driven hundreds of metres into the rock far below the water table. At Zawar, in India, a well-preserved system of hollowed tree trunk conduits channelled the water to collection points from where it could be carried from the mine, probably in clay jars. At Rio Tinto the Romans adopted even more sophisticated techniques, with systems of waterwheels to raise water from one level to another. Where the workings were in a mountain they drove adits (long passages) from the valley beneath the mine workings to drain them. When the workings at Rio Tinto were reopened in the eighteenth century, the mine engineers' first task was to unblock the main Roman adit along its full 2-km length to drain the mines again, and for the next century this adit continued to serve its original function.

At Dariba, in India, the deep mines were augmented by a great opencast mine which extended for about 300 by 100 m, and is of uncertain depth. Until very recently it was flooded, but now that the mine beneath has been reopened the opencast has been drained, revealing along one side a most elaborate and extensive stretch of timber supports, holding back the loose deposits in a series of stepped benches reminiscent of modern opencast mines (fig. 4.7). The flooded condition of the pit and the high concentration of metallic salts in the water has preserved the timbers as if they were only a few years old, but radiocarbon dating shows that this mine was opened as the demand for silver coinage reached a peak in ancient India in the second and third centuries BC.

4.7   Small section of the elaborate timber shoring that ran along one side of the very extensive opencast silver mine at Dariba in India over two thousand years ago.

Iron Age silver smelting

Smelting silver is rather more complex than smelting other metals, as most silver ores contain only a small trace of the metal, which would be lost in the slag unless special provision were made. If lead is present in the furnace it will readily absorb the silver. Fortunately, the two metals are often found together and from an early date man seems to have solved the problem of separating the silver from the lead by the process known as cupellation. Thus ore is smelted in the usual way, with lead added if it is not already present. Then the silver-rich lead is placed in a vessel of refractory clay, the cupel, raised to red heat and subjected to a blast of air. This oxidises the lead to a dense molten mass of litharge (lead oxide), on which the molten silver floats 'like oil on water', in Pliny's apt phrase in the *Natural History*.[20]

The cupels were traditionally made of bone ash, which absorbs the litharge, but most of the ancient examples that have been examined are of clay. The copious lead oxide fumes must have been very injurious to the workers' health, and were probably the major factor contributing to the short lifespan of those '*condemnato per metallica*'. At Agucha, in India, one of the pits excavated, dated to the third century BC, was filled with numerous small clay cupels still with the tuyere attached for providing the air blast, together with parts of the small furnace in which they sat. All were covered in a thick glaze from the all-pervading lead oxide (figs. 4.8 and 4.9). The cupels only have a capacity of a few millilitres and it is likely that they were used to estimate the silver content of ore samples sent up from the mine for testing. This may therefore be debris from the mine assay office of the third century BC.

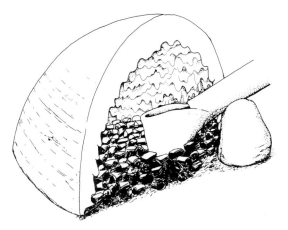

4.8 *left* Small cupel with tuyere attached for separating silver from lead (third century BC), excavated at Agucha.

4.9 *above* Artist's reconstruction, based on fragments excavated at Agucha, showing how silver was cupelled (drawing by Brenda R. Craddock).

At Rio Tinto the Romans mined a complex silver ore known as jarosite which contained many metals but relatively little lead. Thus the Romans had to import lead to the mine to smelt the ore and ingots have been found stamped 'Cartagena', a lead-producing area some hundreds of kilometres distant. Transport costs must have made the lead at Rio Tinto quite expensive, in contrast to mines such as Laurion where the lead was only a by-product of the silver smelting. This is reflected in the composition of the slags: the lead was carefully recovered from the Rio Tinto slags by the Romans, whereas the lead content can often exceed 10 per cent in the slags from other mines.[21]

The jarosite ore contained antimony and arsenic, which created other problems for the smiths at Rio Tinto. These elements reacted with the iron minerals in the furnace to produce compounds known as speiss. Not only was this difficult to tap from the furnace but it also absorbed the silver. In the nineteenth century German metallurgists were recovering silver from speiss by repeated roasting and slagging before treatment with lead, followed by cupellation. There is evidence that the Romans also used this method two thousand years earlier at Rio Tinto.[22] The small fragments of speiss discarded in the main slag dumps or entrapped in the slag itself are rich in silver. However, at one area well away from the main slag heaps the ground is littered with pieces of silver-free speiss, lead and litharge. There is also a little slag, and at another part of the site a large bowl in which speiss has been melted. The suggestion is that the Romans separated the larger pieces of speiss from the slag and recovered the silver from it at this one site, where the de-silvered speiss was then discarded.

Thus the combination of science and archaeology can produce not only basic information on the technology but also new insights in other areas such as the efficiency of the process. For example, at Rio Tinto archaeologists found a heap of ore abandoned in a Roman gallery. The most likely explanation for this was that on assay it was found to be too poor to be worth smelting and it was left. This ore contained about 100–150 parts per million of silver, whereas the contemporary slags contained about 70 parts per million. If we assume that a roughly equal weight of flux was added, then the ore would have needed to contain over 140 parts per million or all the silver would have been absorbed by the slag, confirming that the ore with only 150 parts per million would have been borderline.[21] These are very approximate figures, based on very broad assumptions and over-simplifications, but they do give some indication of the general efficiency achieved by the Romans.

Into the modern world

So far we have considered metals which are molten when smelted and collect as a liquid ingot in the base of the furnace. But some metals, notably zinc, are released from the ore not as a liquid but as a gas. This would be lost up the flue of the furnace where it would promptly re-oxidise. In order to produce metallic zinc it is necessary to remove and condense the vapour in a system from which air is rigorously excluded; in other words, a form

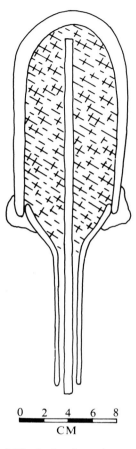

0   2   4   6   8
CM

4.10 Section through a
retort for smelting zinc,
shown with condenser and
stick in place (drawing by
Brenda R. Craddock).

of distillation. This is clearly a much more advanced technology than
traditional smelting and zinc production did not commence in Europe until
the eighteenth century AD. However, zinc was already being imported from
the East, where it had been produced for many centuries, and medieval
Indian scientific texts describe the distillation of zinc in retorts. Modern
mining engineers noted that vast heaps of spent retorts were to be found
at the zinc mine of Zawar near Udaipur in north-west India, and recent
excavations at that mine have helped clarify a most interesting and sophisticated process.[23]

The early treatises described the retort as being shaped like an aubergine
(*brinjal*), fitted with a condenser shaped like a thorn apple flower (*dhatura*);
the Zawar retorts match this description well. Essentially they comprised
open round-bottomed jars of between 1 and 3 litres capacity. After being
filled with the reactants they were closed with a condenser shaped like a
flower or, to modern technical eyes, a filler funnel, sealed in place with
clay (fig. 4.10). A stick was inserted to stop the charge falling out when
inverted into the furnace. The Indian texts give a variety of exotic ingredients for the charge of which this thirteenth-century recipe taken from the
Rasaratanasamuchchaya[24] is typical:

> Zinc ore is to be powdered with lac, treacle, white mustard, the myroblans, natron, salt
> and borax, and the mixture boiled with milk and clarified butter and made into balls.
> These are to be enclosed in a retort and strongly heated.

Although this recipe seems fanciful in the extreme, in principle it is quite
sensible and where possible it can be checked against the surviving contents of the retorts. This shows that the charge was indeed in the form of
small balls. The calcined zinc ore, together with some of the dolomite and
silica host rock, was ground up with charcoal, salt and some sticky organic
binder and rolled into balls. In later times Indian smiths used cow dung
as the organic binder in other smelting operations, but perhaps the more
exotic materials listed above were used in earlier times, at least in the
medieval laboratory. On heating, the organics charred, losing their sticki-
ness, but at the same time the silica in the charge, reacting with the salt,
would have begun to sinter, causing the balls to remain stuck together
and thereby preserving the open structure between the balls through
which the reducing carbon monoxide gas and the forming zinc vapour
could circulate. The stick would char and fall out, leaving a central passage
down which the zinc vapour could escape to the condenser.

The same Indian texts give some information on the form of the furnace
in which the retorts were to be fired:

> Dig a hole in the bottom of a furnace (*koshthi*) and place a water-filled vessel in it, with a
> perforated plate over its mouth. Then fix the filled crucible in an inverted position over
> the perforated plate. Put charcoal, of the *jujube* (*Ziziphus jujuba*), over and around the
> crucible and heat it strongly with the bellows. On heating the zinc extract goes down and
> gets collected in the vessel.

Excavation uncovered an intact bank of seven *koshthi* furnaces, each one
containing not one but thirty-six retorts in a six by six arrangement (fig.

4.11), making a total of 252 retorts fired together. Each furnace was in two parts, a square cool collecting chamber over which was the furnace in the form of a truncated pyramid. These were separated by a floor of four perforated bricks, supported by a central pillar (fig. 4.12). Each of the bricks had nine large and a number of smaller holes (fig. 4.13). The retorts were inverted on the perforated bricks with the condenser necks protruding through the large holes down into the cool chamber. The bricks also acted as a grate, with air and ash passing through the smaller holes. The forming zinc vapour passed down from the retort, sat in the furnace and condensed in the condenser necks in the cooler chamber before dripping into a collection vessel.

Studies of the clay walls of the retorts and furnaces suggest the process operated at a temperature of 1100°–1200°C for about four to five hours. When time for loading the retorts and bringing the furnace up to temperature is added, this makes a full day's work. Figure 4.14 gives an artist's impression of the scene as the furnace block was being charged with retorts one morning some six hundred years ago. This process probably began at Zawar on an industrial scale about a thousand years ago and continued with interruptions until the early nineteenth century. By this time, not only zinc was being exported to Europe but also the secrets of the process by which it was produced, and competition from European zinc proved fatal to the traditional Indian industry. Even so, during the hundreds of years that the process was operating we can estimate from the millions of retorts in the heaps that about 100,000 tonnes of zinc were produced.

How did such a sophisticated process come into being? Almost certainly it was through the interaction and adaptation of several technologies. The

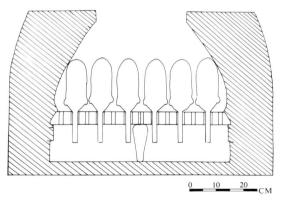

0   10   20
CM

4.11 *left* Bank of medieval zinc-smelting *koshthi*, or furnaces, after excavation of four of the seven present in the bank.

4.12 *above* Section through a *koshthi* showing the arrangement for holding the retorts (drawing by Brenda R. Craddock).

4.13 *left* One of the four perforated plates which each furnace contained. Note the large holes in which the condenser necks sat and the smaller holes through which air was drawn into the furnace and through which ash fell.
4.14 *below* Artist's impression of how the bank of *koshthi* described here would have looked as they were being charged with retorts one morning about six hundred years ago.

principle of smelting a metal by condensation had already been established for mercury, the ore of which decomposes at about 800°C to give mercury vapour, which may be collected in air. The conditions for smelting a chemically active metal such as zinc are much more demanding and required special apparatus. The form of the *koshthi* furnace is clearly derived from the traditional pottery kiln, except that the fire is in the upper chamber rather than beneath. So a combination of the principle of mercury smelting with the form of the humble pottery kiln may have led to one of the most technically sophisticated processes of the medieval world.

Conclusion

This brief survey of the first ten thousand years of metallurgy is, by its selective nature, very incomplete. Metals of major importance such as gold, tin and iron have been omitted (but see Penhallurick on tin[25] and Tylecote on iron[26]). Tin ores are not usually found with copper ore, but those working on placer deposits of river gravels for gold from the fifth millennium BC[3] would sooner or later have encountered dense black pebbles of tin ore (cassiterite) and these would have been easily smelted to metallic tin. Bronze, the alloy of copper and tin, seems to have been first used in the third millennium BC but only became general in the second millennium (see Chapter 5) as the major sources of tin in Western Europe and in South-east Asia became available. The superiority of bronze over copper or arsenical copper probably gave the impetus to the vastly increased scale of production and improved smelting technology observed at sites such as Timna. Similarly, in the highly interlinked world of metal technology, improved copper smelting utilising a highly reducing slag-forming process created the necessary conditions for the smelting of iron. In the West, iron was usually smelted as a solid material and fabricated by hammering and welding alone right up to the end of the medieval period, but in China cast iron has been used extensively for over two thousand years.

The extraordinary technical and industrial developments of the past three or four hundred years, commonly known as the Industrial Revolution, came about partly because of the interaction and cross-fertilisation of advanced technologies, such as cast iron production from China, crucible steel and high-temperature distillation of zinc from India, with the already highly developed metal industries of Europe. As a result of the research outlined here, we can now begin to appreciate how deep in the past lie the roots of the modern industrial world.

Further reading

P.T. Craddock (ed.), 1980. *Scientific Studies in Early Mining and Extractive Metallurgy*, Occasional Paper 20, London, British Museum.

P.T. Craddock and M.J. Hughes (eds.), 1985. *Furnaces and Smelting Technology in Antiquity*, Occasional Paper 48, London, British Museum.

H.C. and L.H. Hoover (eds.), 1950. *Agricola: De Re Metallica*. Reprint of the 1912 Mining Magazine edition. New York, Dover Reprints.

R. Maddin (ed.), 1988. *The Beginning of the Use of Metals and Alloys*. Cambridge, Mass., MIT Press.

R. Penhallurick, 1986. *Tin in Antiquity*. London, The Institute of Metals.

R.F. Tylecote, 1986. *The Prehistory of Metallurgy in the British Isles*. London, The Institute of Metals.

R.F. Tylecote, 1987. *The Early History of Metallurgy in Europe*. London, Longman.

R.F. Tylecote, 1990. *A History of Metallurgy*. London, The Institute of Metals.

References

1. P.T. Craddock, 1989. 'The scientific investigation of early mining and smelting'. In *Scientific Analysis in Archaeology*, J. Henderson (ed.), Monograph No. 19, Oxford, OUCA, pp. 178–212.

2. J.D. Muhly, 1988. 'The beginnings of metallurgy in the Old World'. In *The Beginning of the Use of Metals and Alloys*, R. Maddin (ed.), Cambridge, Mass., MIT Press, pp. 2–20.

3. C. Eluère (ed.), 1989. *Le Premier Or de L'humanité en Bulgarie*, Paris, Editions de la Reunion des Musées Nationaux.

4. R. Maddin, T.S. Wheeler and J.D. Muhly, 1980. 'Distinguishing artifacts made of native copper'. In *Journal of Archaeological Science* 7, 3, pp. 211–26.

5. D.R. Hook, I.C. Freestone, N.D. Meeks, P.T. Craddock, A. Moreno Onorato, 1990. 'Early production of copper alloys in south-east Spain'. In *Archaeometry '90*, E. Pernicka and G.A. Wagner (eds.), Basel, pp. 65–76.

6. P. Crew and S. Crew (eds.), 1990. *Early Mining in the British Isles*. Occasional Paper 1, Blaenau Ffestiniog, Plas Tan y Bwlch Centre.

7. B.R. Craddock, 1990. 'The experimental hafting of stone mining hammers'. In Crew and Crew, *ibid.*, p. 58.

8. A. Lewis, 1990. 'Underground exploration of the Great Orme copper mines'. In Crew and Crew, *ibid.*, pp. 5–10.

9. J. Pickin and S. Timberlake, 1988. 'Stone Hammers and firesetting'. In *Bulletin of the Peak District Mines Historical Society* 10, 3, pp. 165–7.

10. J.C. Ambers, 1990. 'Radiocarbon, calibration and early mining'. In Crew and Crew, *ibid.*, pp. 59–64.

11. S. Timberlake, 1990. 'Excavation and fieldwork on Copa Hill, Cwmystwyth, 1989'. In Crew and Crew, *ibid.*, pp. 22–9.

12. R.F. Tylecote, 1987. *The Early History of Metallurgy in Europe*. London, Longman, especially pp. 31, 33, 128–30.

13. B. Rothenberg, 1972. *Timna*. London, Thames and Hudson.

14. P.T. Craddock and M.J. Hughes (eds.), 1985. *Furnaces and Smelting Technology in Antiquity*, Occasional Paper 48, London, British Museum.

15. P.T. Craddock and N.D. Meeks, 1987. 'Iron in ancient copper'. In *Archaeometry* 29, 2, pp. 187–204.

16. Zhou Baoquan, Hu Yougan and Lu Benshan, 1988. 'Ancient copper mining and smelting at Tonglushan Daye'. In *The Beginning of the Use of Metals and Alloys*, R. Maddin (ed.), Cambridge, Mass., MIT Press, pp. 125–9.

17. P.T. Craddock, I.C. Freestone, L.K. Gurjar, A.P. Middleton and L. Willies, 1989. 'The production of lead, silver and zinc in early India'. In *Old World Archaeometry*, A. Hauptmann, E. Pernicka and G. A. Wagner (eds.), Bochum, Deutsches Bergbau Museum, pp. 51–69.

18. C. Conophagus, 1980. *Le Laurion Antique*. Athens, Edotike Hellados.

19. L.U. Salkield, 1987. *A Technical History of the Rio Tinto Mines*. London, The Institution of Mining and Metallurgy.

20. H. Rackham, 1968. *Pliny: The Natural History*. London, Loeb, especially Books 33 and 95.

21. P.T. Craddock, I.C. Freestone, N.H. Gale, N.D. Meeks, B. Rothenberg and M.S. Tite, 1985. 'The investigation of a small heap of silver smelting debris from Rio Tinto, Huelva, Spain'. In P.T. Craddock and M.J. Hughes, *ibid.*, pp. 199–218.

22. P.T. Craddock, I.C. Freestone and M. Hunt Ortiz, 1987. 'Recovery of silver from speiss at Rio Tinto'. In *I.A.M.S. Newsletter* 10/11, pp. 8–11.

23. P.T. Craddock, I.C. Freestone, L.K. Gurjar, A.P. Middleton and L. Willies, 1990. 'Zinc in India'. In *2000 Years of Zinc and Brass*, P.T. Craddock (ed.). Occasional Paper 50, London, British Museum, pp. 29–72.

24. C. Ray, 1956. *History of Chemistry in Ancient and Medieval India*. Calcutta, Indian Chemical Society, pp. 171, 190.

25. R.D. Penhallurick, 1986. *Tin in Antiquity*. London, The Institute of Metals.

26. R.F. Tylecote, 1990. *A History of Metallurgy*. London, The Institute of Metals.

CHAPTER 5

Metalwork: Artifice and artistry

Michael Cowell and Susan La Niece

Even after overcoming the tremendous technical difficulties of mining and smelting metals, the end result of all this endeavour was a raw material that still required the considerable skills of the metalsmith to turn it into artefacts, whether practical, artistic or both. These skills are perhaps no better illustrated than by the finds from the ship-burial at Sutton Hoo. This burial mound, probably for the Anglo-Saxon King Redwald, contained a rich treasure which gives a startling insight into the wealth of the ruling classes in seventh-century East Anglia. It includes, amongst other objects, drinking vessels, iron weapons and chain mail, huge silver dishes imported from the eastern Mediterranean, a lyre, ivory gaming pieces, fine gold personal jewellery and regalia, and coins.

Understandably, the splendour of the goldwork – inlaid with garnets backed by gold foil to enhance their appearance – attracts immediate attention (plate 5.1). But the skills involved are at least equalled by those lavished on some of the base metal objects, such as the iron sword with its complex design of pattern welding (see p. 88) and the intricately cast and decorated escutcheons on the hanging bowls.

The study of metalwork such as that from Sutton Hoo provides a variety of information about an individual site and the technical competence of the culture which created the artefacts: for example, suggesting the source of materials used, establishing the technology employed to prepare and alloy (mix) the metals, and determining how the artefacts were fabricated and decorated. In some cases this involves experimental work to test particular theories of how certain processes were carried out and the ways that artefacts were constructed.

The quality of many of the individual objects makes the site of Sutton Hoo exceptional. However, their archaeological importance is enhanced compared with that of equally fine stray finds because of the association with other artefacts from an excavated context. The humble iron rivets, for example, were all that remained of the boat at Sutton Hoo. Individually they are of little importance, but collectively, and excavated in their original positions, they are fundamental in establishing the ship's lines.

The amazing variety of metal artefacts in the ancient world was created with only a few different metals: copper, tin, lead, silver, gold, iron, arsenic and zinc. Initially the latter two metals only occur in alloys as they were not generally isolated in metallic form until the medieval period. Copper and iron were most commonly used as both are tough and easily shaped. Silver and gold are rare and were prized for their monetary value, appearance and resistance to corrosion. The remaining metals were mainly used to modify the properties of the others by alloying and for specialised functions in construction such as joining by soldering. All of these metals were already in widespread use in their own right or in alloys over two thousand years ago and some have much earlier origins. Native (natural metallic) copper was probably first used about the eighth millennium BC, and the earliest smelted metals, copper and lead, date from the fifth or sixth millennium BC. Perhaps surprisingly, even today most of these metals are still of considerable importance and few 'new' metals have superseded them except for certain specialised uses; one metal unknown to the ancients which is used in large quantities today is aluminium.

Metal is one of the most versatile materials known; it can be melted and poured into a mould of almost any shape, hammered into thin sheets, drawn into fine wires and extruded as rods and pipes. Most importantly, when a metal artefact is damaged or becomes redundant, the metal can easily be melted down and recycled into another artefact. Furthermore, any number of metal components can be joined together to make complex shapes, leading to an almost limitless variety of products. Some of these basic shaping methods were used to manufacture artefacts in metal from the very beginnings of metallurgy, when only native metals were available. However, the quantity of metal available from native sources was limited in most parts of the world and consequently the major use of metals and alloys for artefacts was dependent on developments in smelting (see also Chapter 4).

Developments in alloying

Copper alloys

Copper was the first metal to become available in quantity for general use and the metal and its alloys have retained their importance to the present day. Much early copper contains a small percentage of arsenic and this, arsenical copper, was the first alloy to be put to practical use throughout the ancient world. Initially the manufacture of arsenical copper was accidental. Arsenic is very volatile and was unobtainable by ancient smelting techniques, but arsenic minerals commonly occur in association with copper ores and an alloy with a few per cent can be obtained by smelting these. However, once the properties of the alloy were appreciated, the ores were no doubt deliberately selected, or arsenic minerals may have been added to molten copper. Arsenical copper could never have been easy to make or work with; during smelting, clouds of poisonous arsenious oxide are produced and in re-melting the alloy some of the arsenic may be lost. It is not surprising, therefore, that tin bronze replaced it. Although tin sources are rarer than those of arsenic (or arsenic-rich copper), the metal is much easier to smelt and can be added in precisely controlled amounts to the copper. Tin bronze had almost completely superseded arsenical copper by the end of the second millennium BC although the scale of this change varied considerably throughout the Old World.[1]

Brass is another important alloy of copper (made with zinc), which first appears during the latter half of the first millennium BC and was widely used from the Roman period onwards. It has an attractive yellow colour and in certain properties, such as its ductility, it is superior to bronze. As with arsenical copper, there were difficulties in the manufacture of brass, because zinc metal is also highly reactive and volatile and was not isolated in quantity until the fifteenth century AD in India.[2] The alloy was produced by a process called cementation. This involved heating zinc ore and charcoal with metallic copper in a closed vessel to about 1000°C. The zinc, which at this temperature is liberated as a gas, is absorbed by the copper to form the alloy. A process essentially the same as this was used for brass-making in Europe until the nineteenth century, when it became more economical to alloy metallic zinc directly with copper.

Iron

Towards the end of the second millennium BC, but particularly during the first millennium BC, developments in smelting technology meant that iron became available. Because of their superior strength and durability, iron and ultimately steel (the alloy with carbon) largely replaced copper-based alloys as the preferred materials for the manufacture of many functional items such as tools and weapons. The greater abundance of iron ores over those of copper also meant that iron was more readily obtainable and cheaper.

Gold, silver and lead

Many other metals and alloys were of course discovered and used throughout the ancient world, though few could rival iron and those based on copper for the sheer amounts used in artefact manufacture. Gold and silver have attracted particular attention because they were used to make prestige items such as jewellery and regalia. As a native metal, gold required no extraction by smelting. However, it commonly occurs as a natural alloy with silver, and methods were therefore developed to purify the gold. This was done by reacting the silver in the alloy with salt at high temperatures, leaving the gold unaffected.[3] Metalworking remains at Sardis in Turkey suggest that this process, called 'parting', was employed there in the sixth century BC to refine gold from the river Pactolus.[4]

Most ancient silver was extracted from argentiferous (silver-rich) lead by cupellation, a process dating back to at least the second millennium BC, which involved oxidising the lead to molten litharge (lead oxide), leaving the relatively unreactive silver as the metal. Lead was first used at about the same time as copper, though it was seldom used to make artefacts in its own right. Lead was far more important as a metal added to bronze to modify its properties and to alloy with tin to form pewter and soft solder. Soft solder is of course an aid to artefact manufacture as opposed to a raw material for overall construction, and is one of a whole range of alloys with more specialised applications in metalwork.

Metal properties and selection

Depending on the materials available, the choice of what metal or alloy to use for a particular artefact would be influenced mainly by its intended function and how it was to be manufactured. Although many artefacts are made of pure metals, rather more are made of alloys. The main reason for using alloys is to modify the mechanical and physical properties of metals to suit the item being manufactured. By mixing metals it is possible to make alloys which are tougher, more ductile, have a different colour, a lower melting point, or flow more easily when molten than the individual component metals.

Bronze

Bronze illustrates the variety which is possible with copper-based alloys. By alloying tin with copper to make bronze we obtain a metal which is much tougher than copper alone. It is also more suitable for casting because its melting point is lower and the tin reacts with gases dissolved in the molten alloy, preventing porosity. The precise properties of the alloy depend on the amount of tin added. Up to about 10 per cent of tin gives an alloy that is red to gold in colour and ductile enough for easy shaping by hammering, provided that the alloy is annealed (heated to remove internal stresses). Working without annealing increases the hardness but also makes the alloy brittle and ultimately liable to crack. By selective working, though, part of an object such as a cutting edge could be made harder. With 15 to 20 per cent of tin or more, the alloy becomes brittle and almost unworkable, although it can still be cast to shape, and as more tin is added it becomes whiter in colour. The alloy is nevertheless still useful for a variety of purposes. It is sonorous and therefore very suitable for making bells. When polished it is also highly reflective and was thus widely used for mirrors. The decorative properties of high-tin bronze were also exploited, for example in the surrounds to the escutcheons on the Sutton Hoo hanging bowl (fig. 5.1).[5]

5.1 The escutcheon from the base of Sutton Hoo hanging bowl number I (INV 110), which has a surround made of a high-tin bronze that would have had a silvery appearance when new.

The properties of bronze can be further modified by introducing other metals such as lead. Adding lead makes the alloy easier to cast because the melting point is reduced and the fluidity is increased. The molten alloy will penetrate all parts of the mould more quickly before solidifying, thus allowing the craftsman to make more detailed and intricate castings. However, lead is only slightly soluble in copper and forms a separate metallic phase in the alloy. This means that leaded bronze is relatively weak and may explain why the statuette in Figure 5.2, which has a particularly high lead content of about 30 per cent, was broken at the neck. Heavily leaded alloys were therefore not generally used for artefacts which required high mechanical strength. In addition, too much lead spoils the finish of mercury- or fire-gilding (see page 90), so leaded alloys were avoided if this particular decoration was to be applied.

Iron

Although the mechanical properties of copper-based alloys are readily modified by working and heat treatment, they are not as versatile as iron in this respect. Provided that iron contains some carbon, introduced by carburisation (heating under charcoal), it can be hardened by quenching, that is by cooling rapidly in oil or water. The metal may be somewhat brittle after this but a final tempering process (heating to a moderate temperature, followed by slow cooling) relieves the internal stresses, leaving a hard and durable finished product which is mechanically stronger than bronze. The whole process produces characteristic structural changes in the metal which can be detected by microscopic study of sections through the artefact. The first known use of carburisation and quenching of iron dates back to the eleventh and tenth centuries BC in Cyprus and

5.2 The head of this Chinese statuette had become detached and then been re-attached with solder. But was this the original head, or a replacement from another similar statuette? An analysis of both parts reveals that their alloy and trace metal patterns are almost identical. The two parts therefore almost certainly belong together (OA 1983.11– 17.1).

Palestine. Although the processes were used spasmodically after that, they were not applied consistently and effectively until the Dark Ages and the medieval period.[6]

The study of metal use

The vast majority of functional objects and many prestigious artefacts have long been manufactured from copper and its alloys. The analysis of these metal objects can range from simply identifying the composition of an individual item or its component parts to studying the general development of metal use. The technique of atomic absorption spectro-photometry (AAS) (see glossary) is often used to analyse copper-based metals. Apart from quantifying the alloying metals, it also measures trace metals which can sometimes be used to 'finger-print' an individual supply of metal (fig. 5.2).

The applications of copper-based metals were extensive, and as new alloys became available through developments in smelting they were exploited in new ways. Evidence of how the properties of these metals were manipulated can indicate the technical level of a society at any given time. To build up an impression of how metal use developed, many and various artefacts covering a long time span need to be examined. The chronological introduction of different alloys can then be compared between different cultures and geographical areas.

A typical study of ancient Egyptian tools and weapons, particularly axes, shows that four copper-based metals or alloys were used from the early third millennium BC to the middle of the first millennium BC: 'pure' copper; arsenical copper (an alloy of copper with up to 6 per cent of arsenic); tin bronze or leaded tin bronze; and iron.[7] In a study of metal development such as this it is essential to examine datable or chronologically ordered artefacts. Some Egyptian axes can be dated by association with datable material in excavation contexts and occasionally by an inscription. However, the principal indicator is often typology, the way axe shapes changed over time to accommodate different methods of hafting and specialisation in use (fig. 5.3).

5.3 Egyptian copper-alloy axes which were in use during the late third and early second millennia BC (EA 1903.8–13.2, 51021 and 67486).

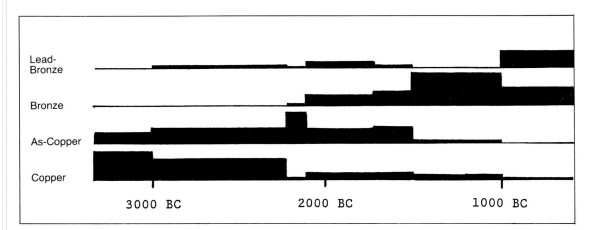

When the proportions of the dated axes made from the four copper-based metals are arranged chronologically (fig. 5.4), a trend is evident. During the third millennium BC most axes were made of unalloyed copper and few were of arsenical copper, but by the middle of the third millennium arsenical copper gradually supplanted copper and this, in turn, was replaced by tin bronze and also some leaded tin bronze. This development was of course gradual and there were long periods when several alloys were in use. The alloys are entirely typical of other cultures in the Near East and elsewhere, but the Egyptians were rather slower to adopt tin bronze. This may have been as much due to tradition as to limited supplies of tin. Consistent with its fluidity and lack of strength, leaded bronze is mainly confined to decorative axes requiring detailed casting which were probably not produced for functional use.

5.4 The chronological development of non-ferrous metals and alloys used by the ancient Egyptians for tools and weapons from the third millennium BC.

Similar studies have been carried out on axes from the British Isles and, whilst the same alloys were used, the time scale of their introduction and use was quite different.[8] The advent of copper began much later, in the middle of the third millennium BC; whilst arsenical copper was used, it was replaced by tin bronze at a much earlier date, by the beginning of the second millennium. Arsenical copper use was therefore very shortlived in Britain, compared with Egypt. Admittedly, the British Isles had substantial tin deposits, a resource which Egypt does not seem to have possessed.

As well as charting chronological developments in alloying, it is also possible to examine those changes dictated by the specialised use of arte-facts. We know, from representations of Egyptian axes on wall paintings, that initially the same type of axe was used as both tool and weapon. Gradually, however, different shapes developed to suit the respective functions, and the visual appearance of the separate tool and weapon types suggests that different alloys were used for each. In fact, the tools turn out to be either simply copper or arsenical copper (none are made of bronze), whereas weapons are never made of copper alone and most are tin bronze. The few weapons that are made of arsenical copper contain more arsenic than the tools, thus making them potentially harder. The weapons were therefore a superior product at the forefront of developments in alloying.

Plate 2.1 The Prunay Vase (Morel Collection, ML 2734).
Height *c*. 310 mm.

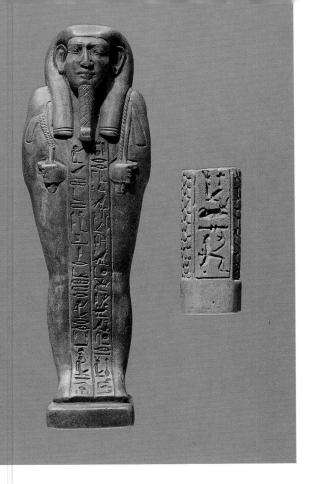

Plate 2.2 Egyptian faience shabti and sistrum, 25th–26th Dynasty (EA 34095 and 26975). The height of the shabti figure is *c*. 155 mm.

Plate 3.1 Fragment of mosaic from San Marco, Venice (MLA 1882.11–1.11). Width *c*. 250 mm.

Plate 3.2 The Lycurgus Cup (MLA 1958.12–2.1): **(a)** *left* in transmitted light and **(b)** *right* in reflected light. Height 165 mm.

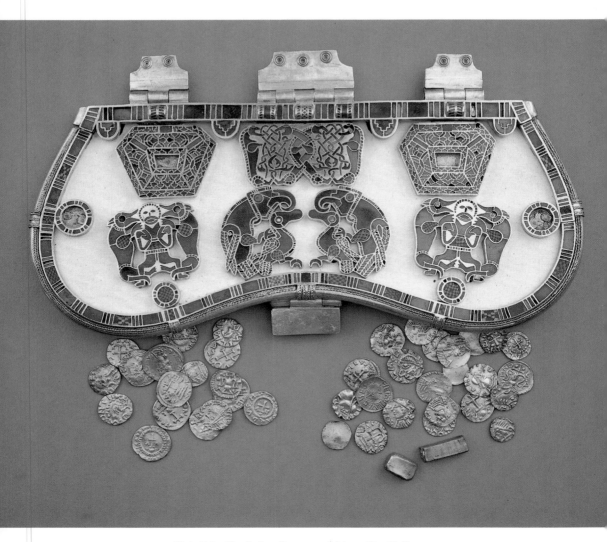

Plate 5.1 The Sutton Hoo purse lid (INV. 2) with the associated gold coins, coin blanks and ingots. This piece is typical of the high quality of the Sutton Hoo goldwork. It is decorated with inlaid garnets and millefiori glass, the garnets backed with patterned gold foil to enhance their colour. Length 190 mm.

Plate 5.2 Japanese shakudo alloy sword guard, with gold, silver and brass inlays (OA 1952.2–11.28). 80 × 60 mm.

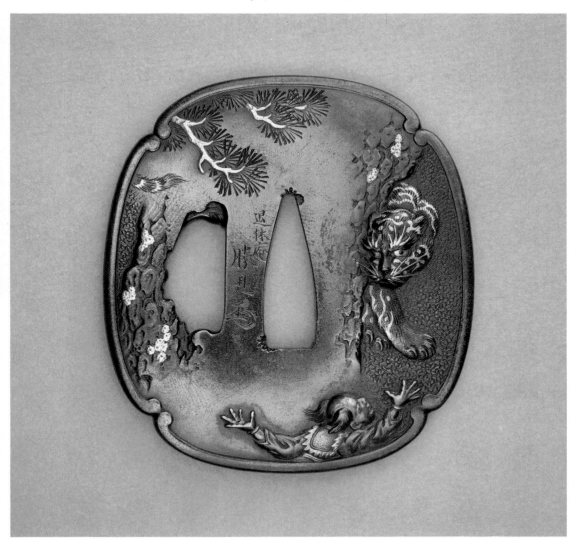

Plate 6.1 Petrographic thin sections of Iron Age pottery sherds from Hengistbury Head, Dorset (on loan from the Society of Antiquaries): **(a)** *above* Locally made Durotrigian ware with very sand-rich fabric. Width of field *c.* 4 mm. **(b)** *below* Cordoned ware, imported from northern Brittany, containing amphibolite rock. Width of field *c.* 1 mm.

Plate 8.1 Contemporary paintings can give us an indication of the original appearance of ancient metalwork, as in this Roman wall painting from Pompeii (from A. de Franciscis, 1963, *Il Museo Nazionale di Napoli*, Naples, Di Mauro). The bronze statues shown in this street scene are not patinated green or black, but are apparently bronze coloured.

Plate 8.2 The fake patina on this Chinese bronze sleeve weight (OA 1894.1–8.8) was put on when the piece was made in the twelfth century AD. China has a long tradition of quite sophisticated faking methods designed to fool the scholar and collector. Diameter 60 mm.

Plate 8.3 These two bronzes are both quite genuine Roman pieces. However, the symbolic hand (GR 1824.4–41.1) on the left was given a false patina by the great collector Richard Payne Knight in order to give it the appearance he felt it would have had originally. Length 146 mm. The statuette on the right (GR 1920.2–18.1), shown for comparison, has a natural patination. Height 140 mm.

5.5 Some of the earliest cementation brass coins from Asia Minor: **(a)** Mithradates VI, mint of Amisus, Pontus (90–75 BC) (CM BMC 79); **(b** and **c)** Pergamum (mid-first century BC) (CM BMC 130 and 144); **(d** and **e)** Apamea, Phrygia (70–60 BC and 56 BC) (CM BMC 85 and 59).

The extra cost of a harder and more lasting cutting edge was a wise investment – warriors would have had little time to re-sharpen their blades in the heat of battle!

An alloy which was not available to the ancient Egyptians because the required technology had not been developed was brass (*oreichalcum* or *oreichalkos* to the ancient writers), the alloy of copper with zinc. The Romans produced coins from this alloy which, in the first century AD, contained about 25 per cent zinc. They did not have to isolate zinc metal to do this but used the cementation process described on page 76. Artefacts made of brass before the Roman period (that is, before the end of the first millennium BC) are rare, although there are numerous historical references to *oreichalcum* before this. Many of these references indicate that the process originated in Asia Minor, in particular the region of Phrygia, near zinc ore deposits which are known to have been worked in antiquity. This association was confirmed by analysis of early first-century BC Greek coins (fig. 5.5) from the region;[9] some of these coins proved to be made of brass typical of the cementation process and they thus pre-date Roman use of the alloy. They are probably the earliest reliably dated brass artefacts known.

A major restriction in the cementation brass-making process was the limited amount of zinc which could be introduced into the alloy. Using the ancient method, the maximum zinc content was about 28 per cent, but as the process developed this increased to about 33 per cent. To make brass containing more zinc than this required access to zinc metal. Another disadvantage of the cementation process was that impurities from the zinc ore, such as iron, became incorporated into the alloy and had a detrimental effect on its mechanical and corrosion-resistant properties.

Such features enable us to recognise brass made using metallic zinc as opposed to cementation. Analyses of Chinese statues and coins show that they did not make much use of brass until about the sixteenth century AD. When they did make extensive use of it for coinage, however, the high zinc and low iron content of the coins indicates that they must have used metallic zinc rather than cementation.[10]

81

Precious metals

In antiquity all metal was a valuable commodity and rarely wasted. Metal extraction was difficult, sources of non-ferrous ores are particularly scarce and these, and the smelting sites, were often far removed from where the majority of the artefacts were eventually used. Even base metals were probably recycled, as evidenced by finds of non-ferrous scrap metal hoards from, for example, the Late Bronze Age in Britain.[11]

Traditionally, gold and silver were the most highly prized metals although occasionally other metals or alloys were equally in demand. For example, Plato, writing in the first century AD, says that some regarded *oreichalkos* (brass) as being above silver, and more recently, in the nineteenth century, when aluminium first became available as an expensive novelty it was used in place of silver for prestige items.[12] As one would expect, the composition of precious metal artefacts has always been heavily influenced by economic factors and it became common practice to modify their value by alloying them with baser metals. However, this also has a desirable practical side-effect. Pure gold and silver are soft metals but, when alloyed together or with copper, a harder alloy is produced that is more resistant to wear and distortion. This is clearly an essential attribute for articles of jewellery and functional items such as tableware. Roman silver dishes, for example, are usually made of high purity silver, typically over 94 per cent, but also contain a small percentage of copper (about 3 per cent). The Roman refining techniques were such that they could easily have produced silver containing only traces of copper (under 1 per cent). Therefore, the small amounts of copper were almost certainly added deliberately to harden the alloy without significantly debasing the silver.[13]

The chemical analysis of precious metal artefacts can be difficult because their value and decorative finish usually prevent sampling. The technique of X-ray fluorescence (XRF) (see glossary) is often used for these because of its non-destructive capabilities (fig. 5.6).

5.6 XRF was used to analyse this fragile balance wheel from an English marine chronometer, made in about 1785 and used by the explorer George Vancouver. For timing accuracy the balance wheel is fitted with a temperature compensator which proved, unexpectedly, to be partly made of platinum, a metal which was still something of a laboratory curiosity in eighteenth-century Europe (MLA 14/104).

Alloys of gold and silver with baser metals have long been controlled by established standards, first for coinage and then for plate, such as the English sterling standard guaranteed by a hallmark. Items were tested for compliance with such standards by assaying, a method of analysis, and by the use of a touchstone, a dark-coloured stone on which the colour of a streak of the alloy indicates its quality. The sterling standard for silver (925 parts per thousand of silver with the remainder being mainly copper) has its origins in the fourteenth century and has continued virtually without interruption to the present day. During the period from 1697 to 1720, however, the higher Britannia standard became the legal requirement. Silver of this period should conform to the Britannia standard but does not always do so. The maker's marks on some English watchcases suggest that some manufacturers continued to make their cases from sterling silver and this has been confirmed by analysis. Occasionally the inner and outer cases of the same watch were made of silver of different standards. Although the using up of old stock may be one reason for this practice, watchcase-makers were probably also reluctant to use Britannia silver because it is a softer alloy than sterling. Apart from the increased likelihood of abrasion on an item being constantly handled, it was also important that the case did not become distorted, thus preventing precise closure.

A guarantee of the quality and quantity of precious metals for the purposes of exchange is coinage. Until the last hundred years or so, the purchasing value of coins was closely related to the intrinsic value of the metal they were made from. The value of this precious metal could be modified by alloying with baser materials. The most direct way of revealing a society's economic state is therefore to study the quality, or fineness, of its currency. The most common pattern is one of debasement, that is, increasing amounts of base metal in the alloy (possibly coupled with a decrease in the weight of the coin), followed by occasional reforms. A classic example of this was the debasement of the English silver coinage by Henry VIII to raise additional money for his treasury. The systematic reduction in the standard from sterling (92.5 per cent silver) to one containing only 33.3 per cent silver caused widespread inflation. The coinage standard was subsequently reformed under Edward VI and Elizabeth I.

Although we are now familiar with coins bearing precise dates, this was not usually the case with ancient coin series. Trends in coin fineness can therefore often help to place an otherwise undatable series in chronological order. For example, a study of the debasement trends of sixth- to seventh-century AD European gold coinage provided a basis for dating the Sutton Hoo ship burial.[14] The thirty-seven Frankish gold coins, three coin blanks and two ingots found in the Sutton Hoo purse (plate 5.1) belong to the Merovingian series. Unfortunately Merovingian coins do not carry explicit dates although some examples can be dated by, for example, association with other coins in hoards. When these dated issues were analysed a fairly steady debasement trend was discovered and this allowed the approximate fineness of the coinage at any particular time to be charted. By comparing the fineness of the Sutton Hoo coins themselves with this trend, it was possible to say that the basest and therefore latest coins in the purse were made in the 620s AD, thus defining the earliest probable date for the ship burial.

Manufacturing techniques

The choice of manufacturing technique is to some extent governed by the metal or alloy used and by the intended finished shape. For objects which need some thickness of metal, like ingots or axes, casting is the obvious method, while others, like fine wire or thin sheet metal, need extensive working. In many cases, however, the method used is not immediately obvious. For example, a bowl may be formed by casting, by hammering up the sides from a flat disc, or by a combination of casting (for the basic dish shape) and working up details, like the rim. In rare instances, there is still evidence of manufacturing methods, for example the clay moulds used for casting bronze bridle bits and other equestrian equipment found at the Iron Age site of Gussage All Saints[15] or stone moulds for weapons (fig. 5.7).

Other clues to the manufacturing process might be found by examining the object itself. In casting, the molten metal may have squeezed between the joins of a mould, solidifying as a seam-like ridge known as a casting flash. Casting flashes can often be seen running down the sides of objects such as bronze palstaves (fig. 5.8), which were cast in two-part moulds. The ends of the chaplets (metal pins used to hold a clay core in position inside the mould of a hollow statue or vessel during casting) may show up as small patches of a different alloy on the surface of the finished piece.

5.7 *left* Stone mould for casting bronze spearheads, from Lough Gur, Limerick (PRB 62.12–6.1).

5.8 *above* Side view of a bronze palstave from Stibbard, Norfolk, with the ridge down its length formed in the metal at the join of the two halves of the mould (PRB 38.2–20.15). Length 114 mm.

5.9 Base of the Achilles dish from the Kaiseraugst mid-fourth-century AD Roman treasure. The radial grooves in the silver were made when the dish was turned on a lathe to remove excess metal (Romermuseum, Augst, Switzerland, inv. no. 62.1). Diameter of dish 530 mm.

5.10 Late Bronze Age stand from Cyprus, made by casting (GR 1946.10–17.1). Height 340 mm.

The clay core is usually removed after casting but the chaplets, which are made of an alloy with a higher melting temperature so that they will not melt during the casting process, become embedded in the metal. Similarly, concentric lines radiating from the central pip on the base of a Roman silver dish reveal that it was finished on a lathe (fig. 5.9), and the impressions left by the craftsman's hammer can be seen on the sides of a brass Islamic jug.[16]

Where none of these clues are apparent, the answer may sometimes be found by examining the internal structure of the metal itself. Polished metal looks as smooth and featureless as glass to the naked eye but, unlike glass, it is a crystalline material; it solidifies as a network of tiny grains which can be seen if the metal is etched with a dilute acid and examined under a microscope (fig. 5.11a). If a lump of cast metal is hammered and annealed, the structure will be modified (fig. 5.11b). The microstructure seen is influenced by the composition of the metal and the treatment it has received.[17]

It was this characteristic of metal which revealed the manufacturing history of a bronze stand of the Italian Late Bronze Age (1250–900 BC). It belongs to a group of stands and tripods made in Cyprus and Sardinia which were probably used to support round-bottomed ceramic vessels. The stands are composed of a series of metal rods (fig. 5.10), and two possible methods of construction had been proposed. Either they were made up of a large number of bronze rods, hammered to shape and soldered together, or they were cast by the lost wax process from a model made of wax rods. There was no decisive evidence from examination of the surface, from analysis or from radiography, of which technique had been used. However, examination of the microstructure of the metal at a convenient break provided conclusive proof that the stands had been made by casting: the structure is typical of a cast bronze, with 15 per cent lead in the alloy (fig. 5.11c).[18]

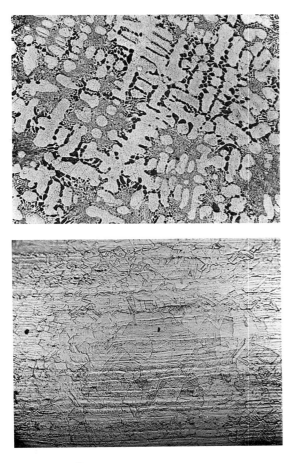

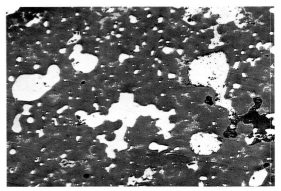

5.11 (a) *above left* Structure of the cast silver-copper alloy of an Egyptian silver figure of Nefertum (EA 66818). Polished and etched sample. Field of view 0.5 mm across.

(b) *left* Structure of worked and annealed silver from a fourth-century AD Roman bowl, showing strongly banded structure and recrystallisation of the silver. Water Newton, Huntingdonshire (PRB P1975.10–2.5). Polished and etched sample. Field of view 0.3 mm across.

(c) *above* Structure of a cast bronze with 15 per cent lead (white areas in the photo). Sample from Late Bronze Age stand (fig. 5.10). Scanning electron microscope BS image. Field of view 0.5 mm across.

Joining techniques

Many metal objects are made of more than one component. Mechanical joins such as rivets are easily recognised but, from as early as 2500 BC in Sumer, smiths developed methods of joining one metal with another of a lower melting point. Soldering alloys are usually categorised as either 'soft' or 'hard'. The main difference between the two is the melting point of the solder. A temperature of 450°C is usually accepted as the upper limit for soft solders, whereas hard solders have a higher melting point. In antiquity, regardless of the metal being joined, soft solder was generally tin or lead or an alloy of the two. Soft solder joins like a glue, without significant interdiffusion (or exchange) with the metals it bonds, leaving the composition of metal and solder essentially unchanged. Hard solders, on the other hand, were usually of the same metal as the object they were used on, but alloyed with a few per cent of another metal in order to reduce the melting point. For example, the ideal composition for a solder to attach a silver handle to a silver jug would be 28 per cent copper and 72 per cent silver. This is the silver copper alloy with the lowest melting point (780°C), known as the eutectic composition. Hard solders join by interdiffusion at high temperatures with the metals being bonded, so that composition at the join will be somewhere between that of the solder and that of the object.

Soldered joints are often difficult to spot visually, but radiography is helpful for detecting them if the solder is denser than the rest of the object or if there is a cavity at the joint. The technique used is much the same as that used in hospitals to find fractures in bones; where the metal is broken the film is blackened by the X-rays which pass unhindered through the break; where the metal is densest, more of the X-rays are stopped and the film remains pale. The image in Figure 5.12 of an inlaid Islamic brass ewer is formed by X-rays passing through the ewer and on to a sheet of film beneath it. Unlike a conventional photograph, an image of both sides of the ewer is produced on the radiographic film. The silver inlays show up as pale areas because they are denser than brass to X-rays. What the X-rays reveal, which cannot be seen on the surface, are the soldered joins at the neck, handle and base as well as around the hole for the missing spout. The tin lead soft solder used on the ewer is very dense to X-rays and appears as white patches on the radiograph.[19]

Radiography can reveal the original construction of an object even when it is so corroded that no external evidence is left. The great ship mound of Sutton Hoo, which was probably the burial place of the East Anglian King Redwald who died in the seventh century AD, contained a wealth of fine metalwork including a sword. Its hilt was decorated with fine garnet work but the blade was broken and rusted. However, a radiograph of the pieces revealed that it had not been made from just one piece of iron,

5.12 Radiograph of a thirteenth-century AD Islamic brass ewer with silver (pale in the radiograph) and copper inlays. It was made up from several pieces of sheet brass, soldered together. The tin lead soft solder is dense to X-rays and appears as white patches, especially on the neck and handle of the ewer. Height 330 mm (OA 1866.12–29.61).

but from many welded together.[20] Using the radiographic evidence, an experimental replica of the blade was made by a modern smith from eighteen laminated rods of twisted wrought iron welded in the same way. The result, when polished, was a beautiful interwoven pattern on the surface of the blade (fig. 5.13).

In most cases metal is joined with metal, whether it is riveted, soldered or welded. However, radiography of the fine pair of Celtic bronze wine flagons from the site of Basse Yutz in France seemed to show that the bottoms of the flagons were not attached to the sides. Further investigation disclosed that they were in fact glued on with a resinous adhesive which appeared transparent to the X-rays. Indeed, use of organic adhesives in metalwork may have been more common than would appear from the surviving archaeological record.[21]

5.13 Sword from the Sutton Hoo ship burial (MLA 1939.10–10.27).

(a) *left* Tip of the corroded iron blade.

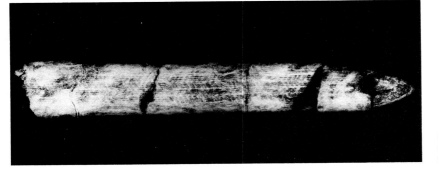

(b) *left* Radiograph of the tip of the blade showing the pattern-welded structure.

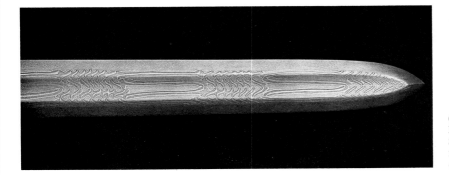

(c) *left* Replica of the Sutton Hoo sword blade, made by Scott Lankton, based on the radiographic image of the original.

Joins on silver or gold objects made with silver and gold solders cannot usually be distinguished by radiography because they are approximately the same density as the metals they join, although they can sometimes be identified by colour difference or porosity when seen at high magnification. Some joins, such as the fine solder work required for gold filigree and granulation, cannot be seen even at high magnification. Spot analysis by microprobe or EDX analysis (see glossary) in a scanning electron microscope (SEM) (see glossary) can detect the solder points by the minor changes in composition. Figure 5.14 shows a panel of gold filigree work from an eighth-century Irish paten as seen in a scanning electron microscope. Etruscan goldsmiths used minute granules of gold, less than 0.5 mm in diameter. The use of conventional solders to attach minute granules of gold presented great difficulties to the goldsmith who had to keep them in position during soldering and avoid flooding the delicate work with solder. These difficulties could be overcome by using finely ground copper carbonate rather than metal, and mixing it with an organic glue. The glue held the granulation in place and turned to carbon when heated, reducing the copper carbonate to metal. The copper metal reacted with the gold to form a bond. There was no surplus solder to spoil the work, but this makes it very difficult to detect.[22]

The most important factor in choosing a solder is that it must have a lower melting point than the pieces to be joined. Where several components had to be soldered together it was vital that the heating for the last piece to be attached did not melt the solder already in place. If the heat could not be sufficiently localised to avoid this, then the first solders had to have a higher melting point than the subsequent ones. X-ray fluorescence (XRF) analysis (see glossary) of solders used on Roman silver suggests that the Roman silversmith did indeed use several different solders which could have given him a working temperature range from the melting point of silver (960°C), down to 180°C. It has to be remembered that the analysis of a soldered joint will not be identical to the composition of the original solder alloy because, unlike adhesives, hard solders bond with other metals by diffusion. This means there will be some exchange between the solder and the metal which will alter the composition of both.[23]

5.14 Detail of gold filigree work on the paten from the eighth-century AD ecclesiastical hoard from Derrynaflan, Co. Tipperary, seen by scanning electron microscope. The beaded wire running diagonally across the top right corner is approximately 0.3 mm in diameter. Solder can be seen joining the end of the strand of wires at the bottom right (National Museum of Ireland, 1980:4).

Decoration and finishing

Metal lends itself to a wider range of decorative techniques than most other materials because of its physical properties, particularly its ductility, which allows it to be twisted into wire or inlaid with other metals and even other materials such as gemstones. It can be engraved, embossed, covered with filigree wire, enamelled, patinated and plated. The range of decorative techniques which have been at some time applied to metalwork is a subject for many books, not just a few pages.[24] This section will therefore only touch on some of the techniques which have become better understood as the result of scientific research. There are several approaches, the first being study at high magnification using an optical microscope or scanning electron microscope (SEM) (see glossary). The second is analysis, for which the method will be dictated by the material, potential sample size and the information needed. Replication experiments are another possible approach. Attempting to copy a decorative technique can confirm or disprove that it produces the same appearance and microstructure observed on the original item, and it is also useful to assess the practical difficulties of the technique. In practice, a combination of scientific approaches is usually needed.

Plating

Gilding, silvering and tinning (all involving the application of a thin layer of metal on to another metal) have been used since the third millennium BC for decorative or practical purposes and also for deception. The earliest examples involved simple mechanical attachment, but it was not long before more permanent and more economical methods of gilding and silvering were developed. In the Roman Imperial period copper and bronze statues and silver and bronze jewellery were commonly gilded. Significant levels of mercury can be detected in the gilding of many but not all these artefacts. The presence of mercury indicates the use of a technique known as mercury- or fire-gilding. Gold dissolves in mercury at room temperature to make an amalgam (an amalgam is an alloy of mercury). This property allows the gold to be applied in semi-liquid form over all or part of the object. The object is then heated to drive off the mercury (which boils at 357°C), leaving a thin surface plating of gold. Because over-heating the gilding will ruin the finish, this stage is not carried to the extent of driving off every trace of mercury, so some evidence of the plating technique is left.

However, analysis shows that not all Roman gilding contained mercury. Pure gold can be beaten out to form very thin sheets; according to Pliny,[25] writing in the first century AD, 25 g of gold could be beaten into 750 leaves each 10 cm square. Burnishing alone can cause gold leaf to adhere to a clean metal surface, but adhesives like egg white were also used. Unlike mercury-gilding, there is no positive analytical evidence which can identify gold leaf, but it can often be recognised when viewed in cross-section at high magnification. Leaf-gilding usually shows only minor variations in thickness and a superficial bonding to the metal below. The overlapping edges of the sheets of gold leaf are very characteristic (figs. 5.15a and b). Analysis of a large number of gilded Roman 'bronzes' has revealed that most of those which are mercury-gilded are in fact made of copper. They contain very low levels of alloying elements, particularly lead, which can dissolve in the amalgam layer and leave unsightly grey patches in the plating. It was found that gold leaf was generally used by the Romans to plate high-lead bronzes,[26] although at later periods the choice of gilding method was not governed by the metal composition.

To identify the method used, it is necessary to see how the plating layer is bonded. This is usually impossible from surface examination of the object. If the edge of the plating does not provide enough information, a minute flake of plating, as small as 1 sq mm, can be mounted on its end in an epoxy resin for easy handling. Once the resin has set hard, the block and sample are ground flat, then polished with fine diamond paste. When viewed at high magnification with an optical microscope or scanning electron microscope, much is revealed about the plating technique which is simply not visible on the surface of the object. This examination technique is illustrated by a pair of micrographs of silver plating (figs. 5.15c and d), both of which are sections through ancient silver coin forgeries. In each case there is a copper core with a plating of silver which superficially appears to be identical on the two coins. But when the cross-section is viewed at high magnification, it becomes clear that different plating methods have been used. In the first example there is a white outer skin of pure silver, with overlapping joins at each end. Between this and the core is an alloy of copper and silver (light grey in the photo). This is a solder attaching two discs of silver foil cupped around the copper core like the foil wrappers around a chocolate penny. The second example has no joins in the outer skin, only a copper-silver alloy coating, indicating that it was plated with molten metal rather than foils.

The mercury method, so popular in the Roman period for gilding, can also be used for silvering bronze and brass. Mercury silvering was certainly practised in the medieval period, but the Romans silvered jewellery, table-

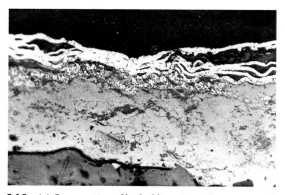

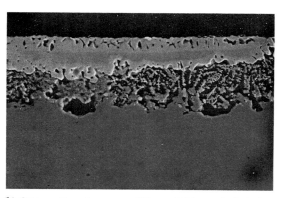

5.15 (a) Cross-section of leaf gilding. Several superimposed layers of leaf (light coloured) remain on this corroded Roman bronze. Field of view 0.14 mm across.

(b) Cross-section of mercury gilding c. 0.01 mm thick (pale band) on corroded copper.

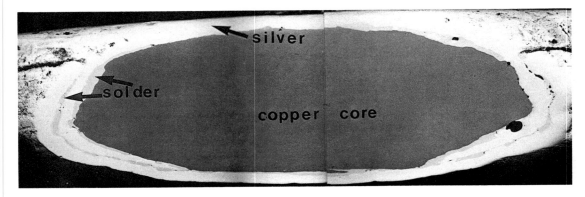

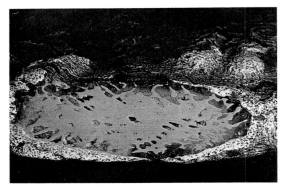

5.15 (**c**) *above* Section at edge of a contemporary forgery of an ancient Greek silver coin of the city of Byzantium, *c.* 400 BC (CM BMC 9). The copper core is plated with two silver foils, overlapping at the edges and attached with silver-copper solder. Field of view 6.5 mm across.

(**d**) *left* Section at the edge of a contemporary forgery of a Celtic silver coin of Epaticus (CM 1972.4–4.1). The corroded copper core (grey) is coated with a continuous layer of copper-silver alloy (speckled, white), applied molten.

(**e**) *above right* Surface of a tinned Roman mirror viewed at high magnification by scanning electron microscope. Field of view 0.07 mm across.

(**f**) *far right* Surface of a high-tin bronze alloy Roman mirror. Field of view 0.1 mm across.

ware and horse trappings by coating the copper alloy with soft solder (tin and lead), wrapping it with silver foil, then heating until the solder melted and secured the foil. The reasons for the difference in treatment of gilding and silvering by the Romans is not clear. Unlike gold, silver needs regular polishing to keep it bright. As the foil plating was thicker it may have been found more durable than mercury plating.[27]

Not all plating was of precious metal. Tin has a low melting point (232°C), and tinning simply involves wiping a thin layer of molten tin over the surface of copper, bronze or brass. It dates back to at least the fifth century BC and is still carried out today at the roadside in parts of Asia. Tinning was used either for decorative purposes, for example on Merovingian jewellery, or for more practical purposes, such as providing a reflecting face on Roman bronze mirrors. Analysis of these mirrors shows high levels of tin on the reflecting surface, but although all these mirrors are superficially similar, there are in fact two quite different types. Many are bronze mirrors with a normal tin content of approximately 10 per cent, which have been tinned to produce a silvery reflecting surface. The second type has no separately applied coating; instead the whole mirror is cast in a high-tin bronze alloy containing about 25 per cent tin. This alloy is naturally silvery in colour and is much more hard-wearing than a thin layer of tinning, but it requires a high degree of skill to control the casting conditions. The two types of mirror look much the same after being

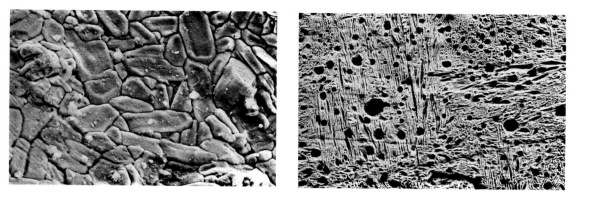

buried for centuries, but when the microstructure is examined at high magnification, as in Figures 5.15e and f, it is possible to distinguish between tinned bronze and the high-tin alloy.[28]

Niello inlay

The scientific research into the history of plating technology relies almost entirely on microscopy and element analysis, but these techniques cannot provide a complete picture of many of the non-metallic inlays used by the ancient metalworkers. One example of this is a black inlay material known as niello, which is found on gold, silver, bronze and brass items from as far apart as first-century AD Rome and nineteenth-century AD Moscow, ninth-century AD Persia and thirteenth-century AD England (fig. 5.16). We know that niello is a metal sulphide, made by heating metal filings with sulphur, but could there be a continuity of tradition amongst the metalworkers of cultures so widely separated by time and geography? Certainly there are visual differences; first-century Roman niello is often poorly preserved but fifteenth-century Italian niello, even in badly damaged pieces, still fills every detail of a finely engraved design.

To study such inlays, the method of analysis must identify any differences without damaging the object. Inlays may be very small in area and are often closely mixed with corrosion products from the metal into which the niello was set, so the analysis technique also has to distinguish the niello inlay from corrosion and the metal of the inlaid object itself. X-ray diffraction (XRD) analysis (see glossary) is ideally suited to this sort of problem as it requires only a minute sample and, most important, it identifies the mineral or compound present. XRD is able to identify the metal sulphide used to make the niello and to distinguish it from the metal and from the oxide, chloride and carbonate corrosion products which contaminate the sample. Thus, where element analysis by X-ray fluorescence of the inlays on two silver Anglo-Saxon disc brooches shows both to have a major component of silver, with some copper and sulphur, XRD analysis identifies one inlay as silver-copper-sulphide ($AgCuS$) and the other as silver-sulphide (Ag_2S) contaminated with copper carbonate ($CuCO_3.Cu(OH)_2$) from the corroding base silver alloy of the brooch.

5.16 (a) *left* A silver charka made by Nyotr Ivanov in Moscow between 1686 and 1708, decorated with niello inlay (MLA 1878.12–30.645). Diameter 70 mm.

(b) *above* The handle of a bronze Roman skillet from Prickwillow, Isle of Ely, with niello and copper inlays (PRB 1893.6–18.14).

A survey of niello composition, from the Roman period to the twentieth century, has identified the beginnings of a change in composition in the sixth century in Northern Europe when, perhaps for economic reasons, copper as well as silver was added to the crucible with the sulphur. A second and more fundamental change occurred in the tenth and eleventh centuries in Europe and in the Islamic world, when lead was added to the ingredients for the inlay. This had the effect of significantly lowering the melting point of the niello, allowing it to be melted into finely engraved designs. Niello produced according to the Roman niello recipe decomposes before it melts. It therefore had to be applied as a paste, not a liquid, and did not bond well to the metal; hence the observed differences in preservation between Roman and later medieval niello.[29]

Paint and patination

Pigment identification is another field to which XRD analysis is well suited. Many early pigments are naturally occurring and brightly coloured minerals, usually metal salts, and often only minute traces remain. We do not necessarily think of pigments in the context of metalwork, but there are traditions of painted metal statues. For example a study of the Buddhist statuettes of Tibet and the Himalayas has identified the blue copper mineral azurite, red lead and cinnabar (red mercury sulphide) on the head-dresses. The blues are normally found on the 'peaceful' deities and the reds on the head-dresses of the 'angry' deities.[30]

A more durable method of colouring metals is to patinate them. This is usually done by chemically inducing a thin surface coating of corrosion.

Metal is easily corroded, but the skill lies in producing an attractive colour which is even in tone and texture. Japanese metalworkers have made the skill of patination into a sophisticated art form, producing naturalistic scenes with flowers, animals and people, using different-coloured inlays (plate 5.2). The best known in the West is probably *shakudo*, which is a copper alloy with a deep black patina, but other copper alloys were pati- nated to produce colours ranging from shades of grey and brown through to green. From as early as the 1860s, Western scientists have been inter- ested in how these colours were produced. Analysis has shown that it is not just the recipe for the pickling solution which affects the colour but, more fundamentally, low levels of alloying elements added to the copper. The shakudo alloy contains 1 to 5 per cent of gold in copper. The greys and browns are produced by varying the proportions of silver added to the copper, often with traces of gold and arsenic.[31]

Patinated metalwork is not just confined to Japan. Pliny describes a much sought-after metal called Corinthian bronze, an alloy of copper with gold and silver, which took on a purplish hue. It has been argued that this is a description of a patinated alloy. Analysis of a small Roman plaque with a black patina and gold inlays proved it to be largely copper with traces of silver, gold and arsenic, adding weight to the view that this patination technique was practised in the West as well as the East.[32]

Another distinctive type of patinated metalwork, known as *bidri*, has been made since the seventeenth century or earlier and is produced in India to this day (fig. 5.17). Again the patina is a deep black and contrasts with brightly polished silver, brass and gold inlay decoration. However, in this case the patinated metal is zinc, which would not be expected to turn black on pickling as zinc has no black corrosion products. This has been explained by analysis of the metal which reveals that copper is also present in the alloy. Experiments in pickling different alloys of copper and zinc have shown that only alloys with between 2 and 10 per cent of copper in the zinc will take on the black patina, and the silver and brass inlays are unaffected by the pickling solution.[33]

5.17 Mid-seventeenth- century AD bidri alloy (black) ewer, inlaid with silver and brass, from the Deccan, India. Height 285 mm (courtesy of the Board of Trustees of the Victoria and Albert Museum V & A 1479–1904).

Conclusion

These are only a few examples of the applications of scientific research to metal artefacts. Clearly one cannot hope to give a comprehensive survey of the history of metals and metalworking in a single chapter. Rather we have attempted to show the potential of analysis and technical studies to increase our knowledge of the past. Such research provides a means of tracing the progress of technological change; for example the development from the early exploitation of native metal to the alloying of copper with arsenic or tin to make bronze and then to the large-scale manufacture of brass (copper-zinc alloy) by the Romans. Metal analysis can reveal fluctuations of economic prosperity, through evidence of coinage debase- ment, the imposition of gold and silver standards, or scarcity of precious metals for prestige items. Study of manufacturing and decorative tech- niques can provide an insight into contacts between cultures. New trade routes may be traced by the spread of metalworking skills and the import of rare and exotic materials such as gemstones and ivory for jewellery. The study of metalwork from an archaeological site, whether a burial site like Sutton Hoo or a major settlement like York, which has a whole range of artefacts and materials, provides an opportunity to build a picture of the place of technology and metals in the context of the economic prosperity and social hierarchy of the society. The potential information which can be extracted from a metal artefact by analytical and technological study extends far beyond providing accurate factual information for museum labels and excavation reports.

Further reading

L. Aitchison, 1960. *A History of Metals*, 2 volumes, London. Macdonald and Evans.

W. Alexander and A. Street, 1989. *Metals in the Service of Man*. 9th edition, London, Pelican Books.

J.W. Allan, 1979. *Persian Metal Technology 700–1300 AD*. Oxford, Ithaca Press.

I.M. Allen, D. Britton & H.H. Coghlan, 1970. *Metallurgical Reports on British and Irish Bronze Age, Implements and Weapons in the Pitt Rivers Museum*. Oxford, Oxford University Press.

V. Biringuccio, 1959. *Pirotechnia* (trans. C.S. Smith and M.T. Gnudi). New York, Basic Books.

Cellini, translated by C.R. Ashbee 1967. *The Treatises of Benvenuto Cellini on Goldsmithing and Sculpture*. New York, Dover.

H.H. Coghlan, 1956. *Notes on the Prehistoric Metallurgy of Copper and Bronze in the Old World*. Oxford, Pitt Rivers Museum.

R.J. Forbes, 1964. *Studies in Ancient Technology*, vols. 7–9, Leiden, Brill.

R.J. Gettens, 1969. *The Freer Chinese Bronzes Vol. II: Technical Studies*. Washington DC, Smithsonian Institution Oriental Studies No. 7.

M. Grimwade, 1985. *Introduction to Precious Metals*. London, Butterworth (Newnes Technical Books).

J.G. Hawthorne and C.S. Smith (trans. and ed.), 1963. *Theophilus On Divers Arts*. New York, Dover.

H. Hodges, 1970. *Technology in the Ancient World*. London, The Penguin Press.

C. Johns and T. Potter, 1983. *The Thetford Treasure*. London, British Museum Publications.

H. Maryon, 1971. *Metalwork and Enamelling*, 5th edition. New York, Dover.

J.O. Nriagu, 1983. *Lead and Lead Poisoning in Antiquity*. New York, John Wiley & Sons.

J. Ogden, 1982. *Jewellery of the Ancient World*. London, Trefoil.

R.D. Penhallurick, 1986. *Tin in Antiquity*. London, The Institute of Metals.

Pliny The Elder, translated by H. Rackham, 1956. *Naturalis Historia*, especially volume 9. London, Loeb.

E.C. Rollason, 1973. *Metallurgy for Engineers*. London, Edward Arnold.

B.G. Scott and H. Cleere (eds.), 1984. *The Crafts of the Blacksmith*. Belfast.

R.F. Tylecote, 1976. *A History of Metallurgy*. London, The Metals Society.

R.F. Tylecote, 1986. *The Prehistory of Metallurgy in the British Isles*. London, The Institute of Metals.

R.F. Tylecote and B.J.J. Gilmour, 1986. *The metallography of early ferrous edge tools and edged weapons*. Oxford, BAR 155.

O. Untracht, 1969. *Metal Techniques for Craftsmen*. London, Hale.

O. Untracht, 1982. *Jewellery: Concepts and Technology*. London, Hale.

T.A. Wertime and J.D. Muhly (eds.), 1980. *The Coming of the Age of Iron*. New Haven, Yale University Press.

H. Wilson, 1903. *Silverwork and Jewellery*. London, Pitman.

References

1. R.F. Tylcote, 1986. *The Prehistory of Metallurgy in the British Isles*. Institute of Metals. J.D. Muhly, 1988. 'The beginnings of metallurgy in the Old World'. In *The Beginning of the Use of Metals and Alloys*, ed. R. Maddin, pp. 2–20. Cambridge, Mass., MIT Press.

2. P.T. Craddock, I.C. Freestone, L.K. Gurjar, K.T.M. Hedge and V.H. Sonawane, 'Early zinc production in India', *Mining Magazine*, January 1985, pp. 45–52. P.T. Craddock, 'Mining and smelting in antiquity', Ch. 4, this volume.

3. R.J. Forbes, 1971. *Studies in Ancient Technology in Antiquity*, vol. 8, p. 180. Leiden, Brill.

4. J.C. Walbaum, 1982. *Metalwork from Sardis: The Finds Through 1974*. Cambridge, Mass, Harvard University Press.

5. J. Reiderer, 'Metallanalysen Chinesischer spiegel (Metal analysis of Chinese mirror)', *Berliner Beitrage zur Archaometrie* 1, 1977, pp. 6–16. W.A. Oddy, M. Bimson and M. Cowell, 1983. 'Scientific examination of the Sutton Hoo hanging bowls (Appendix B)'. In R. Bruce-Mitford, *The Sutton Hoo Ship Burial*, Vol. III, pp. 299–315. London, British Museum Publications.

6. J. Lang and A.R. Williams, 1975. 'The hardening of iron swords', *Journal of Archaeological Science* 2, pp. 199–207.

7. M. Cowell, 1989. 'The composition of Egyptian copper-based metalwork'. In *Science in Egyptology*, ed. A.R. David, pp. 383–402. Manchester University Press. M. Cowell, 1987. 'Chemical analyses (scientific appendix)'. In W.V. Davies, *Catalogue of Egyptian Antiquities in the British Museum*, Vol. VIII, pp. 96–118. London, British Museum Publications.

8. S.P. Needham, M.N. Leese, D.R. Hook and M.J. Hughes, 1989. 'Developments in the Early Bronze Age metallurgy of southern Britain', *World Archaeology* 20, pp. 383–402.

9. P.T. Craddock, A.M. Burnett and K. Preston, 1980. 'Hellenistic copper-base coinage and the origins of brass'. In *Scientific Studies in Numismatics*, ed. W.A. Oddy, Occasional Paper 18, pp. 53–63. London, British Museum.

10. S.G.E. Bowman, M.R. Cowell and J. Cribb, 1989. 'Two thousand years of coinage in China', *Historical Metallurgy* 23, pp. 25–30.

11. Martin O'Connell, 1986. *Petters Sports Field Egham: excavation of a Late Bronze Age/Early Iron Age Site*, Research Volume 10. Surrey Archaeological Society, Guildford.

12. H. Saint-Claire Deville, 1859. *De l'Aluminium*. Paris.

13. M.J. Hughes and A. Hall, 1979. 'X-ray fluorescence analyses of late Roman and Sassanian silver plate', *Journal of Archaeological Science* 6, pp. 321–44.

14. J.P.C. Kent, 1975. 'The date of the Sutton Hoo coins'. In R. Bruce-Mitford, *The Sutton Hoo Ship Burial*, Vol. I, pp. 580–606. London, British Museum Publications. W.A. Oddy and M.J. Hughes, 1975. 'The analysis of the Sutton Hoo gold coins by the method of specific gravity determination'. In R. Bruce-Mitford, *ibid.*, pp. 648–52.

15. J. Foster, 1980. *The Iron Age Moulds from Gussage All Saints*. Occasional Paper 12. London, British Museum.

16. R.F. Tylecote, 1986. *The Prehistory of Metallurgy in the British Isles*, pp. 81–123. London, The Institute of Metals.

17. C. Stanley Smith, 1960. *A History of Metallography*. University of Chicago Press. *Metals Handbook*, vols. 7 and 8, 8th edition 1972/3. Ohio, American Society of Metals. J.T. Norton, 1965. 'Metallography and the study of art objects', and C. Stanley Smith, 1965. 'The Interpretation of Microstructures of metallic artefacts'. In *Application of Science in Examination of Works of Art*, pp. 13–53. Boston, Museum of Fine Arts.

18. E. Macnamara and N.D. Meeks, 1987. 'The metallurgical examination of four late Cypriot III stands now in the British Museum'. In *Report of the Department of Antiquities Cyprus, 1987*, pp. 57–60, Plates XVII–XVIII. Nicosia, Department of Antiquities.

19. A. Gilardoni, R. Ascani Orsini and S. Taccani, 1977. *X-rays in art*. Mandello Lario. (Como) Italy, Gilardoni.

20. R. Bruce-Mitford, 1978. *The Sutton Hoo Ship-Burial, Vol. 2: Arms, Armour and Regalia*, pp. 273–309. London, British Museum Publications.

21. P.T. Craddock, 1990. 'Report on the technical and scientific examination of the Basse Yutz find'. In J.V.S. Megaw and M.R. Megaw, *The Basse-Yutz Find: Masterpieces of Celtic Art*, Chapter 5, Research Report no. 46. London, Society of Antiquaries.

22. H.A.P. Littledale, 1936. *A new process for hard soldering*. London, J. Wolters, 1983. *Die Granulation: Geschichte und Technik einer alter Goldschmiedekunst*. Munchen, Callwey Verlag. J. Wolters, 1981. 'A short history of granulation (in 3 parts)', *Aurum* 6, pp. 8–14, 7, pp. 6–13, 9, pp. 6–13. H. Maryon, 1936. 'Solders used by ancient goldsmiths'. *Goldsmiths Journal*, pp. 72–3. H. Maryon, 1936. 'Soldering and Welding in the Bronze age and early Iron ages'. In *Technical Studies in the Field of the Fine Arts*. 1936, pp. 75–108. Cambridge, Mass., Fogg Art Museum.

23. J. Lang and M.J. Hughes, 1984. 'Soldering Roman silver plate'. *Oxford Journal of Archaeology* 3, pp. 77–107. V. Fell, 1982. 'Ancient fluxes for soldering and brazing'. *Masca Journal* 2, (3), pp. 82–5.

24. See further reading list.

25. Pliny the Elder (translated by H. Rackham), 1952. *Naturalis Historia* (volume 9) XXXIII, XIX, pp. 48–9. London, Loeb.

26. W.A. Oddy, 1981. 'Gilding through the ages'. *Gold Bulletin* 14, pp. 75–9. W.A. Oddy, 1982. 'Gold in antiquity: aspects of gilding and assaying'. *Journal of the Royal Society of Arts* 130 (5315), pp. 730–43.

27. S. La Niece, 1990. 'Silver plating on copper, bronze and brass'. In *Antiquaries Journal* 70, (1).

28. N.D. Meeks, 1986. 'Tin-rich surfaces on bronze – some experimental and archaeological considerations'. *Archaeometry* 28, (2), 133–62.

29. S. La Niece, 1983. 'Niello: an historical and technical survey'. *Antiquaries Journal* 63, (2), pp. 279–98.

30. W.A. Oddy, M. Bimson and S. La Niece, 1981. 'Gilding Himalayan images: history, tradition and modern techniques'. In *Aspects of Tibetan Metallurgy*, eds. W.A. Oddy and W. Zwalf, pp. 87–101. Occasional Paper 15. London, British Museum.

31. R. Murakami, S. Niiyama and M. Kitada, 1988. 'Characterisation of the black surface layer on a copper alloy coloured by the traditional Japanese surface treatment'. In *The Conservation of Far Eastern Art*, eds. J.S. Mills, P. Smith and K. Yamasaki, pp. 133–6. London, IIC. M.R. Notis, 1988. 'The Japanese alloy Shakudo: Its history and its patination'. In *The beginnings of the use of metals and alloys*, ed. R. Maddin, pp. 315–27. Cambridge, Mass., MIT Press. H. Oguchi, 1983. 'Japanese Shakudo'. *Gold Bulletin* 16 (4), pp. 125–32. S. La Niece, 1990. 'Japanese polychrome metalwork'. In *Archaeometry '90*. Basel, Birkhauser.

32. P.T. Craddock, 1982. 'Gold in antique copper alloys'. *Gold Bulletin* 5 (2), pp. 69–72.

33. S. La Niece and G. Martin, 1987. 'The technical examination of bidri ware'. *Studies in Conservation* 32, pp. 97–101.

CHAPTER 6

Tracing to Source

Michael Hughes

The first question one tends to ask about any object in a museum is where did it come from? In many cases, pinpointing provenance, where an object of a particular type was made, enables us to identify it quite specifically. For example, the tin-glazed pottery made in Europe from the Renaissance onwards was produced in many styles[1,2]: that made in the Low Countries (known as Delftware) is of a specific range and type which varies from one production centre to another and is different again from the maiolica of Italy[3] and the lustreware of Spain.

An object's appearance is the first way we recognise where it comes from: a Volkswagen 'Beetle' is an instantly recognisable shape even if the VW badge has fallen off the car; likewise we recognise a Rolls Royce. Much of the expertise of a museum curator or an archaeologist lies in being able to offer a reasonably accurate identification of an object just on the basis of looking at it and handling it. From experience and familiarity he or she builds up a mental pictorial encyclopaedia based on study of museum collections, information from archaeological research and accumulated knowledge from books and papers describing objects of particular periods and cultures.

However, from time to time the curator's instinct for identification comes up against scholarly puzzles. Differences of opinion exist among scholars; sometimes the appearance gives very little to go on – details may have been rubbed off or we may only have a small fragment of a large object to examine; two or more origins may be possible contenders and it may be impossible to decide which on stylistic grounds alone. All such cases need an alternative approach to the problem of origin and it is natural to turn to scientific techniques to see if they have something to offer. The problem then needs to be formulated in scientific terms and this requires the object to have some property which is unique to its origin, but which varies from place to place and is not significantly modified by manufacture; the property must also be scientifically detectable. Either the composition of the object or its microstructure are the obvious candidates.

For metal objects, as we have seen in Chapter 5, the bulk composition was very much under the control of the metalsmith rather than being unique to origin. Hence most provenance studies are of ceramic and stone materials, where the composition and microstructure of the basic raw materials is relatively unaffected by the manufacturing process, although we will see that metals too can be provenanced in some circumstances. If an object is to be sourced, the first step is to determine the composition of the raw materials of the most probable sources. More usually for ceramics, the scientist examines the composition of groups of similar objects of known origin to build up a comparative database.

An appropriate scientific technique has to be chosen for this task, and experience of analysing antiquities suggests that there are certain requirements of such a technique. For example, in most cases only small amounts of material can be removed from an object: the analysis technique must therefore be quite sensitive. The differences in composition are sometimes quite subtle so the technique must also be accurate and precise. Identifications need to be made clearly, which requires us to investigate as many features of the object as possible.[4] This is like forensic science, where the more 'matches' one finds between two fingerprints, the greater the certainty that they belong to the same person. Normally we need to look at large numbers of objects (tens, or perhaps hundreds): the analytical technique must therefore give results in a reasonable amount of time per sample and cope with large numbers of objects. This requirement eliminates a lot of the older classical chemical techniques and indeed some of the ultra-modern high-tech instruments which can only handle a few objects per day.

Different techniques are chosen for different materials. The aim is always to select an appropriate method, one which answers the question as clearly as possible. There is no reason to use a difficult and probably expensive analytical method if a much simpler and quicker visual examination under a microscope provides the same answer. Some materials still resist easy answers – gold is an example. There is a continual need to appraise existing techniques, to seek refinements and to search out new instrumental methods of examination which have more to offer in speed, accuracy or range of elements found. In ten years' time we shall no doubt still be using the techniques discussed in this chapter but we may also have opened up new avenues of research by widening the range of materials examined and by using other scientific techniques which at present are only at the development stage.

Ceramics

Two general approaches have been much used: thin-section petrography and chemical analysis of the body fabric or composition.

Petrography

Thin-section petrography is a standard geological technique, fundamental to determining the mineralogical and textural characteristics of rocks; it can be applied in just the same way to ceramic materials. First, a small fragment of material is removed and stuck to a glass slide; it is then carefully ground away until it is only 0.03 mm thick. At this thickness most rock-forming silicate minerals are translucent and the thin section can be viewed in transmitted light using a polarising microscope. Particular minerals can be recognised by their characteristic optical properties so that individual grains and rock fragments can be identified. Textural characteristics – such as the size, shape and orientation of grains – can also be observed. Although clay minerals are generally too fine-grained to be reliably identified, features such as clay pellets and parallel alignment of the platy clay particles, which may result from forming processes such as wheel-throwing, can be recognised.

Examination of thin sections of ceramic materials may yield information about ancient technology (e.g. type and amount of added temper, mixing of clays, and method of forming). Such examination may also help us to determine provenance by revealing inclusions characteristic of particular geological sources. Textural analysis, which involves studying the size, shape and proportion of the inclusions, can be useful when the inclusions are not distinctive in other respects. It may sometimes be possible to associate together vessels which have inclusions with similar textural characteristics, and even to suggest possible sources. The following example from Iron Age Britain shows how scientists use thin-section petrography to decide whether pottery found at a site is local or imported.

Hengistbury Head is a low sandy promontory jutting out into the English Channel near Bournemouth. Evidence of human occupation here goes back to the Upper Paleolithic and Mesolithic periods (Early and Middle Stone Ages) but its period of greatest activity was in the Late Iron Age, from roughly 100 BC to 50 AD, when it became a trading centre and port for people and goods from the Continent. Today, it is being slowly eroded on the south face by the sea. It was excavated by Bushe-Fox in 1911–12,[5] and has been excavated more extensively within the last ten years by Barry Cunliffe, using the latest archaeological techniques.[6]

During the excavations, the Iron Age settlement yielded large amounts of pottery. Because Hengistbury was a port, we were especially interested in identifying which pieces of pottery were local and which imported, and in trying to find their sources. To do this, a selection of the Late Iron Age pottery (c.100–50 BC) was studied. In thin section a Dorset-based type of hand-made pottery known as Durotrigian ware (named after the Iron Age tribe, the Durotriges)[6] shows a very sand-rich fabric (plate 6.1a: left-hand side). The white or greyish grains embedded in the dark clay matrix are composed of the common mineral quartz. This was probably deliberately added by the potter as sand temper, to 'open up' the clay fabric, allowing water vapour to escape so that the pot would be less liable to crack during firing (see Chapter 2 for further discussion). Most of the hand-made Durotrigian pottery analysed in thin section had the distinctive appearance of Plate 6.1a, with a fairly coarse sand temper. On the grounds of petrology, this sandy ware seemed to be locally produced Dorset pottery, made from the local Tertiary clays of the Poole-Wareham region.

In contrast to these local pottery types, there were also wheel-made vessels decorated with raised cordons or bands on the body. In thin section these have a dramatically different appearance (plate 6.1b). Under the polarising microscope they contain coarse grains which show multi-coloured areas, corresponding to interference colours caused by the presence of particular minerals. While quartz gives grey and white interference colours, the bright colours of Plate 6.1b are produced by an amphibole mineral (pale colour to yellow to red) and the black and white stripey pattern by the feldspar mineral plagioclase. (These two minerals form a rock type known as an amphibolite.)

Other very distinctive thin sections were found for vessels with a distinctive rilled decoration which contain the minerals feldspar, mica and quartz: these are fragments of a granite. Both the amphibolitic and granitic minerals can be matched with the rock types found in northern Brittany but not in Dorset. Taken together, the petrological analysis of the black cordoned and rilled micaceous wares recovered at Hengistbury Head and the known geology of the region leave no doubt that these wares were imported to southern Britain in the Late Iron Age.

Chemical composition

The provenance study of ceramics is one of the most active research fields involving chemical analysis. This is partly because we need to understand and classify the vast amounts of pottery recovered from excavations at archaeological sites, and partly because of the high success rate of such analytical projects. But the real explanation is found in the nature of pottery. On the one hand it is made from clay which, after being extracted and processed, is a durable material which outlives other materials in aggressive soil conditions. On the other hand numerous studies have shown that clay from one locality, if not always of a single composition, has at least a reasonably uniform and limited compositional range, whereas clays from different locations (towns, countries, continents) have different chemical compositions because they reflect differences in the underlying geology. The chemical composition of clay may differ in major elements, like aluminium, iron, sodium or calcium, or in the minor or trace elements present at very low concentrations, such as chromium, uranium, barium or lanthanum (one of the rare earths). Fashioning and firing a pot does not affect the clay composition but care must be taken, since potters frequently mix additives into clay to prepare it, and burial of pottery in the ground has some slight effects on its composition. In ancient times the most common additive, or temper, was quartz sand, which simply dilutes the concentrations of the chemical elements. The chemical effects of burial on the pottery are few and generally well known.

Neutron activation analysis

Neutron activation analysis (see glossary) was developed in the mid-1940s, following the introduction of nuclear reactors. It remains one of the most sensitive methods for chemical analysis ever developed. At present it is also the most popular method of analysis for provenance studies in archaeology,[4, 7] but it may not always be so, since scientists are continually looking for new instrumental methods of obtaining a comprehensive chemical analysis of a material. Mass-spectrometry techniques (see glossary) are currently receiving attention because they are superior to other methods in sensitivity and the range of chemical elements to which they can be applied. However, routine chemical analyses of large batches of samples has yet to be achieved. Instrumental neutron activation is still selected most frequently because of its sensitivity, accuracy and the wide range of elements which can be measured in a single sample.

For ceramic provenance studies, a sample of the ceramic body fabric is taken, using a non-contaminating drill such as synthetic sapphire. This produces a powdered sample of the interior body fabric of the ceramic (about 50 mg are needed). Batches of about sixty samples, each sealed in a pure silica tube, are irradiated, together with six samples of a standard clay of already known chemical composition.[8] Typically, the chemical analysis for each sample yields results on over twenty elements. Laboratories located next to a reactor can increase the number of elements to between thirty and thirty-five. This is because they can include additional short irradiations for elements with isotopes of very short half-lives, from a few minutes to a few hours, although this increases the analyst's work.

A typical provenance project could involve analysis of a hundred to two hundred samples of pottery and it would clearly be impossible to make sense of all two thousand to four thousand quantitative elemental analyses without the use of modern multivariate statistical computer programs. Such programs take a comprehensive analysis (more than twenty elements) on each sample in turn, and compare it with perhaps a hundred to two hundred other samples to try to find a close 'match'. Essentially it is like the forensic scientist trying to find two chemical 'fingerprints' which match for as many elements as possible. Eventually the program will organise all the samples into groups having the same or similar 'fingerprints'. Each of these pottery composition groups represents the same clay. Working out why these different groups have emerged then becomes a matter of closely integrating the archaeological and scientific information: the key to understanding the results is close co-operation between the archaeologist and scientist, who need to work together in order to extract all the latent information in the analyses. The use of neutron activation analysis is best explained by the following case study.

Medieval Spain had a vigorous ceramic industry with many local potters producing ceramics with a galaxy of brightly coloured and lustred designs on a white background. This is tin-glazed pottery and it was exported widely. For example it was packed into the holds of ships sailing to the New World, to satisfy the expatriates' desire for Spanish tableware in their overseas posting. Sherds of such pottery have been found on sites along the eastern seaboard of the United States, including Florida, the Caribbean islands and parts of South America such as Venezuela.[9]

The most famous tin-glazed pottery of Spain was lustre pottery; it was also exported and found its way into the wealthy households of medieval Europe. The first lustre pottery produced in Europe was made by Arab potters working in Spain. The Muslim potters of Malaga in the Kingdom of Granada became justly famous for their wares and lustre pottery was subsequently made by both Muslim and Christian potters in the Christian town of Valencia.[1,2,10] Both lustre and blue-on-white wares were made from the mid-thirteenth century to the late fifteenth century at Malaga and a typical example of a wide dish decorated in lustre and blue is shown in Figure 6.1. The designs fill the surface of the ceramics almost completely.

From the late fourteenth century onwards, however, very similar pottery was produced at Valencia, a long-established pottery-making centre. It is thought that the potters had migrated from Malaga in response to the increasing pressure of the sea blockade of southern Spain by Christian ships. Later, Valencia came to dominate as the major lustreware centre. But before this both centres produced very similar ranges of designs and there are considerable difficulties in distinguishing on stylistic grounds alone between late Malaga and early Valencia lustre pottery.[11] This is where neutron activation analysis enables us to source them with certainty.

As a first step, sherds of known origin from the two centres were analysed.[12] The results were then evaluated using several statistical techniques mentioned in Chapter 9 (see page 158). A preliminary test with principal components analysis was followed by cluster analysis using the program CLUSTAN[13] and finally discriminant analysis to test for chemical differences between the products of the two sites. Figure 6.2 shows the results of discriminant analysis in graph form: the compositions of the pieces of pottery from Malaga, Valencia and Seville can be clearly differentiated from each other. There are also composition sub-groups which for Valencia at least are related to quality of the wares.

The splendid lustreware dish shown in Figure 6.1 has already been referred to. From a purely art-historical viewpoint it presents a puzzle: the shape is Valencian but the style of decoration is Malagan. Analysis showed it to have a definite Valencian chemical composition: in Figure 6.2 it is part of the Valencian sub-group with black filled circles. From this one can infer that it belongs chronologically to that transition period in Spanish

6.1 *left* Hispano-Moresque dish in lustre and blue (MLA G517). The dish has a Valencian shape but the crowded design is Malagan; neutron activation analysis shows it to be Valencian. Diameter 420 mm.

6.3 *right* Two medieval floor tiles: **(a)** from the chapel of Leo X in the Castel Sant' Angelo, Rome (MLA 1883.11–6.9) of Genoese or Spanish origin (140 mm square), and **(b)** *far right* made in Seville (MLA 1900.7–18.1), one of a group analysed for comparison. 115 mm square.

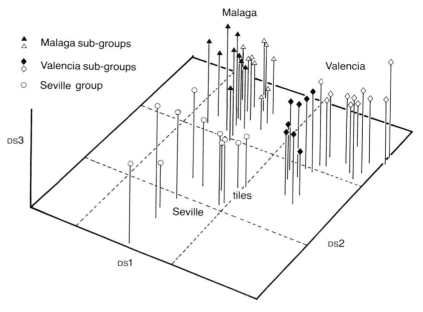

Malaga

▲
△ Malaga sub-groups

◆
◇ Valencia sub-groups

○ Seville group

Valencia

DS3

DS1

DS2

tiles

Seville

6.2 Discriminant analysis results of neutron activation data for Spanish tin-glazed pottery known to be from Malaga, Valencia and Seville. Each symbol represents the analysis of an individual object; samples of unknown origin can be assigned to their source by their position on such a diagram.

ceramics when the displaced potters of Malaga had set up afresh in Valencia but were still using the traditional designs of Andalusia in their new environment.

Analysis has also helped to ascertain the origin of the tiles in the chapel of Leo x in the Castel Sant' Angelo in Rome (fig. 6.3a). It was recently suggested that these might be the products of an Italian maiolica workshop rather than Spanish as has long been believed.

Maiolica made in Renaissance Italy was also tin-glazed and painted with such vibrant colours that the ceramics seem to glow with a Mediterranean light.[3] A neutron activation analysis study of these ceramics (such as the

pharmacy bottle in Figure 6.4) has so far tested pieces known to be local products from over twenty maiolica centres in Italy.[14] The composition of the Leo x tiles does not compare with any of these, including those from the postulated source at Genoa, but they are almost identical to the composition of contemporary tiles definitely known to have been made at Seville, such as the example in Figure 6.3b. In the discriminant analysis diagram (fig. 6.2), these Seville tiles form a compact group into which the Leo x tiles closely fit; this demonstrates that the Leo x tiles are Sevillian. Anthony Ray has recently reached the same conclusion on art-historical grounds[15] and we know that Seville was an important centre for the manufacture and export of tin-glazed pottery.[9]

Among the Italian maiolica ceramics analysed was the pharmacy jar of Figure 6.4, which is one of a number in the same style. Their origin has been disputed but analysis has now shown that their compositions are consistent with being made at Castelli in southern Italy.[3, 16]

Stone

The parallel approaches of petrology (or thin-section petrography) and chemical analysis, which have been so successfully applied to ceramics, have also solved some quesions about stone objects. In addition another technique, stable isotope analysis, has been used to identify the sources of white marble used in the Classical world.

Microscopic study of stone axes

Petrology has been particularly helpful in identifying Neolithic stone axes made from the hard rocks which predominate in western Britain from Cornwall to Scotland. From the seventeenth century onwards antiquarians recognised that the polished stone axes found at numerous sites in Britain were made of stone that was not available locally. They speculated on how far it would have been necessary to travel to obtain the stone, and whether one could precisely locate its origin. Modern petrological studies have gone a long way towards answering this question: polished hard-rock axes seem to have been made from stone obtained from a limited number of outcrops.[17] Sometimes there is actual evidence of extensive roughly pre-pared axeheads (as in the great outcrops towering above the Langdale Valley in the Lake District), while in other cases the geological sources have been identified fairly exactly by petrology even though there is little archaeological evidence of working at the outcrops themselves.

Just how far the raw material travelled from source to customer is illustrated by the outcrop of greenstone rock in Mounts Bay, Cornwall: many axeheads made from this rock are actually found in East Anglia on the Essex coast (some 550 km from Cornwall) and in south-eastern England along the Kent and Sussex coasts. We therefore know that there was long-distance transport of stone axes in prehistoric Britain, which may have begun with carriage of axes from the axe factory to a secondary distri-bution centre, from where they were traded out into the surrounding area.

6.4 Italian maiolica pharmacy bottle of 'Orsini-Colonna' style showing a bear hugging a column (MLA 1852.11–29.2). Neutron activation analysis has now shown that this series of pieces was made at Castelli in southern Italy. Height 450 mm.

Our knowledge of the identification and distribution of stone axes in Britain has been gained from a very long-running co-operative research effort involving archaeologists and petrologists: over the last fifty years more than 7500 axes have been examined petrologically.[17] Well over thirty distinct hard-rock types, each representing a different rock outcrop, were utilised for artefacts in the prehistoric period. Some of these rock types are quite exotic – for example the rare porcellanite from Northern Ireland – whereas others, such as the granite type known as dolerite, occur in many different areas of upland Britain including Wales.

Chemical analysis of flint axes

The most enduring and widespread artefacts from the earliest times are made of flint, a hard rock which fractures to give sharp edges ideally suited for making knives, axeheads and arrowheads. In Great Britain such artefacts are particularly common from the Paleolithic through to the Bronze Age. An astonishing variety of artefacts was made from flint, requiring a craftsman's skill to chip the blocks of flint to the required shape.

How and where were the raw materials obtained and transformed into useful items for hunting, food production, woodland clearance and so on during the Neolithic and Early Bronze Age (roughly 4000–1500 BC)? Enough is known from archaeology to realise that in many cases chance finds of flint nodules or fragments provided the raw material for small tools. On the other hand, archaeological study has also shown that in specific locations across southern Britain (and elsewhere in Europe) there were large-scale exploitations of flint resources, in effect flint mines. Attention has been focused on the composition of these deposits to see if we can link implements to specific mines.

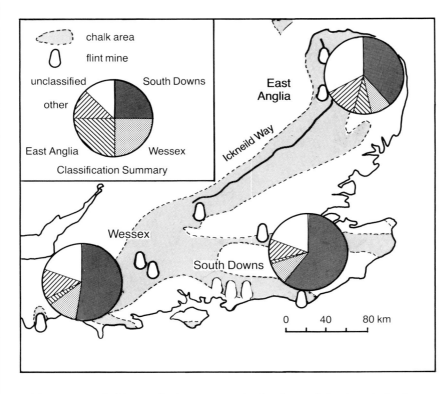

6.5 The distribution of flint axes from the source mines in southern Britain. Each pie chart shows the proportion of axes found in the three areas, classified according to whether they came from the South Downs, Wessex, East Anglia or other mines (after Craddock *et al*, 1983).

Flint is regarded by geologists as a particular form of chert, a chalcedony: that is, a material which is almost pure silica with small inclusions of water. The chemical properties of flint at first seem very unpromising since so much of its chemical make-up is a silicon-oxygen network, and is the same in flint found anywhere. But there are trace amounts of other elements entrapped within the flint. Because it forms slowly over geological time in the Cretaceous chalk, minute amounts of clay dispersed in the chalk are incorporated within the flint. These trace amounts of clay can be analysed chemically and research has shown that the flint taken from the major flint mines scattered across southern Britain (fig. 6.5) has a particular chemical composition for each mine.[18] This composition 'finger-print' is consistently found for flint from the same mine but differs between mines.

As the amounts of these chemical elements trapped in the flint are so small, it is necessary to use a sensitive analytical technique,[18] namely atomic absorption spectrometry (see glossary). This technique has been used to find the amounts of elements such as iron, sodium, potassium, aluminium, calcium, magnesium, lithium and phosphorus in the flint, and it was the concentrations of these elements which were different for different mines. Neutron activation was not chosen[19] because those elements which it can measure in flint (as compared to pottery) are more erratically distributed than those measured by atomic absorption (the major elements in clay), and this makes it harder to distinguish the products of any two mines. Recently inductively coupled plasma spectrometry (see glossary), which is related to atomic absorption, has also been successfully applied to flint analysis.[20]

In this project over a thousand flints from across southern Britain, including unworked flint nodules collected from the known mines, were analysed. All flint mines in southern Britain are located on the Chalk (fig. 6.5). A typical Neolithic mine is not very different from our contemporary idea of a mine even though these are over 4000 years old and the interior of the mine at Grimes Graves is shown in Figure 6.6.[21]

Raw flint from the mines as well as finished artefacts were analysed, mainly hoards of flint axeheads found far from the mines, and there were some unexpected results (fig. 6.5). The pie charts in the diagram show the proportion of flint artefacts which originated from the major flint mining areas of the South Downs, Wessex and East Anglia. In the South-East, as one would expect, the South Downs mines supplied the raw material for more than half the axeheads analysed from that region. However in East Anglia the South Downs group still supplied a large proportion (this time somewhat under 50 per cent of the axeheads), whereas East Anglian sources, such as Grimes Graves, had apparently cornered only a small proportion of the market. Many of the analysed axeheads are datable stylistically to an early period, before mining operations began at Grimes Graves. However there is still the slightly bizarre picture of flint being carefully transported from the South Downs northwards over 350 km, along the Icknield Way into East Anglia on the Chalk ridge which contains countless tonnes of flint nodules perhaps 10 m below the surface.

As well as showing how far flint was traded in prehistoric times in Britain, the analyses have shown that the largest proportion of the flint used to make axeheads was deliberately mined, in many ways like the hard rocks used for axes (see page 106).

Stable isotope analysis of white marble

Sculptures in white marble from the Classical world of ancient Greece and Rome have for centuries delighted and inspired the ordinary observer as well as other sculptors, painters, architects and art historians (fig. 6.7).

6.6 Interior of a typical flint mine gallery at Grimes Graves, Norfolk, showing the black flint seam at the foot of the wall.

That a range of quarries was exploited in the Mediterranean area is not in doubt, but particular sculpted pieces cannot always be attributed to particular quarries on purely visual grounds. Some alternative method of assigning sculpture in white marble to its quarry source has been long sought. Petrographic methods have provided some indications because the grain-size of the white marble from some quarries is very distinctive, but not all quarries can be distinguished in this way.

In 1972 a research paper by American scientists[22] showed that the stable isotope ratios for oxygen and carbon in white marble varied from quarry to quarry, and more extensive research since then has confirmed that such measurements provide a 'signature' for the marble quarries of Italy, Greece and Turkey, which were the main sources of Classical marble.[23]

For convenience the patterns can be shown on graphs (fig. 6.8) as a series of statistical ellipses which represent 90 per cent of the results from each quarry. If a measurement on an 'unknown' marble fragment is then plotted on this graph and it falls within one of the ellipses, the fragment can probably be assigned to that quarry. However the picture is not absolutely clear, as will be obvious from Figure 6.8, since some of the ellipses are rather large and some overlap: without additional information it would not be possible to say which of the pair (or more) of overlapping quarries was the true source. In practice when items of archaeological information, such as the date of the sculpture and its style, are taken into account, we can eliminate some quarries because they are not operational

6.7 *below* Marble horse from the Mausoleum at Halicarnassus, about 350 BC (GR s1002). Height 2.4 m. Identified as Pentelic marble by stable isotope analysis.

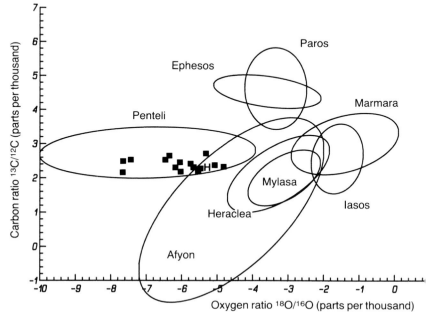

6.8 *above* Stable isotope analysis for carbon and oxygen of the marble sculptures from the Mausoleum at Halicarnassus, including the horse, denoted by H (fig. 6.7), superimposed on the data for Classical marble quarries. The ellipses represent 90 per cent confidence limits for the samples from the named quarries.

at that date or because we know the sculptors were working in certain places and it is highly improbable that they were using distant rather than local sources. Each case has to be considered on its merits where an ambiguous answer emerges from the stable isotope data.

In the last few years trace element analysis of the marble has been introduced as an additional aspect of characterisation. Because marble is ultra-pure calcium carbonate, the technique for trace analysis has to be very sensitive and instrumental neutron activation analysis has proved ideal for this.[24] Quarried blocks of marble and finished sculptures have been analysed by neutron activation and the results have been very encouraging. By a happy coincidence, those quarries which have proved difficult to separate by stable isotope analysis have very different trace element compositions, and some with very different stable isotopes are rather similar in trace elements. Several research groups have concluded that the combined use of visual examination of grain size, stable isotopic analysis and trace element analysis may successfully distinguish all the major quarries of the Mediterranean region.[25]

The application of stable isotopes to white marble is exemplified by the programme of analysis[26] of the sculptures from the Mausoleum at Halicarnassus dating to about 350 BC. (Halicarnassus, modern Bodrum, lies on a peninsula in south-western Turkey.) The Mausoleum was a major structure commissioned by the Mausolus dynasty, consisting of a white marble building surmounted by a series of large sculptured figures and with extensive use of decorative sculpted friezes in the architecture. It was an impressive monument and, as the local area lacks high-quality building or sculptural marble, the white marble used in its construction had to be imported. The aim of the project was to identify the types of marble used for specific functions and to associate unidentified fragments with known parts of the building. The most outstanding decorative element of the Mausoleum was the series of massive free-standing sculptures arranged high up on the podium of the monument, executed in fine marble. At the apex stood a chariot with a four-horse team: one of the horses is shown in Figure 6.7.

Samples from the horse were analysed, and the isotope results showed that quarries high up on Mount Pentelikon were the source, rather than the more numerous and better-known quarries at the foot of the mountain. Penteli was an important quarry near Athens in Greece and recent research has distinguished between the products of the upper and lower quarries. Two fragments of the chariot were also tested: one, a wheel, was also of Pentelic marble but the axle was of Ephesian marble (Ephesus was a major port on the west coast of Turkey, north of Halicarnassus). The impressive free-standing sculptures on the podium of the building were shown to be made of two types of Pentelic marble.

However, the marble used for the building came from these two sources. Analysis has shown that the figureheads are of Parian marble (from the Aegean island of Paros), a particularly fine-quality marble, which was expensive because it was mined from underground. However, the less important constructional blocks with carved decoration were from quarries in the Dokimeion-Iasos region of Turkey. Two different sources of marble within this same quarry group were exploited for the roof and the wall blocks. The overall picture which has emerged from the analyses is of more or less consisent use of the same marble quarry for the same elements of the monument, but that a variety of marble types were selected for different purposes. Finer grades (such as Parian or Pentelic) were used for the most important statuary, and lower-quality and more local marble, mainly from south-western Turkey, was used for the main architectural building blocks of the monument. The analyses have also shown much interesting detail: sub-groups have emerged when marble fragments have been found to have extremely similar isotope ratios, which suggests they came not only from the same quarry but from the same part of the quarry.

Metals

Finding the provenance of metal objects presents a more difficult problem for archaeological science. Unlike stone, flint or ceramics, the raw material has to undergo drastic changes before it is made into the finished artefact. Metals do not, with the exception of gold, a limited amount of copper, and meteoric iron, occur as the free metal in nature: they usually occur as metallic minerals which have to be smelted. The smelting process alters the chemical composition of the original ore so that there is usually no simple chemical correlation between ore and metal. Re-melting and alloying further complicate the situation.

However, there are occasions when the trace element pattern of a metal object bears some traces of the elements in the original ore. The trace elements in Sassanian silver provide one example,[27] copper from the Hartz mountains has a very distinctive pattern of high concentrations of arsenic, cobalt, nickel and antimony, and there are a significant number of similar studies. However, generally speaking, of the numerous ancient metallic artefacts still in existence, relatively few can be provenanced purely through elemental analysis.

Can any other approach help? In the early 1970s geological research highlighted the fact that lead ores carried distinctive isotope ratio 'signatures', depending upon the geological period when they were laid down as deposits. The discovery of the usefulness of lead isotope ratios was quickly applied to archaeology and has proved highly successful in provenancing lead-containing objects from antiquity. Research began on lead objects from the Roman era, lead ingots, and so on. But the technique was soon applied to objects which contain substantial amounts of lead, particular glazes and glasses rich in lead, such as enamels.[28] The search for other materials to analyse has now progressed to copper alloys. Heavily leaded bronzes are obvious candidates for analysis. However research has shown that even in copper objects containing no deliberately added lead, the small amounts of lead present in the original ore (and transferred to the finished metal during smelting) contain a 'signature' in lead isotope ratios of the *copper* ore body. The situation can be complicated if the metalworkers added small amounts of lead, or added pieces of scrap at the

6.9 Large Igbo-Ukwu roped vessel of leaded bronze in the form of a water pot (now in the National Museum of Nigeria, Lagos). Analysis of this unique vessel suggests it was made from local Nigerian copper. Height 320 mm.

casting stage, because the 'signature' of the lead will no longer be that of a single source and sorting this out seems well-nigh impossible.

One recent example is the research on the bronzes excavated in the 1950s at Igbo-Ukwu in south-eastern Nigeria and dated around the tenth century AD (fig. 6.9). These splendid and intricate bronze castings are enigmatic: they appear on the scene without apparent precursors and with no obvious descendants. This, the technical skills required to make them, and the apparent lack of copper resources in Nigeria have prompted many scholars to conclude that they were made away from sub-Saharan Africa, although no convincing stylistic links with other cultures, including those of the Mediterranean, have emerged.

Chemical analysis and technical study of these bronzes[29] have shown that they have an unusually high silver content (up to 1.2 per cent silver) which, by comparison with analyses of other ancient bronzes, suggests that one principal source of metal was involved. Considerable technical skills were needed to make the bronzes, but the metalworkers used a very small range of techniques. Thus, where one would expect a large basin to have been made from sheet metal, it was instead cast with walls of amazing thinness. (Such aspects also suggest technical isolation of the metalworkers.) Recently lead-zinc-copper deposits have been noted in the Benue Rift some 100 km from Igbo-Ukwu, raising the possibility of ancient exploitation of these local copper resources. For some of the bronzes, lead isotope ratios have now been obtained on lead extracted from the samples, and from two lead ore samples from the Benue Rift. This research showed that one group of bronzes had very similar lead isotope ratios to the Benue Rift ores, while others had isotope ratios which, although different to the ores, could result from Benue Rift material being mixed with another (and geologically younger) source. The Benue Rift deposits are spread out along 600 km, so they cannot yet be said to have been adequately characterised, but the technical, stylistic, compositional and lead isotope evidence now points to the Igbo-Ukwu bronzes originating within Nigeria.

Conclusion

This chapter has outlined the range of materials to which scientific techniques have been applied in order to discover a particular object's provenance. Even for the materials described here, all the combined scientific efforts have still only made comparatively small inroads into the accumulating list of unsolved questions. Other materials continue to present challenges to the scientist, including many of organic origin such as tars, waxes and oils. So far virtually only those organic materials with structures visible to the microscope (e.g. pollen) have received detailed attention. However, the range of scientific techniques will also grow, no doubt enabling us to provenance materials with greater speed and accuracy in the future.

Further reading

There are no books dealing exclusively with provenance studies, though the subject is mentioned by Tite, *Methods of Physical Examination in Archaeology* (1972). There are many papers on provenance studies in the proceedings of the International Archaeometry Conferences, the most recent being those edited by Olin and Blackman, *Proceedings of the 24th International Archaeometry Symposium* (1986) and Maniatis, *Archaeometry* (1990). For petrology applied to ceramics, see Peacock, *Pottery and Early Commerce* (1977) and Freestone *et al*, *Current Research in Ceramics: Thin Section Studies* (1982). For neutron activation, see the general textbook by De Soete *et al*, *Neutron Activation Analysis* (1972) and collections of papers in the conference proceedings edited by Olin and Blackman and Maniatis, cited above. Perlman, a pioneer of the technique in archaeology, has written a survey in *Archeological Chemistry III* (1984) pp. 117ff. For stone, see the two volumes by Clough and Cummins, *Stone Axe Studies 1 and 2*, Council for British Archaeological Research Reports 23 and 67 (1979 and 1988). For flint, see G. de G. Sieveking and M. Hart, eds., *The Scientific Study of Flint and Chert* (1986). For marble, see Herz and Waelkens, *Classical Marble: Geochemistry, Technology and Trade* (1988). For lead isotope studies, see the recent survey by N. Gale in J. Henderson, ed., *Scientific Analysis in Archaeology* (1989).

References

1. A. Caiger-Smith, 1973. *Tin-Glaze Pottery in Europe and the Islamic World*. London, Faber & Faber. A. Caiger-Smith, 1985. *Lustre Pottery*. London, Faber & Faber.

2. J.G. Hurst, D.S. Neal and H.J.E. van Beuningen, 1986. *Pottery Produced and Traded in north-west Europe 1350–1650*, Rotterdam Papers VI. Rotterdam, Museum Boymans-van Beuningen.

3. T. Wilson, 1987. *Ceramic Art of the Italian Renaissance*. London, British Museum Publications.

4. G. Harbottle, 1982. 'Provenience studies using neutron activation analysis: the role of standardisation'. In *Archaeological Ceramics*, eds. J.S. Olin and A.D. Franklin, pp. 67–77. Washington DC, Smithsonian Institution Press.

5. J.P. Bushe-Fox, 1915. *Excavations at Hengistbury Head, Hampshire in 1911–12*. Reports of the Research Committee of the Society of Antiquaries of London No. III, London.

6. B. Cunliffe, 1978. *Hengistbury Head*. London, Paul Elek. B. Cunliffe, 1987. *Hengistbury Head, Dorset Volume 1: The Prehistoric and Roman settlement 3500 BC–AD 500*, Oxford University Committee for Archaeology Monograph no. 13, Oxford.

7. J.S. Olin and M.J. Blackman, 1986. *Proceedings of the Archaeometry Symposium, Washington 1984*. Washington DC, Smithsonian Institution Press. Y. Maniatis, 1989. *Archaeometry: Proceedings of the 25th International Symposium (Athens, May 1986)*. Amsterdam, Elsevier. M.J. Hughes, M.R. Cowell and D.R. Hook (forthcoming). 'Neutron activation analysis procedure at the British Museum Research Laboratory'. In *Neutron Activation and Plasma Emission Spectrometric Analysis in Archaeology*, eds. M.J. Hughes, M.R. Cowell and D.R. Hook, British Museum Occasional Paper, London.

8. P.L. Main, and M.J. Hughes, 1983. 'Using a Hewlett-Packard minicomputer for the processing of gamma-ray spectra from neutron activation analysis'. *Computer Enhanced Spectroscopy* 1, pp. 17–24.

9. F.C. Lister and R.H. Lister, 1987. *Andalusian Ceramics in Spain and New Spain – a Cultural Register from the Third Century BC to 1700*. Tucson, University of Arizona Press.

10. A. Frothingham, 1951. *Lustreware of Spain*. New York, Hispanic Society of America.

11. J. Hurst, 1977. 'Spanish pottery imported into Medieval Britain'. *Medieval Archaeology* 21, pp. 68–105.

12. M.J. Hughes and A. Vince, 1986. 'Neutron activation analysis and petrology of Hispano-Moresque pottery'. In *Proceedings of the Archaeometry Symposium, Washington 1984*, eds. J.S. Olin and M.J. Blackman, pp. 353–67. Washington DC, Smithsonian Institution Press.

13. D. Wishart, 1978, 1982. *CLUSTAN User Manual Version 1C release 2 and Supplement*. Program Library Unit, University of Edinburgh.

14. M.J. Hughes, 1991. 'Provenance studies on Italian maiolica by neutron activation analysis'. In *Italian Renaissance Pottery*, ed. T. Wilson. London, British Museum Publications.

15. A. Ray, 1991. 'Francisco Niculoso called Pisano'. In *Italian Renaissance Pottery*, ed. T. Wilson. London, British Museum Publications.

16. M.J. Hughes, 1989. 'Studio sul metodo di analisi per irradiazione neutronica su ceramiche di Castelli/Neutron activation analysis study of maiolica from Castelli'. In *Le Maioliche Cinquecentesche di Castelli*. Carsa Edizioni, pp. 183–4 (Italian, and English translation).

17. T.H. McK. Clough and W.A. Cummins, 1979. *Stone Axe Studies*, Council for British Archaeology Research Report no. 23. London, CBA. T.H. McK. Clough and W.A. Cummins, 1988. *Stone Axe Studies volume 2*: The petrology of prehistoric stone implements from British Isles, CBA Research Report no. 67. London, CBA.

18. P.T. Craddock, M.R. Cowell, M.N. Leese and M.J. Hughes, 1983. 'The trace element composition of polished flint axes as an indicator of source'. *Archaeometry* 25 (2), pp. 135–63. G. de G. Sieveking, P. Bush, J. Ferguson, P.T. Craddock, M.J. Hughes and M.R. Cowell, 1972. 'Prehistoric flint mines and their identification as sources of raw material'. *Archaeometry* 14, pp. 151–76.

19. A. Aspinall and S.W. Feather, 1972. 'Neutron activation analysis of prehistoric flint mine products'. *Archaeometry* 14 (1), pp. 41–53.

20. M. Thompson, P. Bush, and J. Ferguson, 1986. 'The analysis of flint by inductively coupled plasma atomic emission spectrophotometry as a method of source

determination'. In *The scientific study of flint and chert, Proceedings of the 4th International Flint Symposium, Brighton, 1983*, eds. G. de G. Sieveking and M.B. Hart, pp. 243–7. Cambridge University Press.

21. G. de G. Sieveking, 1979. 'Grimes Graves and prehistoric European flint mining'. In *Subterranean Britain: Aspects of Underground Archaeology*, ed. Harriet Crawford, pp. 1–43. London, John Baker.

22. H. Craig and V. Craig, 1972. 'Greek marbles: determination of provenance by isotopic analysis'. *Science* 176, pp. 401–3.

23. S. Walker, 1984. 'Marble origins by isotopic analysis'. *World Archaeology* 16 (2), pp. 204–21. J. Clayton Fant (ed.), 1988. *Ancient Marble Quarrying and Trade*, British Archaeological Reports International Series 453. Oxford.

24. L. Moens, P. Roos, J. De Rudder, P. De Paepe, J. van Hende and M. Waelkens, 1988. 'A multi-method approach to the identification of white marbles used in antique artefacts'. In *Classical Marble: Geochemistry, Technology and Trade*, eds. N. Herz and M. Waelkens. NATO Advanced Science Institute Series E: Applied Sciences vol. 153. Dordrecht, Boston and London, Kluwer.

25. N. Herz and M. Waelkens (eds.), 1988. *Classical Marble: Geochemistry, Technology and Trade*, NATO Advanced Science Institute Series E: Applied Sciences vol. 153. Dordrecht, Boston and London, Kluwer.

26. S. Walker and K. Matthews, 1988. 'Recent work in stable isotope analysis of white marble at the British Museum'. In *Ancient Marble Quarrying and Trade*, ed. J.C. Fant, pp. 117–25. British Archaeological Reports International Series 453. Oxford.

27. P.O. Harper and M. Meyers, 1981. *Silver Vessels of the Sasanian Period*. New York, Metropolitan Museum of Art.

28. I.L. Barnes, R.H. Brill, E.C. Deal and G.V. Piercy, 1986. 'Lead isotope studies of some of the finds from the Serce Liman shipwreck'. In *Proceedings of the 24th International Archaeometry Symposium*, eds. J.S. Olin and M.J. Blackman, pp. 1–12. Washington DC, Smithsonian Institution Press.

29. V.E. Chikwendu, P.T. Craddock, R.M. Farquhar, Thurstan Shaw and A.C. Umeji, 1989. 'Nigerian sources of copper, lead and tin for the Igbo-Ukwu bronzes'. *Archaeometry* 31 (3), pp. 27–36.

CHAPTER 7

Questions of Chronology

Sheridan Bowman

Most people wear watches, some keep diaries: we continually monitor the passage of time and keep records of the sequence of events. Public buildings such as libraries house less personal records in the form of newspapers, parliamentary accounts and other documents. We live in a historical period; written records are kept and we tend to assume that our records are correct and that we can accurately reconstruct the events of the past. However, historical documents are not always true records of the past. For example the so-called 'Dark Age' of European history, following the decline of the Roman Empire, has a dearth of written records, and those that do survive are questionable. In Britain, for instance, unravelling any facts from the many legends associated with King Arthur[1] is no easy task. In this case it is open to question whether the authors of the limited number of extant documents were writing about contemporary events or were recording what they believed to have happened, based on oral tradition. Indeed, the documents themselves could have been transcribed many times through the ages. Inevitably scribes would have corrected what they perceived to be 'mistakes' and undoubtedly the story would also have been embellished on occasion.

Nor were records necessarily kept with the intention of providing a precise calendar of events. For example, the tens of thousands of cuneiform tablets found at Kanesh (modern Kültepe in Turkey) are largely monetary accounts (lists of goods transported and letters regarding merchandise). It is obviously difficult to infer the chronological framework of a town from its stocklists alone.

If history is potentially unreliable and incomplete, what of the prehistoric period for which we have no written records at all? Here archaeology is usually the sole source of information. As in geology, the ordering of the strata (layers) of sediment on an archaeological site provides us with a relative dating technique. A layer high in the sequence will have been deposited later than a lower one, and, provided there has been no disturbance, the artefacts in the higher level will be younger than those underlying. But how much younger, and how do the artefacts on one site relate temporally to those on another? Similarity of style could suggest similar age, but dissimilarity does not necessarily imply the opposite. The style of an artefact does not inherently tell us its age – independent dating techniques are required.

Dating techniques are many and varied, with similarly diverse applications.[2] Some are based upon the effects of seasonal change and are therefore directly related to the orbit of the earth about the sun, which provides us with a useful unit of time, the year. Dendrochronology, varves and ice core dating are such techniques, based respectively on the annual formation of tree rings, lake sediment layers and polar ice-cap layers. Each ring or layer must be differentiable from the adjacent ones and be formed annually. Thus tree rings are differentiated by the types, density and size of cell laid down at different times of the year; varves by the gradation in particle size resulting from sedimentation of debris released into rivers and carried to lakes by the annual melt of glaciers; and ice core layers by differences in dust content and acidity. Dendrochronology is the most directly useful for dating archaeological sites, but, perhaps surprisingly, even polar ice core dating can occasionally be very useful. Ice cores record events, such as major volcanic eruptions, which affect global dust and acidity levels. Thus they have provided evidence that helps to date the eruption of Thera (modern Santorini) which virtually destroyed the Minoan town of Akrotiri in the seventeenth century BC.[3]

Less frequent rhythms in the earth's orbit produce more dramatic climatic changes and form the basis of some of the relative dating techniques. Thus evidence of glacial and interglacial periods, such as the type of flora and fauna present, can sometimes be used to assign a sequence to events, but, as with any relative dating technique, events are only set in order. To assign them to a calendar scale and determine the sizes of the intervals between them requires absolute dating methods, such as those described above or those based on radioactive decay.

A radioactive isotope of a specific element decays in a defined way (see fig. 7.1). Knowing how much was there to start with and how much remains determines how much time has passed. The simplest radioactive methods are based on decay of a radioactive isotope into a stable one. Radiocarbon and potassium-argon dating fall into this category. In the former, to a first approximation, the initial amount of radiocarbon in an organic sample is taken to be that in the atmosphere now, but many adjustments are made to this assumption as will be seen below. In potassium-argon dating of volcanic rocks, the radioactive potassium isotope is in a known proportion to the non-radioactive one and decays to argon. The radioactive potassium has a very long half-life (1250 million years) so that the amount lost is extremely small relative to the total amount of potassium present and cannot be measured. However, argon, being a gas, is at zero concentration when the rock solidifies from the molten state, so the amount of argon produced is measured.

Some radioactive methods, like uranium series dating, involve a chain of decay: one radioactive element decays into another which in turn decays. Uranium series dating is particularly used for dating stalagmitic calcite. When the calcite forms it incorporates uranium dissolved in the ground water. The various decay products in the uranium chain are not present as they are not soluble in water, but they build up in a defined way, according to the decay rates of the individual isotopes in the chain.

From this brief summary of a small proportion of the scientific dating techniques, some common principles of their application emerge. The

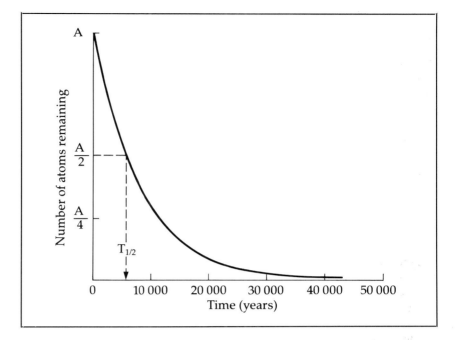

7.1 In radioactive decay, after each half-life ($T_{\frac{1}{2}}$) the number of atoms remaining is halved: if there are A to begin with, after one half-life there will be $\frac{A}{2}$ atoms remaining; after two half-lives, $\frac{A}{4}$ remain; after three, $\frac{A}{8}$, and so on. The time axis shown is for radiocarbon.

dating method itself must have a definable 'zero time point': for example, the tree ring formed this year in dendrochronology; the solidification of a volcanic rock in potassium-argon dating; or the formation of a calcite layer for uranium series. This definable zero-point must have some relevance to the archaeological site being dated: potassium-argon dating of a piece of volcanic rock will date the formation of the rock, but it does not necessarily provide any useful information for the archaeologist; the rock may simply be part of the geological environment of the site. On the other hand, if archaeological finds are sandwiched between two volcanic rock layers, then the dates for them will bracket the date of the archaeology. Whether upper and lower date limits (*terminus* results) such as these provide the archaeologist with a sufficiently detailed chronological picture will depend on a number of factors – the nature of the site and sequence to be interpreted, the archaeological questions being posed, and the samples available for dating – and the relevant dating methods would then need to be assessed.

As the general reading list at the end of this chapter testifies, a whole book could be written on any one of the scientific dating techniques, so selectivity must be exercised when covering the subject in a single chapter. Only radiocarbon and thermoluminescence, the techniques which the British Museum has 'in house', will be discussed in any detail. But this is not simply a parochial choice. Radiocarbon was developed forty years ago and is still the scientific dating method most commonly used by archaeologists. Thermoluminescence is a complementary technique in the material and date range to which it is applicable; it also enables the authenticity of ceramics to be tested. Any mention of radiocarbon dating necessarily involves at least a reference to dendrochronology, and the basic principles of this powerful technique are therefore also outlined (see p. 125).

Radiocarbon dating

Basic principles

Radiocarbon dating[4] is based on carbon – a common yet remarkable element. Together with hydrogen, it is a component of all organic compounds and is fundamental to life. Carbon has three naturally occurring isotopes, that is, atoms of the same atomic number but different atomic weights. These are designated ^{12}C, ^{13}C and ^{14}C in scientific notation, the letter C being the symbol for elemental carbon and the isotopes having atomic weights 12, 13 and 14 respectively. They do not occur equally; modern carbon consists of 99 per cent of ^{12}C and 1 per cent of ^{13}C, whereas ^{14}C is present at the level of only one part in a million million. Unlike ^{12}C and ^{13}C, ^{14}C is unstable and therefore radioactive; hence the name 'radiocarbon' is used for this isotope which, because of its scientific designation, is also called 'carbon fourteen'. Both here and in Chapter 8, the scientific notation (^{14}C) will be used when referring to the isotope itself, and the word 'radiocarbon' when discussing the dating technique generally.

The rather unusual characteristic of ^{14}C is that it is continually being formed. This occurs in the upper atmosphere when neutrons produced by cosmic rays interact with nitrogen atoms. As soon as they are formed, the ^{14}C atoms rapidly combine with oxygen to form carbon dioxide which is chemically indistinguishable from carbon dioxide containing either of the other carbon isotopes. This carbon dioxide mixes throughout the atmosphere, dissolves in the oceans and, via the photosynthesis process and the food chain, enters all plant and animal life known collectively as the biosphere. Under certain circumstances, in particular if the production rate is constant, there is a balance between formation and decay, and the ^{14}C concentration in the atmosphere therefore remains constant. Thus, in principle, all living organisms have the same level of ^{14}C relative to ^{12}C.

When a plant or animal dies it ceases to participate in carbon exchange with the biosphere and no longer takes in ^{14}C. If ^{14}C were stable, its concentration relative to ^{12}C would remain constant after death, but, since it is not, the level falls at a rate determined by the radioactive decay law. This law states that the number of atoms of a radioactive element is halved after a given amount of time has elapsed. This amount of time is naturally enough called the half-life ($T_{\frac{1}{2}}$). The relationship between the number of atoms remaining and time is shown in Figure 7.1. In principle, therefore, if the concentration of ^{14}C atoms remaining and the initial, or equilibrium, concentration can be evaluated by experiment, then one can determine the amount of time which has elapsed since death. For ^{14}C, the best estimate of $T_{\frac{1}{2}}$ is 5730 years.

In general, the materials which can be dated by radiocarbon are those which once formed part of the biosphere, and hence are organic. For example, the most commonly preserved sample types occurring on British sites are bone, shell and charcoal, but on some sites – or in other areas of the world – a different range of materials might remain. Wood and other plant remains such as ropes, cloth, reeds and seeds may be well preserved in arid environments or if waterlogged. Many other materials, such as antler, horn, tooth, ivory, hair, blood residues, wool, silk, leather, paper, parchment, insects and coral, are also datable by radiocarbon.

The principles of radiocarbon dating are fairly straightforward, but in practice there are many problems. One fundamental assumption is that the atmosphere has had the same ^{14}C concentration in the past as now, and this in turn assumes, amongst other things, that the production rate of ^{14}C has remained constant. In fact there have been considerable variations in the atmospheric ^{14}C production rate. Radiocarbon results cannot therefore give a true measure of age and we need some method by which to convert them to calendar dates: this is the process of calibration (see p. 124).

Nor can it be assumed that all parts of the biosphere have the same ^{14}C concentration. Firstly, in any biological pathway, differential uptake (fractionation) of the lighter isotopes of carbon occurs. In addition, some of the carbon available to an organism may come from a source that is not in equilibrium with the atmosphere; the problems caused by this are called the 'reservoir effects'. For example, carbon in fresh water can have a variety of sources, including atmospheric carbon dioxide, but also soil humic material and limestone (calcium carbonate). Thus freshwater shells and aquatic plants may not give true radiocarbon ages (see also fig. 7.2). Whereas fractionation can be accurately corrected for, reservoir effects cannot.

Another factor is whether or not the death of a plant or animal necessarily coincided with the point at which it ceased to exchange carbon with the environment. The outstanding example of radiocarbon age at 'death' (or more usually felling) is wood. It is well known that trees grow by the addition of rings, usually (though not always) annually. Once formed, rings soon cease to exchange with the biosphere. Hence, if one considers a long-lived tree, say a three-hundred-year-old oak, the innermost heartwood will give a radiocarbon result three hundred years older than the sapwood. Indeed, this is as it should be. However, if part of that heartwood were found on an archaeological site, the radiocarbon result would not provide the date of usage of the wood, but rather a date three hundred radiocarbon years earlier, and more if it has been seasoned before use or re-used. This is the 'old wood effect'.

7.2 Whalebone plaque dated to 1480 ± 80 BP (see p. 122); however, the whale could have had an apparent radiocarbon 'age' at death of several centuries (MLA 1987.10–5.1; OxA-1164). Height 320 mm. Marine environments show a reservoir effect due to slow mixing of carbon through ocean waters and upwelling of deep ocean water depleted in ^{14}C.

Measuring radiocarbon

Once a sample is accepted for dating, the first task in the laboratory is to remove any likely sources of carbon contamination, such as carbonates and humic acids from the burial environment. After this pretreatment, the sample is converted to a form suitable for the particular method of radiocarbon dating to be used.

These methods for detecting ^{14}C are based on two fundamentally different principles. The nucleus of a ^{14}C atom is unstable so there is a finite probability at any instant in time that it will decay. When it does, it reverts to nitrogen (^{14}N) and a beta particle is emitted. Because it is electrically charged, the beta particle can be detected fairly easily. This is the basis of conventional radiocarbon dating.

A more efficient method for detecting ^{14}C is to measure the number of atoms present, or a proportion of them, by mass spectrometry. In a magnetic field, a moving charged particle is deflected from the straight path along which it was travelling. When charged particles are travelling at the same velocity, and are subject to the same magnetic field, the heavier particles are deflected the least. Detectors at different angles of deflection then receive particles of different mass. However, normal mass spectrometers are not sensitive enough to detect ^{14}C and to reject all other elements or molecules of very nearly the same weight, such as ^{14}N. As this nitrogen isotope makes up some 80 per cent of the atmosphere it is very common relative to ^{14}C. The techniques of nuclear physics were brought to bear on this problem in the late 1970s, and it was shown that ^{14}C could be detected using what is now referred to as accelerator mass spectrometry, AMS. In AMS the charged particles are subjected to large voltage differences so that they travel at very high speeds. This enables various devices to be used in order to discriminate against the much more abundant elements and molecules which would otherwise swamp the ^{14}C signal.

The disadvantage of AMS is the high cost of establishing such a facility (around a million pounds sterling, nearly two million dollars) and of running it. Its great advantage over conventional techniques is the small sample size needed: typically 1000 times smaller. Most conventional radiocarbon laboratories require a sample that will yield about 5 g of carbon. This is equivalent to about 10 g of charcoal, 50 g of wood or 200 g of bone, but depends on the state of preservation of the sample and degree of sample pretreatment to be undertaken. Small objects (fig. 7.3) that would have been totally destroyed if dated by conventional ^{14}C can now be sampled for AMS,[5] and the benefits in dating art objects are obvious. Likewise in archaeology AMS has enabled us to date samples as minute as individual seeds, which can tell us a great deal about the origins of agriculture and the domestication of cereals.

Whatever the technique, radiocarbon results are given in uncalibrated years BP, where 0 BP is defined as AD 1950 and the half-life used to calculate a radiocarbon result is not the more accurate value of 5730, but the Libby half-life of 5568 years (named after Willard Libby, the founder of the technique). Use of the wrong half-life is automatically taken care of in the

7.3 Horse mandible from Kendrick's Cave[5] (Great Orme's Head, Llandudno, Wales), AMS dated to the late Upper Palaeolithic or very early Mesolithic (PRB 1959.12–3.1). If dated by conventional radiocarbon, it would have been totally destroyed during measurement. It is one of the few examples of mobiliary art of the period from Britain.

calibration of a conventionally calculated date. In addition to determining the radiocarbon 'age', the laboratory must estimate the uncertainty on the experimental measurement. For radiocarbon 'ages' below about 10,000 years, the error term is typically ± 50–100 years (at the 68 per cent confidence level: see glossary). High-precision laboratories can produce results with error terms of less than ± 20 years; they employ very carefully controlled measurement procedures, but they also require samples three to four times the size of those used by normal-precision, conventional laboratories.

In conventional radiocarbon dating the maximum age that can be measured is determined by the count rate, additional to that from ^{14}C, caused by radiation in the environment. It therefore varies from laboratory to laboratory, but is typically in the region of 40,000 years. For AMS, the upper age limit is determined by other factors such as machine stability and the degree of modern contamination introduced in the processing of very small samples; the values tend to be similar to those for conventional radiocarbon laboratories. The lower limit for both techniques is determined by the mutual interference of the fossil fuel and bomb effects. In the early half of the twentieth century, the burning of fossil fuel such as coal, in which the ^{14}C had totally decayed away, diluted the atmospheric ^{14}C concentration relative to ^{13}C and ^{12}C. Nuclear weapons testing had an even more dramatic effect on atmospheric ^{14}C content. The neutrons thereby produced in turn produced ^{14}C by interaction with ^{14}N. This simulated natural cosmogenic production, albeit in large bursts, and roughly doubled the atmospheric ^{14}C content as measured in about 1965. Radiocarbon results of less than two hundred years are therefore usually described as 'modern'.

123

Calibration of radiocarbon results

The existence of radiocarbon in nature was predicted before it was detected, and this prediction was sufficient for an American scientist called Willard Libby[6] to perceive the basis of a dating method. The theoretical aspects were formulated in the mid-1940s and the first dates were published in December 1949. During the 1950s, with advances in techniques for detecting ^{14}C, discrepancies of several centuries began to emerge between radiocarbon ages and historical ages for the Egyptian Old Kingdom. Of course, the validity of the historical ages was not proven beyond doubt, but it was realised that tree rings could provide the truly 'known-age' material needed to test the accuracy of the new technique. The radiocarbon discrepancy was confirmed and it became clear that radiocarbon results would need to be calibrated to convert them to calendar ages. Since there is no theoretical way of predicting the correction factor, empirical calibration curves were needed to link radiocarbon 'age' with known age.

In the 1960s, a continuous tree-ring sequence stretching back some eight thousand years was established by Wesley Ferguson, an American dendrochronologist. The first calibration curve using this was published by an American scientist, Hans Suess. High-precision calibration curves[7] now exist which confirm the two features apparent in Suess's curve. First there is a long-term trend caused by fluctuations in the earth's magnetic field strength. This trend has a maximum deviation from true age of about nine hundred years too recent at the beginning of the fourth millennium BC. On the other hand, in the middle of the first millennium AD, radiocarbon produces 'ages' that are too old by a century or so (fig. 7.4).[8] The second

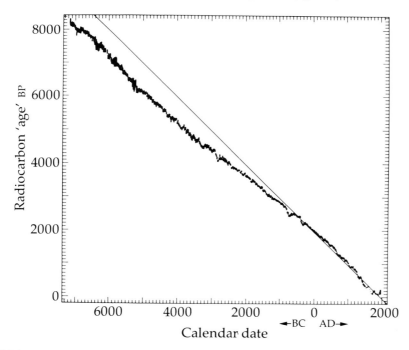

7.4 High-precision radiocarbon calibration curve based on Irish oak[8] (courtesy Gordon Pearson).

feature takes the form of 'wiggles'. These are superimposed on the main curve, and only last a few decades, but can have deviations on the radio-carbon axis of a century or so (fig. 7.5). They are probably produced by variations in sunspot activity.

Any variations in production of ^{14}C are rapidly distributed throughout the atmosphere, so a calibration curve of radiocarbon 'age' versus calendar age for one material and one geographical region will serve as a global calibration curve. Once the calendar timescale has been produced using dendrochronology, groups of ten or twenty tree rings are dated by radio-carbon to provide the y-axis of the calibration curve.

The basis of dendrochronology[9] lies in the fact that, in temperature climates where there is a contrast between the seasons, trees grow by the addition of an annual ring. The growth region is a thin band of cells called the cambium, which lies between the bark and the sapwood. Division of these cells adds new bark to the outer side of the cambium and new sapwood to the inside. The well-defined rings (fig. 7.6) are due to the difference in the cells produced at different times of the year. For some species, the width of each ring depends on prevailing climatic conditions, such as temperature and rainfall. Thus, for a living tree, counting back-wards from the cambium layer gives the age of a particular ring, and its relative thickness indicates whether the growing season was good or bad in that year and locality. Trees of a single species growing in the same locality should have a similar pattern of ring widths, uniquely defined by their common history. This is the basis of cross-dating: being able to associate a tree-ring sequence of unknown age with one of known age by matching one pattern with another. Long chronologies ('master curves')

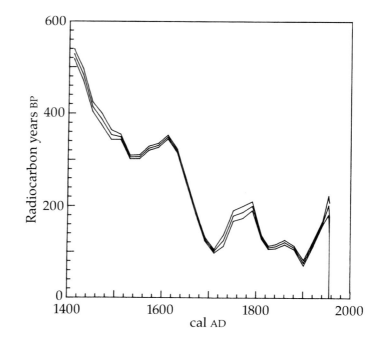

7.5 Section of Stuiver and Pearson's high-precision calibration curve[7] for the recent past (courtesy of the authors). The highest and lowest lines show the error term on the curve (centre line) at each point. Large wiggles mean that a single radiocarbon result can correspond to more than one calendar result (see fig. 7.8); distinguishing between the different calendar possibilities cannot then be achieved by radiocarbon alone.

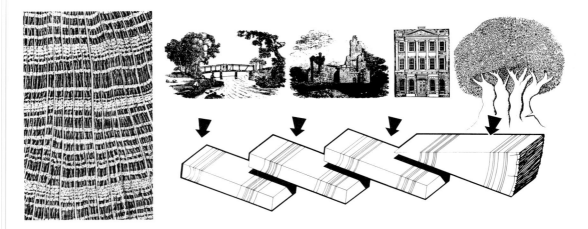

are established starting with living trees, or timbers where the 'zero age' ring is present and the year of felling known (fig. 7.7). The timescale is then extended by using large felled timbers with patterns sufficiently overlapping the existing chronology to be certain of a unique match. In dendrochronology the timescale of the master chronology is accurate to within one year. It is therefore a very powerful dating technique making it possible to date the right archaeological samples (see p. 144) to the year of felling, as well as providing the accurate calendar timescale necessary for radiocarbon calibration.

In converting radiocarbon results to calendar dates, the wiggles in the calibration curve are the real problem. One consequence is that calibrated dates are not central dates with an error term, but a range or ranges of dates. In fact, there is currently no consensus on exactly how to calibrate a radiocarbon result. Essentially there are two approaches: the intercept and probability methods. A brief description of the intercept method should provide a flavour of what happens when a radiocarbon result is calibrated. As shown in Figure 7.8, the calendar dates corresponding to $t + \sigma$ and $t - \sigma$ are found (where t is the radiocarbon result and σ is the error term, which includes the laboratory's estimate of the experimental error on the result and the error on the calibration curve, combined statistically).[10] Using the values $t + \sigma$ and $t - \sigma$ gives 68 per cent confidence ranges (see glossary); for 95 per cent confidence, $t + 2\sigma$ and $t - 2\sigma$ must be used. If the calibration curve is 'wiggly', there will be multiple ranges. Note also the increased size of the calibrated range relative to the uncalibrated one where the slope of the curve is effectively less than 45 degrees, and the decreased size where the slope is steep. It must not be assumed that the most likely date is in the centre of the range; to quantify the distribution of the calendar dates, one of the probability methods[11] (which require computerisation) must be used.

Although calibration complicates the process of interpreting the radiocarbon results, it is essential. There are several periods in the calibration curve where events that are separated in calendar time by several centuries appear approximately contemporaneous from their radiocarbon results.

7.6 *above left* Polished section of the trunk of an oak showing the well-defined rings (courtesy Jonathan Pilcher).

7.7 *above* In dendrochronology a master curve is produced, starting with a living tree and extending the timescale using timbers with overlapping patterns (courtesy Ulster Museum, Belfast).

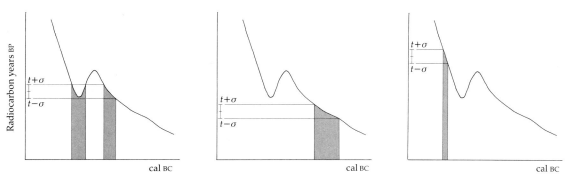

7.8 The intercept method of calibration: the calibration curve is shown schematically without its error limits; these are incorporated in the overall error, σ. Note the effect of the shape of the curve on the size of the calibrated date range; more than one range is possible.

The worst of these is for the period corresponding to the British Early Iron Age (*c.*800–400 BC). There are also periods where the curve is so steep that apparently large differences in radiocarbon results arise from events separated by relatively small amounts of real time. Only after calibration can we begin to assess the true temporal relationship of events dated by radiocarbon.

To distinguish calibrated dates from true historical dates, the conventions cal BC, cal AD and cal BP (where 0 BP is AD 1950) are used.

Using radiocarbon dating

When radiocarbon dating was developed and first used in the late 1940s and 1950s, the complexities of the technique were not fully appreciated. For the best results in a given situation, archaeologists and radiocarbon scientists must work together, from the planning of a sampling strategy to the interpretation of the results. As we have seen, the interpretation is complicated by the need for calibration, and the involvement of statisticians is increasingly valuable.

Once the archaeological problem has been formulated, whether or not radiocarbon can be used to resolve issues of chronology will depend on a number of factors, such as the type of samples available, the nature of the contexts and events to be dated and the likely age range once the radiocarbon results are calibrated. The interplay of these factors is illustrated by the following case studies.

● *British Beaker chronology*

The second half of the third millennium BC saw the introduction of the first metalworking into Britain. This very early phase of the Bronze Age was also marked by the appearance of a distinctive ceramic form called the Beaker, which also lends its name to this period of transition from the Neolithic to the Early Bronze Age. Beaker pottery is characterised by often skilfully made vessels with an S-shaped profile and zones of geometric decoration produced by impressing twisted cords, stamps or combs into the clay. Much time would have been invested in making these fine vessels, and many were apparently viewed as prestige items fit to be placed with burials of the period (fig. 7.9). Often only a Beaker accompanies the body, but occasionally other grave goods occur, such as copper-alloy knives, archers' wristguards of stone and, in some instances, even personal ornaments made of gold.

Beaker pottery is very widespread in Europe and there is little doubt that the style was initially introduced to Britain from the Continent. However, the chronological development of Beaker styles and the possibility of further Continental influence were open to conjecture. Through past study a broadly accepted relative chronology for Beaker pottery had been developed.[12] This was based on classification of the proportions of the bodies of the vessels and the decorative motifs employed. Until recently, there were few radiocarbon results for material directly associated with Beaker pottery. Furthermore, of these few results, a substantial number were for charcoal, with all the attendant problems of possible age offset due to 'old wood' (see p. 121). Hence neither the relative nor the existing absolute dates were totally satisfactory.

To remedy this situation, the British Museum initiated a research programme of radiocarbon dating. The aim was to locate forty to fifty samples well associated with Beaker pottery in a variety of styles. The obvious choice of sample was the skeletal material in the Beaker burials themselves, because for bone there is no time delay between death and cessation of ^{14}C exchange with the biosphere. Also, the association is good between sample and context (bone and grave), and between context and event to be dated (grave and the act of burial). The theoretical basis of the project was

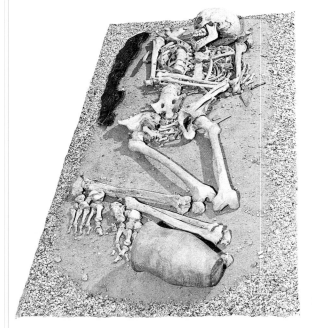

7.9   Beaker period burial from Barnack, Cambridgeshire. Here the body is accompanied by a Beaker, a copper dagger, an archer's wrist guard and other items.

therefore straightforward, but in practice it proved significantly less so. Museums and archaeological collections throughout Britain were contacted and, although many were willing to help by providing samples for dating, problems emerged. Much of our knowledge of Beaker burials derives from excavations conducted in the last century, when the principles of good archaeological practice were only just beginning to be formulated. Where bone from burials had been retained, the frequent lack of adequate documentation made it impossible to associate definitively one particular skeleton with a given Beaker pot. Many frustrating searches and months later, the total number of samples collected was only twenty-eight and, worse still, nearly half of these had to be rejected, either because of carbon contamination introduced during conservation treatments, or because the sample was too small to give a reasonably precise result. Fortunately, samples from recent excavations have subsequently become available, and the project[13] has now produced twenty radiocarbon results: more than doubling the previous total for actual skeletons from British Beaker burials.

What of the results? As always, the need to calibrate the radiocarbon 'dates' means that normal statistical tests cannot be applied. It is therefore impossible to test statistically whether samples associated with a particular type of Beaker pot are earlier or later than those linked to another. However, graphical plots of the date ranges show no clear chronological pattern. The foundation of many theories of Beaker pottery development and the effects of Continental influence must therefore be re-examined.

● *Early mining in Wales*

Trying to be highly selective in the type of sample submitted for radiocarbon dating can be very frustrating, as illustrated by the Beaker project outlined above. It is nevertheless essential in the majority of situations where there is a specific question on the chronology requiring an accurate and reasonably precise answer. Not all contexts allow such careful choice, however, and it has to be decided whether a set of radiocarbon results using less than ideal samples provides better dating evidence than the archaeology alone. One such case is the search for evidence of early mining in Britain. Much is known about the metal artefacts produced in the British Bronze Age, but until recently very little was known of the copper sources exploited (see Chapter 4).

Mines have very few chronologically distinctive features. Unlike habitation sites, they have little domestic refuse and, unlike cemetery sites, they do not normally contain burials. Consequently, there are rarely any really diagnostic ceramic or metal artefacts that can provide any clue as to their age. On the other hand, there are two recurring characteristics of certain copper mines: the use of firesetting and pebble-stone hammers. Some would argue that these provide clear evidence of prehistoric exploitation, whilst others see them as highly practical, and therefore long-lived, mining methods. The problem boils down to a lack of independent dating evidence. Like other debris, there is a limited amount of organic refuse suitable for radiocarbon dating, and what there is tends to be charcoal from mature oak. Although the wood is presumed to have been used for firesetting, the association between mining activity and the sample is rarely certain. Thus, when there were only one or two dates for supposedly early mine sites, their relevance had to be interpreted with care. Now, however, for Welsh copper mine sites alone there are fifteen radiocarbon results,[14] all of which calibrate to the Early or Middle Bronze Age; such a body of evidence cannot be chance. Thus the long and laborious process of collecting anything that might conceivably be datable has paid dividends, placing several Bronze Age mines firmly on the map.

Thermoluminescence dating

Basic principles

The principles of thermoluminescence (TL) dating[15] are reasonably straightforward, but the details of the TL mechanism are not fully understood – even by solid state physicists! The principles of TL dating are here outlined for pottery, for which it was first developed; its extension to other materials is discussed later.

Thermoluminescence is a property of crystalline materials, such as quartz and feldspars, which are found in pottery. These minerals receive radiation both internally, from the ceramic, and externally, from the burial environment and cosmic rays. The ceramic and soil contain minute quantities of uranium, thorium and potassium which are radioactive, and when these decay they produce alpha, beta and gamma radiation (potassium contributes only to the beta and gamma components). These radioactive elements have very long half-lives, so the flux of radiation is effectively constant for the archaeological periods of interest in TL dating. Alpha, beta and gamma radiation, together with cosmic rays, are referred to as ionising radiation because they interact with atoms, removing electrons from them, and the atoms then became ions. In this way the radiation loses energy, which is imparted to the electrons of the material. The amount of energy lost to the material per unit weight is referred to as the 'radiation dose'. When minerals such as quartz and feldspars have received a radiation dose and are then heated, they emit light. This is thermoluminescence ('heat-light'); it is produced because of the radiation dose, and is additional to any red-hot glow produced by heat alone.

Thermoluminescence is emitted because crystal lattices contain defects, and electrons produced by the ionising radiation may become trapped at one type of defect (a 'trap'). This is only one of the things that can happen to the electrons, but it is the one which is of interest in the production of TL. Depending on the nature of the defect, electrons may remain trapped for long periods of time; such a trap would be referred to as 'deep'. If heat is applied, the electron may be able to escape from the deep trap. Again, however, many things can then happen to it; if it is to produce TL, the electron must recombine with another type of defect, and the recombination process must produce energy in the form of light. This type of defect is referred to as a 'luminescence centre'.

The intensity of the TL produced by the deep traps is roughly proportional to three factors: the amount of radiation received per year; the TL sensitivity of the sample (i.e. the amount of TL produced per unit of radiation dose); and the time, in years, that has elapsed since the sample was last heated. The last of these factors is the age of the pot, because its initial firing by the potter in antiquity would have ejected all the trapped electrons (thus 'zeroing the TL clock'), from which time the electron population in deep traps would have steadily built up. The basic age equation is:

$$\text{Age (in years)} = \frac{\text{natural TL signal}}{(\text{TL per unit radiation dose}) \, (\text{radiation dose per year})}$$

where the 'natural TL signal' is the TL measured on the first heating of a sample in the laboratory. In principle, therefore, if the three factors on the right-hand side of the equation can be measured, then the pot can be dated. In practice the situation is not quite so simple, and many measurements and checks must be made by the TL scientist, only a few of which will be mentioned here.

The upper age limit of TL dating depends on the stability of the signal, on the saturation level of the TL material and on the annual radiation dose. The stability of the signal is usually determined by the depth of the trap: the deeper it is, the more stable the signal. However, other factors can also affect stability (see, for example, anomalous fading, p. 133). Saturation occurs when the TL signal no longer increases significantly with the addition of further radiation; this is due to the filling of the traps with time. The radiation dose which produces saturation is related to the concentration of defects in the crystal. However, the time at which this level of radiation dose is reached depends on how quickly the radiation dose is received; the lower the dose rate, the longer it will take to reach saturation. In consequence, it is not possible to attach a single number to the upper age limit of TL; rather it is specific to each type of sample and each archaeological site. The few generalisations that can be made are discussed at appropriate points below.

Determining the TL age

The TL produced by archaeological samples such as pottery is weak and its measurement therefore requires sensitive light-detecting equipment such as a photomultiplier, which converts the light signal to an electrical one. The signal is plotted as the temperature of the sample is increased, up to 500°C typically, and the output is referred to as a glow curve (fig. 7.10). So-called 'artificial' glow curves can be induced in the laboratory using alpha and beta radiation sources. Thus the TL sensitivity of the sample to radiation can be determined. In fact, this involves taking a large number of TL measurements to check or correct for changes of TL sensitivity and non-linear growth of TL with dose. Some of the checks for stability of TL signal involve the use of the plateau test. This compares the shape of

131

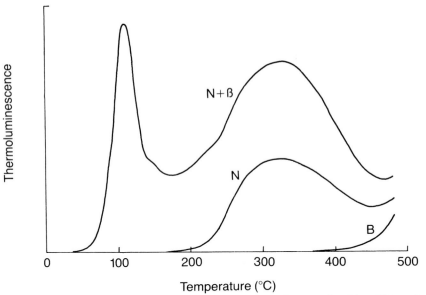

7.10 Natural TL glow curve (N) from a sample of pottery, and one produced by addition of a beta radiation dose in the laboratory to an identical sample (N + β). The additional TL produced by the laboratory dose enables the TL sensitivity of the pottery to radiation to be determined. The thermal glow from the sample, due to heat alone, is curve B.

the natural TL glow curve (see fig. 7.10) with that induced by a laboratory dose: at low temperature the signal is not stable and the ratio of the TL signals varies, but at temperatures above about 300°C there should be a plateau.

The radioactive components in the pottery and the soil are uranium, thorium and potassium, which can be readily detected by analytical techniques such as neutron activation analysis (see glossary), and their contributions to the dose rate then calculated from knowledge of how they decay radioactively. However, particularly for the gamma-ray contribution, more direct measurement of the radiation dose is usually employed. The gamma radiation has a range of about 30 cm, and for a typical sherd of pottery, this means that the soil contributes the majority of the gamma dose. If this contribution is to be representative of the burial environment within a 30 cm radius, it is best measured *in situ*, either using small metal capsules containing a highly TL-sensitive material buried for about one year, or using a calibrated gamma ray spectrometer.

There are many measurements involved in evaluating a TL age, each of which is subject to measurement errors. To improve precision, it is usual to date several samples from the same archaeological level to determine the mean age. Even so, the resulting error term is still typically ± 5–10 per cent of the age, at the 68 per cent confidence level (see glossary). However, occasionally, if it proves impossible to measure any one of the factors in the age equation accurately, no TL date for a site may be obtained at all.

Other TL-datable materials

For a sample to be datable by TL it has to be crystalline but non-metallic. It also has to have some mechanism by which the latent TL signal is zeroed that can be related to an archaeological or geological event of interest. Thus, for pottery dating, quartz and feldspars satisfy the initial criteria, and the zeroing mechanism is the firing of the ceramic. Heat also resets the TL clock in a range of other materials:

- volcanic minerals and sediments underlying a lava flow
- clay, other than pottery, which has been deliberately subjected to heat (e.g. walls and bases of kilns and hearths, metal-production debris such as tuyeres and furnaces, core material remaining in bronzes after casting on a clay core), or heated accidentally (e.g. daub from a house burnt down in a fire)
- stones, such as flint, heated either deliberately (e.g. cooking stones heated in a fire, then used to boil water) or accidentally
- vitrified materials, such as glass itself or slag from metallurgical processes.

At first sight the last category might not seem to fit the dating criteria since glass is strictly speaking amorphous rather than crystalline, but it can have a sufficiently crystalline structure for TL to be produced. However, even if the natural TL signal can be measured, the dating of both glass and slags is rarely satisfactory: glass gives problems because of its transparency, which allows the TL signal to be bleached by light (see below), and slag can be very inhomogenous in its radioactivity content.

The feldspars in volcanic lava flows can also be problematic. Indeed, it was the initial attempt to date these which led to the discovery of anomalous fading. This is the name given to rapid loss of the TL signal from that part of the glow curve normally thought to be stable. A safer approach is to date quartz within the flow, or from the underlying sediment heated by the flow. Dating baked clay and burnt stone are perhaps the most interesting archaeological applications of TL, because these – in particular burnt flint – allow the dating of sites older than about ten thousand years, when the first pottery began to appear. Because of its low internal radioactivity, flint is especially good for dating the Palaeolithic back to at least 250 ka (1 ka = 1000 years).

Apart from heat, there are two other main zeroing mechanisms: crystal formation and exposure to sunlight. Without a crystal structure, there can be no TL; hence, the formation of a crystal such as calcite is 'time zero' for TL dating. It is important to date stalagmites or flow stones, rather than stalactites, since the formation of the latter is not readily relatable to any archaeological event. With stalagmitic calcite, the position of the calcite in relation to the archaeological levels will provide at least a *terminus* result, and in some cases the archaeology may fortuitously be sandwiched between two datable calcite layers.

If there is detrital material in the stalagmite, such as clay and limestone, it will not have a zero TL signal at the time of the stalagmite's formation. The amount of detrital material determines the *lower* level of TL dating of calcite. The useful age range may therefore be 20–300 ka, although its true limits have not been adequately explored.

In some of the early work on TL dating of ocean sediments, it was thought that the TL observed was produced by foraminifera or radiolaria and that the zeroing mechanism was the formation of their shells. In fact it was the sediment particles attached to the shells which were producing the TL. These were most likely to have been zeroed by the action of sunlight prior to their deposition on the sea bed. In recent years, TL has increasingly been applied to the dating of terrestrial sediments. Loess, in particular, is an obvious sediment for TL dating since it is fine-grained. Also, while being transported by wind, it will have been exposed to sunlight for a considerable time prior to deposition. Perhaps more than any other application of TL, sediment dating has fired the most interest. This is largely because of its enormous potential for dating geological processes and sedimentary sequences.

The lower limit of TL dating of sediment is closely linked with uncertainty about how far the sediment was bleached in antiquity, and this led to development of the optically stimulated luminescence (OSL) technique.[16] On the other hand, the apparent upper limit of TL dating of sediment seems to depend on the methodology used, and there is currently no consensus on the matter other than that this limit is at least 100 ka: many dates are being produced well in excess of this value, but there are rarely independent and reliable age estimates against which to compare them.

Having ranged rapidly through the materials that are datable by TL, we must not forget that it is also widely used in authenticity testing of both ceramics and the casting cores of bronzes. These applications are discussed in Chapter 8.

Using TL dating

● *Pontnewydd Cave*

Pontnewydd Cave[17] (fig. 7.11) is situated near Rhyl in North Wales and is one of only two British sites having hominid remains of the Middle Pleistocene period. It also exemplifies the potential, and some of the prob-

7.11 Pontnewydd Cave under excavation (courtesy National Museum of Wales).

lems, of TL dating beyond the range of radiocarbon. Continued involvement of TL scientists through the different seasons of excavation has enabled them to collect samples and bury capsules to measure the associated gamma radiation dose rate, burying a capsule one summer and retrieving it the next. For calcite dating by TL, the use of TL capsules is essential. A gamma spectrometer cannot be used because a hole about 5 cm in diameter is required for the probe; it is extremely hard work to drill the 1 cm hole needed for a capsule, and anything larger would be impossible! Also, many calcite layers are relatively thin and surrounded by non-calcite levels; removal of a 5 cm diameter part of the layer could well result in an unrepresentative measurement of the gamma dose rate.

The chief difficulty in dating Pontnewydd Cave arose because the gamma dose rates varied locally within the cave deposits. The infill of the cave is made up of a wide variety of materials, from silts to large stones, and the radioactive content of these materials is similarly variable. Those which are datable, the stalagmites and burnt flints, have low concentrations of the radioactive elements uranium, thorium and potassium, as does the limestone which is also found within the deposits. However, other stones and sediments interspersed with these contain far greater amounts of radioactivity. It is not always possible to measure the gamma dose rate at exactly the spot where a sample for dating is found, since the excavation of the sample will have removed much of the material surrounding it. Capsules have to be buried as near as possible, but there is no guarantee that the measurement will be truly representative.

The burning of flint samples should be directly associated with the date of occupation of the site. TL dates of three burnt flints have been measured at the British Museum, and these straddle a mean of 190,000 years BP, but there is a large variation about this mean because of the inhomogeneity of the radiation environment in the cave outlined above. Measurements on a single burnt flint, carried out in Oxford, also indicated an age of about 200,000 years.[17]

Some of the deposits from which the burnt flints derived were overlain by an undisturbed stalagmitic floor. The dating of this floor, which has been carried out using both TL and uranium series dating (see p. 118), generally confirms the occupation dates obtained from the burnt flints. By the TL method, the stalagmitic floor is dated to around 170,000 years BP. The uranium series measurements give a slightly older date of 205,000 years BP, but given that the uncertainties in each of these figures are typically 20 per cent, the two techniques can be said to agree with each other.

Such margins of error and variation in results may seem large, but they have to be viewed against the alternative: no independent dates at all. The picture of the history of Pontnewydd Cave that emerges from these and other date measurements is now fairly well established. The occupation of the site, at the cave mouth, occurred around 200,000 years ago. Within a few thousand years, the debris left by the occupants – including some of their remains, their artefacts and the burnt flints – was incorporated in a deposit which was forced into the cave from the outside by water. Upon the upper surface of this deposit, stalagmitic floors formed, and continued to do so intermittently and in different parts of the cave, until a further inflow of material entered the cave between 80,000 and 30,000 years ago. The growth of stalagmites resumed on top of this fresh deposit when the climate warmed up around 18,000 years ago.

- *Bermondsey Abbey*

Although TL really only comes into its own beyond the range of radiocarbon dating, it can also provide answers to specific archaeological problems where no suitable radiocarbon samples exist.

Excavations at Bermondsey Abbey[18] in south-east London uncovered a large drain. Not a prepossessing feature in isolation but, to the archaeologist, understanding the origin of the contents of the backfill of this drain could play an essential part in unravelling the history of activities on the site as a whole. The backfill material contained a considerable amount of pottery, which was stylistically attributable to the second half of the eleventh century AD, along with much burnt clay or daub thought to derive from wattle walls. Stratigraphically the ditch was backfilled before the construction of the first phase of the priory church and was thus before AD 1090. The mystery was the origin of the large quantities of daub. This daub could have come from one of three distinct periods. One possibility was that it was Roman material introduced when the drain walls had collapsed, for the drain had been cut through Roman deposits. A second possibility was an origin in the Middle Saxon period in the first half of the eighth century AD: evidence for this occupation comes from both documentary sources and finds from the site. The third alternative, and the most straightforward interpretation, was that the daub was contemporary with the backfilling of the drain.

Given the possible mixed origins of the backfill, dating the daub by other associated material such as charcoal could not solve the problem. Provided the gamma dose rate, which had possibly changed at some point in the history of the daub, was not a dominant contribution to the TL age, TL could solve the mystery. The gamma dose rate proved to be only about 20 per cent – reasonably typical for clay materials. Three pieces of daub were dated and provided an average age and standard error of 830 ± 40 years. In other words, the true date lies between TL 1080 and 1240, with 95 per cent confidence, clearly demonstrating that the third alternative holds: the daub is broadly contemporary with the backfilling of the drain and coincides with clearance of buildings in the eleventh century AD to make way for the building of the priory church.

Radiocarbon or thermoluminescence?

For a particular archaeological site, the choice of dating method depends largely on the materials available and the age of the site. If we had to choose between radiocarbon and TL dating, then we would have to take into account that radiocarbon is used for organic materials and has an upper age limit of about forty thousand years, whereas TL is applied to inorganic samples and can be used beyond the range of radiocarbon. Another factor to bear in mind is that, unlike TL dating, radiocarbon is independent of the archaeological burial environment, provided that potential contaminants have been removed in the pretreatment process.

In situations where both methods could be used, the choice depends on the association between the sample and the event to be dated, as well as on the likely error terms. TL typically produces an error term of ± 5–10 per cent of the age, i.e. ± 50–100 years for a TL age of 1000 years, ± 100–200 years for 2000 years, and so on. In contrast, radiocarbon typically produces error terms of ± 50–100 years, independent of age, for ages less than about 10,000 years, after which the error increases. However, unlike TL dates, radiocarbon results have to be calibrated and the size of the resulting age range depends on the form of the calibration curve in that period (fig. 7.8), although the radiocarbon age range will generally be smaller than the corresponding TL one. Hence TL is normally used in the following situations: beyond the range of radiocarbon; when no organic material has been preserved on the site; when the association between the event to be dated and the radiocarbon content of the organic samples is poor; or for the few periods where the age range on a calibrated radiocarbon age is larger than the corresponding TL error term.

Whatever the technique – be it radiocarbon, TL, or one of the many others – there are optimal circumstances under which it works best. Occasionally there are situations where two techniques can be used, and there may be good reason to apply both so that they provide supporting evidence for each other (for example, see p. 134 for the use of TL and uranium series dating at Pontnewydd Cave).

Concluding remarks

Scientific dating techniques, and none more than radiocarbon, have revolutionised the archaeologist's understanding of human cultural development.[19] Before the advent of radiocarbon, chronologies for later prehistory in Western Europe were often based on presumed linkages, however tenuous, with those civilisations of the Near and Middle East which had historical calendars. The chronological extrapolation to Western Europe then required the postulation of models about the rate of diffusion of ideas. Thus Stonehenge was presumed to postdate the tholoi of Mycenae, and the time taken for agriculture to spread to Britain was thought to be so great that the inception of the Neolithic was placed at about 2500 BC. Radiocarbon, particularly once the need to calibrate was accepted, has shown that the development of Stonehenge lasted several centuries with Mycenae being only contemporary with the final phase; thus the independent invention of megalithic monuments had to be accepted. Just as dramatically, radiocarbon dating has shown that the Neolithic was introduced to Britain at least 1500 years earlier than previously believed.

Radiocarbon alone cannot provide the absolute dates that archaeologists require. Calibration of radiocarbon results relies totally on the provision by dendrochronology of a reliable calendar timescale, precise to the year.[20]

The origins of dendrochronology lie in climate studies and it was then applied to dating. But the benefits have come full circle, for the long master chronologies subsequently established for archaeological dating and calibration of radiocarbon results are now of just as much value to climatologists studying cycles in weather patterns associated with factors like sunspot activity and variations in the earth's orbital parameters.

Beyond radiocarbon, other techniques such as TL are providing dates that can aid in the understanding of human evolution. For example, it is now known that in Israel anatomically modern humans were present some 90,000 years ago[21] and that there was human occupation of Australia 50,000 years ago.[22] Much earlier still, potassium-argon dating has provided a chronological framework for the early hominid finds in East Africa.[23] Between them, the scientific techniques available thus span very wide time ranges and are indispensable in the continuing search for answers to questions of chronology.

Further reading

Many of the books cited in the references have extensive bibliographies which can provide detailed information on techniques and specific applications.

References

1. L. Alcock, 1971. *Arthur's Britain*. Allen Lane, The Penguin Press, Harmondsworth, Middlesex.

2. M.J. Aitken, 1990. *Science-based Dating in Archaeology*. Longman, London and New York. This book provides an excellent introduction to the full range of scientific dating techniques and their applications.

3. A summary of the dating of Thera is given in M.J. Aitken, H.N. Michael, P.P. Betancourt and P.M. Warren, 1988. 'The Thera eruption: continuing discussion of the dating', *Archaeometry* 30, pp. 165–82.

4. There are a number of recent books specific to radiocarbon dating:
S.G.E. Bowman, 1990. *Radiocarbon Dating*. London, British Museum Publications.
R. Gillespie, 1984. *Radiocarbon User's Handbook*. Oxford, Oxford University Committee for Archaeology.
W.G. Mook and H.T. Waterbolk, 1985. *Radiocarbon Dating*. European Science Foundation Handbooks for Archaeologists No. 3, Strasbourg.
R.E. Taylor, 1987. *Radiocarbon Dating: An Archaeological Perspective*. London, Academic Press.
There is also a journal called *Radiocarbon*, publishing papers and datelists. However, many laboratories do not publish their dates in *Radiocarbon* and computerised databases are being established; one of these is being co-ordinated by Renee Kra, one of the editors of *Radiocarbon*.

5. G. de G. Sieveking, 1971. 'The Kendrick's Cave mandible', *British Museum Quarterly* 35, pp. 230–50. The radiocarbon result (OxA–111) was 10,000 ± 200 BP (published 1985 in *Archaeometry* 27, p. 238).

6. W.F. Libby, 1952. *Radiocarbon Dating*. 2nd edition 1955, Chicago University Press.

7. The curves recommended by the international radiocarbon community are:
G.W. Pearson and M. Stuiver, 1986. 'High-precision calibration of the radiocarbon time scale, 500–2500 BC'. *Radiocarbon* 28, pp. 839–62.
M. Stuiver and G.W. Pearson, 1986. 'High-precision calibration of the radiocarbon time scale, AD 1950–500 BC'. *Radiocarbon* 28, pp. 805–38.
Other curves in the same volume of *Radiocarbon* provide extension of the calibration, but have not as yet been independently verified and internationally recommended. In the near future an agreed curve extending back to about 9000 BC is expected.

8. G.W. Pearson, 1987. 'How to cope with calibration'. *Antiquity* 61, pp. 98–103.

9. M.G.L. Baillie, 1982. *Tree-ring Dating and Archaeology*. London, Croom Helm.
D. Eckstein, 1984. *Dendrochronological Dating*. European Science Foundation Handbooks for Archaeologists No. 2, Strasbourg.

10. See the references in note 7 which use the intercept method to provide tables of calibrated date ranges.

11. A simplified description of the probability approach to calibration is given in S.G.E. Bowman, 1990. *Radiocarbon Dating*. London, British Museum Publications. A full mathematical description can be found in C. Litton and M. Leese (forthcoming), 'Some statistical problems in radiocarbon calibration' (Computer Applications in Archaeology Conference, Southampton, 1990), ed. S.P.Q. Rahtz.

12. D.L. Clarke, 1970. *Beaker Pottery of Great Britain and Ireland*. Cambridge, Cambridge University Press.
J.N. Lanting and J.D. van der Waals, 1972. 'British Beakers as seen from the Continent: A review article'. *Helinium* 12, pp. 20–46.

13. The results of the British Museum's Beaker dating programme are to be published in the near future by Ian Kinnes, Alex Gibson, Janet Ambers, Sheridan Bowman, Morven Leese and Robin Boast.

14. J.C. Ambers, 1990. 'Radiocarbon, calibration and early mining: some British Museum radiocarbon dates for Welsh copper mines'. In *Early Mining in the British Isles*, eds. P. and S. Crew, Plas Tan y Bwlch, Wales.

15. M.J. Aitken, 1985. *Thermoluminescence Dating*. London, Academic Press.
S.J. Fleming, 1979. *Thermoluminescence Techniques in Archaeology*. Oxford, Clarendon Press.
There is also a thermoluminescence newsletter called *Ancient TL* which produces a datelist supplement.

16. D.J. Huntley, D.I. Godfrey-Smith and M.L.W. Thewalt, 1985. 'Optical dating of sediments', *Nature* 313, pp. 105–7.
M.J. Aitken, 1989. 'Luminescence dating: a guide for non-specialists', *Archaeometry* 31, pp. 147–59.

17. H.S. Green, 1984. *Pontnewydd Cave: A Lower Palaeolithic Hominid Site in Wales*. Cardiff, National Museum of Wales. This first report on the site includes

a number of dating contributions such as:
J. Huxtable. 'Thermoluminescence studies on burnt flint and stone' (pp. 106–7).
N.C. Debenham, M.J. Aitken, A.J. Walton and M. Winter. 'Thermoluminescence and uranium series dating of stalagmitic calcite' (pp. 100–105).

18. D. Beard, The Museum of London Department of Greater London Archaeology, personal communication.

19. C. Renfrew, 1973. *Before Civilization: The Radiocarbon Revolution and Prehistoric Europe.* London, Jonathan Cape.

20. The precision and accuracy of dendrochronology is well illustrated by the dating – to the year of construction – of the Sweet Track, a wooden trackway that crossed the Somerset Levels (England).
J. Hillam, C.M. Groves, D.M. Brown, M.G.L. Baillie, J.M. Coles and B.J. Coles, 1990. 'Dendrochronology of the English Neolithic', *Antiquity* 64, pp. 210–20.

21. H. Valladas, J.L. Joron, G. Valladas, B. Arensburg, O. Bar-Yosef, A. Belfer-Cohen, P. Goldberg, H. Laville, L. Meigren and Y. Rak, 1987. 'Thermoluminescence dates for the Neanderthal burial site at Kebara in Israel', *Nature* 330, pp. 159–60.
H. Valladas, J.L. Reyss, J.L. Joron, G. Valladas, O. Bar-Yosef and B. Vandermeersch, 1988. 'Thermoluminescence dating of Mousterian "Proto-Cro-Magnon" remains from Israel and the origin of modern man', *Nature* 331, pp. 614–16.

22. R.G. Roberts, R. Jones and M.A. Smith, 1990. 'Thermoluminescence dating of a 50,000-year-old human occupation site in northern Australia', *Nature* 345, pp. 153–6.

23. For example: G.H. Curtis and R.L. Hay, 1972. 'Further studies and potassium-argon dating at Olduvai Gorge and Ngorongoro Crater'. In *Calibration of Hominid Evolution*, eds. W.W. Bishop and J.A. Miller, pp. 289–302. Edinburgh, Scottish Academic Press.
D.C. Johanson, F.T. Masao, G.G. Eck, T.D. White, R.D. Walter, W.H. Kimbel, B. Asfaw, P. Manega, P. Ndessokia and G. Suwa, 1987. 'New partial skeleton of Homo habilis from Olduvai Gorge, Tanzania', *Nature* 327, pp. 205–9.

CHAPTER 8

Spotting the Fakes

Paul Craddock and Sheridan Bowman

A wide range of scientific methods can be usefully employed to unmask fakes and fraudulent restorations, in much the same way that forensic methods are used in criminal investigations. However there is one obvious question to ask about authenticity testing: if scientific dating methods can be used, why bother with any other techniques? It is, after all, the date of the object that is in question. The simple answer is that not all materials lend themselves to scientific dating. We must therefore resort to more indirect methods, such as the variation with time of copper-alloy composition or technology of production. Indirect methods require the establishment of appropriate databases against which to compare the composition, or other characteristic, of the questionable object. Here, the value of well-documented museum collections or excavated finds cannot be overstated. In contrast, dating techniques do not require this comparative material; they tell us immediately whether or not the object is genuine – at least, they do in theory!

There is another less obvious reason why other techniques might be applied in an authenticity study, even when a dating method can be used. The material with which a major museum has to deal, both within its own collections and on offer to it, will have come from a wide variety of sources. Very often the history of an object is not known at all and there may be reason to believe that it is not all that it purports to be. The problem is often not just whether it is genuine or fake, but rather how much is original, and what has subsequently been done to the object, when, by whom and why. A badly damaged object may have been repaired, or the whole object may be a confection of previously unassociated fragments. A genuine but mundane antiquity can have its value increased enormously by the addition of a unique feature, or of a historical association such as a royal cipher. Given the complexity of many of the objects, and the almost endless possibilities of treatment that could have befallen them, the scientist needs the collaboration of the art historian, in addition to a very wide experience of antiquities and knowledge of the technical processes of the past, in order to reconstruct as much as possible of a particular object's background history.

Some of the scientific methods and problems encountered are exemplified below by specific case histories. The main approaches to the scientific detection of fakes are: the study of composition and methods of construction to see if they match the supposed age of the object; examination for evidence of aging, such as the formation of a patina; and the application of archaeological dating techniques, which can at least give an indication of age and in some cases an actual date.

Scientific dating techniques

The most widely used dating techniques for authenticity testing are thermoluminescence, radiocarbon and dendrochronology: how they work is outlined in Chapter 7. In their application to authenticity testing the first consideration is whether the sample size required is likely to inflict unacceptable damage. The object may prove to be genuine, but this is little consolation to the owner if it has been largely destroyed during the authentication process.

Radiocarbon dating

Until relatively recently, radiocarbon dating would have fallen into the largely destructive category. Conventional radiocarbon dating normally requires sample sizes which will yield a *minimum* of 1 g of carbon. This may not sound much but it is equivalent, for example, to about 400 sq cm of cloth or 50 g of bone. The advent of small sample systems, in particular accelerator mass spectrometry (AMS, see p. 122) has placed all but the very smallest objects within reach of radiocarbon: AMS only requires about 1 *milligram* of carbon. The sample preparation procedures are the same as those used for radiocarbon dating, care being taken to avoid contamination. The range of objects tested covers the whole spectrum of datable materials found on archaeological sites but also encompasses more exotic items such as embroidered silk and carved ivory.

All of the caveats that apply to radiocarbon dating apply to its use in authentication. One might even have to be careful about possible re-use of materials which would produce a radiocarbon result older than the true age of manufacture of the artefact. It was, for example, quite common in the last century for ivory objects to be carved from mammoth tusk that had been preserved in the permafrost of the Siberian tundra since the last Ice Age! The application of radiocarbon dating is usually relatively straightforward, and the dating process will produce a result with an error term that is just as good as for any archaeological sample. In many authenticity studies there is rarely a problem in distinguishing very recent from ancient. Indeed, an artefact made since about 1955 will give an apparent radiocarbon age that is some time into the future because of the excess radiocarbon produced in the atmosphere by nuclear weapons testing (the 'bomb effect', see p. 123). To interpret a radiocarbon result in terms of calendar age requires that it be calibrated (see p. 124). Where problems can arise is in distinguishing between possible dates in the last few centuries, but prior to the bomb effect. A canvas may be perfectly genuine if shown to date to the seventeenth century, but be a fake if it is nineteenth century. Here radiocarbon cannot help. The calibration curve is so wiggly in this region that the possible alternative date ranges encompass both periods (see figs 7.5 and 7.8).

8.1 The facial image of the Shroud of Turin, viewed in negative (courtesy British Society for the Turin Shroud).

The most well-known application of radiocarbon must be the dating of the Shroud of Turin.[1] This linen cloth, some 4.25 m in length, bears the shadowy image of the front and back of a man who appears to have been scourged and crucified, and it is therefore believed to have been Christ's burial shroud. Its history is known with certainty back to about AD 1350, when it was in the possession of the de Charny family in France. Even then it appears to have caused something of a religious furore, being declared by some to be a fake and by others to be the true Shroud. In 1898, the first ever photograph of the Shroud showed that the image, when seen in negative, is strikingly life-like (fig. 8.1). This discovery and subsequent medical findings fuelled suggestions that the cloth could conceivably be genuine.

Despite the large size of the Shroud, removal of the area of cloth needed for normal radiocarbon dating would have inflicted unacceptable damage. Thus it was not until the AMS technique had been perfected that a fragment of the linen could be removed for dating. This fragment, measuring only a few square centimetres, was divided up and samples, the equivalent of about 50 mg in weight, were given to three accelerator laboratories in Oxford, Zurich and Tucson. The British Museum was asked to participate in the certification of the sampling and the statistical analysis of the results. The calibrated radiocarbon result[2] was AD 1260–1390 (at the 95 per cent confidence level: see glossary); this accords well with the Shroud's first appearance in France. However, until it can be properly established how this striking image came into being, the mystery will not be completely solved. Indeed, the controversy raised in the fourteenth century over the authenticity of the Shroud has been revived rather than settled by the radiocarbon date.

Thermoluminescence dating

If AMS is used, there is no fundamental difference between radiocarbon as applied to authenticity testing and archaeological dating. This is not the case with thermoluminescence (TL) dating, which requires several grams of pottery. This is rarely a problem for dating an archaeological site where fragments of broken pottery tend to abound, and it is usual to date several sherds from the same context to provide an average age and better precision. Clearly, however, one cannot remove such a large sample from a fine ceramic artefact on offer to a museum. The other problem is that part of the radiation dose which induces the TL signal is from the environment the object has been kept in, and the precise storage history over the lifetime of most antiquities is not known. These two problems can be overcome but at a price in terms of the overall precision and accuracy of the result.

A sample weighing about 30 mg is drilled from an inconspicuous area of the object, usually the base. This sample size is just sufficient to allow a limited number of measurements to be done. From dating studies on archaeological ceramics, we know that the environment does not make the largest contribution to the annual radiation dose of ceramics, and a likely range of environmental radiation values can be assumed in estimating the TL age. This is normally adequate to distinguish recently made objects – fakes – from those genuinely manufactured in antiquity.

In addition to pottery, the core material from bronzes that have been cast using a clay core (see p. 84) can also be tested by TL, since this ceramic material has normally been fired to a sufficiently high temperature to 'zero the TL clock'. Porcelain can also be TL tested,[3] but it is such a hard ceramic that a drill cannot be used to take the sample because of the heat generated and the spurious luminescence signals produced. Samples can, however, be taken by using a diamond-impregnated coring bit. The small cylinder of sample removed is then sliced, like a loaf of bread, and the slices are used for the TL measurements.

Thermoluminescence has had a major impact on the antiquities market starting from about 1970 when the first tests were made in Oxford.[4] No longer does evidence of authenticity have to rely solely on stylistic criteria, which can be unreliable. Museum collections worldwide have also been shown to have their share of fakes, as the TL testing of the British Museum's collection of seventy Zapotec ceramics can demonstrate.

The Zapotec culture[5] flourished in Oaxaca in southern Mexico between about AD 200 and 800. It produced distinctive pottery vessels in human or animal form, which are now found in large numbers in collections throughout the world. Many Zapotec pottery vessels, however, have long been suspected of being forgeries. The British Museum's collection, much of which was collected last century or in the early half of this century, was shown by TL to contain some twenty forgeries, most of which had, in recent years, been suspected to be modern. That so many museum curators have been deceived by these fakes is less surprising when seen in the context of both the style itself and the history of archaeology in Oaxaca. Relatively little was really known of Zapotec culture until the excavations at the Monte Alban and other sites in the 1930s. Except for the earliest styles, Zapotec pottery was largely mould-made and decorated with applied decorative motifs often cut from flat sheets of clay and easily copied. The use of genuine pre-Hispanic moulds has also caused confusion. The 'basket' with rodents included in Figure 8.2 would attract suspicion because the form itself is not within the canon of Zapotec work. However, the animal figures which decorate the body of the vessel are from a genuine figurine mould and therefore in perfect Zapotec style. There is good evidence that a flourishing trade in false antiquities existed at the turn of the century, and its products filtered through to the United States and Europe. In the 1920s and 1930s a large percentage of the so-called ancient material which would have been familiar to interested collectors was the product of this well-established manufacture.

Dendrochronology

As the name implies, dendrochronology is specific to the dating of wood. This technique is highly precise, to the year or even season of felling, if the sample is adequate. Herein lies the problem: the wood needs to be of a

8.2 Zapotec ceramics tested by TL. From left to right: genuine figure of a deity (ETH 1849.6–27.20), height 320 mm; fake 'basket' of rodents (ETH 1940 Am2.43), diameter 355 mm; and fake figure of a deity (ETH 1946 Am.16–7), height 400 mm.

species for which there is a 'master chronology' (see p. 125) and there must normally be at least a hundred tree rings in the sample to be dated to ensure a unique match with the master pattern. If the date is to be precise to the year of felling, the bark must also be present, otherwise an estimate must be made of the number of missing rings corresponding to likely wastage by the carpenter. Furthermore, to determine the date of actual usage, allowance must be made for seasoning of the timber.

Dendrochronology is most commonly used in the art world to test the authenticity of panel paintings.[6] This is feasible because the panels were prepared from radial sections of the timber rather than tangential ones, since the latter would warp. Many panels have more than enough rings to be datable, and the most popular timber was oak, for which long master chronologies exist.

If the date of felling of the tree can be determined and shown to post-date the death of the artist, the painting is clearly a fake. Indeed, if only heartwood is present but the last ring itself post-dates the artist's death, this too condemns the piece. Interestingly, dendrochronology can also demonstrate when the panels are taken from the same tree because of the close similarity of the ring patterns. It can therefore be used to associate paintings, if not to the same artist, at least geographically.

Other methods of detecting fakes

Anachronistic use of materials

Through the ages, the composition of synthetic materials, such as metals, ceramics and glass, has changed as the sources of raw materials have changed and new processes have been discovered. As already described in

Chapter 5, we are beginning to define the range of composition of materials used by many of the principal civilisations of the past, and to discover when and where particular materials, such as brass, were first used.[7] This information is extremely useful in authentication studies. One can compare the composition of the suspect piece with the range of composition of genuine pieces of comparable period. This applies to both the major components which the craftsman deliberately mixed together to form the final product, and also to the trace elements of which he was probably ignorant, but which can indicate the likely source of some of the materials, thus enabling us to distinguish the genuine from the spurious.

One must be careful to differentiate between compositions which are unusual and those which are plainly impossible. Thus, if one had a bronze with, say, 2 per cent of tin, where the tin content of the comparable genuine bronzes lay between 5 and 10 per cent, this would be unusual and would count against the piece but it certainly would not condemn it. If, however, the suspect piece turned out to be an aluminium bronze (as was recently the case with some coins purporting to be Anglo-Saxon), then one could reject it straight away because aluminium, and thus aluminium bronze, was not known before the nineteenth century.

Sometimes the analysis can be quick and quite definitive. For example, two very similar copper-alloy statuettes both purport to be Etruscan of the sixth century BC (fig. 8.3). Both are technically very fine castings and well finished. But surface analysis by X-ray fluorescence (see glossary) shows that one is a leaded tin bronze, quite appropriate for the period, whereas the other is of brass, the alloy of copper and zinc, which did not become common until the Roman period over five hundred years later. Thus, on these grounds alone, the second figure is most unlikely to be ancient. In all probability it was made as an innocent copy in the nineteenth century.

However, one has to beware of jumping too rapidly to conclusions on the basis of a single surface analysis without considering all the possibilities. For instance, when one of the British Museum's most magnificent Etruscan bronze vessels was similarly analysed on the surface and found to contain zinc, there was understandably some consternation. Subsequent analysis of a sample drilled from the interior showed it was of bronze with no zinc present at all. The explanation was that the vessel had been

8.3 *below left* Two Etruscan banqueteers: the statuette at the back is bronze (GR 1831.12–1.1) but the other is brass (GR 1918.1–1.113). Length 330 mm.

electrochemically cleaned to remove the worst of the corrosion at some time after its excavation in the nineteenth century. In this treatment the vessel would have been wrapped in a zinc foil, placed in a solution of weak acid and then an electric current applied.[8] During the process the bronze was bathed in a solution of zinc salts and, unless it was carefully washed afterwards, some of these zinc salts could persist in the remaining patina on the surface. This example illustrates well that one has to be aware of the range of possible treatments and restorations to which even perfectly genuine objects could have been subjected.

The composition of glass also changed through the ages: most glass from the early civilisations of the Middle East were soda glasses with relatively high sodium contents, and low lime and lead contents compared with modern glass (see Chapter 3). Modern glass also tends to contain a greater range of other metals such as arsenic and zinc. Thus, when a series of Egyptian canopic jars of blue glass purporting to belong to the New Kingdom of the second millennium BC came under suspicion stylistically, they were analysed and found to contain high levels of lead and some arsenic, thereby confirming the doubts of the Egyptologists.

Trace elements can also be diagnostic. For example, almost all sources of silver naturally contain a little gold, and ancient silver artefacts typically have gold contents in the range of 0.1 to 1.0 per cent. Not until after the medieval period was it economically viable to recover amounts as small as this, and so the gold content of silver artefacts can be a useful indicator of their antiquity. A number of supposedly late Roman silver ingots, of the type distributed to the army on special occasions such as the accession of an emperor, appeared on the market fairly recently. All were in perfect condition, and the inscriptions seemed rather unusual: analysis failed to detect any gold at all, strongly suggesting the ingots were made from modern refined silver.

Sometimes the composition of the solders used to hold together the components of the objects can themselves be indicators of age. Modern gold solders often contain several per cent of cadmium, small amounts of which significantly lower the melting point of the alloy without affecting the colour of the metal too badly. Cadmium is a very volatile metal that has to be prepared by distillation; as this was not achieved until 1818, solders containing cadmium cannot be ancient.

A whole series of quite spectacular pieces of supposedly Dark Age jewellery and belt fittings, including the well-known Lombard Treasure, appeared on the art market at the beginning of this century (fig. 8.4). Quite apart from unusual stylistic characteristics, cadmium-containing solders had been used extensively. The British Museum acquired some of these pieces knowingly, as examples of modern fakes, and by examining the pieces in the scanning electron microscope (see glossary) using micro-analysis and digital-mapping techniques it has been possible to plot the concentration of the cadmium over the soldered surfaces. It has recently been suggested that some ancient solders did contain cadmium, using the cadmium sulphide mineral greenockite as source of the metal.[9] However, in many years of examination of ancient jewellery, cadmium has never

8.4 *left* Fake 'Lombardic' brooch (MLA 1930.11–6.1), one of a number of pieces made at the beginning of the century. The brooch purports to belong to the Dark Ages, but uses a modern cadmium gold solder to hold together the components. Diameter 57 mm.

8.6 Three methods of making wire: **(a)** *above* and **(b)** *right* are ancient, **(c)** *far right* is modern. In **(a)** a thin strip of metal is tightly twisted to produce a hollow tube rather like a very thin drinking straw. In **(b)** a thin rod of square section is twisted and then rolled. In **(c)** a thin rod is passed through progressively narrower draw plates. The very characteristic marks left on the wire show how it was made and this can indicate the likely age of a piece.

8.5 *left* Fake Egyptian jackal's head of lapis lazuli (EA 64075). All ancient lapis came from a single source in Badakshan in Afghanistan. However, the composition of this piece shows it came from Lake Baikal in Siberia, a source not exploited until the nineteenth century. Length 98 mm.

been found in pieces from excavation, or from otherwise unimpeachable sources, but only in pieces that were suspect on other grounds.

So far we have considered man-made materials where the composition reflects the processing, but the composition of materials such as stones and gems, which were used without chemical modification, can also sometimes indicate their source, and thereby the authenticity of artefacts made from them. An example of this is a jackal's head, purportedly ancient Egyptian, and carved from the semi-precious stone lapis lazuli (fig. 8.5). X-ray diffraction (see glossary) revealed the presence of the calcium silicate mineral, wollastonite, in the lapis. We know that all the lapis lazuli used in the ancient Middle East came from a single source in the Badakshan Valley, Afghanistan,[10] but this source does not contain wollastonite. However, lapis from the region of Lake Baikal in Siberia does contain wollastonite, although this source was not worked until the nineteenth century. The lapis in the jackal's head is therefore unlikely to be ancient.

The ratio of stable isotopes in marble (see glossary) can also be used to determine provenance, and has been particularly useful in checking the integrity of statuary recomposed from fragments (see p. 109).

Anachronistic technology

The way in which things are made has changed slowly through the millennia and much more rapidly during the last two centuries. Thus the techniques used to manufacture and decorate an object are indicative of its authenticity. To the trained observer, careful study under a binocular

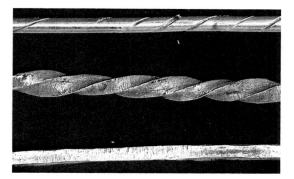

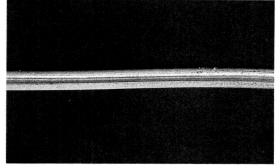

microscope can reveal how an object was made and decorated, and also reveal any discrepancies or anachronisms in a fake antiquity.

For example, since the medieval period, wire has been made by drawing thin metal rods through progressively thinner holes. This leaves long parallel striations running along the wire. In antiquity a variety of methods were used, including strip twisting and block twisting.[11] Both these methods leave very characteristic helical seams which can be seen on examples of wires made by the two methods in Figure 8.6a and b, taken from genuine antiquities. A modern drawn wire from a fake is shown for comparison (fig. 8.6c).

The methods used to cut stone and gems can also be indicative of age. For instance, the teeth on the famous supposedly Pre-Columbian crystal skull, said to be from Mexico (fig. 8.7), have been cut with an abrasive wheel. Although this technique has a long ancestry in the Old World it was unknown in the Americas until the Spanish conquest in the sixteenth century. This would seem to suggest that the head cannot belong to the Aztec civilisation. But this remarkable object may not be a completely modern fake. It could have been made by the indigenous people immediately after the conquest, or alternatively features such as the teeth could have been cut much later on the head.

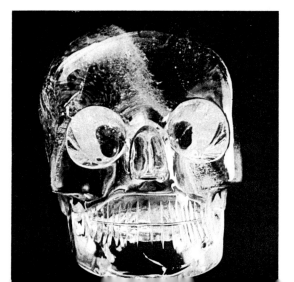

8.7   Crystal skull (ETH 1898–1), said to be from Mexico. This striking head is difficult to parallel stylistically, and the teeth seem to have been cut with an abrasive wheel which would not have been available in the Americas before the Spanish conquest. Height 210 mm.

Artificial aging

Having produced the fake, there is then the problem of making it look old. This is a two-fold process: first the wear that the object could have received during normal usage must be replicated, and then the decay and corrosion of centuries of neglect or burial must be induced. Real wear is the cumulative result of a vast number of very minor rubs and abrasions from a variety of preferred angles concentrated at a number of areas such as extremities or where one component rubs against another, such as on the links of a chain or the catch of a clasp. Wear cannot therefore be simulated by just sand-blasting the whole object, nor even by concentrating on the vulnerable parts with a coarse file. On one fake astrolabe examined recently the faker had clearly got bored and resorted to an angle grinder to wear down the edges, leaving very characteristic scratches; unfortunately most fakers are much more painstaking!

● *Patination*

After long exposure to the air or burial in the ground most materials corrode. Thus, over a long period of time, stone, glass and metals acquire a distinctive patina which the faker must try and imitate. The patinas on copper alloys were often appreciated in their own right and a study of the patination is central to all authenticity studies. It is essential to have a good appreciation of the possibilities of recent treatments, such as over-restoration or repatination, so a brief history of patination is given here.

As far as we know, the ancients intended their metalwork, both artistic and utilitarian, to be kept in a brightly polished metallic state,[12] with the possible exception of special alloys such as Corinthian bronze.[13] We tend now to think of Classical bronze statuary, for example, as being covered with a fine green or deep brown patina, and moreover that this was their original state. But, on the contrary, the evidence suggests that these statues were kept bright. For example, contracts survive to pay for the regular cleaning of the bronzes in Roman temples[14] and where statues are depicted as part of landscapes or street scenes on contemporary wall paintings they are always shown as bronze-coloured, never patinated (plate 8.1).

The first people to have appreciated and replicated patinas seem to have been the Chinese. This is perhaps not unexpected, given their reverence for the past and their long tradition of scholarship and collecting stretching back over several millennia. The bronzes that the Chinese so eagerly collected came from burials and were usually covered in a fine green patina. Supply of ancient bronzes exceeded demand and forgeries were very prevalent. Over a thousand years ago bronzes were being produced in the style of the early pieces and given an artificial patina.[15] This was done by applying a mixture of ground-up malachite and other minerals to the bronze (plate 8.2). The result is superficially quite convincing, but would not deceive anyone with experience of genuine patinas. Very probably at least some of these patinated bronzes should be regarded as legitimate copies rather than as fakes, rather as today the British Museum produces and sells resin copies of some of the more famous antiquities.

Serious study and collecting of antique metalwork only began in Europe during the Renaissance. The patina the bronzes had acquired during burial was much admired, and people assumed that they had originally been patinated. The belief grew that the original patination had been black, possibly based on some rather oblique remarks in Pliny's *Natural History* on treating bronzes with bitumen.[16] Some dealers and collectors were not above altering or even removing the genuine patina and treating the surface to give the appearance they felt it should have had. The collector Richard Payne Knight is a prime example. His superb collection of mainly Classical antiquities passed to the British Museum in the early nineteenth century and includes hundreds of small bronzes. Almost all of these are now covered in a spurious black patina (plate 8.3); indeed one can go through the sculpture galleries of the Greek and Roman Department and pick out the Payne Knight pieces from a distance, before checking against the registration number which invariably begins with 1824. More seriously, the possible repatination of an otherwise quite genuine piece has to be carefully considered in authenticity studies, and demonstrates again the importance of a close acquaintance with antiquities generally, and an especial awareness of the potential vicissitudes that could have befallen them.

Throughout the eighteenth and nineteenth centuries there was a steady increase in the number and sophistication of methods for chemically patinating copper alloys.[17] These techniques were developed for the perfectly legitimate 'bronzing' and 'antiquing' of patently modern metalwork, but could also be used by the faker with less honest motives. Changes in taste, coupled with a general decline in craft techniques, have meant that the use and range of chemical treatments has declined in this century, although in the Far East the beautiful patinated Shakudo alloys (see p. 95) are still produced by the traditional chemical treatments. Partly inspired by this continuing tradition, there has been a recent revival of interest in Europe[18] and North America[19] emanating from art schools, where the subtle nuances of colour and texture of a chemically patinated surface are more appreciated.

The faker has more immediate problems: the false patina must simultaneously look attractive, stay firmly in place, and appear genuine. One method is to grind up a suitable mixture of the correct minerals and stick it to the surface. Alternatively a patina can be induced on the surface of the metal, either by treatment with suitable chemical concoctions or by rapid weathering in an extreme environment. Italian fakers traditionally encouraged the rapid development of a patina by such measures as exposing the bronze on the workshop roof for some months, or by burying the piece in a dunghill.

Fortunately these approaches create difficulties for the faker and also leave clues for the scientific investigator. If the patina has been stuck on, then it is often possible to detect the organic binder or glue quite easily, either by application of various solvents, or by exposure to ultra-violet radiation. Many organic binders contain molecules which fluoresce when excited by ultra-violet radiation. This is well exemplified by the ancient

8.8 Three images of a Chinese *fang ding* vessel (OA 1973.7–26.4) probably made in the eleventh century BC. It was subsequently badly damaged but the clumsy repair is skilfully disguised by deceptive restoration. Height 222 mm.

(a) *left* By ordinary light the *fang ding* appears intact.

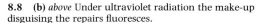

8.8 **(b)** *above* Under ultraviolet radiation the make-up disguising the repairs fluoresces.

(c) *left* X-rays pierce right through the object, revealing the massive breaks. The very white areas in the cracks are lead solder.

Chinese *fang ding* vessel, shown in Figure 8.8a. In Figure 8.8b the make-up used to disguise repairs fluoresces under ultra-violet radiation. Also the junction between the uncorroded metal and the applied patina is very sharp, whereas a patina which has developed over a long period of time will have eaten into the metal in a very irregular and quite characteristic manner that is very difficult to imitate.

One problem for the faker trying to develop a patina *in situ* is that the chemicals which give the most attractive patinas also give totally the wrong minerals, which can be detected quite easily by X-ray diffraction. In addition, rapidly developed patinas tend to be rather loose and powdery.

This section has concentrated so far on metals, reflecting the interest in metal patinas, but other materials also develop distinctive surfaces over time and some work has been done both by fakers to replicate them and investigators to differentiate the fake from the genuine. The early fakers of marble statuary used a variety of treatments to tone down the too obvious freshly carved surfaces, ranging from cold tea to the more sophisticated repeated acid bath treatments used by more recent fakers.[20] However, as with their metal counterparts, the false patinas on stone may look convincing but when viewed under high magnification and analysed are petrologically and chemically quite distinct.

Another branch of stone patina faking is to be found in a very different area of collecting. In the late nineteenth and early twentieth centuries there was a passion for collecting prehistoric flint implements,[21] and quite high prices were paid for prize specimens; not perhaps in the same league as the prices paid for Classical sculpture, but quite enough to encourage the fakers. The products of their industry were of course quite fresh and unpatinated, whereas the genuine flint artefacts had a white or brown patination especially if buried in chalky soil. This could be replicated, at least superficially, by boiling in a concentrated caustic soda solution to give a white patination; the addition of a few rusty nails would then turn the patina brown. However the texture of these patinas is not very convincing as they tend to be rather matt and powdery, and are quite easily recognised under the microscope.

Glass that has been buried usually develops a distinctive iridescence and onion-skin texture. This is caused by the slow leaching of elements from the unstable early soda glasses, and has so far proved impossible to replicate. This patination is very difficult to induce artificially. At best the faker can try and render the surface somewhat weathered and pitted by treatment with hydrofluoric acid, but the presence of fluorides in the surface can be easily detected.

Restoration

Deceptive restoration or alteration and embellishment of antiquities is another area of faking. Scientific examination can be used to assess the extent of repairs or new work, and to pick up the joins and fillers used to disguise them. Where an object has been heavily restored, radiography can frequently 'see' through the carefully applied make-up. This is clearly illustrated by the small Islamic jug in Figure 8.9. To the unaided eye, the

8.9 Restoration revealed by radiography. This small Islamic jug (OA 1952.2–14.1) of the ninth century AD appears intact *below* when viewed by ordinary light, but X-rays show that it is extensively repaired *right*, especially around the rim. Height 117 mm.

jug does appear slightly restored, but the true extent of the restoration is starkly revealed by the X-rays, which pass more easily through the relatively light plaster make-up than through the denser ceramic. Similarly, damage to the ancient Chinese *fang ding* and the lead solder used to repair it are clearly visible on the radiograph (fig. 8.8c), in which the X-rays pass easily through the restorer's plaster and false patina.

Additions and embellishments can be more difficult to detect, and here of course the cooperation of the art historian is essential. It would be of no great help to pronounce the body of an object genuine if the interest, and hence the value, lay in the inscription. For example, a small Egyptian gold pendant in the form of a shell (now in the Egyptian Department of the British Museum, EA 65281) is very probably ancient, but it bears an engraved cartouche purporting to be of the Twelfth Dynasty in the early second millennium BC. The crudity of the cartouche and various internal anachronisms raised suspicion. On careful examination it became clear that the cartouche had been engraved. In this technique a V-profile chisel, the graver, is pushed over the surface of the metal in order to remove a sliver of metal. To do this the graver must be very hard and strong. The technique of engraving was therefore not really feasible until iron and steel tools came into use at the end of the second millennium BC, yet this piece purports to be many hundreds of years older.

Where it is suspected that a piece is made up of unrelated fragments, the composition can sometimes be studied to sort out which fragments are original, or at least which ones belong together. This problem is especially common with Classical marble statuary which in the past was often highly restored before being sold. Stable isotope analysis (see glossary) can be used both to provenance the marble used and to solve some particularly knotty problems caused by over-enthusiastic restoration, where fragmentary pieces were re-assembled, frequently incorporating new pieces of marble, to make the statue appear whole. The British Museum has in its collections a marble panel, recomposed from fragments, belonging to a Roman sarcophagus (GR 1805.7–13.135). The fragments have a long and complex history since their discovery, dating back to at least the sixteenth century. Some earlier drawings show the panel as considerably less complete than it is now, suggesting that pieces were added in the eighteenth century, as was the common practice with fragmentary works. However stable isotope analysis shows that all the fragments belong to one piece of marble, demonstrating the overall integrity of the piece, and also that the marble is likely to have come from the quarries at Carrara in Tuscany.

The limits of scientific expertise

The examples used above to demonstrate particular approaches or methods tend to suggest that each problem has a neat and unequivocal solution. Usually the situation is much less clear-cut. Scientific examination adds another dimension of evidence to authenticity studies which, taken together with the art historical evidence, can allow us to make an attribution with much more confidence. There are the rare cases, as with the

8.10 Life-size bronze figure of a youth. This statue, now in the Kunst Historische Museum in Vienna, was until recently believed to be the Roman statue found at Magdalensberg in the sixteenth century and as such the only complete Roman statue ever found north of the Alps. However, recent scientific examination by an international team of scientists suggests that this is an early copy of an original now lost. Height 1.7 m.

bronze and brass Etruscan statuettes described above, where a few moments spent performing a surface analysis can unequivocally solve a problem, which might have remained a stylistic conundrum for ever. But more often scientific examination will add to the store of information without finally solving the basic problem.

The following example, although not strictly an authenticity examination, uses the same approaches and shows the application of scientific detection in a related sphere of the British Museum's activities. A number of small bronze figurines have been found in several locations in southern Britain. They bear some resemblance to figurines of the Italic culture of central Italy of the mid-first millennium BC. If they were genuine imports into prehistoric Britain then they would be of some importance in suggesting trade networks. However, none of them has been found in an archaeological context and they have aroused considerable suspicion: they could be relatively modern copies loosely based on Italic originals; they could be genuine prehistoric imports; or they could be perfectly genuine figures brought to Britain relatively recently as curios and since discarded or lost. Scientific examination has shown that they are made of bronze similar to that used in genuine Italic figures from Italy and the patination appears to have developed over a long period, suggesting that they are not modern copies. Useful though this information is, however, it still leaves the central question open of whether the figures came to Britain in antiquity or more recently. This particular problem is likely to remain unsolved until a similar figure is recovered from an excavation site.

Usually the art historical and scientific approaches to the same problem reach broadly the same conclusion, even though it may be necessary to rely heavily on one of the approaches to make sense of the other. However, just occasionally, the evidence of the two disciplines is in apparent contradiction. A good example is provided by the famous life-size bronze statue of a youth, found at Magdalensberg (fig. 8.10). It is, or more correctly, *was* the most important antiquity to have been found in Austria and has pride of place in the Kunst Historiche Museum in Vienna.

The piece has an apparently unassailable history. It was dug up in the sixteenth century and achieved fame almost immediately, entering the imperial collections, and being drawn by artists such as Apianus in 1534. Only in the nineteenth century did excavations reveal a major Roman temple to Mercury at Magdalensberg, and the youth was almost certainly the cult statue. Further, the statue has an inscription on one leg mentioning a specific family and once again only much later was this name encountered on Roman pottery as an important family firm of merchants in that region. Thus the archaeological evidence would seem to establish the authenticity of the statue beyond all reasonable question, but some stylistic doubts were raised and the statue was examined scientifically by an international panel of scientists, including members of the British Museum Research Laboratory.[22] Their findings were equally unequivocal. Thermoluminescence dating of the clay core suggested that the statue was only a few centuries old, and this was supported by technical examination and analysis which showed that the casting technology and the metal used were quite typical of the Renaissance, and equally unlike those used by the Romans. Examination of the metal showed that it had always been in a clean condition with no evidence of corrosion, suggesting that it had never been buried. The apparent conflict of evidence is still not completely resolved, but there is a possible explanation. It is known that shortly after its discovery, a copy, now lost, was made and sent to Spain. Is it possible that the statue which was scientifically examined was actually the copy, and the original – the only complete Roman bronze statue to have been discovered north of the Alps – was sent off to Spain, never to be seen again?

Further reading

F. Arnau, 1961. *3,000 years of Deception in Art and Antiques*. London, Cape.

S.J. Fleming, 1975. *Authenticity in Art*. London, Institute of Physics.

M. Jones (ed.), 1989. *Fake? The Art of Deception*. London, British Museum Publications.

O. Kurz, 1948. *Fakes*. London, Faber and Faber.

A. Rieth, 1970. *Archaeological Fakes* (English edition). London, Barrie & Jenkins.

References

1. I.W. Wilson, 1978. *The Turin Shroud*. Gollancz, London. Results of scientific studies (see also note 2) are to be found in: *La S. Sindone-Richerche e studi della Commissione di Esperti nominata dall 'arivescova di Torino, Cardinal Michele Pelligrino, nel 1969*, 1976, Supplemento Rivista Diocesana Torinese. E.J. Jumper, A.D. Adler, J.P. Jackson, S.F. Pellicori, J.H. Heller and J.R. Druzik, 1984. 'A comprehensive examination of the various stains and images on the Shroud of Turin'. In *Archaeological Chemistry – III*, ed. J.B. Lambert, pp. 447–76, Washington DC, American Chemical Society.

2. P.E. Damon, D.J. Donahue, B.H. Gore, A.L. Hatheway, A.J.T. Jull, T.W. Linick, P.J. Sercel, L.J. Toolin, C.R. Bronk, E.J. Hall, R.E.M. Hedges, R. Housley, I.A. Law, C. Perry, G. Bonani, S. Trumbore, W. Woelfli, J.C. Ambers, S.G.E. Bowman, M.N. Leese and M.S. Tite, 1989. 'Radiocarbon dating of the Shroud of Turin'. *Nature* 337, pp. 611–15.

3. D. Stoneham, 1983. 'Porcelain dating'. *PACT* 9, pp. 227–39.

4. M.J. Aitken, P.R.S. Moorey and P.J. Ucko, 1971. 'The authenticity study of vessels and figurines in the Hacilar style'. *Archaeometry* 13, pp. 89–141.

5. A. Caso and I. Bernal, 1965. 'Ceramics of Oaxaca'. *The Handbook of Middle American Indians*, Vol 3, Part 21, *The Archaeology of Southern Mesoamerica*, pp. 871–95. Austin and London, University of Texas Press.

6. Some of the problems that can arise in dendrochronology are discussed in: M.G.L. Baillie, J. Hillam, K.R. Biffra and D.M. Brown, 1985. 'Re-dating the English art-historical tree-ring chronologies'. *Nature* 315, pp. 317–19.

7. P.T. Craddock, 1985. 'Medieval copper alloy production and West African bronze analyses'. *Archaeometry* 27, 1, pp. 17–41.

8. M. Gilberg, 1988. 'History of bronze disease and its treatment'. In *Early Advances in Conservation*, Occasional Paper 65, ed. V. Daniels. London, British Museum, pp. 59–70.

9. N.D. Meeks and P.T. Craddock, 1991. 'The detection of cadmium in gold/silver alloys and its alleged occurrence in ancient gold solders'. *Archaeometry* 33, pp. 95–107.

10. A. Lucas, 1934. *Ancient Egyptian Materials and Industries*. London, Arnold, esp. p. 347.

11. W.A. Oddy, 1977. 'The production of gold wire in antiquity'. *Gold Bulletin* 36, 3, pp. 79–87.

12. D. Kent Hill, 1969. 'Bronze working'. In *The Muses at Work*, ed. C. Roebuck, Cambridge, Mass., MIT, pp. 60–95.

13. P.T. Craddock, 1982. 'Gold in antique copper alloys'. *Gold Bulletin* 15, 2, pp. 69–72.

14. A.C. Johnson, 1936. *Roman Egypt II*. Baltimore, Johns Hopkins Press, esp. pp. 662–4.

15. N. Barnard, 1961. *Bronze Casting and Bronze Alloys in Ancient China*. Canberra, Monumenta Serica, esp. ch. 7.

16. Pliny the Elder. *The Natural History*, trans. H. Rackham 1956. London, Heinemann, esp. Books 34, p. 15 and 35, p. 182.

17. A.H. Hiorns, 1892. *Metal Colouring and Bronzing*. London, Macmillan.

18. R. Hughes and M. Rowe, 1982. *The Colouring, Bronzing and Patination of Metals*. London, The Crafts Council.

19. C. Lewton-Brain, 1985. *Patinas for Small Studios*. Edmonton, author.

20. F. Arnau, 1961. *3,000 years of Deception in Art and Antiques*. London, Cape, esp. pp. 95–6 and 214–15.

21. A. Rieth, 1970. *Archaeological Fakes* (English edition). London, Barrie & Jenkins.

22. A. Vendel, B. Pilcher and J. Weber (eds.), 1987/8. 'Naturwissenschaftliche Untersuchungen an der Bronzestatue ''Der Jungling vom Magdalensberg''.' *Wiener Berichte uber Naturwissenschaft in der Kunst* 4/5, pp. 262–355.

CHAPTER 9

Computing and Mathematics:
Putting two and two together

Peter Main

Centuries ago, mathematics was dubbed 'handmaiden of the Sciences', and with good reason. The earliest discoveries in mathematics were made by the great physicists and astronomers in the course of their work, and in those days great scientists *had* to be great mathematicians. The power and wide-ranging applications of mathematics quickly gave it recognition as a discipline in its own right, whose theorems have now been brought to bear on problems in every field of knowledge. Computers, and the programs that control them, rely no less on the past creativity of mathematicians. The youngster of today who comes to grips for the first time with a personal computer little imagines the wealth of mathematical inventiveness invested in the design of the software and in the electronic circuitry itself. Statistics, a multi-faceted sub-discipline of mathematics, has its own long and proud history, boasting such famous exponents as Isaac Newton, Edmund Halley and Florence Nightingale. Statistics grapples with the quantification of such nebulous concepts as probability, certainty and error.

Computer science, though one of the younger disciplines, relies like so many others on mathematics, and this happy relationship works both ways. Increasingly, the practical application of many mathematical techniques depends on the computer's ability to carry out calculations with faultless accuracy at ever more extraordinary speeds. Applied mathematics and computer science are distinct disciplines, but they are now locked for ever in an inseparable embrace. Together, they underpin rather than oversee the disciplines they serve, and reliance upon them can be so complete that procedures simply cannot be carried out without their aid. For example, neutron activation analysis (see glossary), one of the techniques used to determine the composition of ancient ceramics, would be impossible without a computer program, since the calculations required are so complex and extensive that not even the most resilient individual armed with a pocket calculator could possibly complete them in a single lifetime.

A less obvious aspect of the power of mathematics and computer science derives from the abstract, or generalised, nature of the procedures they employ; in solving one problem one is often, perhaps unwittingly, solving another apparently unrelated problem. We will see some instances of this fascinating phenomenon in the following sections, as we take a brief look at applications of mathematics and computing to the study of museum collections and the wider spheres of archaeology and prehistory.

In the service of museums

Counting loose change

It is standard practice in museums to 'register' objects as they are acquired, and the register is the primary record of a museum's holdings. A small collection can be monitored regularly by carrying out a check of all objects against the register, but in the case of a very large collection this may well be impracticable. The British Museum has (or is believed to have) some 5 or 6 million objects, so that a conventional stock-take of the entire collection could occupy all the qualified staff for five or six years and could be exhaustive only if all other duties were suspended for the duration.

However, a branch of statistics called 'sampling theory' can be applied, which will allow conclusions about the entire collection to be inferred (to within a known degree of certainty) by checking on a small percentage of it. Statistical sampling is widely used in scientific experiments and market surveys. It also has applications in field archaeology where financial or time constraints preclude excavation of more than part of a site, and where it is therefore important that the excavated part yields as much information as possible. Sampling theory has been of value in various areas of museum work, from assessing the long-term resources required for conservation treatment of the British Museum's large collection of Babylonian clay tablets, to ensuring that a given 'kill rate' in insecticides used for paper conservation will provide effective treatment.

A sampling programme carried out in the Coins and Medals Department in 1979 checked some 10,000 of the estimated 600,000 objects in the collections. The results indicated that, with a high degree of probability, more than 99.8 per cent of the total collection could be accounted for. Of course, this can only be verified by a complete inventory, but the important point is that the sampling methods used, and the way in which the results were extrapolated to apply to the whole collection, are based on a sound mathematical theory which is widely used and tested in other fields, and therefore carried sufficient weight to satisfy the Museum and its auditors.

Good housekeeping

A long-term solution to the management of huge collections of material is to enter details of all objects and their whereabouts into a computer database and to keep the information up to date thereafter. Such a project began in the British Museum in 1978, using a computer originally purchased for scientific work, but now transferred to a 'super-minicomputer' which runs powerful database software. The main objectives of the documentation project are threefold. Firstly, and most importantly, it will eventually form a complete inventory of the collections. Secondly, it will enable us to locate each object more quickly and easily. Finally, much extra information is being recorded, such as provenance, cultural associations and so on, which will allow the database to be used as a powerful research tool. To record such information for over five million objects is clearly an immense undertaking which will continue well into the future, and entails considerable staff costs, powerful computer hardware and highly sophisticated software (see Chapter 10).

It is the software that is of most interest here since that is where the 'intelligence' of the facility resides. To give but one example, it allows us to search a database of tens of thousands of objects looking for 'wooden bowls from Ghana which are greater than 12 cm wide', and to get an answer within seconds of posing the question. It will even take account of the fact that some relevant objects may not be described as 'wooden' at all, but as being made of 'beech', 'mahogany', 'deal' or the like. All the information about an object is stored on the computer within what is called a hierarchical database, meaning simply that the information is broken down from broad categories such as 'geography' into more specific ones such as 'continent', 'country', 'region' and so on. One can visualise this as a tree-like structure with broad categories branching out into narrower ones. Such structures are indeed referred to in computer science jargon as trees, and the technical literature abounds with pleasing arboreal metaphors such as roots, branches and leaves. To retrieve our wooden bowls, two other tree-like structures are necessary: an index to the database allowing us to find all wooden objects quickly without checking every one, and a thesaurus which remembers that 'beech', 'mahogany' and so on are all forms of wood. These three types of tree, although slightly different in form, have abstract mathematical properties in common which are embodied in the theorems of a rather obscure branch of mathematics called graph theory. By progressing from the sampling of collections to storing details of every object in a computer database, we have therefore simply transferred our allegiance from sampling theory to graph theory.

From words to pictures

Words are not the only type of information we may wish to include in a computerised record of museum collections. What about pictures? Modern technology allows us to use lasers to record images from photographs or video cameras on to videodiscs, and to access each picture or frame instantly by quoting its frame number. Although this may well be a valuable facility, it really forms no more than an appendage to the database, since we cannot search a videodisc image for details within it in the way we can search text. If we know the frame number corresponding to an object's picture, we can display the picture, and that is that. The possibilities become more interesting when we begin to ask questions such as 'What objects in this database are similar in shape to this one?'. In fact this is a commonly asked question, since shape is of great significance in the study of certain classes of ancient artefacts. It plays an important role in defining typologies which can be then be used to help date or provenance new examples. It should be emphasised that the shape discrimination required is usually much more subtle than could ever be achieved by verbal shape descriptions, and that the heavier tools of mathematics need to be applied. We are in fact attempting to persuade a high-powered calculating machine to imitate the process of human shape perception. While the human eye is extraordinarily good at doing this, the process by which it does so is not well understood and hence can be only imperfectly imitated. If the human eye can do better, why even try? In practical situations, the problem is one of quantity of information. Although it is quite reasonable to ask a human being to search by eye through a moderate number of drawings of artefacts it is not reasonable where thousands are involved. From this point of view, the capacity of an electronic computer for tireless number-crunching should have something to offer. By attempting to imitate a human cognitive process, however, we are straying into the notoriously difficult sub-discipline of computer science known as artificial intelligence, and anyone working in this field would agree that many of its problems have yet to be solved. It is nevertheless of interest to look at one approach to such problems, since this area of research demonstrates, perhaps as well as any, how a close liaison between mathematics and computer science can be of service to the museum archaeologist.

As an example of a class of artefact whose outline shapes are of particular interest to the expert, let us turn to bronze axes dating from the Early Bronze Age of southern Britain (fig. 9.1). The outline of such an axe can be measured very precisely and processed by various techniques of

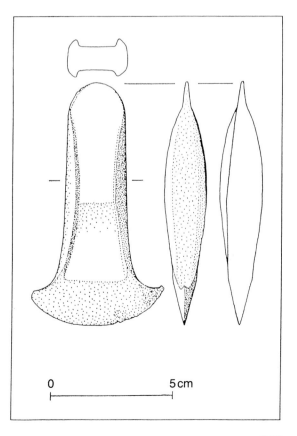

9.1 An artist's impression of an Early Bronze Age bronze axe from Devon. Measurements taken from such a drawing allow a computer to compare axe shapes, and also to draw smooth and accurate reconstructions. (The axe outlines in fig. 9.2 were drawn by a computer in this way.)

0   5 cm

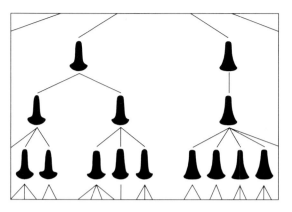

9.2 *left* A schematic impression of part of a computer database of axe shapes, structured as an inverted 'tree'. The database is searched by following the 'branches' of the tree downwards.

9.3 *right* A multi-dimensional scaling configuration of thin sections from Roman tiles, showing six groups of similar tiles. Each spot represents one thin section, and a typical thin section from each group is shown alongside.

coordinate geometry (including, incidentally, one originally invented by marine engineers to measure the shape of ship hulls) to give a final mathematical 'fingerprint' of the axe's shape. These fingerprints are in such a form that they can be easily compared one with another; that is to say the computer can calculate a measure of 'shape difference' between any two axes. This shape difference measure is the fundamental building block by which we can create large databases of outline shapes that can be searched efficiently. Trees return once more to help us in this endeavour. Figure 9.2 shows what a very small part of a large database of axe shapes might look like. The whole should be imagined as a huge and intricate multi-branched tree which has been designed so that axes similar in shape (as determined by the shape difference measure) lie in branches near each other. Suppose now that we wish to search the database for axes similar in shape to some given axe. Since the relevant ones will be concentrated in one area of the inverted tree they can be quickly located by moving from the root downwards and along the correct branches, without ever having to search the whole database.

Shuffling things about

Imagine now a slightly different problem. Suppose we are given some outline drawings of axes. Can we use a shape difference measure to classify the axes into groups of similar types on the basis of their shapes? In other words, can a computer imitate the process the archaeological expert carries out by eye when he constructs his standard typologies? There is more than one way to tackle this problem, but a very widely used and mathematically elegant technique called multi-dimensional scaling can help us. It was invented in the 1950s by psychologists, and solves a more general problem than the one we have posed. Given any group of objects, and the ability to measure difference (or dissimilarity) between any pair of the objects, how can we position the objects in two dimensions in such a way that their physical separation reflects the measure of dissimilarity between them? In other words, we want dissimilar objects to be far apart and similar ones to be close together. If we can achieve this, we have gone a long way towards solving the axe typology problem since groups of similarly shaped

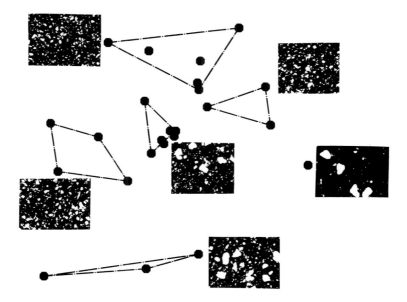

axes would appear as distinct clusters on the page and could be easily identified by eye. Two points about multi-dimensional scaling should be stressed. Firstly, it is perhaps surprising that the procedure is very difficult to do by hand, even for a small number of objects, and is quite impossible for a large number. To appreciate this, imagine that you ask a friend to mark thirty numbered points randomly on graph paper (unseen by you) and that you are required to discover their positions, with no information other than the distances between any pairs you request. The problem can be solved, but quite complex mathematics and a computer are required to solve it. Secondly, the technique can be used for any type of dissimilarity; shape difference is just one example. This means that multi-dimensional scaling has applications in many areas of work, as we can see from the following examples.

When petrological thin-sectioning (see glossary) is carried out, many separate items of data may be collected from each artefact studied, making it difficult to see those groupings of artefacts that have features in common. Multi-dimensional scaling can help to clear the murky waters. The process of examining thin sections is a painstaking and laborious one, since each slide has to be viewed individually under a microscope and various aspects of appearance judged and recorded. The scientist has to remember a great deal of information before he can even begin to look for patterns in the data. The burden can be eased by introducing the following procedure. For each thin section, the scientist makes a decision on what he regards as its significant features (such as size or shape of particular mineral inclusions) and then scores each feature, for each thin section, on a simple scale from one to five, without giving any thought at this stage to similarities and differences. These scores are then combined to give overall measures of dissimilarity between each possible pairing of artefacts – exactly the form of information required for multi-dimensional scaling. The computer then does the hard mathematics and produces a diagram showing broad groupings of similar material (fig. 9.3).

An imaginative application of multi-dimensional scaling by the statistician David Kendall serves to illustrate how widely the technique can be applied. It is known that many medieval villages in England became deserted through decline and shift of population, and the ravages of disease. It is perhaps less well known that a number of them became 'lost' as building stone was re-used and land ploughed over. The lost villages are known to have existed mainly through references in medieval parish records of births, marriages and deaths, but their location is unknown beyond the parish in which they lay. It was common practice for marriage registers to record the places of abode of the newly-weds, and what Kendall did was to use this information to construct a crude measure of dissimilarity between villages based on frequency of intermarriage over a long period. The underlying assumption was that the likelihood of marriage between people from different villages drops off with increase in geographical distance between the villages. The multi-dimensional scaling configuration resulting from processing the 'degree of intermarriage' values might therefore be expected to reflect geographical location of the villages. Kendall was able to check his results to an extent, since much of his data related to villages whose location *was* known, and this gave him some confidence in suggesting the locations of the lost villages. Kendall never claimed, of course, that this method could ever be accurate enough to pinpoint where the archaeologist should sink his spade, but rather that it could help in choosing between a number of possible locations to which the search had been restricted on other grounds.

Weights and measures

Let us now turn to another example of how mathematics, through the breadth of its applications, allows us to attack more than one problem

9.4 Brass gold-weights made by the Ashanti people of Ghana: **(a)** *far left* shows a 'figurative' type (length 106 mm), and **(b)** *above* shows a selection of six 'geometric' types.

with a single weapon. Quantum analysis is a branch of statistics designed to test a very specific hypothesis, namely that a set of measurements is 'quantised', and thus occurs in multiples of some basic measurement unit. The method concerns itself both with what the underlying unit actually is, and also with how likely it is that we are observing a real effect rather than some random one. In the early 1960s, Alexander Thom, a retired Scottish professor of engineering, sparked off a great deal of interest and controversy in the archaeological community through his claims for the existence of a 'megalithic yard', an ancient unit of measurement used by the builders of megalithic monuments. Such claims in fact go back as far as 1926, but it was with Thom's careful measurement of many stone circles and alignments in Britain and Brittany that a scientific analysis of the problem could be attempted. Thom's theoretical analysis was based on the work of S.R. Broadbent, a statistician whose quantum hypothesis allows the extent to which data are quantised to be assessed objectively. There is still some disagreement among experts about whether the methods Thom used were appropriate.

The arguments surrounding the issue, important in assessing Thom's work, were also vital to an investigation of gold-weights made by the Ashanti people of Ghana. These objects are actually made of brass, but are believed to have been used for the weighing of gold dust (fig. 9.4). Like the dimensions of stone circles, the weights of these objects seemed to peak in definite weight bands, suggesting that they were made to preset weight specifications. This observation was the starting point for a study of a large sample of gold-weights from three museums. This study showed up some fascinating differences: the figurative pieces – small models of porcupines, antelopes and so on – showed no convincing evidence for quantisation, but the geometric pieces did, as can be seen in the frequency charts of the weights (fig. 9.5). The geometric pieces were clearly made as utilitarian

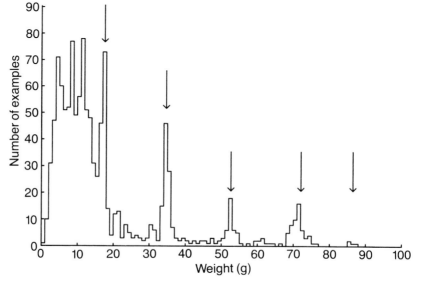

9.5 Distribution chart of the weights of 1208 geometric-type Ashanti gold-weights from the collections of the British Museum. The arrowed peaks show clearly how weights tend to concentrate around multiples of a basic weight unit. No evidence was found of similar quantisation with figurative gold-weights.

165

objects, and in fact were designed to weigh in multiples of 1.46 g. Another conclusion that emerged from this study was that around one thousand objects would need to be sampled to be able to detect the sort of peaks which were actually present. In the gold-weight study there was no problem: by gathering data from the British Museum, the Museum für Völkerkunde in Berlin, and the Pitt Rivers Museum in Oxford, over 2,500 objects were studied.

This leads us to one of the main problems in this sort of computer-based study. The computer allows us to make almost unlimited calculations, and indeed the larger the sample the better for statistical applications. But the labour involved in studying the objects and producing the data, be it weighing, chemical analysis or whatever, means that the scope of investigations has to be limited in some way. So the need to record sufficient data to enable definite conclusions to be reached has to be balanced against the requirement to make the best use of staff time and resources. This is an area where the concepts of sampling theory, mentioned at the start of this chapter, can again prove useful: sampling schemes can balance these two objectives by determining the minimum labour that must be invested to be satisfied that the correct conclusions have been reached.

In the service of archaeology

Rank and position

Let us now move away from the store-rooms of museums to the wider world of archaeology in the field. What do computers and mathematics have to offer us here? Our first example comes from a cemetery complex in Humberside dating from the Iron Age. Computer studies of cemeteries abound, and range from surveys of a number of cemeteries and their geographical distribution to very detailed studies of an individual one. Our site is actually two separate but contiguous cemeteries at the neighbouring villages of Rudston and Burton Fleming (fig. 9.6). These graves and their contents had been studied long before computers became commonplace, and gave indications of two different burial rites: one involving burial with pig bones and metal goods but no pottery, and the other involving sheep bones and pottery. Surprisingly, the 'pig' graves tended to lie with the long axis pointing north-south and the 'sheep' graves east-west. When features are as obvious as this, one hardly needs a computer to detect them. In this project, however, we wished to go further and to investigate whether the pig graves differed from the sheep graves in terms of the age, sex or apparent wealth of the incumbents. The number of cross-tabulations involved is very large, and significant trends are easily lost. If all the data are initially entered into a computer database, the power of a database management system makes it easy to present different views of the data to the researcher, allowing more subtle and complex associations to emerge.

At a more sophisticated level, computerised methods of a technique known as discriminant analysis can be invoked. This is particularly useful where the bodies have to be grouped into categories such as male/female,

9.6 A group of north-south orientated graves within barrows excavated by the British Museum at the village of Burton Fleming in Humberside (courtesy Tony Pacitto).

child/adult, or even into groups with different racial or familial origins. Sometimes it is obvious to which group an individual should be assigned, but where it is not, information such as basic measurements of bone dimensions can be added to the computer's database and discriminant analysis can then predict the group that is most probably correct. This procedure is akin to the methods now being used for computerised medical diagnosis, where the symptoms are fed in to the computer and the most likely illness is predicted. Indeed we hope it may be possible to predict some of the medical problems our Iron Age ancestors were subject to, using just these methods. We can see, then, how computers help to develop and extend information, as well as merely acting as the storage medium. The investigation has now entered a new phase where demographic characteristics of the Iron Age population are being modelled (albeit crudely, since the information available from the Iron Age is very sparse). Perhaps surprisingly, the methods of modern-day actuarial statistics, where 'life-tables' are constructed on behalf of insurance companies to help them estimate the probable lifespans of various classes of individual, have come to our aid in this project.

Getting below the surface

The application of computer technology in the excavation process itself has been a major area of growth over the last decade. Personal computers are now commonly found in site huts, even in remote locations where they can be powered by car batteries. Modern scientific excavation techniques yield prodigious quantities of data, and the abilities of even quite simple personal computer database programs to organise, tabulate and sort this information offer the archaeologist very obvious benefits. Such computer software is rapidly becoming the archaeologist's workhorse, both during the excavation process in circumstances where immediate feedback is desirable, and afterwards to help in preparing the final published report. Invaluable as this sort of computing may be, the archaeologist's spade reveals more interesting and mathematically challenging problems. Much archaeology involves looking for underlying patterns within a jumble of visual detail. In extreme cases the search for order among the chaos can become too difficult for the human eye alone.

At sites such as Petters Sports Field in Surrey, archaeologists have uncovered large numbers of post-holes (remains in the soil showing where wooden posts once supported structures). Such configurations (fig. 9.7) can be difficult to interpret for two reasons. Firstly, the marks one sees in the ground at any particular level may in fact result from many successive building phases, since the holes will commonly have been dug through earlier material and to varying depths. Secondly, an individual post-hole

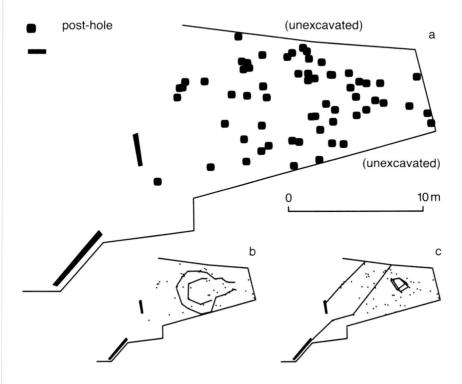

9.7 Distribution of post-holes (**a**) found during excavations at Petters Sports Field in Surrey; (**b**) and (**c**) show an archaeologist's interpretation of the structures that gave rise to medium depth and deep post-holes, respectively.

9.8 Electronic Distance Measurement device in use at the British Museum's excavation at Torbryan Caves, in Devon. As the operator takes readings they are recorded automatically on the attached 'data logger', to be transferred later to a personal computer (courtesy Cath Price).

cannot easily be assigned to any particular building phase, since any datable artefact found within it could either pre-date or post-date the structure for which the hole was dug. Nevertheless, provided that it is possible to make informed assumptions about the likely shapes and sizes of buildings at particular periods, a computer can be programmed to search for particular configurations of post-holes that might result from such a structure and 'peel them off', to reveal a simplified picture of earlier building phases. The mathematical techniques for doing this were invented fairly recently, and, unlike most of those we have so far mentioned, were developed from scratch to solve a particular archaeological problem.

At sites where a number of periods of occupation overlie one another, the archaeologist has to identify and record very large numbers of what are referred to as contexts – divisions of the excavated material that can be distinguished in some way from their neighbours. At Runnymede Bridge, the computer has been brought in to record and check relationships between contexts and to sort them into continuous sequences, thus ultimately helping the archaeologist interpret the sequences as a record of past human activity. Accurate surveying of contexts in three dimensions is clearly a major part of the excavation process. Modern surveying equipment such as Electronic Distance Measurement devices greatly facilitate this, not least because of their ability to store survey readings on data loggers, small electronic devices that record a large number of readings in a form that can later be easily transferred to a personal computer (fig. 9.8). Clearly there are few barriers to filling the site's personal computer with survey data, but what can be done with it? The excavation process is destructive. After a site has been filled in again only artefacts, notebooks and the photographic record remain to aid the archaeologist in the long post-excavation period when he or she has to decide what it all meant, and publish details of what was found. How valuable it would be to be able to reconstruct what the site looked like while excavation was in progress.

Provided that enough information was recorded at the time, we can indeed use the techniques of three-dimensional computer graphics to achieve this. A particular excavated level (corresponding, for example, to a Bronze Age occupation floor) can be 'modelled' on a computer screen and the power of coordinate geometry embodied in a sophisticated computer program allows us to view it from any angle and at any elevation. Distributions of artefacts of particular types can be superimposed exactly where they were found, to help in the search for significant patterns. Furthermore, a digital graph plotter can reproduce the whole visual image on paper, with pinpoint accuracy, in a minute or two. Figure 9.9 shows a computer reconstruction of an ancient land surface.

What does the future hold?

This brief survey has provided at least a taste of current applications of mathematics and computers in the service of museums and archaeology. What does the future hold? Museums and archaeology both suffer from chronic under-funding, and at present there seems to be no cause for optimism that this situation will change. Constrained resources will inevitably act as a brake on research and new developments, but there are other factors which work against this, and give us reason to be encouraged. Field archaeology attracts a great deal of interdisciplinary interest since it offers so many varied and interesting problems. There is greater incentive in archaeology than in many other disciplines for applied mathematicians and statisticians to develop new techniques, or to apply existing ones in novel situations. Since 1973, an annual conference devoted to the applications of computing and mathematics to archaeology has been held at varying locations in Britain. It provides a forum for the sharing of ideas among archaeologists, computer specialists and mathematicians. During the conferences floppy disks containing home-grown software are exchanged like coinage, and between conferences software and messages continue to be exchanged by electronic mail. The attendance has increased steadily over the years and the conference attracts more and more international participants. The will and skill to move forward are therefore not in short supply.

Another major factor offsets the impoverished state of museums and archaeology and in the long term this will have a far more profound effect. Quite simply, computers are becoming cheaper and more powerful all the time. Archaeology and museums have not, of course, contributed to the massive commercial pressures underlying this trend, but to a large extent they can sit back and reap the benefits. Nowhere is the pace of development more apparent than in computer graphics. Software and hardware that allow us to display reconstructions of scenes in three dimensions are, as we have seen, already available, but are steadily increasing in sophistication and falling in price. True integration of text and graphical information within databases is an area of major development effort among

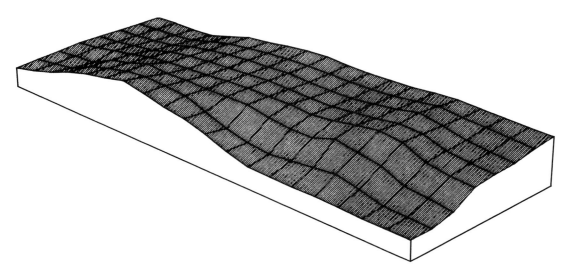

9.9 A computer with graphics software installed can process the data from a surveying instrument and reconstruct a three-dimensional impression of the land surface.

computer manufacturers, and offers great potential benefits for the curation of museum collections. Desk-top publishing already promises exciting possibilities for reducing the cost of publishing excavation reports. Archaeological units are also being tempted by the impressive capabilities of geographic information systems, which in essence allow maps to be stored, displayed, overlaid and updated on a computer screen. Laser light can now give us more than just music in our ears. Compact discs can store data too, and act as a superb archiving medium for large databases, while videodiscs give instant access to thousands of high-quality photographic images on one 14-inch disc. Further in the future, laser light looks set to replace electricity itself, driving computers a hundred times faster than the fastest now available. Developments in the world of computing move close to the speed of light. The challenge for museum curators and archaeologists in the 1990s is to keep abreast of them, and to exploit them to the full.

Further reading

Most of the standard texts relate to mathematics and computing applied to archaeology rather than to museum collections and are not particularly recent. Those dealing with mathematics and statistics have dated less quickly than those dealing with computing, and the following can be recommended. Doran and Hodson, *Mathematics and Computers in Archaeology* (1975) and Hodson *et al.* (eds.), *Mathematics in the Archaeological and Historical Sciences* (1971) give good coverage of techniques such as multi-dimensional scaling and discriminant analysis. The simpler techniques are well covered in Shennan, *Quantifying Archaeology* (1988) and Orton, *Mathematics in Archaeology* (1980). Of particular relevance to statistical quantum analysis is the comprehensive coverage in Heggie, *Megalithic Science* (1981). For the most up-to-date developments, particularly in computing, the reader cannot do better than consult recent proceedings of the annual *Computer and Quantitative Methods in Archaeology* conferences, published by British Archaeological Reports, and *Archaeological Computing Newsletter*, published by the University of Oxford. Papers of relevance also appear in the journals *American Antiquity* and *Science and Archaeology*, and more occasionally in *Archaeometry, Journal of Field Archaeology* and *Computers and the Humanities*.

CHAPTER 10

Computerising the Collections:
The art of successful flea handling

Lea Jones

The British Museum's collections contain a pair of dressed fleas from Mexico. Sceptics may baulk at such an idea, but given the attested presence of such equally implausible-sounding objects as a block of portable eighteenth-century soup (ex Captain Cook), Inuit seal-gut underwear, African cobweb hats and other equally exotic objects, the concept of dressed fleas may seem more acceptable.

This chapter addresses the problem of handling these fleas, not as extraordinary ideas, nor even as physical entities, but as units of information. Each object in a museum comprises a potential body of information, of both administrative and academic significance. These units may be every bit as difficult to define and handle, conceptually at least, as the fleas themselves.

The role of documentation and the devices for handling information in a museum context often remain hidden to visitors, who are nonetheless bombarded with information from the moment they enter any large museum or art gallery – in the form of signs indicating the way to the cafeteria, ground-plans of the premises, or, more obviously, labels and information panels associated with the gallery displays. Few people, however, are aware of how object-related information is generated, gathered, structured and subsequently applied. The processes that generate information about an object within a museum are many and varied, raising problems of both theory and practice, particularly when a major institution considers computerising this information.

The art of information handling is complex. There are no absolutely right or wrong ways to apply it, only good or bad practices. The diversity of museum collections in general requires that these practices be sufficiently flexible to accommodate the unusual object or set of circumstances, and yet sufficiently disciplined to ensure that realistic standards can be established and maintained.

Within every institution (and indeed, individual) may be found the polarised views of the pedant and the pragmatist. The former will cling rigidly to formulae regardless of the situation, nit-picking over tiny detail but sometimes unwittingly missing the larger issues. The pragmatist is more flexible, recognising that exceptions do arise and must be practically catered for. Both attitudes have a valuable role to play when considering an issue such as how to computerise a major corpus of information which exists in a variety of document types of varying degrees of complexity and intelligibility.

10.1 Page from an old British Museum register dating from 1908.

The British Museum has a sound history in the field of documentation, even if our predecessors were on occasions less rigorous in their practices than are current staff. In 1756 the Museum was compiling records of its acquisitions in bound ledgers called 'The Book of Presents' and in 1836 the then single Department of Antiquities began to complete bound Acquisition Registers of a type still in use today (fig. 10.1). There are now ten curatorial departments, and a project of ten years standing, systematically computerising data about the collections, offers the means of sophisticated information retrieval.

There is now a general awareness of the desirability of providing accurate and well-maintained inventories of the holdings of all major publicly funded institutions in order to guard against the loss of objects. However, it has also been recognised that it is impractical to impose a universal method of inventory control across *all* museums and art galleries. The diversity of collections even within a single museum demands instead a flexible series of management devices. These typically comprise the registration of objects, location of the items, stock-taking and auditing processes, as well as the longer-term creation of catalogues and other adjuncts to research. General collections management processes (i.e. the formal documentation of an object on acquisition – or 'accessioning', monitoring object condition, recording of object movement, loan processing, storage environment, etc.) are, however, becoming more generally standardised as a result of the work and influence of bodies such as the Museum Documentation Association. All these processes generate and use documentation. The mere presence of an object on museum premises entails some form of associated documentation.

Not surprisingly, many museums experience difficulty keeping pace with such large-scale demands for recording and, latterly and increasingly, retrieval of this information. However, with recent advances in information technology it has been shown that automation of all or some of these processes will provide an effective way forward.

A major problem facing established museums is the natural variation in recording practices that have developed with time. It may be, for example, that the attribution of inventory numbers follows not one but many forms, each with its own idiosyncratic syntax. Objects may move between departments, as new departments are formed either by evolving from existing ones or merging with others (fig. 10.2). When this happens, items may not be re-registered but will retain their original identity. The original documentation similarly remains with the original department that created it. There are practical reasons for this arrangement: any

10.2 Diagram showing the evolution of the curatorial departments within the British Museum since its foundation in 1753.

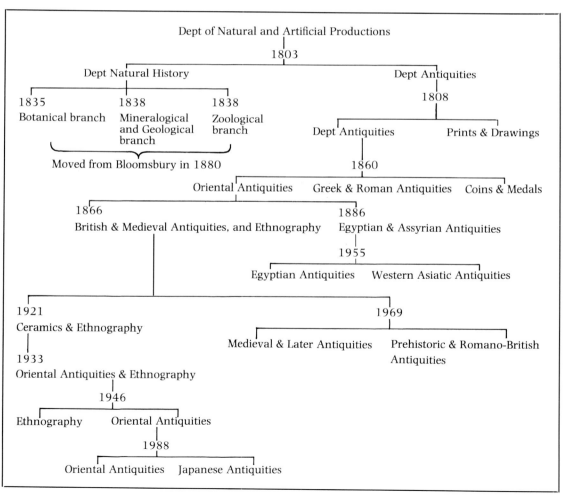

manual system of record-keeping relies either on heavy duplication of information, sited wherever that information may be routinely required, or on a complex system of cross-referenced card-indexes which provide guides to relevant documentation. In either case, the time, expertise and sustained communication required to make this system work place heavy demands on staff who normally have other priorities.

Automation of an information system provides an effective solution to these problems if only by centralising the information concerned. Centralised records provide the means by which many people may have access to the same body of information, regardless of their physical situation. It may also be argued that, provided a computer record is sympathetically laid out, it is more readable than many handwritten entries found in registers, where handwriting, variations in content and idiosyncracies of style may conspire to confuse the reader.

As a preliminary to automation, a major process of review is necessary in order to establish the nature, content and application of the information categories and of the documents containing them. Without such a review there is a serious danger that existing documentation problems may simply be automated along with the data, thus perpetuating rather than resolving them. Equally, this important preliminary is vital to the success of choosing a suitable computer system. Along with the review of existing data, a clearly defined set of objectives needs to be defined. At the most basic level, major museums must satisfy a requirement to produce inventories, regardless of any additional or subsequent developments.

'Great fleas have little fleas...': What is an inventory?

An inventory should contain sufficient information to enable the unequivocal identification of an object. The object name, its identification number, and its location are the very minimum categories of information that may usefully be called an inventory.

The creation of an inventory and an audit trail addresses various problems, both of theory and practice. To be genuinely useful, it is essential to include some reference to the number of elements involved in any one 'object' described as a single item. Without a clear understanding of 'how many' as well as 'what' and 'where', there cannot be a confident system of collections management. This prompts a further question: how should this indication be expressed? How, for example, should one handle the dressed fleas and their garments in terms of a computer record? The pedant might create a separate physical record for each item: the fleas, plus the individual garments. Theoretically (it would be argued) these items may become detached from the flea and be lost in the collections. Should they be found, it would be necessary to have a physically separate record to enable specific identification of this object to be made. The pragmatist might acknowledge this point but would offer the further thought that, under normal circumstances, it is unlikely that a flea's stray garment could be mistaken for anything else, and that the flea, its garments and any other intimately associated paraphernalia would be more sensibly and helpfully handled as a single record. A text description of the item(s) covered by the record should allow the information to be both recorded and retrieved without having to split it between several records. In this way all the fleas and their items of clothing may be recalled successfully. Furthermore, they would be viewed as a single entity from a collections point of view. But (the pedant may pursue the point), what if the flea and its garments were housed in separate locations? Then say so in the record, the pragmatist would counter. In this way the flea gets to keep its clothes on – at least in the records, if not the collections. It is indeed possible for a theoretically single item to have more than one location simultaneously, typically the case with temporary locations and compound objects. A bowl may require conservation, or need to be photographed, but its associated pedestal may not. Thus the bowl will change its location, whilst that for the pedestal remains the same (i.e. the permanent location for both the bowl and pedestal).

However, the true condition and nature of an object can only really be judged by physically checking it. This, too, is a major element in an inventory.

'... upon their backs to bite 'em': Hazards of locating the collections

The collectors of the eighteenth and nineteenth centuries evidently had few qualms about braving remote and inhospitable peoples and places, and their donations to the Museum collections occasionally reflect the intimidations and perils they faced in acquiring them – precisely what Museum staff experience when confronted with some of these legacies. Darts that are literally 'dressed to kill', with curare and other nerve poisons, can be particularly difficult to handle, psychologically as well as physically. Gloves do not provide total protection against accidental nicks. The darts, the lumps of poison and the raw materials from which it is extracted all provide a challenge for others with a taste (figuratively speaking) for excitement. (It should be made clear that, in the vast majority of cases, the poison is so aged that its potency is thought to be negligible.) A frisson of concern ran through the staff when it was discovered that items have only been routinely fumigated against pathogens since the 1950s. Anthrax, it appears, is a remote but potential hazard. Parts of people present another unusual challenge (fig. 10.3). The Egyptian department's assorted examples of the embalmer's art extend from the full body to three lone penises (gilded). These examples vie with other reminders of some of the more arcane uses to which human technical ingenuity has been applied: the production of shrunken human heads from South America, or indeed dressed fleas from Mexico. In all cases, the challenge to the documentation specialist remains the same: how to do justice to the objects in order to create an accurate and sufficiently detailed record of the object to allow it to be identified with confidence.

Possibly more terrifying than the prospect of being run through with poisoned weapons, gassed by noxious organic exhalations from embalmed bodies, or turning black with anthrax, is the very real prospect of an object

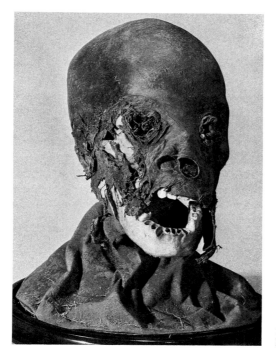

10.3 Mummified head from the Egyptian collections.

disintegrating in (or falling from) one's hands. Museum staff are trained in the handling and care of objects and are well aware of some of the obvious dangers. For example, a crispy one-hundred-year-old nest of leaf boxes that snugly fit their storage device is best left snugly fitted in their storage device and observed *in situ* during inventory checks. Handling objects of this sort may well result in extensive (and expensive) damage. The awful prospect of dropping a priceless Ming vase, everyone's idea of a nightmare, is minimised by working in pairs, with one person observing the necessary details from a safe distance and the other handling the object.

A more recent development in information technology, that of interactive videodisc, may provide the means of avoiding some of these hazards. If an image can be provided of the more inaccessible, fragile or minute objects, students and visitors may view the record and image simultaneously without anyone having to handle the items. This has several advantages: fragile items will be spared the cumulative damage resulting from repeated handling and removal from storage facilities. In addition, museum assistants or other personnel whose task it is to prepare the objects for visitors and to supervise their access to the collections may have more time for other tasks.

'And little fleas have lesser fleas': What price detail?

A limited inventory is exactly that. It cannot offer any greater insight into the object, the circumstances of its manufacture, or the cultural framework from which it derived. The inventory does not constitute 'information' but 'data'. There is no automatic association, for example, between the object's name, its provenance and its physical location within the Museum. Thus, a list of object names from such a database will only be a list of names, not a list of names according to country of origin or date of manufacture. This would constitute information – data plus a contextual framework allowing a larger picture to be revealed. But how detailed should (or can) this information be? Clearly much will depend on the availability of information in the first place. Some register entries are so rudimentary that they are unable to support anything more than a basic inventory. Other registers and sources, such as departmental file cards and reports, can be used to enhance a basic level of data so that it truly constitutes information and, as such, is useful for the production of books, catalogues and as a research tool.

Different departments require a different degree of detail for different research applications. The quantity of detail and the resultant record size will also affect the amount of time involved in the creation of a single record. In a perfect world, where resources are unlimited, all available data could be accommodated. Sadly, this is not possible. Constraints of finance, manpower and time all conspire to limit what may be achieved, and compromises are inevitable. The enhancement of records into research tools must remain secondary if the primary objective is producing an inventory. However, some middle way between a basic inventory and a fully detailed record is possible.

Information about materials and techniques of manufacture, geography of find-spot and manufacture, and a short free-text description of the object are examples of the information categories currently included in the British Museum's inventory. However, the enormous diversity of objects within and between the collections does mean that a degree of flexibility is necessary to provide a sensible selection of fields that reflect the variation in object type. For example, different aspects of a picture, a coin and an Egyptian mummy would need to be emphasised if they are to be distinguished from other objects of the same sort.

Despite limitations imposed upon the *quantity* of information recorded, there are ways to guarantee *quality* and to maximise the usefulness of the available information. How data are input is directly relevant to the way the same information is retrieved from the system. Control of the quality of data can be vitally important. In most systems, if a word is misspelt or miskeyed, that piece of data can only be retrieved if the same format is used during the retrieval process.

One means of controlling the way data are typed into a record is by a so-called 'authority list'. This can be useful in situations where a set number of allowable words or phrases may be used when adding data to a specific part of the record. Any word or phrase not recognised by the computer as being on the authority list will cause the list of available choices to be displayed. The person entering the details must then choose an option from this list and the computer will then add the choice to the record automatically. An example of how this might be applied to an inventory record would be to control the format of named collections, e.g. 'Sloane Bequest, Miscellanea'. Without controlling the way in which this collection name is entered, it is possible that the retrieval of records bearing such information might be wholly or partially unsuccessful.

Another similar but more sophisticated device for use in record systems is a 'thesaurus' (fig. 10.4). A thesaurus (see Chapter 9) is essentially a database in its own right, with each word constituting a record, cross-referenced to other records or terms through a series of relationships which can be broad, narrow or related (e.g. 'metal' is a narrower term of 'inorganic', but it is a broad term of 'iron'. In turn, iron is a related term to 'steel'.) Each term is also designated as either 'preferred' or 'non-

10.4 Example of a thesaurus display.

```
HIERARCHICAL LISTING OF THESAURUS    DO    Materials
From AS
Top terms for this thesaurus are: INORGANIC
                                   ORGANIC
                                   ORGANIC CHEMICAL

NP BARKCLOTH                           BAT HAIR
      PT BARK                                BT HAIR
   BARLEY                                     NT FLYING FOX HAIR
      BT CEREAL                         BAT TOOTH
   BARNACLE                                   BT MAMMAL TOOTH
      BT CARAPACE                             NT FLYING FOX TOOTH
NP BARYTES                              BAUXITE
      PT BARITE                               BT STONE
   BASALT                                     RT ALUMINIUM
      BT STONE                          BEAK
      RT ANDESITE                             BT KERATIN STRUCTURES
         LAVA                                 NT HORNBILL BEAK
         PORPHYRY                                TOUCAN BEAK
         RHYOLITE                       BEAN
   BASS                                       BT SEED
      BT FISH TISSUE                          NT ALGAROBA BEAN
   BASSWOOD                                      COFFEE BEAN
      BT WOOD                                    HARICOT BEAN
      RT BAST                                    LOCUST BEAN
         LIME WOOD                               MUNG BEAN
NP BASSWOOD BARK FIBRE                  BEAN STEM
      PT BAST                                 BT STEM
   BAST                                 BEAN TREE WOOD
      BT BARK FIBRE                           BT WOOD
      NP BASSWOOD BARK FIBRE            BEAR
         BASTWOOD BARK FIBRE                  BT MAMMAL TISSUE
      RT BARK                                 NT GRIZZLY BEAR
         BASSWOOD                                POLAR BEAR
NP BASTWOOD BARK FIBRE                  BEAR BONE
      PT BAST                                 BT MAMMAL BONE
   BAT                                  BEAR CLAW
      BT MAMMAL TISSUE                        BT MAMMAL CLAW
      NT FLYING FOX                     BEAR FUR
   BAT BONE                                   BT FUR
      BT MAMMAL BONE                          RT BEAR HAIR
```

preferred', i.e. deemed suitable for inclusion in a record, or not. Non-preferred terms are not absolutely *forbidden* for use in the records, but no relationships are attached to them, and this has implications during information retrieval. Supposing someone requires a list of all the metal items in a large collection. Without a thesaurus, the records would need to be searched by naming all the metals individually, but without knowing which metals have actually been recorded in the records. This is clearly cumbersome and possibly unsatisfactory and many users might be tempted to abandon the process before achieving their ends. In contrast, use of a thesaurus would require only the broad term (in this case, 'metal') to be stated, plus the relationship to be investigated (in this case the narrower terms). In this way all records with named metals will be retrieved, as well as those that only possess the term 'metal'. An additional element found in the thesaurus is a 'scope note'. These offer the opportunity to record additional insights into the content or application of a term, particularly if there is some ambiguity involved. This is especially useful in a museum context, where vast numbers and types of objects representing different specialisms may be united by the thesaurus.

A particular problem requiring resolution concerns the status given to scientific names for plants and animals. The problem arises when more common, everyday names are available. Take the human flea, or *Pulex irritans*. The pedant's argument might be that *Pulex irritans* is a very specific term for an otherwise undistinguished little insect. It provides precision, 'flea' being too vague and potentially confused with other types of flea, such as the dog flea, or (disaster!) the water flea. The pragmatist might suggest that precision is fine only so long as everyone understands the term: in fact, *Pulex irritans* is less obviously a flea, than 'flea'. The pedant, persistent as ever, could insist that *Pulex irritans* is the proper term for a flea and it therefore ought to be provided for those who understand it. The pragmatist could agree, pointing out that the scope notes for each term could be used for precisely this purpose, adding that, unless a scientific name has no more common alternative, it should remain non-preferred, with an alternative preferred term supplied.

The thesaurus functions not only as a retrieval aid, but also as a reference facility. People are often uncertain as to the exact nature of the enquiry they wish to make concerning the Museum collections. Sometimes this uncertainty is due to ignorance of the contents of the records and the way in which objects are referred to, particularly in large and varied collections. Browsing through the thesaurus allows the user to move between ideas and concepts, on the one hand, and individual terms – either as an alphabetical list, or as separate records in which all the terms that are related in any way are displayed, along with the scope notes. The user is then able to make a detailed search of the database, armed with the knowledge of its potential contents and the spelling of the terms involved. This aspect of information handling in museums is a lexicographic task, involving the definition, refinement and structuring of the terms employed in a computerised record.

'... And so ad infinitum': Where will it all end?

The task of computerising the collections of an institution like the British Museum is a substantial one, but the day will come, some years hence, when all departments have had all their documentation computerised and all their objects checked. However, there will still be the ongoing task of maintaining the system that has been created. A database requires maintenance, not merely because new records will have to have their content assessed and controlled, but because when new ideas permeate the academic disciplines, this too should properly be reflected in the terminology used in the construction of records. A database should be as dynamic as the institution that creates it. Its production is not a once-and-for-all process but a tool in its own right, complementing the many other processes that contribute to the Museum's development.

Further reading

R.B. Light, D.A. Roberts and J.D. Stewart (eds.), 1966. *Museum Documentation Systems: Developments and applications*. London, Butterworth.
E. Orna and C. Pettit, 1980. *Information Handling in Museums*. London, Clive Bingley.
D. Andrew Roberts (ed.), 1988. *Collections Management for Museums*. Cambridge, Museum Documentation Association.

Glossary

The entries in the glossary mainly describe in some detail techniques that are referred to briefly and in more than one place in the text. See the index for references to other techniques which are described more fully within the text.

Atomic absorption spectrophotometry (AAS)

In contrast to X-ray fluorescence (XRF) (*see below*), atomic absorption spectrophotometry (AAS) requires that a sample be removed from the object under examination, but this sample is very small, typically about one-hundredth of a gramme. The sample is dissolved in acids and then some of the solution is sprayed into a flame in the instrument. At the same time, light of a wavelength characteristic of one of the elements to be measured is shone through the flame; some of the light will be absorbed by atoms of that element in the sample. The amount of light absorbed is proportional to the quantity of the element in the sample and, hence, in the artefact. Measurements must be made for each element separately, using the same sample solution, in order to achieve a complete analysis of the artefact. Obviously (unlike XRF) this technique is intrinsically destructive, but there are certain advantages. It can be more accurate and, because it is very sensitive, very low concentrations (as low as 5 parts per million in some cases), in addition to the major components of alloys, can be measured. As with XRF, non-metals such as ceramics and glass can also be analysed.

Confidence level

In the context of experimental data, this is a statistical statement of the degree of certainty that a quoted range of values includes the true value of the quantity being measured. Many experimental measurements can be described by the so-called Gaussian or normal distribution. This is a bell-shaped distribution curve of probability versus measured value: the highest probability is at the centre at the top of the bell, and the probability of observing values on either side of the central one, corresponding to this maximum probability, falls away symmetrically. The central value is the theoretical mean, μ, and is the true value of the quantity being measured. The rapidity of fall-off can be described by the scatter of the values about the mean: this is the standard derivation, σ. An observed measurement or mean, m, of a series of measurements is an estimate of the true value, μ, and its error can usually be assumed to be the standard deviation, σ, of the Gaussian distribution. Confidence statements for the Gaussian distribution are exemplified as follows: there is a 68 per cent probability that the true value will be within the range $m - \sigma$ to $m + \sigma$ and a 95 per cent probability of the true value being between $m - 2\sigma$ and $m + 2\sigma$.

Emission spectrography (ES)

In this technique, a small sample is removed from the object to be analysed, mounted in a conducting graphite electrode and excited either by a spark source or by a continuous DC arc. The spectrum emitted by the elements present is in the visual or ultra-violet wavelength regions and can either be recorded on a photographic plate or electronically.

The method is extremely sensitive for most elements and can give a simultaneous analysis for up to forty elements. However, due to inherent instability in the arc excitation, the method lacks sufficient precision for quantitative measurement of major elements. These problems have now been resolved by inductively coupled plasma spectrometry (ICPS) (*see below*). However, emission spectrography is still useful for the detection and quantification of trace elements, and as such was once the method employed for many of the major analytical studies on antiquities.

Energy-dispersive X-ray analysis (EDXA)

Samples bombarded by electrons (e.g. in scanning or transmission electron microscopes) or by X-rays (e.g. in X-ray fluorescence analysis) emit X-rays which are characteristic of the composition of the sample. These X-rays can be collected by a solid-state detector from which a display of intensity *vs* X-ray energy can be obtained, hence the term energy-dispersive X-ray analysis. The energies of the X-rays depend upon the elements present in the sample, whilst the intensities depend upon how much of those elements is present. Thus it is possible to determine the chemical composition of the sample (*see also* X-ray fluorescence analysis; scanning and transmission electron microscopes).

It is also possible to collect and analyse the characteristic X-rays using a **wavelength-dispersive spectrometer.** In this instrument the principle of determining the composition of the sample is similar, except that the spectrometer is used to produce a display of intensity *vs* X-ray wavelength (the wavelengths of the X-rays are inversely proportional to their energies). Thus the wavelengths can be used in the same way as the energies to determine which elements are present in the sample, and the intensities provide an estimate of the amounts of those elements. Energy-dispersive and wavelength-dispersive analysis each have their own particular advantages and disadvantages, but in general the strength of energy-dispersive analysis lies in its speed and ease of application, whilst the advantage of wavelength-dispersive analysis lies in its greater sensitivity and resolution.

Inductively coupled plasma spectrometry (ICPS)

This is a recently developed analysis technique with particularly favourable features for archaeological objects: it provides quantitative analyses for many elements in each sample (10–30 typically), and it is sensitive, precise and rapid. Solutions must be prepared from samples taken from objects; typically, 50 mg of sample is needed. Spectrometers are either simultaneous or sequential in operation – both are expensive, the former more so.

The **optical emission spectrometers** (ICP–OES) use a very high-temperature plasma flame to excite the emission lines of elements in the UV to visible spectral region. The **mass spectrometer** version (ICP–MS) uses a plasma as the source but a mass spectrometer as the detector, where the actual atoms themselves are separated by mass and then detected.

To date, only a fairly limited number of archaeological applications have been published, although the technique, particularly in the mass spectrometer version, seems to have great potential for the analysis of large numbers of samples down to very low concentrations of elements.

Neutron activation analysis (NAA)

This is a popular analysis technique in archaeology, used mainly for provenance studies of ceramics and rocks such as obsidian and marble. The basic principles are fairly simple: when a material is placed in a dense flux of neutrons, such as within a nuclear reactor, the atoms of the chemical elements of the material capture passing neutrons and are transformed into radioactive isotopes of the same element, which emit radiation. After the material has been removed from the reactor it continues to emit radiation as the radioactive isotopes decay, and, if placed in front of suitable radiation detectors, the radioactivity of each element can be isolated and is a direct measure of the amount of that element in the material. Standard materials of known composition are irradiated at the same time for calibration purposes. The method thus gives the quantity of each element and is also very sensitive: elements which are present at ppm (parts per million) level in the material can be easily quantified, although not all elements produce suitable isotopes for measurement. The size of sample needed is typically about 50 mg.

Scanning electron microscope (SEM)

The magnification which can be practicably achieved with the conventional light microscope is limited to about 1500 times. Furthermore, the depth of focus is relatively small, so that the 'hills' and the 'valleys' on the surface of an object may not be in focus at the same time. The SEM overcomes these limitations.

The basis of the SEM is relatively simple. A very narrow beam of electrons is generated by heating a wire filament (as in a light bulb) to a high temperature under a strong potential difference. This beam passes down a cylindrical 'column' about 1 m long, around which are a series of electromagnetic 'lenses' which allow the beam to be focused and moved. The sample is positioned at the base of the column, and the beam is scanned very rapidly back and forth across the sample. As the electrons hit the sample some are scattered back from the surface, and low-energy electrons are also knocked out of the sample. These 'back-scattered' and secondary electrons are converted into electronic signals which give rise to images of the area scanned on a TV screen.

The magnification is simply the ratio of the size of the image on the TV screen to the size of the area scanned on the sample.

In addition to back-scattered and secondary electrons, the impact of the electron beam on the sample generates other signals. In particular, a spectrum of X-rays is produced, the precise nature of which depends on the elemental composition of the sample. This X-ray spectrum may be processed and analysed, using an X-ray spectrometer in the SEM, to yield the elemental composition of the sample in a manner analogous to X-ray fluorescence analysis (*see below; see also* energy-dispersive X-ray analysis).

Stable isotope analysis of marble

The stable isotope ratios are the relative amounts of the isotopes of carbon (^{13}C and ^{12}C) and oxygen (^{18}O and ^{16}O); these two elements, together with calcium (which does not exhibit useful differences in isotope ratios), form the basic chemical structure of marble (calcium carbonate). The analytical technique requires relatively tiny sample sizes (10–20 mg), but to ensure that a representative sample of a marble object has been taken, a drilling of around 0.5 g of marble is extracted from an inconspicuous part of the sculpture and small amounts of this homogenised powder are weighed out for analysis. After reacting the sample with acid under controlled conditions, the carbon dioxide liberated is collected and analysed using a mass spectrometer. Repeated measurements on marble from the same quarry have been shown to give a consistent pattern. However, the geological conditions prevailing (particularly temperature and pressure) when the marble was formed determined the isotopic ratios. Hence the pattern of isotopic ratios should vary from quarry to quarry like a signature. This is indeed the case, but there is significant overlap of the patterns for some quarries. Assigning the marble of a particular sculpture to one source rather than another may therefore not always be feasible. Stable isotope analysis is now being used in conjunction with trace element analysis by NAA (*see above*) to resolve the products of those quarries which the former alone cannot distinguish.

Thin-section petrography

Thin-section petrography is a standard geological technique, fundamental to determining the mineralogical and textural characteristics of rocks; it can be applied in the same way to ceramic materials. First, a small fragment of material is removed and stuck to a glass slide; it is then carefully ground away until it is only 0.03 mm thick. At this thickness most rock-forming silicate minerals are translucent, and the thin section can be viewed in transmitted light using a polarising microscope. Particular minerals can be recognised by their characteristic optical properties so that individual grains and rock fragments can be identified. Textural characteristics – such as the size, shape and orientation of grains – can also be observed. Although clay minerals are generally too fine-grained to be reliably identified, features such as clay pellets and parallel alignment of the platy clay particles, which may result from forming processes, can be recognised.

Transmission electron microscope (TEM)

The transmission electron microscope is in some ways similar to the scanning electron microscope (*see above*), in that an electron beam, focused using electromagnetic 'lenses', is used to 'illuminate' the specimen. However, the TEM is designed to look through the sample and examine its internal structure, whereas the SEM is essentially an instrument for looking in detail at the surface of the sample. Because electrons are rapidly absorbed, the sample must be very finely crushed or prepared as extremely thin sections, so that generally very small amounts of material are examined. The magnification range of the TEM overlaps that of the SEM but also extends to considerably higher magnifications, allowing very fine inclusions and even details of atomic structure to be imaged. In addition, electron diffraction patterns (cf X-ray diffraction) can be formed and used to provide information on the structure and identity of minute particles and inclusions. As in the SEM, the impact of the electron beam upon the sample generates other signals, including X-rays which can be used to analyse chemically features of interest (*see also* energy-dispersive X-ray analysis).

Units

Mass **g** (grammes), **mg** (thousandths of a gramme), **kg** (thousands of grammes); a **tonne** is one thousand kg.

Length **m** (metres), **nm** (billionths of a metre), **μm** (millionths of a metre), **mm** (thousandths of a metre), **cm** (hundredths of a metre), **km** (thousands of metres).

Time **s** (seconds), **ks** (thousands of seconds), **a** (years), **ka** (thousands of years).

ppm parts per million (this is not in fact a unit, but a concentration ratio, cf 1 per cent = 1 part per hundred).

Xeroradiography

Xeroradiography is essentially similar to conventional X-ray radiography (*see below*) except that instead of film a special electrically charged, selenium-coated plate is used to capture the image. The different intensities of X-rays penetrating different parts of an object differentially discharge the electric charge on the plate, producing a latent X-ray image. The latent image is transferred from the plate to a sheet of paper using fine toner powder in much the same way as a photocopy ('xerox') is produced and hence the name xeroradiography. Although inherently a low-contrast technique, it has the particular property of enhancing discontinuities ('edge-enhancement') and has been found to be particularly useful for the examination of ceramic materials. Xeroradiography can be used to detect such features as joins between different pieces of clay, the orientation of voids or inclusions due to wheel-throwing, and the manner of affixing handles; it can thus be a valuable aid in determining how a ceramic vessel or object was formed.

X-ray diffraction (XRD) analysis

The particular advantage of XRD analysis is that it can be used to identify the mineralogy of very small samples (less than the size of a pin-head when using an X-ray camera), thus allowing virtually non-destructive sampling. XRD analysis makes use of the fact that crystalline materials diffract X-rays and produce patterns which are specific to their mineralogical composition. These patterns can be recorded on film using an X-ray camera or on a chart using an X-ray diffractometer. By reference to standard data from samples of known mineralogy, these patterns can be used rather like fingerprints to identify the unknown samples.

X-ray fluorescence (XRF) analysis

X-ray fluorescence has been called the curator's dream instrument because the actual measurements are non-destructive and usually the artefact itself is analysed rather than a sample taken from it. The analysis is carried out by aiming an X-ray beam at a small area about 2 mm in diameter on the artefact's surface. Interaction of the X-rays with the metal causes other (fluorescence) X-rays to be generated, which are detected as a spectrum. The energies of the fluorescence X-rays are specific to the elemental composition of the artefact. Thus the position and relative heights of the peaks in the spectrum can be interpreted, using reference materials of known composition, to give a chemical analysis – which elements are present and their quantity. xRF is accurate and fast (a result can be obtained in a few minutes), but it is not sensitive enough to measure low concentrations such as trace elements (i.e. those present in concentrations of less than about 0.1 per cent). However, it will quickly determine the alloy of a metal artefact and can also be used to analyse non-metallic materials such as ceramics and glass. It is often used for a rapid preliminary analysis and is particularly applied to small artefacts or those made of precious metal for which a non-destructive analysis is important. One limitation is that only a thin layer, less than 0.1 mm, is actually analysed. This can give misleading results on corroded or plated metal unless the surface is abraded, but it may be an advantage if the surface plating or other applied decoration is the feature of interest.

X-ray radiography

X-ray radiography is familiar as the technique used to examine people with suspected bone fractures. X-rays passing through the appropriate part of the patient do not penetrate denser materials such as bone as well as they do the less dense soft tissues; they therefore penetrate breaks in the bone better than the surrounding bone. An X-ray-sensitive film beneath the patient records the relative intensities of the X-rays that emerge.

The technique works just as well for antiquities and paintings, displaying such features as components of different densities, soldered joints, repairs and overpainting.

Index

Figures in bold refer to illustrations.

adhesive 88, 89
adits 66
Agucha silver mines, India 65
Alchorn, Mr 11
Alderley Edge copper mines, Cheshire 59
Aldrevandini Beaker 51–2
alum 43
aluminium 82
analytical techniques
  in authenticity testing 146–8
  early use of 11–13
  see also glossary
antimony
  in glass 42, 46, 47, 50
Apianus 156
archaeometry 13
Arretine pottery 23
arsenic 75, 95
arsenical copper
  Egyptian 79
  manufacture of 75
  properties 75, 79
artefact
  shape 160–2
  typology 160, 162–3
artificial intelligence 161
ash
  in glass manufacturing 40, 41
Ashanti gold-weights 165–6
assay of silver 67, 68, 83
atomic absorption spectrophotometry (AAS)
  description of technique 182
  of flint 108–9
  of metal 79
authenticity testing 141–57
  by composition 145
  by dendrochronology 144–5
  limits of expertise 154
  by patination 150
  by radiocarbon 142–3
  restoration 152
  by thermoluminescence 143–4, **145**
authority list 178
axes
  chemical analysis of flint 107–9, **108**
  Early Bronze Age 161
  Egyptian 79–81
  petrography of stone 106–7
  shape analysis 161–2
Aztec 149

Badakshan Valley, Afghanistan 32, 148
Baikal, Lake, Siberia 148
Basse Yutz wine flagons 88
Beaker burials 25, 127–9, **128**
bellows 63
Benue Rift, Nigeria 113–14
Bermondsey Abbey, London 136
bidri 95, **95**
bitumen 151
black-burnished pottery 22–3, **22**
bone, radiocarbon dating of 121, **121**, **123**, 127–9, **128**
brass
  cementation 81
  Chinese 81
  Etruscan fibulae 11
  fake Etruscan figure 146
  India 76
  iron in 81
  Roman 81
Britannia silver standard 83
Broadbent, S. R. 165
bronze
  authenticity studies on 143, 144, 146
  casting 84–5
  Chinese **32**, 152
  Corinthian 95, 150
  Cullen, Ireland, bronze from 11
  Cypriot stands 85, **85, 86**
  definition and origin of 11
  Egypt 80
  high-tin bronze mirror 92–3, **93**
  Horses of St Mark's 11
  Igbo-Ukwu, Nigeria 113–14, **113**
  Jungling statue, Magdalensberg 155, **155**
  leaded 78, 80
  microstructure of **86, 93**
  moulds 31, **32**
  palstave **84**
  patination of 150
  Payne Knight, Richard, collection of 151
  properties of 77
  provenance studies of 13, 113–14
bronzo 11
building materials
  brick and tile 17–19, **19**, 103–4
  mortar and concrete 19–21
  see also lime

burial
  Beaker, dating of 127–9, **128**
  'Red Lady' of Paviland 25
  see also cemetery
Burton Fleming, Humberside 166

cadmium
  in modern gold solders 147
calcite
  TL dating of 133, 135–6
canopic jars, fake 147
carburisation 78–9
Carrara marble, Italy 109–12, 154
Cartagena, Spain, lead ingots from 68
cassiterite 71
Castel Sant' Angelo, Rome 105, **105**
casting 84–5
  casting core 84–5
  casting flash 84, **84**
  lost-wax 85
  moulds 31, **32**, 84, **84**
cementation brass 81
cemetery
  Burton Fleming 166
  Rudston 166
  statistics 166–7
ceramics
  definition 16
  see also firing, porcelain, pottery
Cherchel, N. Africa, pottery from 21–3
China
  brass 81
  coins 81
  glass in 37, 54
  patination on bronzes 150
  porcelain 27–9, **26**
  restored *fang ding* 152
  statues 81
  Tonglushan 65
classification
  see typology
clay
  chemical composition 102
  petrography 100–2
  physical properties 16
  see also pottery
cluster analysis 104
cobalt
  in glass 43, 45, 47, 52
coins
  Chinese 81
  contemporary forgeries 91, **92**

coins – *contd.*
  fake Anglo-Saxon coins 146
  Frankish 83
  gold 83
  Greek 81
  Henry VIII 83
  Indian silver coins 65–6
  Merovingian 83
  Sutton Hoo 83–4
collections, computerisation of 172–81
compact disc 171
computer
  early use in archaeometry 13
  graphics 170–1
  multivariate statistics 103–4, **105**
  use in archaeology 158, 166–70
  see also computer database
computer database
  hierarchical 160
  index 160
  of museum collections 13, 159–62,
    172–81
  shape 160–2
  thesaurus 160, 179–80
computer science 158
confidence level 126, 143, 182
conservation
  effects on surface composition
    146–7
  history of 12
  statistical sampling 159, 166
context
  archaeological 76, 169
cooking pots 21–3
copper
  alloys 75–9
  in Egyptian faience 32, 33
  in glass 43, 47
  lead isotopes in 112–14
  mining 59
  native 58, 75
  ores 58
  provenancing 112–14, **113**
  refining 65
  smelting 60–5
Corinthian bronze 95, 150
cow dung 69
Crystal Skull 150
Cullen, Mr 11
cupellation 76
cupels 67
cuprite **43**
Cwmystwyth copper mines, Wales 59–
  60, 129–30

Dariba silver mines, Rajasthan 65–6
data logger 169
database
  see computer database
dating 117–40
  dendrochronology 118, 125–6,
    126, 138
  early palaeobotanical methods 12
  potassium-argon 118

radiocarbon 118, 120–30, **121**,
  123–8, 136–7
thermoluminescence 130–7, **132**,
  134
uranium series 118, 135
see also authenticity
Davy, Sir Humphrey 11
dendrochronology 118, 125–6, **126**,
  138
Derrynaflan, Ireland 89, **89**
desk-top publishing 171
discriminant analysis 104, **105**,
  166–7
distillation of zinc 69

Egypt
  alum 43
  cobalt 43
  copper-alloy axes 79–81
  Egyptian blue 11
  faience 32–3, **33, pl. 2.2**
  fakes 147–8
  glass 38, 43
  natron 41
  Wadi Natrun 41
electronic distance measurement (EDM)
  169
emission spectrography 12, 182
enamels
  on glass 51
  medieval 49
  Mosan **49**
energy-dispersive X-ray analysis (EDXA)
  in SEM
  description of technique 183
  of Egyptian faience 32
  of porcelain 28
  of pottery 24
  of solder 89
Etruscan
  brass fibulae 11
  bronze figures 146
  bronze vessel 146

Fabroni, G. 11
faience, Egyptian 32–3, **33**, 37, **pl. 2.2**
figurines, ceramic 16, 31, **pl. 2.2**
firesetting 59, **61**
firing
  determination of conditions 30–1,
    30, 31
  lime 19–20
  porcelain 28
  pottery 22
fleas 175–6, 180
flint
  axe provenancing 107–9, **108**
  faking of 152–3
  mines 107–9, **109**
  TL dating 133, 135
fluorite 37
frame number, videodisc 160
fuel
  acacia 63

charcoal 63, 69
coke 63
cow dung 69
furnace
  Bronze Age 62–3, **63**
  copper 62–4, **63**
  koshthi 70–1
  primitive 61
  zinc 30, **30**, **31**, 70–1

gangue 64
geographic information system 171
gilding 90–1, **91**
glass
  antimony in 42, 46, 47, 50
  beads 38
  Bronze Age 43
  Byzantine 47–9
  cameo 44
  colorants 41–4
  composition 39
  copper in 43, 47
  dichroic 52
  Egyptian 38, 40
  fake Egyptian canopic jars 147
  fake patina on 153
  enamelled 51
  forest glass 40
  glass-blowing 38
  glass-making 39
  gold in 48, 53
  iron in 41
  Islamic 51
  lead in 46, 47, 52
  manganese in 42
  medieval 40, 49
  melting 39
  Mycenaean 43
  opacifier 43–4, 45, 47–8, 50
  origins 37
  potash 40, 50
  properties of 38
  Roman 41, 44–6, 50, 52
  ruby 53
  soda-lime-silica 40
  stained glass windows 42
  structure of 38
  Venetian 46, 52
glaze
  colorants 29
  on Egyptian faience 32–3
  on Islamic pottery 27–8
  opacifiers 29
  on porcelain 28–9
  see also glass
gold
  alloys 82, 95
  filigree 89, **89**
  first usage 58
  in glass 48, 53
  granulation 89
  parting 76
  Sardis, gold working 76
  solder 89, 147

gold – *contd.*
  sources 71
  wire 150
gold-weights
  Ashanti 165–6
  quantum analysis of 165–6
gossan 59
Gowland, W. 11
Granada, Spain 103
graph theory 160
Great Orme's Head copper mine, Wales 59–60
Greece
  Bronze Age 43
  Hosias Loukas 47
greenockite 147
Grime's Graves, Norfolk 109, **109**
Gussage All Saints, Dorset 84

Haifa, Israel 37
Halicarnassus, Turkey **110**, 111
Hartz Mountains, Germany 112
Hawkes, Christopher 13
hematite
  in glass 52
  in red finishes on pottery 24, 26
Hengistbury Head, Dorset 101–2, **pl. 6.1**
Henry VIII coinage 83
hierarchical computer database 160
Horses of St Mark's, Venice 11

Igbo-Ukwu, Nigeria 113–14, **113**
index computer database 160
India
  bidri 95
  brass 76
  glass 54
  silver 66–7
  zinc 76
inductively coupled plasma spectrometry (ICPS)
  description of technique 183
  of flint 108
ingot, fake Roman silver 147
inventory
  museum collections 159, 173–8
iron
  in brass 81
  carburisation 78–9
  in glass 41
  hardening 78–9
  production of 71
  sword 87–8, **88**
Iron Age
  mines 66
  pottery 22, 23, 25–7, 101–2, **pl. 2.1, pl. 6.1**
  silver smelting 67
Islamic
  glass 51
  imitation of Chinese porcelain 27
  jug 153–4
Israel 37, 47

jade 37
Japan 95
jarosite 68
Jungling, statue from Magdalensberg 155

Kendall, David 164
Klaproth, M. 11
Konigliche Museum, Berlin 12
koshthi 70–1
Kunst Historische Museum, Vienna 155

lapis lazuli 32, 37
  authenticity 58
laser 171
lathe turning 85, **85**
Laurion silver mines, Attica 65
lead
  extraction of silver from 67–8
  in glass 46, 47, 52
  isotope analysis 112–14
  ores 67–8
  solder 86–7
  tin yellow 47, 52
  wort 59
Libby, Willard 13, 124
lime
  production 19–20
  uses 19, 20–1, **20**, 32
litharge 67
location of objects 176
Lombard Treasure 147
lustreware 99, 103–5, **104, 105**
Lycurgus Cup 52, **pl. 3.2**

Magdalensberg, Austria 155–6
maiolica 99, 105–6, **107**
malachite 43
Malaga, Spain 103–5
manganese
  in glass 42
marble
  neutron activation analysis of 111
  quarries 110–12
  stable isotope analysis of 110–12, **110**, 184
  trace element analysis of 111
  white 109–12, **110**
Marco Polo 27, 32
mass spectrometry
  AMS radiocarbon dating 122–3
  for stable isotope analysis 109–12
mathematics
  in archaeology 158, 166–70
  in museum collections 159–66
Mausoleum **110**, 111
measurement of shape 162
megalithic yard 165
Mesopotamia 38, 41
metal
  analysis 79, 82, 112–14
  casting 84–5
  decoration 90–5

extraction 61–5, 67–71
forming 84–5
joining 86–9
lead isotope analysis 112–14
microstructure 85, **86**, 93, **93**
mining 59–60, 65–6
native 58, 75
patination 94–5
plating 90–1
precious 82–3
properties 77–8
quality 83
recycling 16, 75, 82
selection 77
standards 83
microstructure
  of Chinese bronze moulds 31, **32**
  of Egyptian faience 32–3, **33**
  of furnace lining 30, **30**, 31
  of glass **43, 45, 47, 51, 53**
  of lime 20, **20**
  of metal 85, **86**, 93, **93**
  of porcelain 28, **28**
  of pottery 26, **26**
mines
  adit 66
  Agucha, India 65, 67, **67**
  Alderley Edge, Cheshire 59
  Cwmystwyth, Wales 59, 60, **61**
  Dariba, India 65, 66, **66**
  drainage 66
  experimental mining 59
  flint 107–9, **109**
  gold 71
  hammers 59
  Iron Age 66
  Laurion, Attica 65
  Mitterberg, Austria 60
  radiocarbon dating of 129–30
  opencast 66
  Rio Tinto, Spain 66, 68
  Timna, Israel 62
  tin 71
  Tonglushan, China 65
  Zawar, India 69, 70
mirrors 92–3, **93**
mosaic 47–9, **pl. 3.1**
Mosan workshops 49
multi-dimensional scaling 162–4
museum collections
  computers and 158
  computer database 13, 159–62, 172–81
  statistical sampling 159
Museum Documentation Association 173

native copper 58, 75
natron 41, 48
Neolithic stone axe provenancing 13
neutron activation analysis (NAA)
  description of technique 184
  of flint 108
  of marble 111

neutron activation analysis (NAA) – *contd.*
  of pottery 102–6
  of Romano-British tile 18
niello 93–4, **94**
Nigeria 113–14, **113**

Olhausen, H. O. W. 12
oreichalcum 81
ores
  cassiterite 71
  jarosite 68
  locating 58
Oxford Research Laboratory 13, 144

Pactolus river 76
patination
  bronze 150–2
  Corinthian bronze 95, 150
  false patinas 150, 151
  flint 152–3
  Japanese *shakudo* 95, 151, **pl. 5.2**
  of metal 94–5
  Payne Knight bronze collection, false patina on 151
  Pliny on 95, 151
pattern welding 88, **88**
Payne Knight, R. 151
Percy, J. 11
petrography *see thin-section petrography*
Petters Sports Field, Surrey 168
phosphate soil analysis 12
Phrygia 81
pigment 94
Pliny 37, 39, 67, 90, 95, 151
Pontnewydd Cave, Wales 134–6, **134**
porcelain
  Chinese **26**, 27–9
  Islamic imitation 27
  thermoluminescence of 144
Portland Vase 44–6, **44**
post-hole distributions 168–9, **168**
  mathematics 168–9
potassium-argon dating 118
pottery
  Arretine 23
  authenticity testing 143–4, **145**
  black-burnished 22–3, **22**
  Cherchel, N. Africa 21–2, 23
  cooking pots 21–3
  Durotrigian 101, **pl. 6.1**
  Iron Age 22, 23, 25–7, **pl. 2.1**
  Italian maiolica 99, 105–6, **107**
  Prunay, Champagne 25–7, **pl. 2.1**
  samian 23–4, **23**
  Spanish lustreware 99, 103–5, **104**
  tablewares 23–4
  technique of decoration 23–4, 25–7, **26**
  thermoluminescence dating 130–2
  tin-glazed 99, 103–6, **104, 105, 107**
  xeroradiography of 26
  see also ceramics, porcelain
pozzolana 21

prospection techniques, history of 13
provenance studies
  in authenticity studies 146
  flint 107–9, **108, 109**
  history of 13
  lapis lazuli source 148
  marble 109–12, **110**
  metal 112–14, **113**
  pottery 100–6, **104, 105, 107, pl. 6.1**
  Romano-British tile 18–19
  samian pottery 23
  stone 106–7
Prunay vase 25–7, **pl. 2.1**
purple of Cassius 53

quantum analysis 165
quartz 37, 39, 40, 47

radiocarbon
  authenticity testing 142–3
  dating 118, 120–3, **121, 123–8,** 136–7
radiography 85, 87–9, **87**, 152–4, 187
  see also xeroradiography
Ramesses II 62
rare earth elements 102
Rasaratanasamuchchaya 69
Rathgen, F. W. 12
refractories 29–31, **30, 31, 32**
registration
  of museum objects 159, 173
retorts 69, **69, 70, 71**
Rio Tinto, Spain 58, 65, 66, 68
River Belus 37, 41
River Meuse 50
rock crystal 37
Roman
  brass 81
  glass 41, 44–6, 52, 60
  mortar and concrete 20–1
  niello 93–4
  plating 90–2
  pottery 21–4
  silver production 66, 68
  solders 89
  tile 18–19
Rudston, Humberside 166
Runnymede Bridge, Berkshire 169

samian pottery 23–4, **23**
sampling theory
  see statistical sampling
sarcophagus 154
Sardis 76
scanning electron microscopy (SEM)
  in authenticity testing 147
  of bronze moulds 31
  description of technique 184
  determination of firing conditions 30–1, **30, 31**
  of Egyptian faience 32–3, **33**
  of glass **43, 45, 47, 51**
  of lime 20

of metal 89, **91, 92, 93**
of porcelain 28, **28**
of pottery 23–4, 26, **26**
Scott, Dr A. 2, 12
sediment, TL dating of 134
Seville, Spain 104–6, **105**
shakudo 95, 151, **pl. 5.2**
shape analysis 160–2
Shikmona, Israel 47
silver
  Achilles Dish 85, **85**
  alloys 82
  assay 67, 83
  cupellation 67, 76
  extraction 76
  fake Roman ingot 147
  hallmark 83
  in glass 53
  microstructure **86**
  mining 67
  refining 76, 82
  smelting 68
  speisse 68
  watchcases 83
silvering 91–2, **92**
slag 64, 133
smelting
  air supply 63
  copper 60–5
  fuel 63
  furnaces 62–4, **71**
  silver 65, 68
  slag 64
  temperature determination 30–1, **30, 31,** 64
  tuyere 62, 67
  zinc 68–71, **69, 70**
solder 78, 86–9, **87, 89**
  cadmium in 147
Spain
  pottery 103–5
  silver smelting in 66–8
stable isotope analysis (SIA)
  description of technique 184
  differentiation of fragments 154
  of marble 109–12, **110,** 149
statistical sampling 159, 166
statistics
  actuarial 167
  cemetery 166–7
  cluster analysis 104
  discriminant analysis 104, **105,** 166–7
  multi-dimensional scaling 162–4
  multivariate 103–5, **105,** 109, **109**
  quantum analysis 165
stone axe provenancing 13, 106–7
Suess, Hans 124
surveying
  in archaeology 169
Sutton Hoo 74, 96
  coins 83, **pl. 5.1**
  purse 83, **pl. 5.1**
  sword 87–8, **88**

Syrian glass 38, 51, 52

temper 22, **22**, 23, 101, **pl. 6.1**
textural analysis 101
Theophilus 40, 50
thermoluminescence
    authenticity testing 143–4, **145**,
        155, 156
    dating 130–7, **132**, **134**
thesaurus
    computer database 160, 179–80
thin-section petrography
    of bronze moulds 31
    description of technique 100–1, 185
    of pottery 21–2, **22**, 26, 100–2,
        pl. 6.1
    of stone 106–7
    of tile 18, 163
Thom, Alexander 165
tile
    Romano-British, roof 18–19, **19**
    tin-glazed floor 105–6, **105**
Timna copper mines, Israel 62, 65
tin
    in glass 43, 47, 50, 52
    production 71
    solder 86–7
tinning 92–3
TL *see thermoluminescence*

Tonglushan copper mines, China 65
touchstone 83
transmission electron microscope (TEM)
    application to glass 53
    description of technique 185
Turin Shroud 143, **143**
Turner, W. E. S. 52
turquoise 37
Tutankhamen 12
typology of artefacts 160, 162–3

units 186
Ur, Iraq 12
uranium series dating 118, 135

Valencia, Spain 103–5, **104**
Venice
    glass of 45, 46, 47, 51, 52
    Horses of St Mark's 11
videodisc 160, 177
village, lost medieval 164

watchcases
    English silver 83
wire, authenticity of **148**, **149**, 150
wood
    dendrochronology 118, 125–6,
        126, 138
    radiocarbon dating of 121

Woolley, Sir Leonard 12

xeroradiography
    application to pottery 26
    description of technique 186
X-ray diffraction (XRD) analysis
    description of technique 186
    of Egyptian faience 32
    of niello 93
    patination identification 152
    of pigment 94
    of pottery 24, 26, 27
    provenance of minerals 149
    smelting studies 65
X-ray fluorescence (XRF) analysis
    description of technique 186
    of metal 82, 89, 93
X-ray radiography 187

Zapotec ceramics, Mexico 144, **145**
Zawar, India 30, **30**, **31**, 69
zinc
    and authenticity 146
    bidri ware 95
    in brass 76, 81
    production 30, **30**, **31**, 68–71
    use in conservation 147
    Zawar 30, **30**, **31**, 69